RECORDS OF CIVILIZATION, SOURCES AND STUDIES

EDITED UNDER THE AUSPICES
OF THE DEPARTMENT OF HISTORY, COLUMBIA UNIVERSITY

GENERAL EDITOR

W. T. H. Jackson
Professor of German and History

PAST EDITORS

1915-1926
James T. Shotwell
Bryce Professor Emeritus of the History
of International Relations

1926-1953
Austin P. Evans
Late Professor of History

1953-1962
Jacques Barzun
Seth Low Professor of History

RECORDS OF CIVILIZATION
IN NORTON PAPERBACK EDITIONS

Method for the
EASY COMPREHENSION
of HISTORY

By JEAN BODIN

TRANSLATED BY

BEATRICE REYNOLDS

W · W · NORTON & COMPANY · INC · *New York*

It is a pleasure to give thanks to Mr. Roger Howson, formerly Librarian of Columbia University, for permitting me to borrow the editions of 1583 and 1595; to Drs. Lynn Thorndike and P. O. Kristeller for a critical reading of the manuscript; to Dr. A. P. Evans, editor of the "Records of Civilization," for his editorial labors; to various colleagues from whom I have sought information, as well as to the staffs of the libraries of Columbia and Yale universities and Connecticut College.

Beatrice Reynolds

New London, Conn.
January, 1944

CONTENTS

CONTENTS

INTRODUCTION

JEAN BODIN, by birth Angevin, acquired his legal education at the University of Toulouse and later lectured on Roman law in the same town, spending there about a decade of his life. The university, in the sixteenth century, was one of the largest in France, comprising more than four thousand students, both French and foreign, but the traditional method of instruction was under fire. A new way of interpreting the *Code* had been introduced at the universities of Bologna and Padua, and the older ways of Toulouse received unfavorable criticism. Visiting professors from Italian institutions and French scholars who had studied in Italy under Alciati were making the attack.

The school of post-glossators, of whom the greatest was Bartolus of Sassoferrato, had attempted to apply the *Code* and the *Gloss* to fourteenth-century conditions, with interpretations necessarily somewhat strained. In addition, they used the scholastic method. But the humanists of the Italian Renaissance reproached the legists for their neglect, on the one hand, of the conditions producing the law and, on the other, of the value of the Roman statutes as a source for historical knowledge. One of the most outspoken critics of the Bartolists was Laurentius Valla. Politian and Budé both undertook to reform legal instruction, the latter publishing a work on the first twenty-four books of the *Digest,* which he treated in the light of the revived knowledge of classical antiquity.

From Alciati developed the historical school of law. He studied classical culture at Milan, under Parrhasius, and obtained his legal training from Jason of Mayno and Philip Decius at Pavia. His humanist and juristic interests led him to believe that the literature and the history of antiquity, as well as purity of diction, could make a weighty contribution to the interpretation of Justinian's *Code.* The newer method he taught at Avignon in 1518 and at Bourges in 1529, as well as at Italian universities. His influence is reflected in the teaching of several French professors, such as Cujas and Duaren. As Lemonnier suggests, they sought to place a given text in its proper sequence in the life work of a jurist, then the jurist in his proper school, and the school in its own epoch. This was a very different thing from attempting to apply an old law to current conditions. Co-operation between humanists and lawyers was essential for the success of a method which led Le Caron [1] at least to proclaim that the ultimate philosophy was Law.

[1] Loys Charondas Le Caron, 1536–1617, a poet and jurisconsult, composed *Le Grand*

This conclusion might also have occurred to Bodin, who lived in Toulouse from 1550 to 1560. The university, while conservative in its appointments, was nevertheless aware of the importance of Alciati and of his followers, since Cujas was lecturing in Toulouse in 1547. Bodin's desire to achieve a synthesis of universal law may well have developed from a similar interpretation of its significance.[2] As a humanist, with some training in theology and a greater emphasis on law, he was stirred to integrate the three into a philosophy of history. His interest in the question of method is evidenced by his *Oratio de instituenda in republica juventute,* a plea to open a school of classical culture in connection with the legal faculty.

France, at the mid-century, was passing from the exuberance of her first Renaissance under Francis I into a more troubled period when the court ceased to be tolerant of nonconformity. Henry II, less sympathetic to innovation, actively persecuted dissent. During the reigns of his two young sons Catherine de' Medici strove to retain for the dynasty the powers which Francis had firmly grasped, but by the time Bodin was moving from Toulouse to Paris, the kingdom was on the eve of civil and religious warfare.

In addition, then, to the universal and eternal question of the interpretation of history, there was also the narrower and more timely problem of the nature of government in France. Both these questions, I think, were in the mind of Bodin when he wrote his treatise in 1565. It is only in the light of increasingly alarming political conditions, from 1565 to 1576, that one can explain the change that took place in his political philosophy between the writing of the *Methodus* and of the *Republic.* Too much stress has been placed upon Bodin as the author of the *Republic;* too little notice has been paid to his earlier and more liberal work, which was issued in thirteen Latin editions between 1566 and 1650.[3] In a prefatory notice in the 1608 edition of the *Republic,* the author disclaimed any support of absolutism, quoting book and chapter to prove that he objected to the increase of royal power. He called attention to his activities on behalf of the Third Estate during the meeting at Blois, where his resolute

---

Coutumier de France, Pandectes du droit français, and some works on Roman law. The quotation is given in Lavisse, *Histoire de France,* v (2ᵉ partie), 313.

[2] Francis Baudouin in *De institutione historiae et coniunctione eius cum jurisprudentia* (1561) is another who supports this opinion.

[3] Thomas Heywood, in his introduction to an English translation of Sallust in 1608, translated chapter IV of the *Methodus.*

stand exposed him to some peril. An alleged *Apologie de René Herpin pour la République,* really written by Bodin and published in 1599, complained that his critic, Auger Ferrier, had used the least accurate edition of the work, and built against the author a case actually based on the printer's errors.

The feudal regime, in allying itself with the Huguenot constitutionalists, was making its last stand against concentration of authority in the hands of its overlord. Calvin's ecclesiastical pattern had furnished to his French followers a model for distributing governmental functions in a manner which would grant to their faction some voice in administrative policy. A large number of the nobles, particularly those without influence at court, saw in the program of federalization offered by the Huguenots a chance to revive provincial strength and their own claims to local authority. It was therefore the problem of sovereignty which Bodin had to consider in analyzing the government of France. He dealt with this vital problem against the wider background of an interpretation of history.

His expressed aim in writing the *Methodus* was the study of universal law, for in the narrative of human affairs, he said, the best part of universal law lay hidden. Furthermore, he had not been able to discover any historian who explained the art and the method of his subject, or anyone who derived a lesson therefrom. The book is of value in that it gives us the intellectual content of a mind of the transitional period between the medieval and the modern age. To some extent he took all knowledge for his province—with a consequent loss in specialization—and his division of knowledge into human, natural, and divine led him to write books in all three fields. Chapter VI of the *Methodus* was a draft of the later *Republic;* chapter VIII foreshadowed the *Theatrum naturae.* Throughout are scattered sentences and paragraphs leading toward the *Heptaplomeres.* He revealed the trends of his era in that his philosophy of history moved away from the authoritarian toward the natural—in this case, toward the pseudoscientific—for, while he devoted an entire chapter to the theory that the course of events was determined by popular traits, and these in turn by climate, yet he added as further natural causes the influence of numbers and of heavenly bodies propelled by the Prime Mover. The medieval theory of a providential determination of history was not entirely foreign to his thought, although he introduced variables not immediately derived from the Prime Mover.

As he borrowed from the past, so future writers borrowed from him.

Even the eighteenth-century rationalists found some of his theories accept-able. One might, for instance, trace the lineage of the influence-of-climate idea from Hippocrates down to the twentieth century.[4]

Since knowledge of human affairs, or history, was in this book his chief concern, he wished to establish order and manner in historical events; that is, their time sequence, which involved an investigation of chronologi-cal systems, and their logical correlation, which required a critical ap-praisal of the degree of objectivity of the historian.

His second chapter and a large part of the third deal with methodology. An elaborate program of reading on the deductive plan is indicated. The reader should move from brief general accounts to more detailed nar-ratives; he should start with stories of earliest times and advance through the centuries. Biographies are of value in furnishing guides to conduct. Subjects allied to history, such as cosmography and geography, are es-sential for a proper comprehension of the whole. Here again the ap-proach is from universals to particulars. The reader should study the entire universe, then the geography and the topography of separate por-tions, as he studies universal history before the histories of different countries. Such voluminous reading entails systematic arrangement of notes. Human activities concentrated upon the defense of society may be classified under forms of control: self-discipline, familial discipline, and civic discipline. Here the author digressed to analyze government into its three functions—ruling (*imperium*), counseling, and fulfilling orders. Thus he recognized specialization, but left responsibility with those having *imperium*. There is no division of final authority, for sovereignty rests in one group only. The reader should arrange his notes in accordance with a main heading, following the above classification.

Before the notes are taken, however, the material must be critically appraised. Chapter IV quotes Aristotle's advice to readers of history—do not believe all or discredit completely. One should take into con-sideration the background and training of the historian. What are his qualifications for writing? Natural ability developed by education and practical experience produces the most suitable type of writer. Lack of emotional bias is desirable, and it is more nearly attained when the au-thor deals with a period long past or a country not his own. He should make use of official records and should avoid prejudicing the reader by

[4] See, for instance, H. Busson, in his introduction to Pomponazzi's *Les Causes des mer-veilles de la nature*, p. 25, and Lucien Febvre, *A Geographical Introduction to History*, p. 108, where he says of Montesquieu, Buckle, and Miss Semple, "It is Bodin, revised, cor-rected, and considerably enlarged, but it is never anything but Bodin."

offering moral judgments, unless he has authority in that field, as Caesar had on military matters.

The rest of chapter IV is devoted to criticism of many historians. If Bodin actually read them all, he spent years in preparation for his task, and he did reveal a nice acumen in his estimates of the ulterior motives behind the statements of many authors. Prejudices against race, classes, and political affiliations did not escape him. It is true that he himself was not free from nationalist bias, and we detect his childlike pride in the achievements of famous Angevins along with a more serious exaggeration of the virtues of the Celts, the Franks, and the French, who to him represented the Aristotelian mean.

It is in the fifth chapter that we meet a seminaturalistic theory of history. The author carried on the thought of the previous chapter—criticism of historians—by saying that the disagreement among writers necessitated the establishment of standards for the reader. If we could decide upon the fundamentals ordinarily motivating the trend of events and the course of empire, we could then judge the probable accuracy of the account of a single country given by any individual writer. The destiny of a nation is determined partly by the character of its people. This is implicit in his discussion. His main emphasis, however, was on the means whereby character is formed. These were, of course, nature and training. But what shaped the nature? Why was the training of a given type? He found his answer in the influence of geography.

Other factors affecting the course of empire were the harmony of numbers and the stars in so far as they reflected greater forces beyond them. Bodin denied the Ptolemaic theory that the triplicities of the zodiac exercise compulsion, and he did so on grounds in part philosophic, but in part scientific, based on actual astronomic data. He revealed here an acquaintance with the writings of Jerome Cardan,[5] whom he challenged more often than he accepted.

Racial peculiarities, the influence of the planets, and Pythagorean numbers fit into the pattern of the Platonism of the Renaissance. It is in his treatment of geographic determinism that he made a contribution somewhat more ample, by combining with Platonic doctrines the theories of Hippocrates and Strabo.

The earth was divided into areas of thirty degrees from the equator

---

[5] Jerome Cardan, 1501–1576, an Italian physician and astrologer. In addition to his more celebrated work on the solution of cubical equations, he produced *De subtilitate*, and *De rerum varietate* to summarize his ideas on metaphysics.

northward according to temperature. This, of course, was an imitation of the Ptolemaic zones. The author did little with the southern hemisphere, but he was aware that it existed and that some sections were inhabited. Each of these thirty-degree areas was in turn divided into two parts, the fifteen-degree units around the pole and below the tropic being most sparsely inhabited. From the tropic north to seventy-five degrees he found it possible to make generalizations as to the character of the inhabitants. They differed in coloration, going from dark to medium, to blond, to reddish, with more variety in the mean area than elsewhere. They differed in temperament: those in the south were contemplative and religious, developing great wisdom, but lacking in energy. They were "the old men." Those in the north were active and strong, but of no great sagacity, corresponding to youth. Men dwelling in the intervening lands were endowed with the good qualities of both and showed no excess. They were like men in middle life, prudent and most fit to take control. Other parallels with wisdom, prudence, and activity he found in the attributes of the planets Saturn, Jupiter, and Mars, which were assigned, respectively, to south, temperate, and north, or in what for him were the physical functions of the brain, the heart, and the liver. Thus, in analyzing the population of his own hemisphere he found that different peoples complemented each other in the same way as did parts of the body, or the classes of a well-constituted state, or the celestial spheres.[6] Men from south, north, and the intervening area formed the republic of the world.[7]

Throughout, he stressed the superiority of the inhabitants of the temperate zone. They were the mean between the extremes, the virtue between vices. They showed more varied types and more versatility in talents. These advantages they owed partly to fusion with immigrants, but more to a proper blending of the elements within themselves and around them. Hence he linked history to man, man to his nature, nature to the cosmic powers working through the elements. The concept of unity in plurality is interpreted as unity in diversity, a world where each group fulfills a function determined by its geographic environment. Such a world corresponds to the microcosm; it is an extension of the Platonic republic; it displays in miniature the concord existing throughout the universe.

Education would in time alter the customs and ideas of a people, but unless it was consistently maintained, primitive traits would reassert themselves. The Romans once rose to a position of eminence in many arts and skills, but through neglect of training they lapsed into comparative mediocrity.[8] Therefore, the customs and the nature of each people determine the trend of events. We can judge of the probable truth of any account from its recognition of the prevailing attributes of the people under discussion.

To achieve an understanding of history it would be necessary to dwell at some length upon the art of government. Then, too, we must study the rise and the fall of former states in order to make more effective present-day administration. This is one of the great benefits of the historical discipline. Chapter vi should illustrate the conclusions of chapter v, but the author became so engrossed in his study of governments, past and present, that he shifted his emphasis away from the government peculiar to a given geographical area and placed it on the best type of government, as demonstrated by the ages,—a topic in which he as a Frenchman was interested.

The study of the state involved definition of such primary terms as "citizen," "magistrate," "city," and so forth. The Aristotelian concepts were reviewed and rejected as too narrow. For Bodin a "citizen" was one who enjoyed the common liberty and protection of authority. He compared the rights of the inhabitants of various countries and decided that all were citizens regardless of the special rights of separate groups. His text was the law which he attributed to Antoninus Pius: "Those who are in the Roman world, let them be Roman citizens." [9] Foreigners were those who did not acknowledge the government and usually did not pay taxes.[10] Bodin's idea of the position of a citizen in the state was based on the analogy of the child in the home.

A magistrate was one who had part of the public authority, but had not the final authority. He might arrest and condemn; he commanded, but others were the agents. He might delegate his share of authority in the field of equitable justice, but in statutory cases he was bound to judge according to the law.

The description of a magistrate and of his share of authority led to the concept of sovereignty, which is the main interest of this chapter and Bodin's chief contribution to political thought. The word existed in Italian and in French, and it even had two forms in Greek and in Latin; yet men who wrote about the state had overlooked its paramount importance.[11] Aristotle himself gave no precise definition of sovereignty, unless he intended to do so when he divided the activities of govern-

[8] *Ibid.*, p. 145.   [9] *Ibid.*, p. 162.   [10] *Ibid.*, p. 164.
[11] *Ibid.*, p. 172.

ment into counseling, appointing, and giving justice.[12] But this concept was vital to the classification of types of state, for the incidence of sovereignty determined the monarchical, aristocratic, or democratic character of the government. Bodin would have been consistent had he emphasized the theory that northern countries, for instance, exemplify one given type, because of the nature of the people, as do all the different zones. However, he avoided this logical development from chapter v, and after indicating the criteria of sovereignty he proceeded to analyze various well-known empires in order to establish the type of each by the use of these same criteria. He refused to recognize the so-called mixed state, on the ground that, while there could be separation of function, there could be no division of ultimate responsibility, that is, of sovereignty.

This he indicated was involved in five functions: creating and defining the duties of officials; proclaiming and annulling laws; declaring war and peace; receiving appeals from lower magistrates; and pardoning those condemned by the laws. The people or group or man who controlled these powers was sovereign, and thus the type of government was ascertained.

The origin of the state he traced to the family. The patriarchal authority of the father, with its parallel duty of protection, was the prototype of the beneficent, all-powerful monarch. Association of members of the family was due to mutual sympathies, and the same bond brought together the guild, or *collegium*. A state was merely a group of families or guilds subject to the same rule.[13] This applied equally to towns and to principalities, for statehood was not conditioned by size. It was not even necessary for all peoples within a state to have the same set of laws, provided that they were under the protection of the same authority. The Turkish Empire is given as evidence. This larger type of empire comprised the lesser within it. The state was the genus; villages, towns, city-states, and principalities were the differentia.

Progressing from the beginnings of society, we find infinite gradations of change. Contiguity and sympathy decreased as increased numbers involved an extension of territory. When men's pleasure in the society of their fellowmen was spoiled by quarrels, they had to find protection from violence. Some of the weak fled to the strong; but others fled to the most just. Hence came two forms of state—one founded on force, the other on equity. States founded on force must, to endure, be

[12] *Ibid.*, p. 156   [13] *Ibid.*, p. 157.

maintained by justice; the early states therefore were under the control of one man, whose title indicated that his primary function was the dispensing of justice. When he or his descendant ceased to fulfill that mission, conspiracies were formed among powerful cliques to overthrow the despot. Factions gained supremacy, one after another, until the plebs, weary of quarrels and corruption, set up a popular state. These were usually short-lived, since the people were inexperienced and easily fooled by ambitious politicians. Orators quickly obtained control and spent money to please the citizens; they secured office through no merit of their own. They kept the plebs busy working and building fortifications, lest they should have leisure for speculation; they fomented discords between nobles and plebs; they undertook wars for the sake of exacting money.[14] If anyone attempted to intervene, he was corrupted with gifts or forced to abandon his opinion. Thus the cycle goes endlessly on—changes induced sometimes by pressure from within the state, sometimes by violence from without.

Each of the three types of government had a degenerate form, but each had at the start an excellent cause for being and passed through a useful period. Which of the three was best and most generally adopted? If we were to inspect nature closely, we should find monarchy everywhere. Every type of animal life followed its leader. The family was governed paternally. Great empires of the past were under royal power. A majority of contemporary states were ruled by kings and had been so ruled for centuries. This is the summary of Bodin's arguments. He granted that a few writers, such as Machiavelli, preferred a republic. He noticed that democracies and aristocracies had developed in the western portion of the middle zone, but only recently and not for long. This conflicting evidence was dismissed very lightly, and he resumed his study of the most excellent form of government.

There were two main types of monarchy: sovereignty was vested in one man, who commanded either illegally or legally. Of the kings who commanded legally, there were in turn two kinds: those restrained by no law at all and others who were bound by the laws.[15] This gave us the tyrant, the absolute king, and the constitutional king. The first, Bodin repudiated in no uncertain terms. The second and third should rule in accordance with divine precepts. In early times the entire state and the rights of citizens depended upon the will of the prince. Royal power prevailed without any system of legislation. Later, laws were

---

[14] *Ibid.*, p. 219.   [15] *Ibid.*, p. 201.

introduced, much against the wishes of those in authority. Theoretically it was easier to control the magistrate than the ruler, for the former had his authority from the prince, whereas the prince was his own source.

It was really dangerous, however, to create a king who was held by no laws at all, because men are wont to be diverted from justice by all sorts of emotions. There are arguments in favor of the dispensing power, but once the statute had been approved by the common consent and the people were restrained by it, why should not the prince also be held? Bodin leaned away from uncontrolled rule, but he admitted that many absolute kings did exist—and he mentioned the English king as an example. He recognized that absolutism did not violate law provided that the prince fulfilled his complementary duty of protecting his people at his personal hazard.

The type of monarch who won Bodin's approval bound himself by oath to govern the state in accordance with the fundamental laws of the country and the public good. This gave the author the opportunity to enlarge upon the perfections of the French monarchy. There the king could not destroy the laws peculiar to the entire kingdom or alter any municipal customs without the consent of the three estates. Public lands might not be alienated at the caprice of the occupant of the throne. Royal decrees must reflect current concepts of equity and truth, or the magistrates would not have recognized them. Judicial officers would seem, in Bodin's opinion, as later in Coke's, to have an influence both formative and stabilizing on constitutional practice. The more the power of the prince was decreased, the more was his authority augmented and firmly established. The most effective check of all was fear of God, for an unscrupulous ruler would defy any human restraint. It is noticeable that in Bodin's description of the Roman Republic he allotted a position of semi-independence to religious officials, whereas in France it was the judicial official who was significant. He had little to say about the contacts of the government and the Church, other than to urge piety in the prince and the magistrates. Awe of the Deity was to him the most important factor for limiting despotism. It should be inculcated at an early age.

While fear of God was an end in itself, it was also the means by which royal power was best held to its task of working for the good interests of the nation. The other means were the magistrates and the laws. Since men of the middle region were born to manage affairs, they could not easily endure absolutism. The western independence had either driven

away kings of this type or had forced them to obey laws—an arrangement infinitely desirable.[16] Here we find a clear connection with the
characters of people as developed in chapter v. Although Bodin preferred the limited monarchy, he did not go so far as to suggest that a
nation should select its own king. Power should descend from father to
son in order to avoid the dangers of an interregnum and other weaknesses so apparent in Poland and in the Holy Roman Empire.

Change, then, was brought about by inner structural weakness or out-
ward violence. At all events, there was a rise, a period of grandeur, and
then a decline and a fall. Bodin inquired, can these cycles of empire be
calculated from Pythagorean numbers? He dismissed as erroneous
Plato's belief that the ruin of a state is brought about by mathematical
forces. Although God arranged all things according to number, this was
not due to their power, but to express His divine will.[17] When Plato
eliminated internal weaknesses which might bring about the overthrow
of a government, he should have removed from his ideal state that
ancient blight of communities, unequal distribution of wealth. Elsewhere
Bodin said that since neither the sun nor the eccentrics were at all important in the changes of empire, it must be confessed that the whole
thing depends upon immortal God. If on investigation we should find
any correlation between revolution and the conjunctions of the stars, we
could only infer that He had used them as His instruments.[18]

In chapter v Bodin disposed of Ptolemy's triplicities, as enunciated
by Cardan,[19] and showed that the precession of the equinoxes had altered
the position of these groups, yet the traits of the peoples living within
the assigned quadrants had remained constant. In chapter vi he attacked
another supposition of Cardan's—that every great empire depended
upon the tail star of the Great Bear. When this was "vertical" to a city,
it brought power thither, according to Cardan. But in the case of Rome
it could be shown from the tables of Copernicus that this star was not
above the city when the foundations were laid. Furthermore, those countries directly under the Great Bear, the Scandinavian lands, had reaped
no benefit from this position, but, on the contrary, were weaker than
their neighbors.

Having refuted the bizarre theories of Cardan, Bodin proceeded with
perfect gravity to defend others imposing an equal tax on our credulity.
The state should be built with relation to the concord of numbers. The

---

[16] *Ibid.*, p. 217.   [17] *Ibid.*, p. 223.   [18] *Ibid.*, p. 234.
[19] Probably in Cardan's *Commentaria in Cl. Ptolemaei . . . IIII de astrorum iudiciis
. . . libros* (1554).

three types of progression—arithmetic, geometric, and harmonic—he called the three daughters of Themis, representing order, justice, and peace. The middle term included the other two. The arithmetic progression was more suited to a democratic state, since it denoted equality. Plato, in building an aristocratic state, preferred that it should be governed according to the geometric system. But the harmonic ratio, developed from the other two, portrayed the relationship of overlord and vassal and was therefore suited to a monarchy. It represented peace, and this was the highest objective of all empires. Here Bodin entered upon a discussion of musical intervals, probably drawn from Boethius or Macrobius, which sought to show a parallel between the well-tempered state and concord in music.[20] Elsewhere he attacked Forester [21] for making blunders in number theory as applied either to music or to the state.[22] The conclusion is that a state can best avoid danger from within or from without if it is built on harmonic principles, which for Bodin meant a monarchy administered in the interests of all. The parts of this world are so interrelated that if the appropriate dissimilarity is destroyed, the whole structure collapses. Another simile is found in song: unison is monotonous, but variety gives a pleasing harmony. In the same way, the best republic is the result of differentiation, the association of unlike minds.

But granted that governments were not always well balanced, granted that many states have gone to ruin, what is the factor that appears to determine their rise and fall? In order to derive this, Bodin reverted once more to the microcosm, natural man.

The number six concerned women; seven, men. Throughout all nature these symbols had great power. If we noted the age at death of famous men, we should find that it was a multiple of seven or of nine. Cycles of states also had a periodicity depending upon mystic quantities. Sometimes the fatal year fell at the square or cube of seven or nine, or a multiple of the two, or even on a perfect number. The "great number" of the academicians had significance, for no empire has lasted longer than 1,728 years. Bodin proceeded to a long list of illustrations. If the case seemed not exactly to fit, he distorted the figures. If his authorities differed, he supported the Biblical account. The number of Daniel,[23] with the addition of the perfect number six, gave us 496, which Bodin felt was really crucial for empires. The ancients said that the

---

[20] See below, p. 287.   [21] See Chapter VI, note 115.   [22] See below, p. 224.
[23] Daniel 9: 24, where he refers to seventy weeks, or seventy times seven days.

cycle was 500 years, but they had no skill in mystic quantities; 500 was not made up of nines or sevens. What they really should have given was the perfect number 496.

Just as in a fever the crisis occurred on a decisive day, so we must base the cycle of empire in some way upon mathematical relationships. States suffered from disease, or they might have violent ends suited to their natures. Human affairs did not take place in haphazard fashion, but by divine wisdom which, while it arranged all things in proper sequence, might nevertheless reverse them at will.

Chapters v and vi contain Bodin's material for a philosophy of history. The following three chapters attempt to refute older theories or to dispose of complications standing in the way of acceptance of his own. In dealing with these obstacles, he exhibited the same blend of rationalism and superstition that marked his interpretation of history. The Book of Daniel presented a prophecy accepted by early Church Fathers, but elaborated and reinterpreted by later expounders, particularly by German historians with a nationalist bias and by Protestant reformers. This vision of four beasts and another of an image had both been interpreted as indications of empires to come before the end of the world. Bodin was extremely skeptical as to the validity of this explanation with respect to the number of empires and their identification. As usual he wished to define terms before the argument was opened. What was the meaning of "empire"? Or was it rather a monarchy which was under consideration? Size was another factor of importance. If we were looking for a successor to Rome, the most likely counterpart was not the Holy Roman Empire, but the Turkish, in so far as extent and location were concerned. This passage appears to be the reaction of a French nationalist to the assertion of the Germans that they will establish dominion over central Europe.

He then discussed the second vision, the image with golden head and feet of clay, but he had no sympathy with the fable of a Golden Age. Was not the flood caused by the wickedness of man? Were there not barbarous customs in the so-called Silver Age? Were not some French heroes the equals of Alexander? Here, of course, he was involved in the battle of the ancients and the moderns. He did not concede overwhelming superiority to either. Men of old made remarkable discoveries, particularly in astronomy, but more recent research and inventions had eclipsed them. In astronomy further advance had been made. Modern men had investigated the magnet and built engines of war.

Printing alone was of tremendous significance. The farthest recesses of India had been opened up, so that sixteenth-century man sailed over the whole world and had developed a profitable commerce with its most distant quarters. Interdependence born of trade made the world like a city state. So, instead of constant deterioration from gold to silver and down to clay, Bodin found actual progress from the isolation and brutality of earlier eras to the humane customs and law-abiding society about him. The path of change was cyclical, and those who sighed for the Golden Age were comparable to old men who sigh for their youth.

If we were to establish a philosophy of history based on cycles, it was highly important, both for comparative and developmental purposes, that we should reconcile the various calendars in vogue among different peoples. The first step in building up a universal system of time was to determine the start, and the most obvious initial point was the Creation. But could we feel certain that the world had a beginning? Was it perhaps eternal?

Chapter VIII, which develops this subject, is peculiarly difficult to analyze. Bodin found so many interesting digressions from his main theme that its organization is not clearly apparent. In addition there are ellipses which seem to result in contradictions. Somewhat less than half the chapter is devoted to the problem of the world, created or noncreated. Plato's authority was invoked for belief in an actual creation. Philosophically, anything which had a beginning must also come to an end, but by the divine will the world would be immortal. On the other hand, Aristotle argued that a world which is not perishable could not have had a beginning. In presenting this point of view Aristotle had denied to God free will to determine the course of events, an attitude reprehensible to Bodin.

In considering these matters the Peripatetics assumed that nothing was born of nothing. This introduced the constitution of primitive matter and form, their relationship to each other and to the Creator. By reference to Aristotle it is ascertained that at least in the case of man form was achieved from some agent other than matter. In Bodin's opinion both the work and the idea came from the mind of the artificer. The existence of the world was necessary or possible or impossible. In the first case, it had always been; in the last case, it would never be; in the second case, possibility, the potentiality must have resided in some being. Bodin put it in the everlasting effective Cause, who was incited by Himself into action. God was infinite and could not be part of any finite body. From Him sprang the lesser intelligences, from which, since they were finite, the spheres started and ceased to be moved. We could not, however, establish with certainty when the end of the world would come.[24] God protected the universal forms, but neglected the separate things, which were changing and transitory. At all events, the world had a beginning. This was what was wanted for the universal system of chronology.

The calendar had to be built up from historical documents. The Greeks did not recall the days before the Trojan War, and even that was partly fable. By comparison it was found that the Egyptians, Chaldeans, and Phoenicians agree fairly well with the Scriptures on relationships of time. They set a limit of about 5,700 years for the earth's age. The next disparity to be corrected was the different position of the New Year in the various calendars—Greek, Latin, Moslem, and Christian. Again Bodin selected the Jewish custom: the New Year started in September, for the Creation must have occurred then.

Other causes of confusion were the overlapping reigns of kings, with frequent interregna, such as we find in the accounts of Berosus and Manetho; the practice of the Greeks of using lunar years, corrected somewhat by intercalary days; and the occasional intervention of bissextile years. The latter half of the chapter is on the whole a faithful account of the difficulties met by the historical student in reckoning time.

The last chapter of text makes some slight contribution toward, or rather against, the modern doctrine of nationalism. The author had observed in historical works and elsewhere a tendency to disassociate one group of peoples from the others on the ground that one was autochthonous, the other intrusive. Natives felt themselves superior to the others because of this very trait. The land was rightfully theirs—they were the pure stock. Other peoples, migrating to them or living beyond the frontiers, were treated with scorn and vilified. Bodin decried this attitude, but in almost the same breath he artlessly delineated the French and their forerunners, the Franks and the Celts, as the conquerors of Europe, patterns of all virtues, military and civil.

He refuted the doctrine of nationalism on Scriptural grounds. Moses taught us that we are all of the same blood, born of peoples who have migrated hither and thither from their original habitat in the Near East. We should therefore discard the word "indigenous," founded on nothing but national vanity, and recognize our common brotherhood.

[24] See below, pp. 314, 333.

He made a strong plea for international amity based on recognition of kindred blood and mutual interdependence. "Nowadays . . . no region is so fecund that it does not urgently need the resources of others. . . . For what purpose . . . if not that the . . . self-interest of peoples may produce peace among them by mutual exchange of goods . . . ?"

On Biblical evidence the Chaldeans were the most ancient race. The sons of Noah established families which spread throughout the eastern hemisphere. This diffusion of the descendants of Noah gave us the Hamitic, Semitic, and Japhetic races, indeed, but they had a common stock. There was, then, no difficulty in identifying the oldest people. If we wished, however, to investigate relative priority of occupation, there were three tests to make; the first was the reliability of the historian. Considerable attention is devoted to this topic in chapter iv. Another guide was the topography of the region occupied. Obviously the best lands would be taken over first, so that the occupants of Greece and Italy represented an older race than those of Germany, or "Scythia." That criterion to which Bodin attached chief importance is language. He attempted to trace Jewish words to Greece, Greek words to France, and Celtic words to Germany in support of his favorite thesis that the Jews are the oldest race. The study of language as a guide to racial origin is of course an excellent device, but Bodin's philological equipment was hardly equal to the strain imposed upon it. We pursue him with constantly decreasing interest through a maze of preposterous derivations, by which he thought he could prove that the Jews settled in Spain, that the Celts were Greek, and that the Germans were descended from the Gauls. Through war, captivity, and migrations peoples had been so fused that none except the Jews had preserved its isolation.[25] None could boast of the great age of its race, except the Jews. Not even the crowned heads of Europe could trace their lineage back so far, although the race of Capet, the most ancient in Europe, could claim eight hundred years.

While this chapter repeats the lesson of objectivity contained in chapter iv, at the same time it stresses that partiality for Scriptural history which invariably introduces an exception to the author's generalizations. It violates Bodin's preference for the people of the middle zone toward the west, who are so eminently fitted to rule; it runs counter to his professed dislike of nationalism; it leads him to accept Jewish chronology for ancient times; finally, it constitutes an important infringement of the cyclical theory with which he invests all history.

[25] *Ibid.*, p. 362.

To summarize the foregoing, the scheme of the book follows: the Dedication and the Preamble state the aim of the author; chapters i through iv explain a method of studying history; chapters v and vi give Bodin's philosophy of history; chapters vii through ix attempt to eliminate difficulties within his philosophy; chapter x contains his Bibliography.

It must be recollected that this book is Bodin's first major work, the product of his early middle age. He was thirty-six when it was published. Taken in isolation, it is not strikingly important; but it gains in significance when considered in relation to other works of that period and to later works by the same author. Earlier in this Introduction reference was made to the germinal nature of certain passages in the *Methodus*. From the ideas contained within it were derived three other books of Bodin's maturity and old age. In this one we have an image of his early interests—scholarly, political, supernatural, and religious. His was a keen intellect, not without an occasional flash of humor, closely in touch with the many-sided learning of his day and sufficiently profound in some phases thereof. He seems weakest on the side of organization. His very profusion of interests is responsible for the lack of articulation. I have indicated what seems to be the plan of the *Methodus* as a whole. Bodin himself gives an outline on the last page of the Preamble; there is one for chapter v on the first page of that chapter and one for chapter vi on page 212. Contradictory opinions with regard to limited monarchy,[26] to the Creation,[27] to the formation of ethical judgments,[28] and to other matters are due more to the scholastic method than to hesitation on the part of the author. There are, however, passages in which the logical sequence is not clear, owing to ellipses of thought. What the sixteenth century took for granted quite naturally must be supplied for the twentieth, with its different background of information.

The stand of Bodin with regard to certain theoretical phases of history was not original with him. Patrizzi and Baudouin had published works in similar vein a few years earlier. The Platonic doctrines which shape the thought are also typical of that time. Bodin must have encountered them in his university life and heard them from friends in Paris. The equipment he brought to the formation of a philosophy of history was, then, juristic knowledge (his specialty), acquaintance with the classics, indispensable in his day, and a cosmology according to which

[26] Ibid., pp. 202–3 and 217. [27] *Ibid.*, pp. 303, 310, 312, 316.
[28] *Ibid.*, pp. 51, 53–54.

he saw the universe as a series of interrelationships, from the first inspiring influence without to the lowest element of earth. This hierarchy of superimposed powers composed a world both endless and transitory, for it maintained the type while the individual members thereof passed through a cycle of birth, rise, decline, and death.

His religion is an unsolved problem, open to much speculation. Certainly he spent a few youthful years in a monastery.[29] He died a confessed Romanist and was interred in a monastery at Laon. In the intervening forty-five years he appears to have wandered far from the fold. On the basis of the *Methodus* alone, one can observe his acquaintance with German writers, many of them Protestant, and with some French Huguenots. There is indicated an admiration for Calvin and the city state of Geneva. Much more emphasis is placed on the authority of the Old Testament than on that of the New. These admissions may put him in the Calvinist camp, particularly since he sympathized with their desire to limit the monarch. But as we read on into the last chapter, on the origin of races, we may well wonder if he had not become a convert to Judaism. He is obviously well versed in medieval Semitic works, in addition to the Talmud, the Apocrypha, and the Old Testament.

These qualifications, then, he brought to the making of his philosophy of history. It is a doctrine based on the nature of peoples, recognizing the effect of climate in producing different types. This in turn leads to different political structures. The combination of these diverse peoples, playing their specialized roles, makes up the complete world. This explanation of the situation at any given moment hinges upon the Platonic hierarchy previously mentioned, according to which the elements (of which man is composed) are controlled by the stars, and these, in turn, by the spirit world.

Such is his interpretation of the state of affairs at any instant of time. But it was necessary to consider what occurred throughout centuries of time. What was going to happen to the states which temporarily complemented each other? Reasoning from the microcosm man, who was born, flourished, and decayed, Bodin evolved a cyclical theory for states. He did not reckon human life at three score years and ten, but found a fatal significance in multiples of seven and nine. By transferring this number mysticism to states, he concluded that they had a periodicity of 496 years. The importance of numbers led to the digression on a system of universal time, and the cyclical theory introduced his ideas on prog-

[29] A. Ponthieux, "Jean Bodin," *Revue du seizième siècle*, XV (1928), 56–99.

ress in civilization. It was true that the separate units disappeared, but the type remained; states (and men) of the present had achieved as much, or more, than those of the past.

This is the major part of his historical philosophy. There is another strain, considerably at variance with the foregoing. Bodin's obscure religious convictions have grafted onto his Platonic teachings a theory of continuity not exactly that of universals versus particulars. In his discussion of the periods of states and, later, on the origin of races, his patriotism made him give rather special treatment to the French people and their royal house. The race is better poised than other races, even within the same climatic belt; the dynasty is the oldest in Europe. These are slight digressions from the climatic and cyclical theories, but what seems an absolute contradiction is his diffusionist philosophy with regard to the Jews. Here his religious sense of eternity led him to predicate a continuity and a distinction which he did not grant to other races, not even to his own. We have, thus, for the course of civilization a major wave motion, involving slow progress, with a minor linear motion, whose continuous extension is authenticated by revealed religion.

The few known facts of Bodin's life I have not itemized in this account, which attempts to stress his intellectual interests. They are treated fully in various books and articles, of which may be mentioned: Chauviré, R., *Jean Bodin;* Garosci, A., *Jean Bodin, Politica e diritto nel Rinascimento francese;* Brown, John Lackey, *The Methodus ad facilem historiarum cognitionem of Jean Bodin;* Reynolds, B., *Proponents of Limited Monarchy in Sixteenth Century France.*

I have consulted four editions of Bodin's book published in his lifetime, the editions of 1566, 1572, 1583, and 1595. Of these the New York Public Library has the first; the second and third are at Yale; the third and fourth are at Columbia. Since it was not possible for me to obtain the first or second edition long enough for my purposes, for the translation I have used the edition of 1583, and have referred to the other editions for the elucidation of difficult passages.

The title page of the 1583 edition bears the description "accurately reprinted anew" by Marshall of Lyons (or Heidelberg?). On the other hand, the edition of 1572 was revised by the author himself and had some additional material, according to the title page. Comparison with the first edition (1566) confirms this. Authorities are quoted where statements were previously unsupported, and there are some interpolations in the way of expansion of arguments. Both the first and the second edition were published by the same Parisian house, that of Martin Le Jeune.

Collation of difficult passages in the four editions gave me the impression that while that of 1583 contains the additional material of 1572, it makes additional syntactical errors, such as *globo* for *globus,* in chapter v, note 92. This error reappears in the Geneva edition of 1595, which has more inaccuracies than its predecessors. Chapter x, Bodin's bibliography, has the greatest number of variants in the several editions, the dates being omitted or misplaced and the digits reversed. Some of these errors were due to difficulties inherent in the arrangement in corresponding columns on a small page.

There were other occasions during the author's lifetime when the *Methodus* was reprinted, but in volumes containing essays by other writers. These I have not seen. The fourth chapter was translated by Thomas Heywood as the Preface to his version of Sallust (1608).[30] During the present hostilities, a French translation was published (1941) by Pierre Mesnard, which, I believe, has not yet reached this country. It is worthy of notice that the *Methodus* appeared on the *Index* of Sixtus V in 1590.

The translation of proper and place names from the Latin has presented a problem. Modern usage is not entirely consistent, and perhaps the same charge may be made against this translation. For instance, from the Renaissance period we are accustomed to read Guicciardini and Machiavelli, but Aeneas Silvius, Pomponius Laetus, Beatus Rhenanus, and so forth. In the case of the more famous figures I have attempted to follow precedent. For those not so familiar I have for the most part used Latin for the early medieval writers and the native form for men of the Renaissance, when they can be identified at all. In some cases the Latin form may represent several men, for example, Garcaeus. If the context does not throw light, the Latin form is retained, in the hope that the ingenuity of the reader may exceed that of the translator.

Place names have been altered to their modern form, except where the reference is to classical times. Institutional names offered similar difficulties. In comparing the constitutions of various states, Bodin wrote of the "Senate," of the Romans, of the Venetians, and of the French. While the name did not exist in France, Bodin wanted to draw analogies between councils of older and supposedly wiser men, so he applied the

[30] Dean, "Bodin's *Methodus* in England before 1625," *Studies in Philology,* XXXIX (1942), 160n.

same name to all three courts. In general, I have kept close to the original text, assuming that the only possible readers will be those interested in all the characteristics of a sixteenth-century author.

Greek forms have in most cases been translated without indicating any difference of language except where there is no English equivalent, or for philological reasons. Where the author gave Greek with a Latin equivalent, I have omitted the Greek. Bodin, in his Dedication, confessed that he had required assistance with Hebrew, and for the most part he has given Latin equivalents, which I have translated, omitting the original. Where Hebrew appears in the translation, I have left it, as I have left some Greek, for philological reasons.

The identification of the many authors referred to by Bodin and the verification of his quotations have taken considerably more time than the translation itself, and it has not been possible to find them all. Some are so familiar that they require no note; others have been identified as to time and their more important works have been listed. One might swell the notes indefinitely with interesting information as to the historical philosophy of some of these men, their desire for calendar reform, for codification of customary law, and so forth; but there are limits to one's space and time, and a work which has continued throughout seven years must sometime find an end.

METHOD FOR THE EASY
COMPREHENSION OF HISTORY

DEDICATION

Jean Bodin conveys his compliments to Jean Tessier,
President of the Court of Inquests

IN THIS *Method*, oh most excellent President, I planned to deal with the way in which one should cull Flowers from History to gather thereof the sweetest fruits. If indeed I seem to have accomplished my purpose, it must be credited to you, who often urged this goal upon me, bringing conviction by your serious speech, supported as it was by the unbelievable gentleness, benevolence, and excellence of your character. But if the result has not fulfilled my wishes, I recognize that this has come about through my own fault. I thought, however, that the fault might be less flagrant in the eyes of the other judges if I should justify my case first before you, that is, before the most clement judge of your court. Thus, if you gave more heed to truth than to friendship, I might then, with the help of this previous judgment, escape the others by objecting that the matter had already been adjudicated; or if, laying aside the role of judge, you should favor more your love for me, you would aid me with your patronage, though against my own wish and contrary to expectation circumstances have forced me to digress from a somewhat more important plan to write on the laws. My purpose, however, was to explain this plan to you briefly so that in judging the *Method* you might be fairer to me (although you could not be more just); then, too, in order that you might encourage to these most excellent studies men who have ample leisure, but much more talent, knowledge, and judgment than I.

When I came into the law courts, in order to live in the public eye, as the saying goes, and serve the people, I first proposed to myself that I should put all the time free from forensic business into legal studies and that either by writing or in whatever way I could I should make return to the state, to which, after immortal God, we owe all things. But when I observed that there are, in all, three kinds of writing: first, discovering things and collecting materials; second, arranging things in correct order and in polished form; last, in eliminating the errors in old books—it seemed to me remarkable that there were and always have been so many searchers, but rather few who have reported their findings artistically and logically. To omit the other disciplines, we have almost countless writers who by their commentaries have augmented the civil law of the Romans to such an extent that it seems to suffer from no one thing more, from no more serious malady, than its own huge size. Indeed, the more inept each one was in writing, the more did he pour forth a multitude of books; yet I see no one who has compressed into graceful form the scattered and disjointed material found. The people who gave promise in a showy title that they would present such a work, have forfeited their bail. Moreover, they are so far from the goal they proposed that they seem not even to suspect what the art itself is.

The arts and the disciplines, as you are well aware, are not concerned with particulars, but with universals. Nevertheless, these men have tried to deal with the subject of the Civil Law, that is, the legislation of one particular state. How wisely, I do not now discuss. Yet nothing can be conceived further from the dignity and value of an art. I disregard the absurdity of attempting to establish principles of universal jurisprudence from the Roman decrees, which were subject to change within a brief period. It is especially absurd, since almost all the laws of the Twelve Tables were supplanted by an infinite multitude of edicts and statutes, and later by the Aebutian Rogation [1] also; repeatedly the old regulations were replaced by new ones. Moreover, we see that almost all the legislation of Justinian was abrogated by following emperors. I pass over how many things are absurd in the statutes which remain—how many were declared outworn by the just decrees of almost all peoples and by long disuse. The fact remains that they have described the laws of no people except the Romans, and these, indeed, in the wrong order. They should have read Plato, who thought there was one way to establish law and govern a state: wise men should bring together and compare the legal framework of all states, or of the more famous states, and from them compile the best kind.

To this objective I directed all my studies—all my thoughts. At the beginning I outlined in a table a form of universal law, which I have shown to you, so that from the very sources we may trace the main types

---

[1] The Aebutian Rogation was a procedural statute of uncertain date (c.150 B.C.) which enabled suitors to find their causes of action formulated in the Praetorian Edict instead of seeking among the more limited *legis actiones* of an earlier period. See F. de Zulueta in *Cambridge Ancient History*, IX, 855, and Sohm, *The Institutes*, p. 81.

and divisions of types down to the lowest, yet in such a way that all members fit together. In this exercise, truly, I have appreciated the saying of Plato—nothing is more difficult or more nearly divine than to separate accurately. Next I have established postulates, on which the entire system rests as on the firmest foundation. Then I have added definitions. Afterward I laid down as briefly as possible precepts called "rules" according to the proposed form, as if to a norm.[2] At one side I added, in brief notes, the interpreters of Roman law, so that from the same sources whence I have drawn, each man can take to his own satisfaction.

Then from every source I collected and added the legislation of peoples who have been famous for military and civic disciplines. In this connection, also, I made use of the standards of the jurisconsults, as well as of the historians, so that consideration is given to the decrees of the Persians, the Greeks, and the Egyptians, no less than to the Romans. From the Pandects of the Hebrews, also, chiefly from the books of the Sanhedrin, I planned to take all the best things. In this matter Jean Cinqarbres[3] and Mercier,[4] royal doctors of the Hebrew tongue, have promised me their aid. Not to be without the statutes of the Spanish and of the British and of all the more famous states of Italy and of Germany (for it would be endless to seek the more obscure), I trusted to be able to join them to our own at the same time. I wish that we might also possess the civil code of the Turks. Certainly by some means we should have the public law on which that flourishing and powerful empire has been established. To these will be added the legal doctrine and the supreme authority of the decisions in your court, as well as of those in the Imperial court. I have obtained them partly from the work of our men, partly from Guarino[5] and Münsinger.[6] Thus,

[2] This is *normam* in editions of 1566, 1572, and 1595; *formam* in the edition of 1583.

[3] Jean Cinqarbres (Quinquarboreus) was professor of Hebrew and Syriac at the Collège de France in 1554; he published *Institutiones in linguam Hebraicam*, as well as an earlier. *De re grammatica Hebraerorum opus*. He died in 1587.

[4] Jean Mercier, the successor of Vatable in the chair of Hebrew at the Collège de France. He was obliged to leave France on account of his religious opinions. He was the author of *Commentarii in Salomonis proverbia, ecclesiasten et canticum canticorum* and died in 1570.

[5] Possibly the reference is to Guarinus Piso who taught law at Pisa in the sixteenth century and wrote *Tractatus de Romanorum et Venetorum magistratum inter se comparatione* and *In feudorum usus praeludia methodice conscripta*. I cannot find that the more celebrated Guarino of Verona wrote on imperial law.

[6] Joachim Münsinger, 1517–1588, German jurist, who wrote *Observationes iudicii imperialis camerae* and *Apotelesma, hoc est Corpus perfectum scholiorum ad institutiones Justinianeas pertinentium*.

by the rule of Polycletus, we have decided to examine laws and actions
of law; but by the Lesbian rule, to examine equity and the office of
judge.[7]

All this material, then, approved and confirmed by the opinions of
jurisconsults and historians, makes that branch of learning more famous
and more worthy of honor [8] than if it had depended upon the will of
one people, the Romans—especially when our Roman material for the
most part is found to be suppositions of the later Greeks. At a time when
all things suffered from the crudest barbarism, fifteen men appointed by
Justinian to codify the laws so disturbed the sources of legislation that
almost nothing pure is dragged forth from the filth and the mud. From
this condition has originated that immense and diffuse abundance of decrees to eliminate discrepancies among the laws themselves and to put
together in some way members torn from the entire body. From this we
can understand that the ancient interpreters had great talent, but an almost incredible task. We obtain the same impression from their writings, which they poured out in such abundance that they seem to have
spent all their days in writing and saved none for reading. Moreover,
since they lived in the most miserable times, when there was no opportunity for the good arts or for culture, their writings have frightened
many away from this branch of knowledge. When youth was called from
the fairest flowers and gardens of eloquence and philosophy to those
thickets and rocky crags, it was naturally cast down in mind; and the
more unusually each man was endowed by nature, or the more richly
by training, the more did he flee from the approach to this discipline,
half closed by brambles and thorns. But after investigators started to
clear the approach, then the statutes of the Romans seemed to be restored to their early value.

Of interpreters, therefore, of whom we have a choice and whom we
use for citing the laws, there are four kinds. One consists of those who
have trained their memory in the schools in perpetual discussion of
enactments, yet are without exercise and forensic practice. The second
group is made up of those who by continual practice of forensic matters,
but very few precepts, have developed within themselves the wisdom
for judging. The third kind consists of those who have learned from
the latter the practice, from the former the precepts: of this type we

[7] Aristotle *Nicomachean Ethics* v. 10. 1137b 30.
[8] The edition of 1595 has *angustiorem* instead of *augustiorem*.

have, among our men, Durand,[9] Du Faur,[10] Guy Pape,[11] Chasseneux,[12] Bohier,[13] Baron,[14] Connan,[15] Tiraqueau,[16] his colleague Brisson,[17] and the ornament of our college, Du Moulin.[18] From them we have learned valuable lessons in teaching and judging civil causes; from the others [19] almost nothing. Indeed, those who think they have acquired a knowledge of law without forensic training are obviously like men who have exercised constantly in a gymnasium, yet have never seen the line of battle and have never undergone the fatigue of military service. They cannot bear the sight of the enemy any more than can the man who had such a fine reputation in the schools of Bourges (as among the

[9] William Durand, called Speculator, was a French jurist, born about 1232. He wrote a *Speculum iudiciale* (published in Strassburg in 1473), which brought him fame and gave him his name.

[10] Guy du Faur, or Fabre, 1529–1584, Seigneur de Pibrac and councillor of the royal privy council, to whom Bodin dedicated his *Republic* in 1576. Du Faur studied under Alciati at Padua and represented Charles IX at the Council of Trent. He wrote *Aimable accusation . . . des . . . évènements de la France, pour monstrer que la pais et reunions des subjects n'est moins necessaires à l'Estat qu'elle est souhaitable à chacun en particulier.* He also did important research on customary law and wrote a commentary on *The Institutes* of Justinian.

[11] Guy Pape, 1402–1487, was another French jurist who worked on customary law. He was councillor at the Parlement of Grenoble, and wrote *Decisiones Gratianopolitanae.*

[12] Barthélemy de Chasseneux, 1480–1541, was first president of the Parlement of Provence. He published *Consuetudines ducatus Burgundiae* and suspended the operation of the law against the Vaudois.

[13] Nicholas Boyer, or Bohier, 1469–1539, was professor of law at Montpellier, Bordeaux, and Bourges. He wrote *Tractatus . . . de auctoritate magni concilii et parlamentorum regni Franciae.*

[14] Eguinaire Baron, 1495–1555, was professor at the University of Angers in Bodin's youth and wrote *Coustumes generalles des pays et duché de Bretaigne* and works on the Justinian *Code* and *Digest.*

[15] Francis Connan, 1508–1551, was maître des requêtes under Francis I and author of *Commentaria juris civilis.* Moreau-Reibel thinks that he had considerable influence on Bodin. See his *Jean Bodin,* chap. i.

[16] André Tiraqueau, 1480–1558, was called the Varro of his century and was appointed to the Parlement of Paris by Francis I. His chief work is *De nobilitate et jure primogenitorum.*

[17] Barnabé Brisson, 1531–1591, was président à mortier of the Parlement of Paris and was sent abroad on various diplomatic missions. The so-called *Code of Henri III* was compiled by him.

[18] Charles du Moulin, 1500–1566, was perhaps the most eminent French jurist of his day. He was one of the leaders in the movement to compile and codify the customary laws of France, with a view to maintaining local liberties against the encroachments of Roman law. He wrote *De feudis, Coustumes de la prevosté et vicomté de Paris,* and similar works on other parts of France. His Protestant faith caused his exile in the reign of Henry II.

[19] The edition of 1583 omits *ex illis.*

blind a squinter sees most clearly), and who when he came into court and was consulted about the most trifling matter could not answer, incurring a biting rebuke from Riant.[20] Your colleague John Ferrier, a man of great prestige who now is ambassador to the Venetians, used to disabuse such jurisconsults of the false concepts of legal theory which they had developed for themselves with a serious warning, when he candidly confessed to many listeners that he himself had not known the law until he had over a long period acquired legal and senatorial training in your court. In this he resembled Demades the orator, who boasted that he had gained knowledge of managing public affairs, not in schools and at leisure, but in the clear light of the public gaze.

The last type consists of those trained not only by precepts and forensic practice but also in the finest arts and the most stable philosophy, who grasp the nature of justice, not changeable according to the wishes of men, but laid down by eternal law; who determine skillfully the standards of equity; who trace the origins of jurisprudence from ultimate principles; who pass on carefully the knowledge of all antiquity; who, of course, know the power and the dominion of the emperor, the senate, the people, and the magistrates of the Romans; who bring to the interpretation of legislation the discussions of philosophers about laws and the state; who know well the Greek and Latin languages, in which the statutes are set forth; who at length circumscribe the entire division of learning within its limits, classify into types, divide into parts, point out with words, and illustrate with examples. If the ancient interpreters had had these rare gifts, there is no doubt but that the neglected forest of commentaries through which we struggle would be pleasanter to elegant young men and more useful to the state. Yet from this we have borrowed golden definitions for the outline of our plan, and we bear deep gratitude to those men, because they freely gave some fruits of their studies to the state. Oh, that your Papinians,[21] Scaevolas, and Labeos (for they ought not be called by other names), who were naturally endowed with equity, shaped by training, and accustomed by experience, may also be inspired by their example to do as much as they can. What can escape such great wisdom? Or who, since men were born, more deservedly have enjoyed the name "jurisconsult"? No part of the world is so famous [22] for all kinds of learning as Europe. No part of

---

[20] Denis Riant was the king's advocate; he died in 1557.

[21] Papinian, etc., were Roman jurists under Augustus and the Antonines.

[22] This is *floret* in the editions of 1566 and 1583; *flores*, in 1595.

Europe was ever more famous for knowledge of laws than is present-day France (which even foreigners now admit). Nor is there any arena of France more brilliant than this very city [Paris], on account of the glamor of this court, and also because of the contacts of this city and its associations, really, with the whole world. Since these things are so, I think that Plato's plan to care for the people and to shape the laws, and the goal of both Solon and Lycurgus to supply much-needed legislation from the observations of a long journey, as well as the purpose of the decemvirs in traveling throughout Greece, cannot be achieved more conveniently or more easily than in these learned days and in this legal school. Neither Hadrian nor Justinian had any interest in foreign law, but it cannot be doubted that had the elder Francis lived longer he would have undertaken this additional task of correlation and would have completed it. It would not have been necessary to invite jurisconsults from Greece or to summon legislators from elsewhere.

But since so great a king has been snatched away, a wretched change has come upon us. Although he scattered seed in the fields of letters, those who ought to have gathered the teeming harvests and hanging fruits of the sciences preferred to let them decay, of course taking the rewards away from the producers, so that the revenues were given to ignorant and base men. I cannot recall without the bitterest sense of grief that those brilliant flashes of talent which shone throughout all France have been extinguished in desolation and want.

Since you have no time free from public duties, you can only use your high authority to urge the Semelorii, the Portae, the Canaii, and the Mangones,[23] whose affluence gives them leisure, to strive by their writings to do good service to the laws. Or rather they should give thanks to laws, meriting their gratitude, by means of which they have become such as they are. As for the fact that they warn their consultants carefully lest they be deceived, they do what is worthy of their virtue and wisdom; but it is also part of that virtue and wisdom to arrange that posterity receive those inspired decisions which they allow to reach the throng producing not only everlasting fame but also the safety of the state.

This achievement is not to be expected from men whom no one wishes to consult about justice; who prefer to be regarded as grammarians rather than as jurisconsults; who assume a false reputation of

[23] I have not been able to identify these worthies in Pauly-Wissowa or other classical encyclopedias. They were obviously Roman jurists with literary abilities.

knowledge and none of equity; who think that the state is served, judgments decided, and lawsuits settled by the quantities of syllables. Clearly this grammatical pest begins to infest the approaches to all disciplines, so that instead of philosophers, orators, mathematicians, and theologians, we are forced to endure petty grammarians from the schools. The men who ought gently to have cleaned the stains and spots from the old record, so that the ancient scene would be recognized, have with a steel pen so heavily glossed all books with worthless and, indeed, misleading notes that almost no image of antiquity remains.

But omitting those who voluntarily remove themselves from the list of learned men, I come back to history, whence started our discourse. From this subject then we have collected the widely scattered statutes of ancient peoples, so that we may include them also in this work. Indeed, in history the best part of universal law lies hidden; and what is of great weight and importance for the best appraisal of legislation— the custom of the peoples, and the beginnings, growth, conditions, changes, and decline of all states—are obtained from it. The chief subject matter of this *Method* consists of these facts, since no rewards of history are more ample than those usually gathered about the governmental form of states. I have written more on this topic than on the other topics, because few have treated the problem, so vital to comprehend, and those few only superficially.

If this discussion seems to some too extensive and apparently diffuse, they should realize that endless problems, like the history of human affairs, cannot be compressed in a brief treatise. But if Galen composed more than thirty books merely about the method of his branch of learning, which is included within definite limits, and Diomedes actually poured forth six thousand books about grammar, certainly what I have written about universal history ought not to seem too lengthy.

Of course I am aware that this work which I have already offered to you will be in all respects insufficient, in the light of the fame you have won for your remarkable erudition and virtues. My enthusiastic tribute to these virtues I have decided neither to disclose in a publication so obscure nor to proclaim before you. Farewell.

February 1, 1566.

PREAMBLE ON THE EASE, DELIGHT, AND ADVANTAGE OF HISTORICAL READING

ALTHOUGH history has many eulogists, who have adorned her with honest and fitting praises, yet among them no one has commended her more truthfully and appropriately than the man who called her the "master of life." This designation, which implies all the adornments of all virtues and disciplines, means that the whole life of man ought to be shaped according to the sacred laws of history, even as to the canon of Polycletus. Certainly philosophy, which itself is called the "guide of life," would remain silent among dead things, even though the extreme limits of good and evil had been set, unless all sayings, deeds, and plans are considered in relation to the account of days long past.[1] From these not only are present-day affairs readily interpreted but also future events are inferred, and we may acquire reliable maxims for what we should seek and avoid. So it seemed to me remarkable that, among so many writers and in so learned an age, until now there has been no one who has compared famous histories of our forbears with each other and with the account of deeds done by the ancients. Yet this could be accomplished easily if all kinds of human activities were brought together and if from them a variety of examples should be arranged, appropriately and each in its place, in order that those who had devoted themselves entirely to crime might be reviled by well-earned curses, but those who were known for any virtue might be extolled according to their deserts.

This, then, is the greatest benefit of historical books, that some men, at least, can be incited to virtue and others can be frightened away from vice. Although the good are praiseworthy in themselves, even if they are acclaimed by no one, nevertheless it is proper that both living and dead, in addition to other rewards offered to excellence, should attain due meed of praise, which many people think is the only real reward. The wicked may observe with annoyance that the good who have been oppressed by them are exalted even to the heavens, but that they themselves and the name of their race will suffer eternal disgrace. Even if they dissemble, yet they cannot bear this without the bitterest sense of grief. What Trogus Pompey [2] reported about Herostratus and Titus

---

[1] Philosophy would lack vitality without illustration from history.

[2] Trogus Pompey was a historian of the time of Augustus. In the *Historiae Philippicae*

Livy [3] about Manlius Capitolinus is not true, not even probable, I think
—that they were more eager for great fame than for good fame. I believe that despondency and madness impelled the former; the other was
led by a hope of increased prestige through ruling his fellow citizens.
Otherwise it must be confessed that men eager for glory bear insults with
equanimity, which is a contradiction in itself. If the minds of the wicked
were revealed, as we read in the pages of Plato, we should see there
welts and lacerations from the scourge, bloody marks on the beaten
body, or even impressions of a burning iron; [4] it is unbelievable to what
extent the fear of infamy rends and consumes those among them who
are more eager for glory. Even if they have no taste for true praise, yet
they strive for empty fame. Although some are so stupid that they believe their souls die along with their bodies, yet as long as they live they
think posterity's opinion is of the utmost importance, and they often
pray that a conflagration of the world may follow their death. Nero, indeed, used to hope for this in his own lifetime. Tiberius Augustus is a
case in point: although he did many things cruelly and lustfully, due
to his weak character, yet he would have been worse if he had not cared
for fame. So he sought a hiding place for his crimes in some remote
isle, and since he judged himself unworthy to rule he obstinately refused
the power and title of "father of his country" (as Suetonius said) [5] lest
at a later day, as a greater disgrace, he should be found unequal to such
high honors. There is extant a speech of his, delivered in the Senate, in
which he says one thing must be won by a prince—a favorable reputation. Otherwise his virtues are ignored through his neglect of fame.
Letters exist, written by him in mournful mood, in which he miserably
laments his past life and complains that he already feels the grave scorn
of posterity, yet cannot change his habits. This princely fear of infamy,
this lesson of history, seemed to Cornelius Tacitus so significant that it
alone ought to incite men to read and write on the subject.

But of what value is it that this branch of learning is the inventor
and preserver of all the arts, and chiefly of those which depend upon
action? Whatever our elders observe and acquire by long experience is
committed to the treasure house of history; then men of a later age join

---

he covers the story of the Near East from Ninus to Philip of Macedon. This exists only
in the epitome made by Justin.

[3] Titus Livy *De urbe condita* VI. 11.

[4] The idea is that the tyrant suffers within his own soul the tortures he has inflicted
on others. See Plato *Gorgias* 525.

[5] Suetonius Tranquillus *Lives of the Caesars* III. 67.

to observations of the past reflections for the future and compare the causes of obscure things, studying the efficient causes and the ends of each as if they were placed beneath their eyes. Moreover, what can be for the greater glory of immortal God or more really advantageous than the fact that sacred history is the means of inculcating piety to God, reverence to parents, charity to individuals, and justice to all? Where, indeed, do we obtain the words of the prophets and the oracles, where the unending vitality and power of minds, unless we draw them from the fount of the Holy Scriptures?

But beyond that boundless advantage, the two things which are usually sought in every discipline, ease and pleasure, are so blended in the understanding of historical books that greater ease or equal pleasure does not seem to inhere in any other body of knowledge. The ease, indeed, is such that without help of any special skill the subject is understood by all. In other arts, because all are linked together and bound by the same chains, the one cannot be grasped without knowledge of the other. But history is placed above all branches of knowledge in the highest rank of importance and needs the assistance of no tool, not even of letters, since by hearing alone, passed on from one to another, it may be given to posterity. So Moses, in one chapter of the law, says you will tell these things to your sons, though it foretell the ruin of their state and their books.[6] Yet even if empires, states, and cities perish, this story nevertheless abides forever, as he says. Most accurately Cicero foresaw that Salamis would perish before the memory of the deeds done at Salamis,[7] for it was deeply engulfed by a whirlpool, as the waters have covered Aegira, Bura, and Helice, and a great part of Crete itself— which once on account of the multitude of towns was called "hundred-citied" [8] but now may be called "three-citied"—and in our century much of Holland also. But the story of the past, unless the ruin of the human race first comes about, will never die, but will linger forever, even in the minds of countryfolk and the unlearned.

To ease is added the pleasure that we take in following the narrative of virtue's triumphs. This, I suppose, is so great that he who once is captivated and won over by the delights of history can never suffer himself to be torn from her sweet embrace. Moreover, if men are impelled by such eagerness for knowledge that they now take pleasure even in

[6] All four editions, 1566, 1572, 1583, 1595, agree on *librorum* rather than *liberorum*.

[7] Cicero *Tusculan Disputations* I. 46.

[8] Pliny *Natural History* IV. 20. The editions of the *Methodus* of 1583 and 1595 read *nubium*, whereas the edition of 1572 reads correctly *urbium*.

unreliable tales, how much greater will it be when events are recounted truthfully? Then, too, what is more delightful than to contemplate through history the deeds of our ancestors placed before our eyes as in a picture? What more enjoyable than to envisage their resources, their troops, and the very clash of their lines of battle? The pleasure, indeed, is such that sometimes it alone can cure all illnesses of the body and the mind. To omit other evidence, there are Alphonso and Ferdinand, kings of Spain and of Sicily; one recovered his lost health through Livy, the other through Quintus Curtius, although the skill of physicians could not help them. Another example is Lorenzo de' Medici (called "the father of letters"), who is said to have recovered from an illness without any medicine (although history is a tonic) through the narration of that tale told of the Emperor Conrad III. This ruler after he had in a long siege defeated Guelph, the duke of Bavaria, and would not be diverted on any terms from the proposed and attempted razing of the city, finally was won over by the prayers of noble ladies and permitted them to go away unharmed, on condition that they might take out nothing from the city which they could not transport on their backs. Then they, with greater faith, shall I say, or piety, started to carry off the duke himself, their husbands, their children, and their parents, borne on their shoulders. In this the emperor took such pleasure that, shedding tears of joy, he not only cast cruelty and wrath completely from his mind but also spared the city and formed a friendship with the bitterest of his enemies. Who, then, doubts that history may fill with the most exquisite delight the minds of even the most ferocious and boorish of men?

There is more danger that while we revel in too great appreciation, we may overlook the utility (although in delight, also, there is use). This happens to people who dwell on the details of trifling matters, as though they were feeding on condiments and spices, neglecting more solid food. Therefore, passing over the pleasure of this kind of reading, I go on to the utility. How great it is, not only in the most accurate narratives, but even in those where only a likeness to actual fact and some glimmer of truth shines, I shall make plain—not with countless proofs, since each one can draw these things from the same sources as I, but by bringing forward the example of Scipio Africanus alone. When he had grasped firmly in mind the *Cyropaedia* of Xenophon and had learned from it the vast treasure of all virtues and glories, he became such a great man that not only was a formidable war kindled in Spain for no other cause than awe of Scipio and contempt for other generals (thus Livy writes), but also he lived respected and unharmed by the robbers themselves. When brigands approached his country house and the serfs, gathered together, resolutely repulsed from the entrance men who apparently were hostile to Scipio, the latter, as suppliants, begged from the serfs permission to behold and to venerate that divine man; when he understood what was wanted, he consented, in order to transform to human kindness the barbarity of the robbers (although by his virtue he had already mitigated their barbarism). The benefit of real glory was produced by the story of the older Cyrus—a work not true to fact so much as expressive of the ideal of a very just and brave king.

But, not to concentrate on ancient times, there is no example more recent or more famous than that of Selim, prince of the Turks. Although his ancestors always avoided history on the ground that it is false, he himself first had the deeds of Caesar translated into the vernacular, and by imitating that general in a short time he joined a great part of Asia Minor and of Africa to the dominion of his ancestors. Moreover, what drove Caesar himself to such valor, if not emulation of Alexander? When he read of his victories, he wept copious tears because at an age when his hero had conquered all the world he himself had not yet done anything. Likewise, what was the cause of so many victories for Alexander, if not the valor of Achilles, depicted by Homer as the model of an excellent general? Without this work Alexander could not even sleep. What, lastly, to avoid foreign examples, brought Emperor Charles V to such glory, if not emulation of Louis XI, king of the French, from the book of Comines?

Now, indeed, since history has boundless advantages, is read with great ease, and gives even greater pleasure, it has not been open to anyone's reproach. Although many have misrepresented the other arts as dangerous or useless, no one has yet been found who has marked the record of the past with any stain of infamy—unless perchance the man who accused this art of mendacity when he had declared war on all the virtues and the disciplines. But such a reproach is for fables, not for history; if the account is not true, it ought not even to be called history, as Plato thought. He says that every product of thought is either true or false: he calls the latter poetry, the former knowledge.[9] But why argue? When so much of advantage may be extracted from the very fables of Homer, which take unto themselves the likeness of information and truth, then what sort of reward must we hope from history? Since this teaches us clearly not only the arts necessary for living but

[9] That is, fabrication, poesy (from ποιέω, to make) in contrast to information founded on investigation, history (from ἱστορέω, to inquire).

also those objectives which at all costs must be sought, what things to
avoid, what is base, what is honorable, which laws are most desirable,
which state is the best, and the happiest kind of life. Finally, since if we
put history aside the cult of God, religion, and prophecies grow obsolete
with the passing of centuries; therefore, on account of the inexpressible
advantage of such knowledge, I have been led to write this book, for
I noticed that while there was a great abundance and supply of historians, yet no one has explained the art and the method of the subject.
Many recklessly and incoherently confuse the accounts, and none derives
any lessons therefrom. Formerly men wrote books about the proper arrangement of historical treatises; how wisely, I do not discuss. They
have, perhaps, a possible excuse for their project. Yet, if I may give an
opinion, they seem to resemble some physicians, who are distrustful of
all kinds of medicine: resolutely they once again examine their preparation and do not try to teach the strength and nature of the drugs which
are proposed in such abundance or to fit them to the present illnesses.
This applies also to those who write about the organization of historical
material, when all books contain ample information about the past and
the libraries contain the works of many historians whom they might
more usefully have taken to study and imitate than to discuss oratorically
the exordium, the narrative, and the ornaments of words and sentences.

Then, in order that what we are going to write about the historical
method may have some outline, we shall at the beginning divide and
delimit the subject, then indicate the order of reading. After this we
shall arrange similar instances of human activities from history, so that
this may be an aid to memory. Afterwards we shall consider the choice
of individual writers. Then we shall discuss the correct evaluation of
works in this field. Following this we shall speak about the governmental
form of states, in which the discipline of all history is chiefly engaged.
Then we shall refute those who have upheld the idea of the four monarchies and the golden age. Having explained these things, we shall try
to make clear the obscure and intricate sequence of chronologies, so that
one can understand whence to seek the beginning of history and from
what point it ought to be traced. At length we shall refute the error of
those who maintain the independent origin of races. Finally we move
on to the arrangement and order of reading historians, so that it may
be plainly understood what each man wrote about and in what period
he lived.

CHAPTER I

WHAT HISTORY IS AND OF
HOW MANY CATEGORIES

O F HISTORY, that is, the true narration of things, there are three kinds: human, natural, and divine. The first concerns man; the second, nature; the third, the Father of nature. One depicts the acts of man while leading his life in the midst of society. The second reveals causes hidden in nature and explains their development from earliest beginnings. The last records the strength and power of Almighty God and of the immortal souls, set apart from all else. In accordance with these divisions arise history's three accepted manifestations [1]—it is probable, inevitable, and holy—and the same number of virtues are associated with it, that is to say, prudence, knowledge, and faith. The first virtue distinguishes base from honorable; the second, true from false; the third, piety from impiety. The first, from the guidance of reason and the experience of practical affairs, they call the "arbiter of human life." The second, from inquiry into abstruse causes, they call the "revealer of all things." The last, due to love of the one God toward us, is known as the "destroyer of vice." From these three virtues together is created true wisdom, man's supreme and final good. Men who in life share in this good are called blessed, and since we have come into the light of day to enjoy it, we should be ungrateful if we did not embrace the heaven-offered benefit, wretched if we abandon it. Moreover, in attaining it we derive great help from history in its three phases, but more especially from the divine form, which unaided can make mankind happy, even though they have no experience of practical affairs and no knowledge of secret physical causes. Yet if the two latter are added, I believe that they will bring about a great increase in human well-being.

Therefore it would follow that we should turn our first inquiries to the history of divine things. But since in man mother nature engenders first the desire for self-preservation, then little by little due to awe of

---

[1] The word is *assensio*, which in philosophical parlance means the reality of sensible appearances. See Cicero *Academica* II. 12. These manifestations parallel the three divisions: human, which is not absolutely certain, but only probable, developing the use of foresight or prudence; natural history, exact, and therefore inescapable, giving us knowledge; and divine, which is beyond human appraisal and therefore requires faith.

Nature's workings drives him to investigate their causes, and since from these interests she draws him to an understanding of the very Arbiter of all things—for this reason it seems that we must begin with the subject of human affairs as soon as there shall have dawned in the minds of children perceptions of God, the All-Highest, not only probable but also inevitable for belief.[2] So it shall come about that from thinking first about ourselves, then about our family, then about our society we are led to examine nature and finally to the true history of Immortal God, that is, to contemplation. How difficult is the last to men who have not yet been admitted to the mysteries of revealed philosophy is understood well enough by those who have trained themselves somewhat in meditation on great matters. While they raise their minds little by little above their senses, as though over the waves in which the majority of mankind are submerged, they can, however, never liberate themselves far enough to avoid images created by their senses, like nebulae, placing themselves in opposition to the light of truth. On this account it happens that those who start with divine history, without thinking about human affairs and natural science, and explain to boys or unlearned men difficult problems about divine matters, not only are mistaken in their expectations but also discourage many by the very magnitude of these problems. In the same way that we urge those who come from a thick blackish mist into the light to observe attentively the splendor of the sun first on earth, then in the clouds, then on the moon, in order that, having strengthened their vision, they may be able some time to gaze upon the sun itself, we must act for the benefit of the unlettered also. They should first notice the goodness of God and His pre-eminence in human affairs, then in manifest natural causes, then in the arrangement and splendor of the heavenly bodies; after that, in the admirable order, motion, immensity, harmony, and shape of the entire universe, so that by these steps we may sometime return to that intimate relationship which we have with God, to the original source of our kind, and again be united closely to Him. Those who interpret history differently seem to me to violate the eternal laws of nature.

Since eminent and learned men have expressed concisely in written works this threefold classification of the subject, I have proposed to myself just this—that I may establish an order and a manner of reading these and of judging carefully between them, especially in the history of human affairs. For, in general, divine and natural history differ

[2] Compare the three manifestations of history mentioned in note 1.

greatly from human, particularly in this respect, that they not only deal
with origins but also are comprised within definite limits. Natural history presents an inevitable and steadfast sequence of cause and effect unless it is checked by divine will or for a brief moment abandoned by it
and, so to speak, yielded up to the prince of fluid matter and the father
of all evils. From the abandonment are derived spectacles of distorted
nature and huge monsters; from the interposition, outstanding miracles
of God. From both are engendered in us the beginning of religion or
superstition and awe of an inescapable divine will, so that the resplend-
ent and manifest glory of God may become more visible to the race of
men (even though it cannot be more shining or more clear).

But because human history mostly flows from the will of mankind,
which ever vacillates and has no objective—nay, rather, each day new
laws, new customs, new institutions, new manners confront us—so, in
general, human actions are invariably involved in new errors unless they
are directed by nature as leader. That is, they err if they are not directed
by correct reasoning or if, when the latter has deteriorated, they are not
guided without the help of secondary causes by that divine foresight
which is closer to the principle of their origin. If we depart from this,
we shall fall headlong into all sorts of infamy. Although the mind of
man, plucked from the eternal divine mind, isolates itself as far as possible from earthly stain, still, because it is deeply immersed in unclean
matter, it is so influenced by contact with it, and even distracted within
itself by conflicting emotions, that without divine aid it can neither up-
lift itself nor achieve any degree of justice nor accomplish anything according to nature. Consequently it comes about that as long as we are
handicapped by the weakness of our senses and by a false image of
things, we are not able to discern useful from useless or true from false
or base from honorable, but by a misuse of words we attribute our action to prudence in order not to trespass. Since for acquiring prudence
nothing is more important or more essential than history, because epi-
sodes in human life sometimes recur as in a circle, repeating themselves,
we judge that attention must be given to this subject, especially by those
who do not lead a secluded life, but are in touch with assemblies and
societies of human beings.

So of the three types of history let us for the moment abandon the
divine to the theologians, the natural to the philosophers, while we concentrate long and intently upon human actions and the rules governing
them. Investigation into human activity is either universal or particular:

the latter includes the memorable words and deeds of a single man or, at the utmost, of a people. As the Academicians wisely did not assume any generalized concept of old women's affairs, so history should not concern itself with actions equally futile. Universal history narrates the deeds of many men or states, and in two ways: either of several peoples, for example, Persians, Greeks, Egyptians, or of all whose deeds have been handed down or, at least, of the most famous. This also can be done in many ways. That is to say, when events are listed according to time—for each day, or month, or year—then the accounts are called ephemerides, or diaries, and annals. Or writers may trace from the origin of each state, or as far as memory permits, or even from the creation of the world, the beginnings, growth, established type, decline, and fall of states. This also is done in two ways: briefly or fully, and the books are accordingly called chronicles or chronologies, respectively. Other writers achieve the same end in a slightly different way. Verrius Flaccus [3] called history a "tale spread abroad," in which the importance of affairs, persons, and places was weighed by whoever was present at these events. But Cicero gave the name "annals" to accounts reporting the deeds of each year without any ornament or troublesome inquiry into causes. History, said Cicero, is nothing but the making of annals. Diaries, or ephemerides, are the deeds of each day, as Asellio explained in the writings of Gellius.[4] But *fasti* are annals in which all memorable things, the greatest magistrates, the most famous victories, defeats, triumphs, and secular games are briefly mentioned. Such are the works of Verrius Flaccus, Crator,[5] Ausonius,[6] Cassiodorus,[7] and Cuspinian,[8] yet they are generally called histories.

[3] Verrius Flaccus was a lexicographer, probably of the first century B.C. His work is embodied in *De verborum significatione*, by Sextus Pompeius Festus.

[4] Aulus Gellius was a Latin grammarian who lived under Hadrian. The reference is to *Noctes Atticae* v. xviii. 8.

[5] Crator was a freedman of the time of M. Aurelius Verus. He wrote a history of Rome from the foundation to the death of Verus, in which the names of consuls and other magistrates were given.

[6] Ausonius lived in Gaul in the fourth century A.D. and wrote *Tetrasticha* on the Caesars from Julius to Elagabalus.

[7] Cassiodorus, c.486–575, a Roman noble who influenced the intellectual development of medieval Europe through the library which he established at Vivarium. To teach those who were working there he wrote the *Institutiones*, covering the practices of the *scriptorium*. Under his supervision the ecclesiastical histories of Socrates, Sozomen, and Theodoret were translated into Latin under the title *Historia tripartita*.

[8] Cuspinian (Joannes Spiesshaymer), 1473–1529, German diplomat and scholar, was the author of *Commentarii de consulibus Romanorum*.

The above-mentioned division is equally appropriate for natural and divine histories. Either they tell the origin and development of one religion, that is, the Christian, or of several, or of all, especially the most famous—although there cannot be more than one religion which strikes a mean between superstition and impiety. In the same way the natural history of one thing can be collected—for example, of a plant or animal, or of all plants or animals. Such are the books of Theophrastus [9] and Aristotle, or we may even have an account of all the elements and of the bodies made from them, or, finally, the description of all nature, such as Pliny encompassed.

If anyone does not wish to include mathematics with the natural sciences, then he will make four divisions of history: human, of course, uncertain and confused; natural, which is definite, but sometimes uncertain on account of contact with matter or an evil deity, and therefore inconsistent; mathematical, more certain, because it is free from the admixture of matter, for in this way the ancients made the division between the two; finally, divine, most certain and by its very nature changeless. And this is all about the delimitation of history.

[9] Theophrastus, a pupil of Aristotle, and author of *History of Astronomy* and *History of Plants*.

CHAPTER II

THE ORDER OF READING
HISTORICAL TREATISES

THE SAME system and method which is generally employed in treating the arts should, I think, be used in the discipline of history. It is not enough to have a quantity of historical works at home, unless one understands the use of each and in what order and manner each ought to be read. At a banquet, even if the seasonings themselves are most agreeable, yet the result is disagreeable if they are put together in haphazard fashion; so one must make provision that the order of the narratives be not confused, that is, that the more recent portion be not assigned to an earlier place for reading or the central portion to the end. People who make this error not only are unable to grasp the facts in any way but even seriously weaken the power of their memory. So in order that the understanding of history shall be complete and facile, at the start let us apply that pre-eminent guide to the teaching of the arts which is called analysis. This, in general, shows how to cut into parts and how to redivide each part into smaller sections and with marvelous ease explains the cohesion of the whole and the parts in mutual harmony. We must not attempt a synthesis, since the parts of all historical movements are nicely adjusted to each other and cemented into one body, as it were, by the great industry of scholars; but by some people they are unskillfully separated. There is, however, such great cohesion of the parts and of the whole that if they are torn asunder they cannot possibly stand alone. So Polybius reproached Fabius Maximus [1] and other writers on the Punic War because of this very thing—that they specialized on one or another phase of that struggle. He wrote that they were in a sense depicting the eye separated from the head, or some other member torn from the living being, so that one cannot properly understand of what it is a part. Dionysius of Halicarnassus [2] made the same

[1] Q. Fabius Pictor flourished 225 B.C. He was the most ancient writer of Roman history in prose and carried the story from Aeneas down to his own time. The reference is to Polybius *The Histories* I. i. 14. The rivalry between the house of Scipio and the Fabii is reflected in Polybius's unfavorable comments about Fabius.

[2] Dionysius of Halicarnassus flourished 30 B.C. He was the author of *Roman Archaeology*, a great work on Roman history in twenty books, coming up to 264 B.C. and preceding Polybius. He emphasized the Greek origins of Rome.

charge against Polybius, Silenus,[3] Timaeus,[4] Antigonus,[5] and Jerome,[6] who had left mutilated and imperfect commentaries on Roman history. Somebody might make a like comment against Dionysius also. But they are not to be blamed, because not all subjects should be treated by every writer, nor can they be, since each with infinite labor and diligence collects only as much as he can gather. I believe that this reproach applies, not to the writing, but rather to the reading of histories, whose fragments, if they are torn apart, will not cohere to each other or to the whole. What they set down concerning Roman history let us in turn state about the universal history of all peoples. I call that history universal which embraces the affairs of all, or of the most famous peoples, or of those whose deeds in war and in peace have been handed down to us from an early stage of their national growth. Although many more things have been omitted than are included in any work, nevertheless so many remain that the life of a man, however prolonged, is hardly sufficient for reading them.

First, then, let us place before ourselves a general chart for all periods, not too detailed and therefore easy to study, in which are contained the origins of the world, the floods, the earliest beginnings of the states and of the religions which have been more famous, and their ends, if indeed they have come to an end. These things may be fixed in time by the creation and the founding of the City, then by the Olympiad, or even, if reason demands, by the year of Christ and the Hegira of the Arabs (which in popular chronicles is omitted). Conforming closely to this type are the works commonly called chronicles, characterized by spaces between the lines, brief indeed, but easy for beginners. Although their chronology is not exact, yet they approach fairly close to the truth of the matter. After this representation we shall use a somewhat fuller and more accurate book, which covers the origins, conditions, changes, and fall not only of illustrious peoples but also of all peoples, yet with a brevity such that one can see almost at a glance what was the established form of each state. Many have written works of this kind, but no one, it seems to me, more accurately than Johann Funck,[7] who collected in

---

[3] Silenus was a Greek historian mentioned by Cicero (*De divinatione* I. xxiv. 49). The reference is to Dionysius I. vi.

[4] Timaeus flourished 260 B.C. He was a Sicilian who wrote a history of Sicily from the earliest times, using the Olympiads as a system of dating.

[5] Antigonus was a Greek historian of Italy of the third century B. C.

[6] Jerome of Cardia, a historian of the Hellenistic era. See below, p. 370.

[7] Johann Funck, 1518–1566, author of *Chronologia, hoc est omnium temporum et annorum ab initio mundi usque ad hunc praesentem . . . annum 1552.*

a definite scheme of chronology the things which have been recorded by
Eusebius,[8] Bede,[9] Lucidus,[10] Sigismund,[11] Martin, and Phrygio.[12] He
carefully corrected many errors in these writers. But since he sometimes
lost himself in details, let us pass them over and touch upon only the
most important. Having been somewhat informed by this writer about
the condition of all states, we shall run through the history of Carion,[13]
or rather, of Melanchthon, with a like care. He was sometimes too
prolix on theological disputes, as he was much given to religion and
piety. If these accounts seem objectionable, it is very easy to skip them.
The other things which can be said in general about famous states, it
seems to me, he has covered briefly and accurately. If there is any other
author (there are some) who has written universal history more fully
than Melanchthon, I think that he ought to be read.

Then from the general we move on little by little to the details, still
in the order in which they are arranged in the tables of chronicles. Since
the system of governing a state, knowledge, and lastly civilization itself
have come from the Chaldeans, Assyrians, Phoenicians, and Egyptians,
at first we shall study the antiquity of these races, not only in writers
who have written of them especially, such as Berosus,[14] Megasthenes,[15]
and Herodotus, but also from the Hebrew authors, whose affairs have
much in common with the rest. Many more definite things about the
neighboring peoples are commemorated in the *Antiquities* of Josephus [16]

---

[8] Eusebius of Caesarea, historian and theologian of the fourth century, was author of
Chronographia and the chronological canons as well as *Historia ecclesiastica* in Greek.

[9] Bede, 673–735, historian and theologian, was author of the *Ecclesiastical History of
England* in Latin and *De temporum ratione*, which divided history into six ages from the
creation, using the birth of Christ as the dividing point in dating.

[10] Johannes Lucidus Samotheus, a famous mathematician of the sixteenth century, was
the author of *Emmendationes temporum*.

[11] Sigismund Meisterlin was the author of *Chronicon Augustanum ecclesiasticum*. He
died c.1488.

[12] Paul Constant Seidenstücker, 1483–1543, called himself Phrygio. He wrote *Chroni-
cum . . . ab exordio mundi temporum seculorumque seriem complectens.*

[13] Johann Carion of Lübeck, 1499–1537, was author of *Chronicorum libri tres*. This
was edited by Philip Melanchthon and Gaspar Peucer, and brought up to the time of
Charles V.

[14] Berosus was a priest of Bel in Babylon in the third century B.C. There are extracts
from his *Chaldaica* in Josephus and in Eusebius.

[15] Megasthenes was a historian of about 300 B.C. who wrote *Annalium Persicorum
liber I.*

[16] Flavius Josephus, c.37–c.95, was author of the *Wars of the Jews* and other works
dealing with Jewish history. He won the favor of Vespasian, and lived during his later
years in Rome, where a statue was erected to him, on the authority of Eusebius, *Ecclesiastical History* III. 9.

and in his *Books against Apion* than in any other writers. Afterwards we shall investigate the history of the Hebrews, but in such a way that we shall study at first the system of establishing a state rather than a religion, which belongs to the third type of history and requires a more exalted state of mind. Then we shall come to the empires of the Medes, Persians, Indians, and Scythians. From these we turn to the Greeks, who propagated their kind from the Araxes, the Euphrates, and the gates of Syria even to the Hellespont, and from the Hellespont even to the Danube, the Acroceraunian, and the Aemian Mountains. They filled with a multitude of colonists the nearby isles of Asia and of Europe and then Italy itself. There is a threefold division of these: the first are called the Ionians; the second, the Aeolians; the last, the Dorians. From the Greeks we come to the Italians, who are surrounded by the Alps and both seas. Since they excelled all peoples in the majesty of their empire and the glory of their deeds and through their great reputation for justice became so pre-eminent that they appear to eclipse all other nations not only in laws and institutions but also in the superiority of their language until the present, the entire antiquity of this people must be diligently investigated. Moreover, since they waged long and costly wars with the Carthaginians, the history of both races is practically covered by the same writers.

I think that the Celts are nearest to the Romans, and they may be older than the Italians themselves. Certainly they were famous for military training before the Romans were, and they sent colonies not only into Italy but also into Spain, Germany, Greece, and Asia, as we shall recount in its proper place. Although Caesar confined them within the frontiers of the Garonne and the Seine, nevertheless they extended their rule from the Pyrenees and the ocean to the Rhine and the Alps. Next come the Germans, who are surrounded by the Alps, the Rhine, the Vistula, the Carpathian Mountains, and the Baltic Sea, and the people who are neighbors of the Germans—Danes, Norwegians, Swedes, and Scandinavians. Then come the peoples who trace their origin from these— Goths, Franks, Vandals, Huns, Heruli, Lombards, Burgundians, Angles, and Normans, who have done great deeds and established most flourishing empires in France, Britain, Spain, and Italy. Although the Spanish and the Britons are renowned on account of their past, yet their deeds have not been so famous as those mentioned earlier. In a similar category are the Arabs, who were noted for the antiquity of their race, but for a long time remained hidden away in slothfulness, until, bursting forth from the deserts, they drove the Persians and the Greeks from the control of Asia and Africa and won great victories in Europe. They spread not only their arms but also their religion, customs, institutions, and finally their own language throughout the whole world. The common man calls them Saracens; they are, however, a combination of various peoples, but the Arabs themselves hold the controlling position, as we shall make plain later.

From these we move on to the Turks, who, advancing from the shores of the Caspian Sea into Asia, little by little penetrated with their armies the regions of Asia Minor, all Greece, and Egypt. Nor shall we omit the empire of the Tartars, who rule far and wide beyond the Imaeus Mountains and the Caspian Sea, or of the Muscovites, who advanced their frontiers from the Volga River and the Don to the Dnieper and recently annexed Livonia. Last are the Americans and those who control the shores of southern Africa and India, whose history also it will be useful and pleasant to understand.

All these things ought to be run through lightly at first, then they must be examined more accurately, so that when we shall have grasped the most important heads of the narrative, as it were, we may come gradually to the details. We shall investigate not only the great states but also certain mediocre and unimportant ones, for example, the principalities of the Rhodians, Venetians, Sicilians, Cretans, Helvetians, Achaeans, Genoans, Florentines, and the like. Pausanias [17] has described with a fair degree of accuracy the separate states of the Greeks. When the history of all countries has thus been learned, it remains for us to inquire into the deeds of the men who achieved fame through power, or by the splendor and riches of their race, or finally by their valor and conspicuous talent. Of these each reader will make selection according to his judgment and apply the words and deeds of each hero to his theories of life. After the history of human affairs, if anyone has leisure to scrutinize the natural sciences, he will find them much easier approaches to theology. If, on the other hand, the difficulty of the matter and the circumstances of life shall call him from this undertaking, he will enter upon his professional career. Or if for him no place is left in life's activities, let him be the spectator of others in order that with his own eyes he may survey those human affairs whose dead image he has seen in books. We can gather the most valuable fruits from history in no other

[17] Pausanias was a native of Lydia in the second century A.D. His main work was *Description of Greece*.

way than by first taking a modest part in practical affairs or by diligently observing, as Pythagoras warned.

The last step will come when, having comprehended human and natural affairs, we approach the divine, as though with clean hands. First let us collect the chief teachings of each religion. Then let us see who was the author of each; what beginnings, what advances, finally what form and what end it had; what in each is accessory to virtue, what foreign. To these we shall add opinions of illustrious philosophers concerning religion and the highest good, so that from all their opinions, revealed to view, truth may shine forth the more clearly. From this material one may usefully garner many things from which to offer trophies to all-powerful God, as did the Hebrews from the loot of the Egyptians. But in this kind of learning we shall progress further by frequent prayers and the turning of a clean mind toward God than by any course of study.

The things which we have said about the arrangement of history are understood very easily on account of the analogy to cosmography. For such is the relationship and affinity of this subject to history that the one seems to be a part of the other. Indeed, we have plucked and wrested from the geographers alone the accounts of the Scythians, Indians, Ethiopians, and Americans. In addition to these things, historians use geographical data, and they always describe regions of the earth, so that if any art is essential to them I suppose geography must seem so in the highest degree. For this reason then, like a man who wishes to understand cosmography, the historian must devote some study to a representation of the whole universe included in a small map. Then he should note the relation of the celestial bodies with reference to elemental things and separate uranography from the elements: from the air, that is, the waters, and the lands. From these he must deduce anemography, hydrography, and geography, but must apportion the latter into ten circles and as many zones. Afterwards careful observation must be taken of the order of the winds, and the nature and the extent of both seas, and the distribution of the lands. Then the earth must be divided first into four or five parts approximately, that is to say, into Europe, Asia, Africa, America, and the southeastern land, and their situation must be compared with reference to each other and with the configuration of the heavens. Next, that part of the earth which is more temperate and better known, due to the fame of the inhabitants, that is to say, Europe, divide into Spain, France, Italy, Greece, Germany, Scythia, Scandinavia, Denmark, and the islands lying adjacent to each region. Likewise partition Asia into major and minor: the former can be divided into Assyria, Persia, Parthia, Media, Hyrcania [part of Persia], Ariana, Gedrosia, India, and Scythia, hither and farther Imaeus; the latter, into Phrygia, Lydia, Lycia, Cilicia, Caria, Pamphylia, Syria, Galatia, Cappadocia, Pontus, and Armenia. In the same way divide Africa into Mauritania, Libya, Cyrenaica, Egypt, Ethiopia, Numidia, and the regions of the Negritos. In this delimitation it will be sufficient to indicate noteworthy rivers, mountains, and seas as boundaries and to designate for each region suitable meridians and parallels of the heavens.

From geography finally to chorography, that is, to the description of the regions, the approach is easy. Unraveling our pattern more subtly, we shall describe each region. For example, Spain, which is the first part of Europe, we shall divide into Betica, Lusitania, and the Tarraconian province. This last, again, into Galicia, Castile, Navarre, and Aragon, having indicated the bounding rivers, the Ebro, Guadiana, Tagus, Guadalquivir, and Douro, and that mountain (popularly called Hadrian's) which separates hither from farther Spain. Then we shall define the central latitude of the region as forty [18] degrees, but the longitude as fifteen; [19] the size in length, fourteen degrees, in width, seven. A similar system must be used for other regions.

Finally we shall move from chorography to topography and geometry, that is, to the description and dimensions of separate places. First we shall cover the famous towns, ports, shores, straits, gulfs, isthmuses, promontories, fields, hills, slopes, rocks, peaks, open country, pastures, woods, groves, copses, prairies, thickets, hedgerows, parks, orchards, green spaces, willow plantations, and all fortified towns, colonies, prefectures, municipia, citadels, basilicas, villages, cantons, and manors (if the matter shall so demand). Not otherwise shall we define and delimit universal history. As they err who study the maps of regions before they have learned accurately the relation of the whole universe and the separate parts to each other and to the whole, so they are not less mistaken who think they can understand particular histories before they have judged the order and the sequence of universal history and of all times, set forth as it were in a table.

We shall use the same analysis in the detailed account of each race, so that if anyone wishes to understand clearly and to commit to memory

---

[18] The edition of 1583 gives xi; the editions of 1566 and 1572 give xl.

[19] The prime meridian was reckoned at the Azores. See Jervis, *The World in Maps*, p. 31.

the history of the Romans, let him read first Sextus Rufus,[20] who in four pages covered the entire story; from him to the epitome of Florus,[21] and then to Eutropius.[22] Afterwards let him undertake Livy and Polybius. I offer similar advice concerning the deeds of the Franks, which Jean du Tillet [23] covered briefly in one little book. I think that this should be read before Paul Aemilius,[24] and Xiphilinus [25] before Dio,[26] Justin [27] before Diodorus [28] or Trogus, whose writings, however, have entirely disappeared. It is not enough, however, to understand universal history unless we understand also the details. But if the two kinds are joined together, Polybius said, they produce an unparalleled advantage. This view of the matter formerly escaped many who read the chief heads in Rufus or Florus, but overlooked Livy. On this account Livy's work has almost entirely perished. Likewise, Justin seems to have caused the disappearance of Trogus Pompey, and Xiphilinus of Dio.

Finally, it will happen that all sayings and deeds worthy of recall we shall consign to certain general repositories of memory as to a treasure chest. From these we shall appropriate whatever amount seems best to our judgment. Moreover, this cannot be done more conveniently than by putting before our eyes a classification of human activities.

[20] Sextus Rufus was the little-known author of *Breviarum de victoriis et provinciis populi Romani*, dedicated to the Emperor Valens.

[21] Lucius Annaeus Florus was the author of *Epitome rerum Romanarum* in the second century A.D.

[22] Eutropius was the secretary of the Emperor Constantine. He wrote *De inclytis totius Italiae provinciae ac Romanorum gestis* and *Historiae Romanae libri x*, which compresses into brief space 1,100 years of Roman history. It was enlarged by Paul the Deacon.

[23] Jean du Tillet, d.1570, was bishop of Meaux and author of *Chronicon de regibus Francorum*. The edition of 1550 is bound with the *History of France* of Paul Aemilius, frequently quoted by Bodin.

[24] Paul Aemilius of Verona, d.1529, was chancellor of Paris and historiographer of France. *De rebus gestis Francorum usque ad annos 1488 libri xx* is his chief work.

[25] Xiphilinus was a monk of Constantinople in the eleventh century. He made an abridgment of Dio.

[26] Dio Cassius flourished in the third century A.D. He wrote in Greek a history of Rome from Aeneas to A.D. 229.

[27] Justinus Frontinus composed an epitome of the work of Trogus Pompey on the Macedonian monarchy in the first century A.D.

[28] Diodorus of Sicily flourished in the first century B.C. He was author of *Bibliotheca historica*, an attempt at world history.

CHAPTER III

THE PROPER ARRANGEMENT OF
HISTORICAL MATERIAL

SINCE THE forthcoming discussion concerns primarily accounts of human affairs, let us define somewhat narrowly the word "history," itself of wide import, by the activities of men only and, in the popular manner of speaking, by the truthful narration of deeds of long ago. Moreover, such is the multiplicity and disorder of human activities, such the abundant supply of histories, that unless the actions and affairs of men are confined to certain definite types, historical works obviously cannot be understood, or their precepts long retained in mind. What scholars, then, are accustomed to do to assist memory in the other arts should, I think, be done for history also. That is, similar instances of memorable matters should be placed in a certain definite order, so that from these, as from a treasure chest, we may bring forth a variety of examples to direct our acts. Of course we do not lack the studies of erudite men, who from the reading of historical treatises have extracted sagacious opinions known as apothegms. But although in human activities three things are ordinarily noticed—plans, words, and deeds—from which we study the virtues of thinking well, speaking well, and acting well, yet only the words have been collected by writers; they have omitted what is implied in plans and in deeds. Some have recorded the sayings and the deeds of illustrious men, but rather ineffectively and without orderly arrangement. Then, too, they confuse human affairs with divine, and descriptions of nature with both the other two. They do not even suggest the intended actions, although the safety of the state often depended upon the counsel of one man. And so I think an arrangement ought to be made such that in three books we should cover the range of all fields: in the first, human affairs; in the second, natural, which often intervene in history; in the third, divine. Because there is greater disorder and obscurity in the affairs of men than in other fields of inquiry, it is agreed that we should put aside natural and divine history and concentrate upon a topical arrangement of human interests and actions. When these have been set in order, we should indicate how the flowers of history [1] may suitably be grouped, each in its proper place.

[1] Edition of 1583 gives *historiam;* the editions of 1566 and 1595 give *historiarum.*

"Activity" is defined as something which is an end in itself; [2] it does not leave any actual result of labor, like speech. "Production," on the other hand, they define as that which results in work, like writing. However, since all our discourse is phrased in popular terms, let us abandon subtility of speech and define the word "activity" more broadly, as embracing plans, words, and deeds growing out of the will of man. This applies whether the will is unpolluted and free from all passion, like that of a wise man, or diverted by emotions (for example, by lust or anger), as it is in many who are called intemperate, or even mad, and, as they say, do nothing wicked willingly, but, influenced by a certain weakness of character, will their act, nevertheless. Or perhaps something is done through fear of impending misfortune, as in the case of those who throw away precious things. [3] They do not act voluntarily or because of emotion, but having undertaken a course, they choose to lose their riches rather than themselves. If anyone is altogether out of his mind (such as the insane and those unaware of what is happening), his activities seem to be not so much human as divine, or gone awry from their proper nature, or due to a devil's compulsion. As nature's activities in attracting or repelling are not due to human agency, neither are these. Again, if any man fells another after he has been struck by that other, the original act is not his and he has not sinned. Likewise, when God or divine fury inspires someone to prophesy, the action is not human, but divine, since it is not controlled by the will of man.

Those activities are human, then, which spring from plans, sayings, and deeds of men, when volition leads the way. For will power is mistress of human activity, whether it follows reason or the lower faculty of the soul, in seeking and avoiding things.

And because nature has engendered first in every being the desire for self-preservation, the earliest activities of men are related to things impossible to forego. Later they are directed to matters without which we can, indeed, live, but not at all comfortably; or if comfortably, not splendidly; or if splendidly, still not with that keen joy which delights the senses most sweetly. Hence the desire to acquire riches. Since, however, there is no limit to our desire for pleasure, or because this is equally common to man and to beast, the more noble each man is, the further he disassociates himself from the level of the beasts, and little by little he is carried forward by eagerness for glory, so that he may eclipse the rest. From this comes the lust for domination and the vio-

---

[2] Aristotle *Politics* VII. 3. 1325b.   [3] Aristotle *Nicomachean Ethics* III. 1. 1110a.

lence inflicted upon the weak. Hence, also, come the discords, wars, slavery, and massacres. But this kind of life is turbulent and full of danger, an empty glory which cannot satisfy a man of lofty soul; as a result a man naturally well endowed is gradually carried over to activities of moral and intellectual excellence, which earn true praise and lasting fame. Many make this their highest objective.

And so, as nature is eager for repose, it is plain that these virtuous activities ought at some time to be directed to rest. For this reason it happens that a man, little by little distracted by cares and the society of his fellow men, seeks solitude that he may enjoy a tranquillity in consonance with nature. Then, looking upon human affairs and their inconstancy and unpredictability, he turns to survey the exact causes of nature. In contemplating these he takes so much delight that, devoting all his energies to understanding such studies, he neglects the power and fortunes of kings. Moreover, many who swayed great empires willingly chose to retreat to this kind of life rather than to reign. Hence come those systems of knowledge and virtue which, because they rest solely in the recognition of truth, are called speculative. Of course it is not enough for a man well endowed by nature to progress no further than those disciplines whose subject matter is apprehended by the senses. But by these steps he is carried on to things grasped only by the mind—that is, to the strength and power of immortal souls—until he is snatched upward on swift wings and, seeking the first causes of his origin, is closely united to God. In this consists the goal of human action, the final peace, and the highest felicity. Toward this all plans, words, deeds, toward this human strivings, toward this training and virtues are directed. Although contemplation is not very appropriately called activity, yet Aristotle so called it, lest inconsistently he should define a happy life otherwise than as activity.[4]

Let us then arrange these things in order. Occupations of the first kind belong to the arts relating to the protection of men's lives and to the avoidance of illness and attack, such as hunting, cattle breeding, agriculture, building, gymnastics, and medicine. The second kind belong to trade, piloting, weaving, and the mechanical arts. The third, to defense and a more splendid life, especially to the acquisitive arts, in which we are taught to amass riches and to use in magnificence what we have acquired. In this third the elaboration of the former arts is included. Ac-

[4] Aristotle *Politics* VII. 3. 1325b.

tivities then follow which are efficient causes [5] of delight. They gently exert an influence on senses or mind or both; for taste, of course, the arts of Apicius; [6] for touch, the Milesian [7] erotic (*sordida*) delights; for odor, unguents; for sight, arrangement of line and variety of color, suitably mingled, which pertain to painting, engraving, ornamental gardening, founding, statuary, then even to the various arts of dyeing and embroidering; for the ears, elegance of speaking, conveyed in rhythms or figures of speech or both. Harmony weakened and overdone by excessive elaboration exerts an influence, for while one both simple and natural is wont to cure serious illnesses of the mind, on the contrary one contrived from a medley of sounds and rapid rhythms usually drives a mind insane. This happens to men too anxious to please their ears, who dislike the Doric mode and dignified measures. They affect the Ionian, so that it ought not to seem remarkable if many become insane. Moreover, since isolated men cannot obtain from isolated men the delights and advantages of life, much less the individual from himself alone, they therefore seek an opportunity to come together in society. This, however, is not an end in itself, for those advantages are attained also by gatherings of beasts which come together in flocks. But because man has been endowed by God with the immortal gift of a soul and is associated with Him in a certain likeness, it is inconsistent with his superiority to unite him with the beasts in the same desired goal. This, indeed, would be the case if in political groupings he should live happily, but not nobly also.

Then it is not remarkable that the chief activities of men are directed toward defending their common society, the efficient cause of so many great advantages. The interests are divided among civil, domestic, and moral training: the one teaches him to control himself; the second, his family; the third, the state. It is fitting, indeed, to impose upon oneself the rule of reason, in which the culmination of all justice and of all laws resides, before it is possible to rule a wife, children, and servants, and one must control the family before he can control the state. In fact the first command is of one man over one; the second, of one man over several, to direct a wife through marital love, the children by paternal affection, the servants by the master's rule, and even to acquire riches

---

[5] Aristotle *Nic. Ethics* VI. 2. 1139a, and *Metaphysics* V. 2. 1013a.

[6] Apicius Caelius was a contemporary of Augustus and a noted epicure. He is possibly the author of *De re coquinaria*, discovered in the fifteenth century, although it may be the work of another Apicius, who lived under Trajan.

[7] Perhaps the reference is to Aristotle *Nic. Ethics* VII. 7. 1151a.

for help in life and to use the acquired riches frugally. The last reaches far and wide, embracing the union not only of one family but also of several families through relationship [8] and through the practice of trade among them, and fosters and defends this union. That, however, is brought about by civil training, in other words, by the highest discipline of command and restraint.

I do not, as many do, call civil training jurisprudence (for it is a small part of this), but a moderator of all arts and human activity, whose three subdivisions are dominion, counsel, and execution. Dominion is exercised in many ways, yet there are altogether four, and as many kinds of activity, in which are reflected the attributes of sovereignty. The first lies in creating magistrates and assigning to each his jurisdiction; the second, in promulgating laws or abrogating them; the third, in declaring war and making peace. The last consists in distributing fines and rewards and in the highest power of pardoning.

But counsel is usually held on those functions in which we have said sovereignty consists. It is one thing to declare laws, another to take counsel concerning legislation. The latter is for the senate, the former for the people or the prince or whoever has the sovereignty. Consultation takes place also about imposing or diminishing taxes, about collecting an army, receiving ambassadors or dismissing them, concerning defenses and repairing buildings—finally, about the direction of other skills and activities of citizens in the state, which cannot all be included in the laws.

But the most important of these activities are ruling, dispensing justice, summoning an assembly, and performing rites. The former activities are related to coercion; the latter, to persuasion, which has no less power, and sometimes even greater. The former deter from crime by laws and arms; the latter, by reason and religious ceremonies, impel to honor and virtue. At first men wild and barbarous as beasts must be kept from cruelty and rapine by a soldier's hand; the second method rests on the verdict of law and equity; the last is association and religious awe. Human society is held together chiefly by the arts of a general, by jurisprudence, by oratory, and by faith, if soldiers act bravely, judges equitably, priests devoutly, and speakers wisely; so it is as easily disintegrated unless they are guided by civil discipline and control. This branch of activity also directs the business of moving in and out the common necessities; agriculture, cattle breeding, medicine, piloting, and after-

[8] Aristotle *Politics* I. 2. 1252b.

wards crafts which secure either essential or convenient protection for life. Civil discipline directs literary matters, too: for example, the interpreters of divine and human law and those who were called sophists by the ancients, and later, in a single word, grammarians—the rhetoricians, I say, poets, grammarians, philosophers, and mathematicians. The ancients properly called this training architectonic, because it prescribes laws to all masters of all arts that they may direct their activities to the common good and not foment trouble to the disadvantage of the state.

In addition, this discipline defines the function of each man. Offices are civil or military. The latter care for martial affairs, but the former, domestic rule, counsel, judgments, the annual supply of the city, expenses, treasury, fields, houses, the education of youth, and religion. That entire division of functions contains seven classes. The first kind is without honor or money or power and must be undertaken by men who supervise taxes, military training, guard duty, the defense of the city, and offices of this kind without salary. The second kind includes those who have some public office with pay, but without prestige. Of this sort are the lictors and those who usually look after the disposal of the city's rubbish. The third kind is made up of those who have some paid public office, not entirely without prestige, but not associated with any particular dignity, as the publicans, scribes, notaries, public agents, and adjutants. The fourth kind is associated with honor and reward, but yet is without supreme power, such as the priests and the ambassadors. The fifth has great honor, without profit and power; such an office is that of the president of the senate or of the doge of Venice. The sixth has honor and authority, without salary—an arrangement which is proper for magistrates. Such are the consuls, praetors, censors, tribunes, archons, ephors, and others of this sort. The last class is composed of men who have honor and power and receive an income, such as the one hundred and twenty men for judging cases among the Venetians and everywhere else; it includes those who exercise jurisdiction. All these offices are guided by the might and power of the man who holds the sovereignty of the state.

We should not consider religion a part of civil training even if we see priests and pontiffs controlled by the power of the magistrates; this happens because the sacrifices and approved rites in the state must be zealously defended. But religion itself, that is, the direct turning of a cleansed mind toward God, can exist without civil training, without association, in the solitude of one man, and he is thought, by the agreement of great men, to be happier the farther he is removed from civil society.

But civil life demands perpetual action; the whole state cannot be engaged in contemplation, as the body or all faculties of the soul cannot be given to thinking. If we define "good" as contemplation alone, the same happiness will not result for the whole state as for the individual man. This difficulty troubled Aristotle very much, and he could not extricate himself from it. So, on the authority of Varro [9] (Marsilio [10] attributed it to Plato also) the ideal for a man living in society is not leisure alone or activity, but must be defined by us as mixed in character if we wish to have the same ideal for a man and for the whole city. The mind cannot enjoy pure contemplation before it shall have been entirely wrested away from the body.

Then human activities are limited to the foregoing classes. If anything has been omitted, it can be easily related to the above. Wherefore, when we have planned three books—for human, natural, and divine histories—we shall set up in the first book the separate acts of man and human events, in the order given above. The first topic will be the obscurity and the renown of the race; the second, life and death; the third, the conveniences of life; then, riches and poverty; after that, luxury of living and parsimony, games and spectacles, pleasure and pain, glory and infamy, beauty and deformity of the body, strength and weakness, crudity of manners and culture, ignorance and knowledge, gifts of genius and the lack of them; later, moral training and, in general, discussion about virtues and vices. There will follow a consideration of domestic training, of the mutual love of husband and wife, or the mutual feeling between parents and children, of the rule of the master and the compliance of servants. Or if it seems best we shall consider the mutual duty of the strong and the weak toward each other, the financial arts, love and hate, societies and trade, and relationship through blood and marriage.[11]

Afterwards we shall deal with civil knowledge. First we shall speak about dominion, royal prerogatives and despotic rule, the condition of

---

[9] M. Terentius Varro was born in 116 B.C. and became a busy man of affairs as well as the most learned man of his time. He wrote *De lingua Latina, De re rustica,* and *Antiquitates Romanae.*

[10] Marsilio Ficino, 1433–1499, was a Platonist. He translated the Greek philosophers and composed *De religione christiana.*

[11] Bodin may be quoting from the contemporary treatise of Giovanni della Case, *Trattato degli ufici communi tragli amici superiori e inferiori.*

the people and of the turbulent plebs, the rule of the optimates and the ambitions of a few. We shall discuss taking counsel for the state; proposing or annulling laws; magistrates and private citizens; war and peace; and, generally, the protection of citizens and repelling of foes; defeat and victory, rewards and punishments; imposing taxes or decreasing them; admitting or dismissing embassies; setting up or abolishing guilds and corporations; the direction of arts and disciplines; public and private trials; punishments mild and severe; sanctuary and pardon; assemblies and speakers. Finally we deal with agriculture and cattle breeding, by which states are chiefly supported; trade and naval affairs; building and workmanship; spinning and weaving; medicine and drugs; music and gymnastics; painting and statuary; perfumes and other arts giving pleasure; literary matters; the interpreters of divine and human law; philosophers and mathematicians; poets and grammarians.

The second book will cover in a suitable division the history of natural things, which are encountered rather often in reading the works of historians; first it will treat the principles of nature, time and place, rise and fall, and generally motion and change; the elements and their nature; imperfect bodies; metals and stones; the types of plants; living things separated into three groups; the heavenly bodies; the size and shape of the world. All these things it is easy to explain by more accurate distinctions, on account of the extreme exactness of natural things.

The last book concerns divine things: first about the human mind, which is the culmination of all natural developments, but the lowest of the divine, then about the threefold order of intelligences; afterwards of God and His deeds and prophecies; finally about religion and impiety.

These topics having been arranged in each book under headings in this order, or as seems more suitable to each reader, the next step will be to indicate in its own place whatever memorable fact is met in reading histories and in the margin of the book of human activities to add notes of the plans, sayings, and deeds, and put this in capitals. (Thus the relevant material is easily referred to the proper activity.) Then we can see what in the details is honorable, base, or indifferent, and a note should be made in this way, "C.H." (that is, *consilium honestum*, honorable opinion). Or if anyone—repudiating the teaching of the Stoics—prefers to separate honorable from useful, base from useless, I shall not quarrel with him. Then he will establish four types—base, honorable, useful, and useless. For example, the plan of Themistocles about burning the ships, which on behalf of the state at the command of the people he had communicated to Aristides—since it seemed useful to Aristides, yet not honorable, we shall place this subject under the heading, "concerning plans taken on behalf of the state," having added in the margin the letters "C.T.V.," that is, a base, but useful plan (*consilium turpe utile*).

Moreover, counsel is in a sense the basis of words and deeds. It may exist without them, but they cannot exist without counsel, unless something is said or done rashly. Plans of great matters are almost always secret. They are not revealed without hazard, and not until the deed is done are they clearly known. For instance, the useful advice of Cincinnatus in great storms and crises often saved the state of the Romans. When the plebs, carried away by emotion, wished to double the number of tribunes and Appius the consul vigorously resisted them, Cincinnatus, having told his plan to a few, said, "Approve it, for the more tribunes there are, the more limited will be the power of each, since the intervention of one can shatter or slow down the power of all." Of course the plebs did not realize that they were misled, but thanked the senate as though for a great favor. Let plans of this sort about the state be called useful and honorable. As for the deed of Q. Mutius—when he bought a house and, led by conscientious scruples, paid the vendor more than he asked—let this be called honorable and useless. So the plan of Themistocles, when he secretly warned the king of the Persians that the Greeks wished to cut the bridge by which he had united Asia to Europe, was not only honorable, but also most useful, both to Themistocles himself for keeping the favor of the prince, if he had conquered the Greeks; useful also to all Greece, because immediately Xerxes thought of flight. Almost always useful things coincide with honorable. Sometimes in the same episode, plans, sayings, and deeds are of similar classification. For instance, the plan of Sextus Tarquin against Lucretia was base, his speech was baser, and his act basest of all. Sometimes spoken words may vary from plans or deeds, as when Augustus wished to establish his own perpetual power, having defeated Mark Antony at Actium. He devised unusual methods, plainly contrary to the speech which he delivered in the senate. In the speech, indeed, he repeatedly refused to take control and continued to ask a release from the state; finally, conquered by the entreaties of those whom he had bribed, he called on the gods to witness that after ten years, when affairs had quieted down, he would hand over the rule. Hence those decennial vows by which he extended his rule for forty-five years. Here Cicero, impatient of servitude, would say that an honorable speech corresponds not at all with a base plan.

And since the same part of history very frequently may be listed under different heads, we must watch for the main issue: as this one, which Plutarch reported about Antiochus, in the life of Demetrius and Appian [12] in the Syrian wars. Antiochus, inflamed with an incredible passion for Stratonice, wasted away and seemed about to die, had not Erasistratus, the son of Aristotle's daughter, judged the strength of his love from his very pulse. To the father, Seleucus, he said, "It is all over with your son." Said Seleucus, "How so?" Quoth Erasistratus, "He is desperately in love with my wife." "And do I then deserve so badly of you," said Seleucus, "that you cannot indulge the love of the young man?" He in his turn, "Not even you would yield to the love of some one else." "Oh that the gods would turn his love toward my very dear Stratonice," exclaimed Seleucus. At this point Erasistratus said, "You can be at the same time father and physician." And so Seleucus yielded the stepmother to Antiochus. But Erasistratus was given 60,000 gold pieces. This story concerns love, the cure of a serious illness, paternal affection, filial reverence of a son, prodigality, finally the acute and witty speech of Erasistratus. Yet because the great power of love was the cause for all these acts, we shall refer to this pleasing and memorable history, not under the heading "virtues," or "prodigality," or "medicine," but under the heading "love," lest we indicate the same thing an endless number of times.

There are likewise in speeches many things, bitter, disgusting, and shameless, which are also called base; but certain urbane and witty things are recognized as honorable. Those, however, which are witty or spicy, if they do not fit the appellation "base" or "honorable," I usually place intermediately, as "indifferent." Like this remark of Demosthenes to Phocion— "The people will destroy you, if ever they begin to rage." "You, on the contrary, if they recover their senses," was the reply. And to a man who stupidly asked "Who is the best of the citizens?" his answer was, "The one most unlike you." These and similar things belong to the graces of speech.

It is more convenient to refer to human examples those fortuitous cases (although nothing can be fortuitous, but we use a common word) which happen to men and seem to be drawn partly from divine sources

[12] Appian was born A.D. 95, at Alexandria. The reference is to *Roman Histories*, "The Syrian Wars," chap. x.

and partly from nature. An illustration in point is the passage in which Tacitus writes that among the Fidenates fifty thousand men died in the collapse of an amphitheater.[13] This would come under the caption we have made "About Death." The same classification will be made for loss, shipwreck, and accidental defeats. But under the same headings we have included contrary things, because they almost always appear together in history—that is to say, virtues and vices, base things and honorable—so that by making a list of these one can speak at one and the same time about contraries, for example simplicity, prudence, and cunning; cowardice, bravery, and recklessness; overconfidence, hope, and despair; fickleness, constancy, and stubbornness; stolidity, temperance, and intemperance; arrogance, modesty, and self-depreciation; cruelty, clemency, and indulgence, which Seneca sagely called a vice of the soul; avarice, liberality, and prodigality; buffoonery, urbanity, and boorishness; flattery, affability, and surliness.[14] Even if many characteristics are nameless, yet frequently extremes are implied within the name of the means, as in greatness of a lofty soul, friendliness, virtue, clemency, and faith, which either have no extreme at all or only one included in the word.[15] In certain cases extremes do not admit of an intermediate, as in the words envy, malevolence,[16] garrulity, taciturnity, lack of decency, and shyness, which is excluded from the virtues because it does not befit every age—a thing which is implicit in the definition of virtue.

But if someone is not pleased with this division of vices and virtues, let it embrace four classes, that is to say, prudence, temperance, bravery, and integrity. Philo,[17] avoiding ambiguity of words, preferred to call the supreme good that justice which is nothing else than a certain rectitude and integrity in all plans, words, and deeds. When Plato taught that each man develops justice in himself first (as the Hebrews would have it that each man initiates charity in himself), he placed prudence in the higher soul, as a guide to the desirable and a warning of danger, bravery in the heart, temperance in the liver; but he made common to all that justice which assigns command to reason, compliance to the rest.

[13] Tacitus *Annals* IV. 62.

[14] An analysis based on Aristotle *Nic. Ethics* II. 8. 1109a.

[15] *Ibid.* IV. 4. 1125b appears to be the basis of this passage, "the character in the mean has no name, and we may almost say the same of the extreme."

[16] *Ibid.* II. 6. 1107a. "It must not be supposed that every action . . . is capable of subsisting in this mean state . . ."

[17] Philo the Jew was born in Alexandria shortly before the Christian era. The reference here is to *The Posterity of Cain and His Exile*, chap. XXIV.

That is, he gave to each its own.[18] But either this means nothing at all, or justice has been utterly confused with prudence. That virtue by which one can judge what everybody should give to everyone else jurisconsults do not call moral virtue, but prudence. The man who restores their own to others, or orders it to be restored, is not good, since he would be wicked who did otherwise, unless we are to say that there is virtue in rogues who boast that they have given life to those from whom they did not take it. If we grant this type of justice to the lower soul, the difficulty will arise that we shall join brute beasts, which have that lower power, in an association of law and justice with men. But if any virtue is common to both souls, certainly prudence is the bond, as well as between all virtues and bodies of knowledge. If, indeed, we grant this, we shall eliminate from philosophy that obscure argument as to whether prudence is a virtue or not. We shall have as authority for this opinion Plato himself, who in the last book of the *Laws* [19] measured all activities of everyone by virtue alone, and all virtues by prudence. Now, having repudiated the opinion of the Stoics, we shall divide in the way that I have said the virtues pertaining to the intellect, called disciplines, into theoretic, practical, and those productive of works.[20]

So it will come about that nothing in the reading of history may occur, whether worthy of praise or of blame, which cannot be listed suitably in its proper place. If in history base things seem to be joined with honorable, useful with useless, we must eliminate discussion and adapt it to the popular manner of speaking. There is, for instance, the counsel of the Roman senate, which commanded Gallus the proconsul to destroy the common alliance of the Achaeans; yet if he had followed the goodness of his nature, he ought to have maintained them in their common friendship and conciliated them when they were quarreling. We shall say that it was useful to the Romans, since the Lacedaemonians, Venetians, and almost all peoples used this same counsel; and Demosthenes, in his speech against Aristocrates and in his speech for the liberty of the Rhodians, shows that it had been useful to the Athenians. If, however, the rights of nations were violated, this would have to be judged useless and base. In the opinion of inexperienced men it was useful to Emperor

[18] Plato *Republic* IV. 443–444, "Justice . . . means . . . he should dispose well of what in the true sense of the word is properly his own."

[19] Plato *Laws* XII. 963, where it is said that all our laws must have a single objective, virtue, and that virtue consists of four parts, of which the chief is reason.

[20] Aristotle *Nic. Ethics* VI. 8. 1142a appears to make a distinction between practical wisdom and its application.

Charles V to kill the ambassadors Rincon and Fregoso, or to conceal that they had been killed by his people, because they were said to be inviting the aid and the troops of the Turks. Yet this crime was not only base but also most harmful to him and to the state and proved the occasion for a great war, by which the Christian commonwealth was set aflame. The destruction of Corinth and the defeats of Tarentum occurred from no other cause than injuries against ambassadors. If there is anyone who prefers to follow, not the judgment of the people, but of wise men (although about what is base or honorable not even the wise men themselves agree), very often he will err in managing the state. Lastly, in reading the works of historians, lest we be called too often from reading to writing, we should add notes of similar passages in the margin. Then we can easily refer each fact to its heading. We shall also attain the benefit that through repetition we shall fix all the most important matters more deeply in memory.

CHAPTER IV

THE CHOICE OF HISTORIANS

THERE WAS one special grievance which led the Scythians to attempt the destruction of all letters and documents of the ancients—they were angry that the libraries and the bookshelves of the Greeks and the Latins were filled with praises of their own heroic achievements, but all the other peoples, although they also had accomplished great and memorable things, had been unfairly overlooked or else commemorated in hostile and scornful phrases. It is true that the Greeks and the Latins were effusive in their own praise. The others, except the Hebrews, in olden times recorded almost nothing about themselves. And it came about, I know not how, that men who were occupied with war and the administration of affairs avoided writing, while those who habitually devoted more time to letters, taken captive by their snares and delights, could hardly ever be enticed from them. Indeed, very often it happened that nations which had long cultivated arms lost strength and force of spirit after they became interested in literature, either because they relaxed into peace and inertia, or because people who are so much occupied in the contemplation of divine and natural objects not only avoid slaughter and bloodshed but also outgrow barbarity and ferocity altogether. It is evident that this happened first to the Greeks, then to the Latins, and afterwards even to others. Therefore General Phocion encouraged the Athenians, more eager than skilled in war, to fight the enemy with a torrent of words, in which they excelled, not with arms, in which they were inferior. Demades, indeed, used to say that they were like flutes, which were useless once you removed the tongue. Even softer were the Asiatics, who chattered incessantly. The Spartans, however, although altogether lacking in literary knowledge, achieved famous deeds at home and abroad, which have been lauded, not by the actors, but by their enemies. At the same time we see that the illustrious deeds of the Celts and the Germans, as well as of the Arabs and the Turks—their wars and their victories are lost in oblivion or scantily commemorated, and that by their enemies. But the contrary befell the Greeks, who detailed the battle of Salamis or of Marathon with so elaborate an account that no more memorable deed seems ever to have taken place. Yet even so, the great Alexander, when as victor he sat on the royal throne of Persia, urbanely answered the ambassadors of the Greeks, who were announcing that Greece was ablaze with a great war, that it seemed to him a war of mice and frogs. In turn the wars of Alexander against the soft Asiatics and Persians (whom Cato used to call womanish and Caesar despised) are insignificant in comparison with those which were fought by Celts, Germans, Turks, and Tartars. This is easily understood by men who remember that their victories were recorded with little consideration by their enemies. In order, then, that the truth of the matter may be gleaned from histories, not only in the choice of individual authors but also in reading them we must remember what Aristotle sagely said, that in reading history it is necessary not to believe too much or to disbelieve flatly.

If we agree to everything in every respect, often we shall take true things for false and blunder seriously in administering the state. But if we have no faith at all in history, we can win no assistance from it. In the one direction erred the writers who elaborated all records of the past with fables; in the other, the Turks, who are said to have no memory of antiquity and to have abandoned interest in it because they believe that a reliable account cannot be written by men who follow hearsay, much less by writers who were present or had command of events, since they lie about themselves in many respects or are influenced to deviate from the truth by fear, or bribes, or hate of princes.[1] Plutarch himself kept these ideas in mind, and in a way avoided the snare. But what prevents writing for posterity, rather than for contemporaries? Among so many writers it is probable that someone is attracted to writing by neither entreaty, nor bribe, nor envy, nor emotion. The cautious reader of history, then, will strike a mean between the vices vanity and stupidity and will make individual choice of the best authors; he will not form an opinion concerning the work until he has understood clearly the character and the talent of the historian. It is to the common interest that evaluations of writers who reach the public shall seem uninfluenced and not at all partial, in order that we may not frighten away the best men from writing when we wish to impose a limit upon the activity of others. In the choice of writers, which each man must make, I myself should like, not to express a judgment (this requires a somewhat greater art and talent), but merely to make use of some reasonable standard and principles likely to be accepted. If some people do not approve these, I shall not feel vexed to change my opinion. Just as the man who gazes

[1] The edition of 1595 gives *principium*; the editions of 1566 and 1583, *principum*.

intently at pictures, their drawing, lines, and colors, must not be ignorant of painting to express a judgment, since many things escape the
sight and sense of the most acute—so also the man who wishes to judge
the virtues and the vices of historians not only must be well informed
in every branch of history but also must have been engaged for a long
time in administrative work.

There are, then, three kinds of historian, I think: first, those very able
by nature, and even more richly endowed by training, who have advanced to the control of affairs; the second group, those who lack education, but not practice or natural gifts; the last is composed of those
who, endowed to some extent by nature, lack the experience of practical
affairs, yet with incredible enthusiasm and labor in collecting the materials of history have almost brought themselves level with men who
have spent all their lives in public affairs. There is, however, an infinite
variety of any one type—the more so because each man has more or less
integrity, learning, and experience. The best writers are fully equipped
on all three counts, if only they could rid themselves of all emotion in
writing history. It is difficult for a good man, when writing of villains,
to refrain from imprecation or to avoid bestowing love and gratitude
on heroes. The first attempts to embroider history occurred when it was
thought fine to use an honorable lie for the praise of virtuous characters
and the vituperation of evil. But if good writers fail in this type of writing, what must we judge about the evil ones? It is a matter of importance, therefore, whether the historian has written a treatise about his
own concerns or those of others; whether his work deals with compatriots or foreigners; enemies or friends; military discipline or civil;
finally, whether it is of his own age or of an earlier period; for his contemporaries or for posterity.

I call a man thoroughly experienced in public affairs if he has shared
in public counsels, executive power, or legal decisions, or at least has
been privy to them. For in these three are involved the gravest concerns of the state. Yet he is even more skilled if he himself has ruled
the state and still more expert if he has added to this practice the profound study of letters and public law. Without books we can hardly attain the very complex knowledge of governing the state, since the span
of human life is too short for us to acquire this by a prolonged tour of
countries and a varied acquaintance with peoples. Lycurgus, Solon, and
Ulysses, however, did achieve this knowledge without books. The last

of the three was called "sagacious" by Homer, because he had seen cities and the customs of many men.

People attach importance to diversity in countries or in the nature of animals and plants, and to the foundations of building and of pyramids, and to the worn coins of the ancients. They consider valueless laws and the jurisprudence of peoples, the condition of states, and the changes in them, yet from these can be obtained real knowledge for directing the state. In addition, by holding office not only within the executive branch and the public counsels but also within the law courts, we may more readily understand the customs of the people and the type of the state. Those who are engaged in litigation, as Arcadius said, have known all evils; not only evils, but also good things, without which the former can in no way exist or be understood. Moreover, between the extreme limits of good and evil all human wisdom is contained. From this we comprehend that he is the poorest type of historian who without experience or knowledge of good literature undertakes (with insufficient preparation) the writing of history. This is the most important criterion in the selection of historians.

But since it is somewhat difficult to be free from all emotion—a condition which we require in this author whom we seek—at the very beginning we must beware lest we too easily agree with the writer as to what things were admirable about himself, his compatriots, and his friends or what was base concerning the enemy. On the other hand, we may have unlimited faith in the deeds which it is acknowledged were effected nobly and even gloriously by the enemy. For the rest, I do not want evaluations from the enemy or from one's own side, but from some third person, like an arbiter, who may be free from all bias. So Dionysius of Halicarnassus (who held no political office) evidently wrote about the Romans much more truthfully and better than did Fabius, Sallust, or Cato, who were affluent in their own country. Polybius, a Greek, often accused Fabius and Philinus of mendacity, because the Roman and the Carthaginian wrote about the Punic War in such a way that the former told all the excellent things about the Romans and the unfavorable factors about the Phoenicians; Philinus, on the other hand, wrote that the Phoenicians had acted in all cases gallantly and bravely (thus Polybius reported), but the Romans basely and without spirit.[2] Yet in the opinion of Polybius, Fabius was a man of

---

[2] Polybius *The Histories* I. 14, 15.

great integrity and sagacity, from whom no plans of state or of the enemy were concealed.

Furthermore, each prepared himself to write in the same way as do orators who carefully guard against making any remark or expressing any opinion unfavorable to themselves. Yet by no means can it happen that one and the same man fills the office of good orator and that of good historian. I cannot approve those histories which commemorate perpetually the praises and the virtues of a man, but do not mention his vices, since no one is of such great integrity and sagacity that he will not often err. Eginhard [3] and Acciajuoli [4] heaped such eulogies upon Charles the Great, Eusebius upon Constantine, Lebrija [5] upon Ferdinand, Iovius [6] upon Cosimo de' Medici, Philostratus [7] upon Apollonius, Procopius [8] upon Belisarius, and Staphylus [9] and Leva upon Emperor Charles V that they seem to act like orators, not like historians. Therefore the wise examiner will test the record of each man not only on the authority of his compatriots and friends but also of his enemies. He will not agree in all respects with Philippe de Comines when he writes the praises of Louis XI, but will consult also Le Maire, [10] the writer of Belgian affairs; and not him alone, but also Paul Aemilius, for the one, indeed, is full of encomiums of Louis; the other rejects these altogether; the third takes the middle course. Le Maire calls him a perfidious man and the murderer of his brother, to whom nothing was more important than to establish a tyranny through crime after he had violated both human and divine law. Moreover, he calls Comines himself the betrayer of his country and a deserter. To neither the one nor the other do I think we

[3] Eginhard, 770–840, studied in the school of Alcuin and at Fulda before he became associated with Charlemagne's court. He was the author of *Vita Caroli Magni*, for which he used as model the *Life of Augustus* by Suetonius.

[4] Donato Acciajuoli, 1428–1478, was a Florentine who wrote a commentary on the life of Aristotle and a *Vita Caroli Magni*.

[5] Antonio de Lebrija, 1444–1522, was a Spanish humanist and the alleged author of *Chronica de los . . . reyes catholicos.*

[6] Paul Jovius, 1483–1552, was the author of *Historiarum sui temporis tomi iii.*

[7] Philostratus wrote a life of Apollonius Tyanaeus in the first century A.D.

[8] Procopius was a Greek, born in Palestine in the fifth century A.D. He wrote *The Histories*, including that of the Persians, Vandals, Goths, etc., and *Historia arcana*, an unfavorable account of the reign of Justinian.

[9] Friedrich Staphylus (or Stapellage), d.1564, was a German convert to Catholicism. He was the author of *Historia de vita, morte, et justis Caroli V.*

[10] Jean Lemaire de Belges, 1473–1525, wrote *Les Illustrations des Gaules et singularités de Troyes.*

should give credence in this matter, because the former was endowed by the king with great riches and honors; the other was his enemy and extended his scornful words even to the charge of crime, with a vindictiveness unseemly in a historian. Aemilius was neither enemy nor friend (for he came from Verona), and he spoke prudently and moderately in this manner. "The duke stirred up distrust against the king, charging parricide: that he had corrupted the sons of his brother, to poison him through them." He affirmed nothing rashly; he did not omit rumors heard everywhere. The first two wrote in the lifetime of Louis, the other a hundred years later, so that he was not influenced by favor or fear or hate. Cornelius Tacitus admitted the distortion of the deeds of Tiberius, Claudius, Caius, and Nero, composed during their lifetime with swelling praise, on account of fear. After they had died, his account was colored by hate. Therefore he planned to report without wrath or enthusiasm matters whose setting was not his personal concern. He wrote a hundred years after the lifetime of his characters. Perhaps Aristotle meant the same thing when he said that histories were no less displeasing and unreliable when they were too old than when they were too recent. For those who permit histories of present-day affairs to circulate publicly, it is really difficult to write the truth, lest the report should injure the name of someone or damage his reputation. On this account Cicero did not mention any famous orator who was living, fearing, as he himself said, the anger of those who had been overlooked.

Moreover, who seeks for truth from historians in a state where it is base to say what you do not think, but imprudent and dangerous to say what you do think? It is better to avoid all fear of the present and to entrust one's account to posterity. Or if there is anyone who prefers to enjoy the glory of his labors in his own lifetime, let him, when he has investigated all the public and private records, recreate the deeds of a former period and from the tradition preserved by older men write history. Famous writers have done just this: Livy, Suetonius, Tacitus, Arrian,[11] and Dionysius of Halicarnassus. We can rely more readily upon the last author than on the others, because he wrote, not of his own state, but of another and collected all the commentaries and secrets of state from the official documents.

In this class also are Polybius, Plutarch, Megasthenes, Ammianus,[12]

---

[11] Arrian of Bithynia, c.96–c.180, was a disciple and a friend of Epictetus. He wrote *History of the Anabasis of Alexander.*

[12] Ammianus Marcellinus, c.325–c.391, was a native of Antioch and the author of *Rerum gestarum libri xxxi*, a history of the Roman Empire from Nerva to Valens.

Polydore,[13] Ctesias,[14] Aemilius, Alvarez,[15] and Louis the Roman.[16] But the narratives are less to be trusted in the case of those who obtained all their information at second hand—from the talk of others, as Polybius said—and had not seen the official records. So the best writers say that they have collected their material from the official records, to obtain more credit for their writings. Thus, Ammianus asserted that he had brought to light the antiquities of the Gauls from their official documents. Likewise, Arrian at the very beginning of his work wrote that he had read the previously unknown commentaries of King Ptolemy, who shared the adventures of Alexander the Great everywhere. Appian did the same with regard to the writings of Augustus; Megasthenes and Ctesias, the public records of the Persians; Diodorus vowed that he had seen the secret archives of the Egyptians concerning whom he wrote. Onesicritus [17] and Aristobulos, the ambassador of Alexander the Great, boasted of what they had seen in Egypt and in India. For the same reason Palaephatus [18] often said "We ourselves have seen with our own eyes." Of course the actual historical truth ought not to be sought from the commentaries of kings, since they are boastful about their many exploits, but we should investigate only those matters which in no way, or only slightly, pertain to their praise or their blame, as the sequence of time, provinces, governments, ages of kings, lineage, and public accounts as a whole, in which the secrets of the state lie hidden. Here we ought to revert to the words of Megasthenes, who said, "It is true that all authors who write about kings need not be accepted, but only the priests to whom is entrusted preservation of the public annals. An illustration is Berosus, who restored the whole history of the Assyrians from the annals of the ancients." So much said he.

[13] Polydore Vergil of Urbino, 1470–1555, wrote *Historia Anglica*, in twenty-six books. He went to England as sub-collector of Peter's pence and became archdeacon of Wells.

[14] Ctesias was a contemporary of Xenophon. He lived at the Persian court and wrote a history of Persia.

[15] Francisco Alvarez, c.1465–c.1541, was a Portuguese historian and a member of a mission to Abyssinia. He wrote in Portuguese a work, a French translation of which was published by J. Bellère at Antwerp, in 1558, under the title *Historiale description de l'Ethiopie contenant vraye relation des terres . . . du grand Roy et Empereur Prete-Ian*.

[16] Louis Barthema (or Varthema), "Roman patrician," who flourished in the early sixteenth century. He travelled extensively and compiled an important *Itinerary* covering considerable portions of northern Africa and western and central Asia.

[17] Onesicritus accompanied Alexander the Great on his expedition and made scientific observations.

[18] Palaephatus was a Byzantine Greek historian and grammarian, author of *Concerning Incredible Things*.

But if any account has so many witnesses that it cannot be disproved, although it may seem unbelievable, there is every likelihood of its truth, especially if authors disagree about the rest of the story. Who would believe that the senate of the Romans, due to the dream of some country fellow who said that he had been warned by Jupiter, was moved to have the games celebrated anew bcause in the earlier games a public dancer had performed unskillfully? In accordance with his dream, the senate decreed that the games should be repeated. Perchance it would not be believed if one man said it; but on this point are agreed Plutarch, Livy, Dionysius, Valerius,[19] and Pliny, who could not be mistaken in such agreement about the senate and the Roman people.

Someone may say, however, that one author has been misled by the error of another? This, of course, can happen, not only in the narration of human history but also in natural science. There is an old story that swans about to die sing their dirge sweetly, a thing to which all testify, poets and painters from Aeschylus onward, as well as the very leaders of the philosophers, Plato, Aristotle, Chrysippus,[20] Philostratus, Cicero, and Seneca. Yet Pliny first, then Athenaeus,[21] proclaimed from long experience that it was false, and so we accept it. But of course it is very easily understood, whether natural history is true or not. On the contrary, in accounts of human affairs, which fluctuate widely, errors are not so easily recognized. Many have written that Charles, duke of Orleans, was executed at Paris for the crime of lese majesty; not only one or two, but almost twenty historians have said this. However, it appears that thirty years after he was captured by the English this man returned to France and died peacefully. G. du Bellay,[22] my compatriot, criticized the great lack of discrimination of historians in writing down as fact what a recent rumor had spread abroad. Posidonius,[23] Eratosthenes,[24]

---

[19] Valerius Maximus wrote *De factis dictisque memorabilibus libri ix* in the first century A.D.

[20] Chrysippus, c.280–206 B.C., was a Stoic philosopher. Only fragments of his work are extant.

[21] Athenaeus of Naucratis lived at the end of the second and the beginning of the third century A.D. and wrote the *Deipnosophists*.

[22] Guillaume du Bellay, 1491–1543, was a diplomat and historian who wrote *De l'antiquité des Gaules*.

[23] Posidonius, c.130–50 B.C., continued the universal history of Polybius. He was an eminent Stoic, one of the teachers of Cicero.

[24] Eratosthenes, c.274–194 B.C., was librarian of the Alexandrian Library, the author of *Geographica* in three books and of the *Chronographia*. His works are extant only in quoted fragments, but we have his map of the world.

and Metrodorus [25] are reproached by Strabo for the same error, because they handed down as true history the lies of trifling men. Posidonius, however, quoted the authority of Cn. Pompey in order that he should not write without support. So in a matter in which writers disagree among themselves I should think that we ought to believe the more recent account if the author gives evidence either irrefutable or at any rate more acceptable for approval. For such is the power and the nature of truth that it is not brought forth into the light except after a long period, when of course common errors, flatteries, and discords have sunk to rest. And since the chief quarrels are among men who dispute about religion, we do not seek the opinions of the heathens about the Jews, or of the Jews about the Christians, or ours about the Moors and the Mohammedans, but having compared all the most trustworthy writers, we see who they are and whether they themselves have really carried out investigations in this field. In this respect, however, many have tripped more through error and ignorance of antiquity than from the desire to lie.

As for those things which the ancient Greeks reported about the Romans and the Celts, or the Romans reported about the Chaldaeans and the Hebrews, they were for the most part wrong, since any one people was ignorant of the ancient history of the others. Moreover, when we read things about the enemy that are reprehensible, we must withhold assent unless, indeed, we have perfect faith in the author. But as writings of the enemy are not wholly approved, so they are not to be entirely disapproved. Caligula wisely ordered the works of Cassius and Labienus about Caesar to be circulated among the people, although condemned by order of the senate, since he said it was of interest to the state that the deeds of every man should be known to all. Yet if the testimony of the former or of the latter about Caesar were extant, I should in no way approve of it—or that of Caesar, who wrote that the followers of Pompey had made no distinction between divine and human things and had carried off money from the temples, although he himself had despoiled all the temples of the Gauls, with no dread of religion or of the Gods, and had even rifled the sacred treasury, which Pompey had refused to open. Caesar made these accusations and others so that he might seem to have a just cause for engaging in war (although no one can have any just cause of taking up arms against his

[25] Metrodorus was author of a *periegesis* of the first century B.C. The reference is to Strabo *Geography* XVI. iv. 16.

country). But the things which he wrote about the wars he waged are for the most part acknowledged to be true, especially since the commander-in-chief was forbidden by the Portian Law to report a false number of killed to the tribunes of the treasury; otherwise he would be deprived of a triumph and imperium (for the sake of which Caesar thought crime was justifiable). Even though this law was violated with impunity, yet fear of infamy would restrain a man very eager for glory, especially when he suffered his writings to circulate freely in his own lifetime and had countless enemies who could convict him of mendacity. It is admitted that he composed *Anticato* in answer to the *Cato* of Cicero, but, as Tacitus said, he wrote this in the same way that a defendant would plead his cause before the justices. So what we have said about the evidence of an enemy is pertinent, unless a man has been corrupted by money when a prisoner, as people think about Froissart. It is doubtful whether the English owe more to him than he to the English, since he openly confessed that he received lavish gifts from them. Leonardo Bruni [26] acted in the same way when he also boasted of receiving gifts from a man whom he had complimented (though he did this involuntarily).

In conclusion, I think this: one can write of all matters most reliably when he has spent a great part of his life either in affairs of state or in warfare. I think, however, that no one can completely forget the praises of his country or treat them indifferently. For when Polybius, who is considered the most truthful among the best writers, wrote about his compatriots, he could not refrain from inveighing very bitterly against Phylarchus,[27] because he concealed the valor and the bravery of the Megalopolitans in the war against Aristomachus. The same motive, unless I am mistaken, drove Plutarch to write *About the Malignity* against Herodotus. In this work he attacked nothing so much as the material about the Boeotians and the Chaeroneans. Then who can refrain from smiling in reading the works of Sabellicus,[28] where he compares the wars of the Venetians with the deeds of the Romans? Not even Donato Giannotti,[29] a Venetian citizen, could tolerate this comparison. Almost

---

[26] Leonardo Bruni, called Aretinus, 1369–1444, was an Italian humanist and historian, author of *De bello Italico adversus Gothos* and *Historia Fiorentina*.

[27] Phylarchus was a Greek historian of the third century B.C. Only fragments of his work exist.

[28] Marcus Antonius Sabellicus, 1436–1506, an Italian scholar, author of *De situ urbis Venetae*, and *Rerum Venetiarum ab urbe condita libri xxxiii*.

[29] Donato Giannotti, 1494–1563, author of *Libro de la republica de' Venetiani*.

all historians struggle with this weakness (if it is a weakness to defend the dignity of one's own people with an honest lie). Under these circumstances I agree willingly with Caesar when he describes the customs of the Gauls, or with Tacitus on the Germans, or with Polybius on the Romans, or with Ammianus on the Franks, since they were foreigners and obviously had knowledge of the ancient history of the peoples about whom they wrote.

But grave doubts trouble me whether historians ought to praise or to vituperate and to express judgments about the matter under discussion, or whether they should leave to the reader the formation of an unbiased opinion. As this bears closely on the choice of historians, I will bring forward the essential argument on each side and leave the matter to individual judgment. Since history ought to be nothing else than the image of truth, and, as it were, a record of events which is placed in the clearest public view for the decision of all, I suppose that the prejudice of the historians detracts greatly from the events, because they seem to wish to inculcate in the minds of inexperienced [30] readers opinions that are questionable. But to the cautious, who are not willing to be deceived, such historians are strongly suspect on account of this very thing —that they gave an opinion, although not asked. It is no small blemish that many historians, acting like rhetoricians or philosophers, break off the thread of the incompleted narrative and draw elsewhere the thoughts and the memory of the readers, so that Timaeus has rightfully been censured for both faults. Because he digressed too often from history to reproaches, he has been called ἐπιτίμαιος and "traducer." Since nothing is more difficult than to judge equitably, who will not severely censure a historian for expressing an opinion about the greatest directors of the state, when he himself has borne no share of public office or counsel? Moreover, what is more inept than for those who never saw the line of battle of the generals to decide upon their defeats and victories? The man (I omit his name) who related the wars of Henry waged with Emperor Charles V, making himself judge of both of them, surrounded the king with such fulsome flattery—or rather overwhelmed him—that not even Henry himself could endure these praises without disgust. On the other hand, he attacked Charles with all contumely as wicked and ignoble. The good man does not understand how insult of this sort flows back to his own prince, for whom it would be base to wage war with such an enemy, more base to be conquered by him, but most base to contract

---

[30] The edition of 1595 reads *imperatorum* instead of *imperitorum*.

any relationship by marriage.[31] For this he is unanimously decreed untrustworthy as historian and unfair as judge. No less recklessly did Jovius write when he meted out according to his own opinion odious comparisons between Selim and Ishmael the Wise, and then between Charles V and Pope Paul and other princes. I contrast with these Xenophon, Thucydides, Suetonius, Caesar, Guicciardini,[32] and Sleidan,[33] who somewhat rarely, and then only implicitly and cautiously ventured an opinion. Caesar, abounding in military glory and thorough master of the arts of a general, could indeed venture an opinion about military matters by his own right, as it were. He did not need to fear the reproach of being a novice. Yet he did this very prudently and moderately. When it was said that P. Sulla might have been able to obtain a victory if he had pursued the followers of Pompey, Caesar said, "It does not seem possible to find fault with his counsel. The roles of a lieutenant and of a general are different. The one does all things according to order. The other ought freely to take counsel for the most important matters." Likewise, when Pompey ordered a soldier in the line at Pharsalus to stand, not to advance; to receive the enemy, not to attack him, quoth Caesar, "This seems to us to have been done without good reason, because there is some stirring of the soul and alacrity naturally inborn in all of us which would kindle in the zest of battle. Generals ought not to repress this, but to foster it." [34] Here Caesar fought with Pompey not only in battle, but also regarding the art of waging war. We do not lack examples which strengthen the testimony of Caesar, especially the victory of Epaminondas against the Lacedaemonians, but granting that they are countless, what is so inept as when some Phormio,[35] who has never seen a camp, gives an opinion about such men as though he were arbiter? Or when a man from the schools wishes to correct the laws of Lycurgus and Solon, the wisest directors of the state? When Aristotle did this, he incurred the hostility of many, and he was rebuked implicitly by Polybius, but openly by Plutarch. How wisely, I do not know.

[31] This passage probably refers to Francis I, who married the sister of Charles V.

[32] Francesco Guicciardini, 1492–1539, had military, diplomatic, and administrative experience and was the author of *Istoria d'Italia*.

[33] John Sleidan, 1506–1556, was a disciple of Erasmus. He translated Froissart and Comines and composed a work on the Reformation called *De statu religionis et rei publicae*, which traced the history of the Lutheran movement from the political angle. There is a short treatise by him called *De quatuor summis imperiis*.

[34] Reference is to *De bello civili* III. 92.

[35] Phormio was a philosopher who delivered a lecture on the art of war in the presence of Hannibal.

Only this, however—it is absurd to advance an opinion about things little known to oneself; to judge is really dangerous. In this respect Vives,[36] the tutor of Charles V, reproached Comines because too often he wandered from the historical subject selected and discoursed about the customs and virtues of princes and in general about the happy life in the manner of philosophers. Yet this man, unlike Vives, spent all his time in affairs of state, either in wars or in official missions, so that he, if anyone, could rightly pronounce judgment. If a reproach is due, it would be more suitable for a historian to make a mild criticism after the narrative has been given or to withhold his opinion altogether.

But the authority of Polybius draws me in the opposite direction. He chided Phylarchus because he omitted the eulogies due to each hero, and he [Polybius] thought the chief value of annals was encouraging good people in paths of virtue by praises for their like, but terrifying the wicked by vituperation and scorn. This system Tacitus and Procopius accepted, and all the most serious writers did express their opinions about the matter in hand. Moreover, Agathias [37] wrote that history unadorned seemed to him like the idle speech of old women, at which I marvel. But this author is not of so much value to me that I can be convinced by his opinion, especially since by the solemn testimony of Cicero, Caesar seems to excel all historians for this very thing—that his history, bare, simple, straightforward, and as it were devoid of all ornament, is set forth for the judgment of each reader. Like this is the history of Xenophon, following that of Thucydides, where he interposed no judgment of his own, never digressed, and made no rhetorical flourishes. Although many think that the praise of good and the vituperation of evil are among the advantages of history, this service can be performed more truthfully and better by philosophers, whose particular function it is, than by historians. However, any writer vituperates Nero more than enough when he recounts that he murdered the most honorable men, his tutor, two wives, his brother Britannicus, and finally his mother. All these things Suetonius wrote in a simple unadorned prose without any unnecessary verbiage. But when Appian stated that Mithridates had murdered his mother, brother, three minor sons, and as many daughters, he added "Bloody and cruel towards all was he." [38] He undermined

---

[36] Vives, 1492–1540, was a Spanish humanist and professor at Oxford. He wrote *De causis corruptarum artium.*

[37] Agathias of Smyrna, c.536–582, wrote *De imperiis et rebus gestis Justiniani imperatoris*, taking up the story where Procopius ends.

[38] Reference is to *Roman Histories*, "Mithridatic Wars," XVI. 112 end.

faith from the foregoing passage no less than Jovius, who in a long speech, with very scornful words, enlarged upon all the cruelties of Selim, the prince of the Turks. To me it would seem enough for the everlasting disgrace of his name and indeed more convincing simply to narrate that he killed three pashas bound to him by the greatest loyalty and closest affinity, two brothers, five nephews, and his father bent with age, rather than to elaborate oratorically, in a manner not at all befitting a historian, an account which seems to readers false or uncertain. May I indicate my preference, with the indulgence of those who think that nothing is more insipid than bare history.

Of course I would not impugn the judgment of great men about events if only they are such as can rightly give a decision. In civil training the following are pre-eminent: Dionysius of Halicarnassus, Plutarch, Livy, Zonaras,[39] Dio, and Appian; in military training, Caesar, Paterculus,[40] Ammianus, Froissart, Hirtius,[41] Du Bellay; in both, Xenophon, Polybius, Thucydides, Tacitus, Comines, and Guicciardini; in the secrets of princes and the life of the palace, Suetonius, Lampridius, Spartianus,[42] Sleidan, and Machiavelli; in the customs of the people and in differentiation of countries, Diodorus, Pomponius Mela,[43] Strabo, Leo the African,[44] Boemus,[45] and Alvarez; in religion, Philo, Josephus, Eusebius, Theodoret,[46] Socrates,[47] Sozomen, Nicephorus

---

[39] Zonaras, twelfth-century monk at Mount Athos and private secretary to the Emperor Alexius I Comnenus. He wrote *Annales* from the Creation to the death of Alexius in 1118.

[40] Velleius Paterculus, c. 19 B.C.–c. A.D. 31, was the author of *Historiae Romanae*, the story of Rome from the Trojan War to A.D. 30.

[41] Aulus Hirtius, c.90–43 B.C., was an officer with Caesar in Gaul and the author of the eighth book of Caesar's *Gallic War*.

[42] Lampridius Aelius lived at the end of the third and the beginning of the fourth century, and was a member of an alleged group called *Scriptores historiae Augustae*, in which Spartianus is also included.

[43] Pomponius Mela flourished 43 A.D., a native of Spain in the time of Claudius. He was the author of *Cosmographiae liber*.

[44] Leo the African, c.1485–c.1554. He wrote *De totius Africae descriptione libri ix*.

[45] Johann Boemus (Beham), a German Hebraicist, lived at the end of the fifteenth and the beginning of the sixteenth century. He wrote *Omnium gentium mores, leges et ritus . . . tribus libris absolutum opus, Aphricam, Asiam et Europam describentibus*.

[46] Theodoret, bishop of Cyra in the fifth century A.D., wrote a Greek work called *Selected Questions on the Difficulties of the Holy Scriptures.*

[47] Socrates and Sozomen were both lawyers and Greek historians of the fifth century A.D. The former wrote an ecclesiastical history from 306 to 439, the latter, borrowing freely from Socrates, wrote one covering the years from 323 to 423. They and Theodoret continued the chronicle of Eusebius. They were sources of knowledge of the Arian controversy for Cassiodorus.

Calistus,[48] Orosius,[49] Sidonius,[50] Gregory of Tours,[51] the Abbot of Ursperg,[52] William, bishop of Tyre,[53] Antonine the Florentine,[54] and then the writers of the *Magdeburg Centuries*. But as the ancients happily said, let the cobbler stick to his last. Therefore I cannot approve the judgments of Polybius about religion or of Eusebius about military things. So much, in general, about historians.

Now let us turn to the choice of the best authors. To hope for better than those we have, I think, is indeed foolish; to wish seems wicked, and I do not think there is any real value in the studies of people who create for themselves the ideal of a finished historian, such a one as never has been or ever can be. At the same time they overlook those whom we have close at hand. Who doubts that a historian ought to be a serious and an upright man—austere, intelligent, fluent, and, as it were, provided with knowledge of everyday public and private life, as well as of all great things? Rather stupid are those readers who admire nothing in history but eloquence or invented speeches or pleasing digression. I have made up my mind that it is practically an impossibility for the man who writes to give pleasure, to impart the truth of the matter also—a thing which Thucydides, Plutarch, and Diodorus criticized in Herodotus. I wonder why Cicero called him the father of history, when all antiquity accuses him of falsehood. There is no greater evidence of an untruthful historian than to be disapproved unreservedly by all writers, and yet I do not think that he ought to be rejected altogether. There are in his writings, besides eloquence and the charms of Ionic grace, very many

[48] Nicephorus Calistus Xanthopoulos flourished 1320–1330. He wrote a *Historia ecclesiastica*, down to 610, dealing mostly with the Greek Church and compiled from Eusebius, Sozomen, Socrates, Theodoret, Evagrius, and others.

[49] Orosius was a fifth-century historian, associated with St. Augustine. His *Seven Books of History against the Pagans* expressed the theory that the days of the past were more wretched the further they were removed from the consolation of true religion.

[50] Sidonius Apollinaris, c.430–487, was bishop of Arverna and historian of Gaul. We have his letters and panegyrics of emperors.

[51] Gregory of Tours, 538–594, was the author of *Historia Francorum*, which shows the transition from Roman to medieval culture in Gaul.

[52] The abbot of Ursperg wrote a chronicle from the reign of Ninus to his own time. He flourished in the thirteenth century, but the work was continued by other chroniclers, who carried it to the reign of Charles V.

[53] William, archbishop of Tyre, c.1130–1185. He was born in Syria and became chancellor of the kingdom of Jerusalem under Baldwin IV. His book, *Historia rerum in partibus transmarinis gestarum*, covers the years 1095–1184 and is the main authority for the Latin kingdom after Fulcher of Chartres.

[54] Antonine the Florentine, 1389–1459, was archbishop of Florence and author of a *Chronicon, sive opus trium partium historialium*.

pictures of olden times, and many things written most truthfully by him are repeated in later books.

But it is an indication of an excellent writer to have the approval of all, especially of men of the period when participators in the events are still living. In this class I think Thucydides, Sallust,[55] Xenophon, Comines, Guicciardini, Caesar, and Sleidan are placed. Although the Athenians complained that Thucydides had made statements in favor of the Spartans, they thereby gave emphatic testimony of the truthfulness of the writer. Since he was Athenian, not Spartan, had served as ambassador and judge in the Peloponnesian War, was prominent on account of wealth and royal blood, had seen the actual events as from a watchtower, and at great expense had paid able investigators to ascertain the truth of the matter; since, finally, he published his writings in a free city to be judged by the survivors of the events—who would impair faith in his history? But he did not favor the Spartans to such undue extent that he altogether forgot his own compatriots. Although he was sent into exile by them while he was writing the book, he not only spared from calumny Pericles, the author of his exile and the greatest adversary of all, but even showered praises upon him after his death, so that he predicted very truly that because of his loss the state itself would fall. Diodorus, however, implicitly condemned the invention of speeches. This same reproach Trogus Pompeius brought against Livy and Sallust (as we find in Justin)—that by incorporating direct and indirect speeches in their work they had exceeded the limits of their subject. As Cicero said, there is nothing in history pleasanter than simple and shining brevity.[56] But if you take the speeches out of Livy, there will be very little left. This reason led Caligula to remove the writings and the busts of Livy from almost all the libraries. His digressions ought to seem the more remarkable because in the forty-first book he [Livy] asserted that he had decided to write nothing except the history of the Romans.

Concerning Sallust, since almost all his writings have perished, we cannot judge so easily. Yet from those which we have it is evident that he was a most honest author and possessed experience of important affairs. In order that he might write the more truthfully about the great war with Jugurtha, he journeyed as far as Africa. He made rather frank statements, however. What is bolder than to lodge in Caesar and in Cato

[55] Sallust was a Caesarian politician of the first century B.C. He wrote *Catilina* and *Jugurtha.*

[56] Cicero *Brutus,* paragraph 262.

alone the valor of all the Romans of that age? In contrast, Thucydides extolled Pericles, and Sleidan, King Francis, the duke of Saxony, Du Bellay, and Jean Laski with true and appropriate praises, while they rejected disagreeable comparisons. If anything infamous was alleged of anyone, they confirmed it with requisite proofs or reported it accepted implicitly on rumor. It is common to them, along with Guicciardini, Plutarch, Machiavelli, and Tacitus, to bring into the clearest light many plans of many men and various obscure stratagems. Sleidan was the representative of King Francis and very often undertook embassies for his country. But because he planned to write chiefly about religion (since he was dutiful and God-fearing), he covered with what brevity he could not only direct and indirect speeches but also books written by both sides about religion. This is distasteful to many.

Nothing, however, ought to seem troublesome to a man interested in ancient times and affairs of state. There is in our writers, such as Aimoin de Fleury,[57] Monstrelet,[58] Froissart, and Chartier,[59] a great hodgepodge of trifles, in which is concealed a picture of antiquity and former days not to be rashly despised—a picture which I do not find in Aemilius, who granted that he omitted many things others have reported. Of this character, too, is the history of Leo the African, of Alvarez, and of M. Gazius, who covered matters great, small, and indifferent and could fill the ears of the inquisitive with an infinite variety of details. But these things appear more rarely in the Greeks and the Latins, who deal only with civil and military training and the matters relating to some memorable event: as in Livy, the burning of the Capitol in the Social War; and in Tacitus, the great fire which consumed twelve sections of the city. Meanwhile, however, not only commonplace but even famous authors tell of prodigies plainly incredible; like Caesar himself, who wrote in the Civil War that the statues sweated at Tralles—a man otherwise scornful of the gods and of men. In this respect Livy exceeded them all in piety, or shall I say in superstition. For in many passages he stated that cows talked, staffs of office burned, statues sweated (which often

---

[57] Aimoin de Fleury or Haemo was a Benedictine monk of the tenth century. He wrote the first part of the chronicle *De regum procerumque Francorum origine gestisque clarissimis usque ad Ph. Augustum.* His own contribution, based on classical authors and Gregory of Tours, went as far as the middle of the seventh century. It is written in comparatively good Latin. The account was continued by other monks to 1165.

[58] Enguerrand de Monstrelet, c.1400–1453, was a chronicler of the fifteenth century, following Froissart.

[59] Alain Chartier, c.1392–c.1430, was archdeacon of Paris, poet, historian, and diplomat. He wrote the *Quadrilogue-invectif*, a picture of France in the Hundred Years' War.

happens on a rainy day), a god appeared to Hannibal, a child of six months cried triumph; so that not unfairly Polybius called writers of this description "tragedians," since they summoned the gods by some artifice when they could not extricate Hannibal from difficulties. Polybius himself, however, wrote impiously about religion. They are more worthy of indulgence, because it is better to be fettered by superstition than by complete irreverence and to have a false religion than no religion at all. At the same time, Livy is occasionally too fulsome in unsuitable praises. When he preferred Publius Sempronius to all the citizens (whereby he seemed to do injustice to the others) he asserted that this man was endowed by nature and by fortune with all the human virtues heaped together. Not content with this, he amplified very fully the details with respect to the splendor of his race, riches, eloquence, stature, age, greatness of soul, and military training. It is true that he extolled Furius Camillus to the skies and Africanus even above the skies, so it ought not to seem strange if Augustus called him a follower of Pompey,[60] because in praise of Pompey he could not say enough. But in censuring he was moderate and dignified. For instance, when M. Livius and C. Claudius assailed each other with mutual accusations before the censor; on this occasion he said, "Here took place an unseemly struggle to stain the reputation of another at the cost of one's own fame." Elsewhere the same author commented on the former reverence of the plebs toward the patricians: "Where now will you find in any man this unassuming conduct and loftiness of soul, which then was common to the entire population?" And about Calvin Campanus: "He is a wretched man, but not sunk to the lowest depths, since he preferred to rule a fatherland unharmed rather than after it had been destroyed." In addition, we admire in Livy his varied style. Sometimes he was very detailed, but at others concise. In the first ten books he covered 460 years from the founding of the city; in the second decade, seventy-four; in the third, eighteen. As if he were approaching his subject in earnest, he covered in the remaining one hundred and ten books 192 years. At no time did the Roman people cease from wars. Notwithstanding this arrangement, many more things occurred from the expulsion of the kings from the city to the time of Appius Caecus than from him to Caesar. But I think this apparent decrease occurred because he fitted together into one account, as it were, the commentaries of older writers, which were

---

[60] The reference is to Tacitus *Historia* IV. 34.

scanty for the early days of the empire, but abundant for its zenith. When, however, he happened upon those who had written better, he took them over bodily. One can see an instance of this in the Punic War, which indeed he seems to borrow word for word from Polybius.

Polybius, on the other hand, was not only equable at all times, and uniform, but also intelligent, serious, sparing in praise, bitter in criticism, and like a sagacious legislator and good general he discussed many things about military and civic training and many about the function of the historian. In addition, he wrote accounts of almost all peoples who flourished in his times and a little before, from the 124th Olympiad, or 3,680 years from the Creation, even to the year 3766. But of the forty books which he wrote, thirty-four have perished. He seemed, however, to assume the role of philosopher no less than that of historian. In the case of the alliance of the Carthaginians, he warned the leaders and the directors of the republics that they should consider carefully whether those with whom they were forming an alliance were urged on by necessity or drawn by hope of friendship. The sixth book is full of precepts of this sort, in which he expressed himself very fully about the military and the civic training of the Romans. Furthermore, no one of the old writers explained more carefully the characteristics of special sites and regions. Then, too, he often criticized adversely the ignorance of earlier days and of historians, who had written many preposterous things about the Romans. From the same man we discover the deplorable error of Titus Livy and Appian, who reported that the legions of the Gauls had been sacrificed by Brennus and that not a man survived from such a slaughter to boast that the city had been taken.[61] Justin fell into a like error, as well as Callimachus [62] and his scholiasts, who narrated that the troops of Brennus, having devastated Italy, invaded Greece and after they had robbed the temple at Delphi were all stricken by lightning and perished. Yet Polybius showed by the clearest and most convincing evidence that these same troops, having burned the city, advanced as far as the Hellespont and, enticed by the convenience of the site, settled around Byzantium, where, once they had conquered the Thracians, they maintained a kingdom even to the time of Clyarus.[63] This fact ought not to

---

[61] Livy v. xlix. 6. There were two Gallic chieftains by the name of Brennus.

[62] Philip Buonaccorsi, called Callimachus, 1437–1496, wrote *Attila, De bello Turcis inferendo* and *Historia de rege Vladislao.*

[63] I have not identified Clyarus. Polybius IV. 52, mentions a Cavarus at Byzantium. Bodin's next sentence is a reference to the fourth crusade and the conquest of Constantinople.

seem remarkable, for when Baldwin was leader, not so long ago, the Gauls took Byzantium and for a long time were in control of the Greek empire.

In our time Paul Jovius followed Polybius in that he dealt with the general history of his own period. But there is this distinction between them, that the latter either was present at the events, or in charge of the situation, or saw public and private records everywhere; the former wrote many things that he had heard—or had not heard. Polybius had long engaged in military and civic training; the other man had experienced neither. Polybius had been a leader in his state, the other a private citizen. The former was a general, the latter a physician. Polybius traveled over a great part of Europe and the shores of Africa and Asia Minor that he might study the customs of the people, but Paul Jovius, as he himself boasted, remained in the Vatican for thirty-seven years. The other was the director and the companion of Scipio Africanus in his wars everywhere; but this one was the daily companion of the popes. When, however, he was asked why he fabricated things that were false or concealed what was true, he answered that he had done this because of his friends. Although he knew that witnesses would destroy confidence in his writings, yet he understood that these things would be believed by an endless posterity, which would bring praise to him and to his compatriots. Gohorry of Paris [64] certainly gave final proof of this when he expressed confidence that the fables of Amadis, which he had invented, would be no less true and credible than the writings of Jovius. It might have been more excusable if he had been inventing falsehoods on behalf of the state, a thing which Xenophon and Plato permitted to magistrates; but to lie for the sake of flattery is base for anyone—for historians it is very base, indeed. As Cardinal Bessarion [65] said when he observed how many whose lives he condemned were raised to the gods by some stupid apotheosis at Rome, he really doubted very much whether the things reported from the ancients were true. In this way deceitful historians destroy faith in the rest. If Jovius had been imitating Polybius, he ought to have remembered what that author admitted at

[64] Jacques Gohorry of Paris edited or translated cantos 10–11, 13–14 of the *Amadis de Gaule*.

[65] Cardinal Bessarion, c.1395–1472, was titular patriarch of Constantinople. He attempted to reconcile the Latin and the Greek churches, in order to fight the Turks. He later settled in Italy, as archbishop of Sipontium, and visited the court of Louis XI on a political mission. He was a Platonist and wrote *In calumniatorem Platonis* against George of Trebizond, an Aristotelian.

the beginning of his work—that he who takes away the truth from history has taken away the eyes from a most beautiful being. How truthfully Jovius has written can be ascertained, not from the man who calls him an author of tales or from Sleidan or Bruto [66] of Venice, who often accuse him of falsehood, because the former is stirred by religious motives, the latter by hatred of tyranny—but he can be refuted from that very father of history, Guicciardini, who by the judgment of all is thought to have written most accurately. If his writings are compared with those of Jovius, they do not resemble each other more than a circle a square. They are especially at variance in speeches, letters, treaties, and decrees, which Jovius invented at his own caprice. In these, however, he so violated fitness that rude soldiers seem to be scholastic rhetoricians, in the judgment of his panegyrist, Alciati himself. I omit the stupid encouragement of the Emperor Charles to Jovius—"You must play the pipes, Jovius," and then his quarrels and conversations with Jovius, which seem to me as probable as the more than two hundred lions killed by Muley Hasan or that 600,000 sheep, as well as 200,000 cattle, were carried off by the French from the field of Brescia. He himself affirmed this, but he did not give any authority. Many things he reported of the empires of the Persians, the Abyssinians, and the Turks, but whether they are true, not even he knew, since he accepted rumors. He did not see the plans of princes, the speeches, the letters, the deeds, or any public records; yet he wrote as though he had taken part in these affairs and did not leave any room for doubt. He did not want to write the things which he could have recounted truthfully, for example, the events taking place in Italy; but he was unable to handle what he wished to treat, that is to say, external affairs. Nevertheless he wrote that he would be indignant to be compared with the authors of his own time.

This, I think, was composed in imitation of Arrian, who thought himself as superior to other historians who had written the life of Alexander as was Alexander to other generals. Arrian was indeed a man of superior genius, highly educated, as his commentaries on Epictetus reveal. Furthermore, he joined experience to erudition; and on account of his great sagacity he was advanced by Hadrian Augustus through all grades of honor to the consulship when the empire was in its heyday. I omit the flowers of Attic speech and the eloquence which in him were so great

[66] Giovanni Michele Bruto, c.1515–1594, wrote *Le difese de' Fiorentini contra le false calunnie del Giovio*, a *Historia Fiorentina*, and *Historia Hungarica* (1490–1552), at the request of Stephen Bathory. There is also a book on method, *De ratione legendi scriptores historicos*.

that he was called another Xenophon. If Jovius is to be compared in any way with Arrian, he ought not to be annoyed at comparisons with others, which I will allow him. Not that many things written by him were not truly and elegantly written, but he earned the reward of mendacity, so that even when he wrote true things he was regarded as suspect. Yet it is rather annoying and unfair that when he put a history on sale he reaped a richer reward from lies than any other man from telling the truth.

I return, however, to the ancients, whom I will compare with our writers and with one another, as the case warrants. First, indeed, comes Dionysius of Halicarnassus, who, in addition to his moderate manner of speaking and his Attic purity, wrote of the antiquities of the Romans from the very foundation of the city with such diligence that he seems to excel all Greeks and Latins. The things which the Latins neglected as almost too commonplace—for example, sacrifices, games, triumphs, and magistrates' insignia, as well as the general training of the Romans in governing the state, taxes, auspices, assemblies, the difficult division of the whole population into classes and tribes, then, too, the authority of the senate, the orders of the plebs, the rule of the magistrates, and the power of the people—he alone seems to me to have reported most accurately. In order that these things might be more plainly understood he compared the laws and the rites of the Greeks with Roman institutions: for instance, when he derived from the Athenians and the Thessalians the laws of patronage which Romulus had established (although Caesar affirmed that these laws were common among the Gauls also). He thought that the dictator of the Romans had power equal to that of the harmost of the Spartans, the archon of the Thessalians, and the *aesymnetes* of the Mitylenians.

Furthermore, the laws of Romulus, Numa, and Servius, along with the early origin of the Romans, would have been entirely lost except for this author. The Latins negligently omitted these matters as if they were too commonplace, and this charge we see affects almost all historians: they pass over the institutions of the state which are commonly known, as if they judged these things to be known equally well to foreigners and to citizens, or even standardized. In this connection Sleidan acted quite rightly. After the mass had been discontinued at Strassburg for twenty years and then under stress of arms again permitted, the people rushed forward in throngs as though to a new spectacle; he seized the opportunity and proposed to leave to posterity the secrets of the mass, lest if it should be again abandoned, or disregarded, or altogether lost, we should afterwards lack knowledge of the ceremony. Although many things were carelessly overlooked by him, yet he would be entitled to indulgence if he had forgotten this sacrament, at which he had not been present except as a boy.

In the same way Dionysius, Plutarch, Polybius, and Dio, all Greeks, diligently investigated the general institutions of the Romans which the Latins had overlooked. I have often desired the same thing in our writings and those of the Italians—that they would take Dionysius as a model. After he had collected detailed historical material everywhere, he recalled all sayings, deeds, and plans relating to a well-established state, especially those indicating religious awe and fear of God. What more divine and awe-inspiring could be said, when Roman justice is under consideration, than that it was decreed by some eternal law of nature never to perish, so that the control of states might be carried over from unjust possessors to just? That, indeed, was the old prophecy of Sirach, the master of wisdom. We ought to admire the goodness of God and that care which he uses in human affairs chiefly on this account, that in all ages and centuries we see dominion given to each best man to the great advantage of the lowly. Thus, God governs the angels; the angels, men; men, beasts; and in general the soul, the body; reason, lust; and the intellect, reason.

This is all about the history of Dionysius. If it were extant in entirety, there would be no reason why we should complain that the treasures of Varro had perished. Dionysius was not only on excellent terms with Pompey the Great and Tubero, but even with his master Varro, so that he seems to have drawn all his famous passages from his walks and conversations.

Plutarch showed an almost equal diligence for the antiquity of the Romans. It is perfectly obvious, I suppose, how we should appraise this author. Since he was the tutor of Trajan, the best of princes, had had a long experience in the palace of the rulers, and was finally made prefect over Istria there is no doubt that he joined experience in managing affairs to the highest zeal for knowledge. He dealt especially with the history of the most illustrious peoples, although this was not continuous, but in sections, suitable for the imitation of princes. Moreover, we admire in him his frankness in judging each matter, so that he seems to be not so much a historian as a censor of princes. Indeed, I think that if anyone was suited to be arbiter of such matters, it was Plutarch or no one. What could escape so much wisdom? It is patent to all who read only his serious discussions about the state and his profound philosophy. But he also carefully explained the causes of wars, the start, the progress, the defeats, and the victories, like a good general. Sometimes he digressed even to the smallest details of domestic affairs. Of this sort is that tale about Cato the Censor, who sowed discord among the slaves purposely, lest they should deliberately attempt anything worse in conspiring together. He narrated often unbelievable and clearly preposterous things about Pericles, who used to sell for his own convenience the annual harvest which he received from the farms and buy the necessities of life. But he used the phrase "they say," lest anyone should incautiously accredit the tale. For another instance, in the life of Lycurgus he wrote that a Spartan boy had borne unto death the cruelest tearing and mangling of his vitals to conceal the theft of a fox. Agesilaus was punished by the ephors because he had won over to himself alone the minds and wills of his fellow citizens. Yet it is worthy of notice that he compared the Greek princes with the Greeks and the Romans with each other in good faith, but not so the Greeks with the Romans. This can be easily noted in the comparison of Demosthenes and Cicero, Cato and Aristides, Sulla and Lysander, and Marcellus and Pelopidas. But what difference is there between comparing Agesilaus to Pompey and a fly to an elephant? Sometimes he even erred about the ancient history of the Romans; still this ought not to seem remarkable in a Greek, who confessed in the life of Demosthenes that he did not understand the Latin tongue very well. He wrote that Gracchus allied the knights to the senators by the Sempronian Rogation concerning trials, but by this law the trials were taken away from the senators and given only to the knights, as Velleius Paterculus, Appian, Asconius,[67] Tacitus, and Florus confirm. So he mistook the Livian law for the Sempronian and Gracchus for Drusus. A similar case is that in which he equated a drachma to the denarius of the Romans and a mina to the pound, in the lives of Fabius and Antony. This blunder greatly misled Budé, for countless errors follow reasoning from fallacious premises. He was wrong again when he reported in the life of Cato the Utican that among the Romans it was permitted to lend wives and that Cato did this for Hortensius, so that from Martia, the wellborn and fertile wife of Cato, Hortensius may have had children. I can hardly be persuaded to believe this, especially when by the law of Rom-

[67] Q. Asconius Pedianus was an Italian of the first century A.D. He wrote *Commentarii in Ciceronis orationes.*

ulus concerning adultery and the custom of the ancients, which Tiberius revoked, agnates could punish adulterous wives on their own responsibility. Cujas speaks rather rashly in ordering P. Manutius to stick to his own craft, because he [Manutius] thinks that by the Romilian law about adultery capital punishment may be inflicted on a wife by her husband and relatives. Yet this law is quoted by Gellius in these words: "If you catch your wife in adultery, you may with impunity kill her without trial. If you commit adultery with respect to her, she dares not touch you with a finger; this is not allowed." [68] In the speech of Cato about the former life and customs of women, justice permitted the husband to kill women taken in adultery, for ζημιοῦν does not signify merely to fine (*multare*), as Cujas would have it, but in some way to punish. However, this is more plainly understood from Dionysius himself, who wrote that the husband was the final judge of the severity of the punishment, in regard to adultery and intoxication. In these words is given the power of life and death. Nevertheless, Tacitus affirmed in his second book [69] that adulteresses were usually treated more gently and sent off by relatives beyond the two-hundredth milestone. Plutarch, as well as Strabo, said that the Parthians, like the Spartans, were accustomed to lend their wives to their friends. But the Roman decorum, I think, did not permit this custom.

Nor do I agree with Appian when he wrote the same things about the Romans, since he often made errors regarding their early history. In the *Civil Wars*, Book II, he stated that Caesar, disagreeing with Marcellus in the senate, moved his hand to the hilt of his sword and in a threatening manner said to the senate, "If you will not grant [it], this will." These are Antony's words, since Caesar at that time was in Gaul. Likewise, he reported that P. Clodius had had illicit relations with Caesar's Calpurnia and was taken at the festival of the Bona Dea. These matters really related to Pompeia. Moreover, Appian was an Egyptian; only in later life in the principate of Aurelius was he a pleader of forensic cases at Rome, as he himself admitted in his book on the Libyan War. He was, however, the one man of all the historians who spreads before us, to survey as in a picture, the provinces of the Romans, the riches, the armies, and a description of the whole empire. Strabo, Pliny, and Rufus did indeed touch upon the provinces, but they omitted the resources. Appian, in his book on the Libyan War, declared, "The Romans have forty thousand knights, two hundred thousand infantry.

[68] Aulus Gellius *Noctes Atticae* X. 23.   [69] Tacitus *Annals* II. 50.

Their strength of arms is greater by twofold. Of lesser ships, two thousand; a thousand triremes; five hundred quinqueremes; naval equipment for many more; more than eighty fine ships with golden prows and sterns. To these are added three hundred elephants and two thousand armed chariots, and in the treasure house of Egypt 74,000 talents." [70] We have, however, lost a great part of his history, for the books on Sicily, Macedonia, Spain, and Carthage are lacking.

These losses the works of Dio Cassius could repair, if the damage to this author were not greater than to the former. However, Xiphilinus included in his epitome what he could. For since Dio had spent his entire life in affairs of state and had advanced through all the grades of honor to the consulship, which he held twice, then as a proconsul made an excellent record as governor of the provinces, and finally combined with experience the greatest knowledge of the liberal arts, who would hesitate to list him among the best writers? He collected carefully information about the assemblies and the Roman magistrates and the entire public law, of course. But he alone reported on the consecrations of the princes and the deifications, and almost alone he made public those things which Tacitus calls the arcana of the empire. He was indeed a diligent investigator of the public counsel. Yet it seems that he deliberately chose to support the side of Caesar against Pompey on every occasion, and the part of Antony against Cicero. Those portents which took place in the battle against the Marcomanni he attributed to Arnuphu the Egyptian, not to the Christians, contrary to what Tertullian,[71] Eusebius, Orosius, Justin, Paul the Deacon,[72] and Marcus Aurelius himself testified in his letter to the senate.

There are those who think that Diodorus ought to be placed with the foregoing, and many place him first; yet I do not see what they admire so much in him, whether they refer to his manner of speaking, which is extremely commonplace, or to his system of histories. Correctly and in order, it is true, he set forth at the beginning of each book those things which he was about to say, and he could compress his material into brief

[70] Appian *Roman History*, Preface, paragraph 10. The statement is paraphrased and somewhat inaccurate.

[71] Tertullian was born in Carthage, of pagan parents, and flourished in the time of Caracalla. He became converted to orthodox Christianity, but abandoned it for Montanism. He wrote *Adversus Judaeos, apologeticus adversus gentes.*

[72] Paul the Deacon, c.720–c.794, was a Lombard who became a monk at Monte Cassino and was an important figure in the Carolingian Renaissance. He wrote *Historia Romana,* which supplemented Eutropius to 553.

compass, as may be seen at the commencement of the first book, where he divided the entire work into forty books. In the six earlier books he included everything before the Trojan War; in the eleven following, from the Trojan War to the death of Alexander; in the remaining twenty-four, from Alexander as far as the Gallic War. This period includes 1,130 years, in addition to the events before the Trojan War which the ancients call fabulous. From this to the return of the Heraclidae he counted 90 years, following Apollodorus; [73] from this point up to the first Olympiad, 328; from the first Olympiad to the Gallic War, 730. This portion he covered carefully. The chronologies of the famous philosophers, historians, and poets he alone of the ancients contributed to history. For instance, in his fourteenth book he wrote that Ctesias calculated the beginnings of history from Ninus, in the archonship of Lysiades. He [Diodorus] collected into one book the six books of this author on Assyrian affairs, and the same number on Persian, in which the author differed from Herodotus almost everywhere. Plutarch, Pausanias, Athenaeus, and almost all Greeks quote the authority of Ctesias. We have at least his epitome. But Diodorus said that Thucydides placed the beginning of his history in the archonship of Charis, Quintus Furius and M. Papyrius being consuls; Ephorus,[74] in turn, from the return of the Heraclidae to the siege of Perinthus; Theopompus,[75] from the first year of King Philip of Macedon, in the archonship of Calimedes, in the one hundred and fifth Olympiad, Cn. Genutius and L. Aemilius being consuls.

But the same thing that Diodorus criticized in Theopompus can be charged against Diodorus. He said that of fifty-eight books there are five which are of doubtful accuracy; so of forty books of Diodorus, of which we have barely twelve entire, the first five seem to be put together almost from fables, so that, as Vives thought, no author was more trifling than this one. Yet by the judgment of Pliny he was the first among the Greeks who ceased to trifle. Although he had proposed to write the history of the world, the entire work, nevertheless, is Greek history. More-

---

[73] Apollodorus of Athens flourished in the second century B.C. and produced *Bibliotheces sive de deorum origine*, a chronicle from the destruction of Troy down to his own time.

[74] Ephorus of Cumae, c.400–c.334 B.C. We have only fragments of this author's ancient geography, the *Periplus maris Mediterranei* and of the *Hellenica*.

[75] Theopompus of Chios, c.378–c.305 B.C. His most important work is a history of Greece, which supplemented Thucydides. It extended to the time of Philip of Macedon, but exists only in fragments. There is another longer work giving details of the reign of Philip.

over, he was more detailed in the speech of one Gilippus, a Spartan (forgetful of the Laconic brevity and his reproach against Thucydides), than in the history of the wars which were waged throughout Italy for almost three hundred years, though he examined in a long digression the pest of the Athenians and its causes. I omit the absurdity of his interpretation of the lunar year, when men were believed to have lived twelve hundred years, as if sometimes in these days also many had not exceeded this age. But since he confessed that he spent thirty years in writing history and traveling, I wonder why he neglected to investigate the history of neighboring Italy, especially since he lived during the heyday of the Roman Empire, that is, in the dictatorship of Caesar. If anyone compares Livy and Dionysius with Diodorus, almost everywhere in the ancient history of the Romans one will observe discrepancies, particularly in the calculation of *fasti* and Olympiads, in which he erred very often. This I think happened probably because of inexperience with the Latin language, so that he did not investigate the writings of the Romans more diligently; it serves as evidence that everywhere he wrote *phrourios* for "fury," just as though the word were Greek; likewise, Ancus Horace for Marcus, Sp. Manius for Melius, Lactuca for Luctatius, Trigeminus for Tricostus. Granting that this may be attributed to errors of copyists (for thus I suppose), yet the same excuse could not hold with respect to consuls, decemvirs, and tribunes of the soldiers with consular power. In enumerating these, he omitted three and sometimes four and confused the whole system of consular *fasti*. But these matters can easily be corrected through the studies and efforts of Charles Sigonius [76] and Onofrio Panvinio.[77] Both have won the highest acclaim of genius, of course, in explaining the antiquities of the Romans.

In this respect Cornelius Tacitus aids us greatly. For when he wrote the events of one century, from Tiberius to Nerva, he investigated most thoroughly all the most important, minor, and most trifling things. In his fourth book he promised not to tell of war, or sieges of cities, or routed armies, or struggles of the plebs and optimates. His labor would be inglorious, but yet not useless. And a little later—"We have put together despotic commands, incessant accusations, faithless friendships, the ruin of the guiltless, and developments alike in outcome." How-

---

[76] Charles Sigonius, c.1520–1584, wrote *Fasti regum, consulum, dictatorum, ac censorum Romanorum* and *De antiquo jure civium Romanorum.*

[77] Onofrio Panvinio, 1529–1568, wrote *Fasti et triumphi Romanorum a Romulo rege usque ad Carolum V* and *Reipublicae commentariorum libri tres.*

ever, he carefully described all wars which occurred in those times in which he had a share or actual direction. After the victory of Actium there was no historian who treated more fully the military or legal system. He was schooled for a long time in military and civic training, and as proconsul he controlled lower Germany. In that time he described the customs, institutions, and rites of the Germans with such diligence that the Germans owe their ancient history to Tacitus alone. He is worthy of even greater glory, because Tacitus Augustus, who was created emperor on account of his great wisdom, with the unqualified assent of the senate and the legions, traced the origin of his race from this man and filled all the libraries with his books. However, he could not bring it to pass that we might have the work entire. The style of Tacitus is wonderfully keen and full of sagacity. Let this serve as evidence: "It is easier to pay off an ill turn than a good turn, because gratitude is regarded as a burden, injury as an advantage." Moreover, what can be said more briefly and more bitterly about Sejanus than that his good will could not be obtained except by crime? [78] Or of Poppaea, that she did not distinguish between her husbands and her paramours, but where she saw an advantage, thither she transferred her lust? The adultery, lust, drunkenness, and cruelty of Vitellius he bitterly condemned, but nothing too severe can be said against a man who, in addition to natural vices, very marked in him, won over the senate to the law of incest and the marriage of an uncle with a niece. When the same ruler made his way between the bodies of slaughtered citizens and no one else could bear the noisome odor, he said openly that a dead enemy smells good, a citizen still better. If we seek the opinion of Tacitus about the laws and the republic, what more weighty can be said than that every great example contains some injustice which is imposed upon the individuals for the public advantage. Plato's opinion varies but little from this. "They cut off the head of a hydra who think that all inconvenience can be removed from the laws." If we seek the legal and the senatorial arts, if we seek the antiquity not only of the Romans but also of other peoples, there is never a richer harvest than in Tacitus: for instance, when he discussed the ratification of a league among the Armenians. "It is the custom," said he, "to tie the right hands of the kings, bind their thumbs together, and fasten with a knot; soon, when the blood has run into the end of the member, with a light stroke they draw it and lick it in turn." This league is regarded secret as if consecrated by their blood.

[78] Tacitus *Annals* IV. 68.

Why say more? Certainly no historian seems more useful to the magistrates and the judge.

But I am grieved and alarmed by the reproach of certain people, which would need refutation less if their authority were not so great. In the letter which he wrote to Jovius, Alciati [79] dared to call that clearly divine history a thicket of thorns. It is true that on account of his unpolished manner of speaking Tacitus usually is repudiated by those who prefer the lighter trifles of grammarians to the more serious accounts of those who have spent the whole of their lives in public affairs. However, I do not see why Alciati should despise such a man; he is the very one to rejoice about his eloquence, unless, of course, his opinion was due to the fact that Decius [80] removed him from the list of jurisconsults, calling him Ciceronian. A similar case is that of Jerome, who wrote that he himself was beaten with rods before the tribunal of Christ, because he was Ciceronian, not Christian. But he suffered rods and Tacitus scorn, without having deserved them. Joking aside, Budé [81] sharply called Tacitus the most wicked of all writers, because he wrote something against the Christians. I think this was the reason why Tertullian called him most deceitful, Orosius, a flatterer. But just as the jurisconsult Marcellus answered that a prostitute did evil in being a prostitute, yet, granted that she was such, her acts were not base, so Tacitus acted impiously in that he was not a Christian, but he did not write impiously against us, since he was tied to pagan superstition. On the other hand, I would judge him lacking in scruple if he did not try to maintain whatever religion he considered to be the true one and to overthrow the contrary. Since the Christians and the Hebrews were daily dragged to punishment like poisoners and were associated with all crimes and lusts, what historian would refrain from contemptuous words? If ignorance deserves an excuse, then I suppose that Tacitus ought to be excused, although he inferred that the Jews (Iudaeos) are from Mount Ida of the Cretans, as if Idaeans. He resembles Nicolaus of Damascus, who thought that Jerusalem was so named from ἱερόσυλα παρὰ τοῦ ἱερὰ συλεῖν.

[79] Andreas Alciati, 1492–1550, was an Italian jurisconsult who taught at Bourges and Avignon. He wrote *Emblematum liber* and *Index locupletissimus super commentariis codicis Justiniani imperatoris*. For his work in the teaching of law see the Introduction.

[80] Philip Decius, 1454–c.1535, was a Milanese who incurred papal displeasure and left Italy for France, where he became councillor to the Parlement of Grenoble. He wrote *Commentaria in Decretales* and *De regulis iuris*.

[81] Guillaume Budé, 1467–1540, was a philologist who wrote *Annotationes in xxiv libros Pandectarum*, in which he applied philology and history to the interpretation of law. There is also a monetary treatise, *De asse*, written by him.

If this, then, is a crime, Ulpian [82] is guilty of a much greater crime, since he wrote the seven books about torturing Christians, not for historical research, but for the rigor of the punishments.

Sinful indeed was Suetonius when he talked of the Christians, yet his history is greatly admired, so that impartial appraisers of affairs confess that nothing more accurate was ever written by any historian. It does not please certain people that he investigated each trifling thing, but among the sayings of princes and their deeds, nothing ought to seem trifling, nothing small, because these sayings and deeds reach the common people and by the example of the prince the customs of the people are always shaped. It will, perhaps, not meet with favor that he detailed too eagerly certain very horrible princely lusts which Cornelius Tacitus omitted. But in this class he was easily outdone by Lampridius, who described so many monstrous new desires introduced by Heliogabalus that it seems he told them for no other purpose than to propose imitation to each man. Both authors, however, were educated in the intimate, royal circle of princes, especially Suetonius, who was secretary to Hadrian, but was dismissed from this office because he was said to have acted more familiarly with the wife of the emperor than the dignity of palace etiquette permitted. Those who have written in sequence the lives of the successive emperors—that is, Dio, Spartianus, Capitolinus,[83] Herodian,[84] Trebellius, Vopiscus, Eutropius, Lampridius, Volcatius, Ammianus, Pomponius Laetus,[85] Orosius, and Sextus Aurelius [86]—were not of the same rank as Suetonius, and Vopiscus confessed this naïvely when he deservedly called him a most faultless writer.

Suetonius wrote in such a way that he seemed unmoved by the rank or the shortcomings of anyone or by any disturbance at all. He asserted

[82] Domitius Ulpian, 170–228, a Syrian who became a Roman jurist, and wrote *Ad edictum praetoris*. The *Digest* quotes him largely. Bodin apparently knew the passage in Lactantius *Divine Institutes* v. 11, where it is said that Domitius in his seventh book wrote about the penalties to which Christians were subjected.

[83] Capitolinus, Volcatius, Trebellius, and Vopiscus comprised four of the alleged *Scriptores historiae Augustae*. Lampridius and Spartianus were the other two. Cf. note 42.

[84] Herodian, c.170–c.240, wrote *De Romanorum imperatorum vita post Marcum usque ad Gordianum nepotem*.

[85] Pomponius Laetus, 1428–1498, was an Italian philologist, influenced by Laurentius Valla. He wrote *Romanae historiae compendium ab interitu Gordiani junioris usque ad Justinum tertium*.

[86] Sextus Aurelius Victor was of African pagan origin and flourished in the second half of the fourth century A.D. He composed *Breviarium historiae Romanae a Jano et Saturno urbeque condita usque ad consulatum Constantii*, at least in part, in the form of lives of the emperors from Augustus to Constantius. The earlier portions were presumably by other writers.

that Caligula's virtues of soul and body at the beginning were such that
no one excelled him; he stated that the same man's vices, which afterwards developed, were so many and so heinous that no monster of nature seems to have been more dreadful. In the same way, he proclaimed
the first five years of Nero as praiseworthy. Then, too, he wrote that
Claudius was so dull that the frivolous pleaders called him simple when
he was seated before the tribunal, yet he commemorated the noble judgment of the same man, whereby he drove to confession a woman who
would not acknowledge her son, when the evidence was dubious on both
sides, by ordering her marriage with her son.[87] What could be judged
more wisely by that very master of wisdom, Solomon? Herodian did
not have the same zeal for seeking truth; usually he could not recount
the vices and virtues of the same prince, and rather often he was convicted of error by Spartianus and Capitolinus. There is also in Suetonius
many a picture of Roman antiquity and ancient law, many statutes,
edicts, *senatus consulta* which are not found elsewhere; and Suetonius
almost alone, except Tacitus, revealed of what sort was the cognizance
and jurisdiction of princes, from which much light is shed on the writings of jurisconsults.

To these I think we shall join Velleius Paterculus, who, in addition
to a liberal education, held offices and great honors at home and in the
field. I omit mention of his prose, which flows very evenly and pleasantly. He covered the antiquities of the Romans from earliest beginnings
with such brevity and perspicacity (if, indeed, his book were extant in
its entirety) that he seems second to no one. Praise of famous men he
usually gave also, in some unusual speech worthy of a hero, as may be
seen in the praises of Pompey, Caesar, and Cicero. Yet what he has written does not rank as history, but as a plan to comprehend the entire
subject. Following his example, G. du Bellay, viceroy of Milan, in a
short book covered the antiquities of the Gauls, according to the form
of a history, or rather ichnography, by which he gave to the writers of
histories a distinguished model to gaze upon and to imitate. With a
somewhat remarkable fertility of genius and sagacity he wrote, both in
Latin and in the vulgar tongue, of the expedition of Emperor Charles
V into Provence. Indeed, he could not do otherwise, since he had a
sparkling talent, the highest erudition, and unusual experience of managing affairs. He spent all his life in the royal council, in diplomatic

---

[87] Suetonius *Lives of the Caesars* v. 15. 2.

activities, in military office, or in the pursuit of the liberal arts. Finally, he is said to have brought it about that the French nobility flourished no less in the glory of literature than of soldiery, and as one of our leading men he gave arms to the lettered and letters to the armed. Yet, lest anyone should think that my compatriot (for he was Angevin by race) is unduly praised by me, Sleidan went further. He loaded the man with every sort of compliment, then called him the ornament of the French nobility. This author, therefore, we shall join to Polybius, Thucydides, Xenophon, Caesar, and Tacitus, especially since he examined the causes of things, the origins, the progress, the inclinations, all the plans of everyone, the sayings and the deeds, at their just weight. Nor does it affect the choice of historian that this man of ours wrote little, since from the claws we know the lion.

The works of Guicciardini are very detailed and might have been written in imitation of this man if the authors had not been contemporaries. Although he always remained within the territory of Italy and cannot be compared in military renown with Du Bellay, nevertheless, in the judgment of serious people he excelled his contemporaries in writing history (and I do not know whether or not he excelled the older historians also). For where anything came under deliberation which seemed inexplicable, just there he showed the keenest subtlety in discussion, and everywhere he sprinkled sage opinions appropriately like salt. To collect a few from many: since he was most skilled in military and civil training, he implicitly accused our men of recklessness because they extended their power easily by arms, but could not retain it; they did not observe that the dominion acquired by those who do not know how to apply civil disciplines has always been not only useless but even a dangerous responsibility. Truly an unusual opinion and one worthy of a great man! Oh, that it were well known to princes! In another place he castigated the imprudence of the Venetians in these words: "When the affairs of Italy were disturbed, the Venetians idly looked forward to the end of the wars, so that they themselves might obtain the booty, thinking that there would be no one who would dare to harm them. But it is necessary to be the more powerful or to work in alliance with the more powerful." These reproaches have nothing of scorn or bitterness. He did not bestow praise or vituperation upon any living person, and he wrote without any indication of emotion; this may be seen in the case of Pope Leo, through whom he attained great riches and even greater honors and offices. By him he was put in charge of the papal army and the ecclesiastical provinces with full authority. Nevertheless, he stated that Leo was a prince in whom you could praise many things and condemn many. Moreover, he alone revealed to King Francis the pope's perfidy in abandoning the alliance; yet he reported that he had been not less disloyal to Charles V, because with his help he had driven the French from Italy in order that he might the more easily drive out the Spanish afterwards. Furthermore, what more candid remark can be made about Ferdinand than that he clothed all his cupidity with the appearance of religion and public advantage? It is another proof of his integrity and of a mind free from rancor that when he ought to have been really angry with the French (for he had been besieged by them for a long time when he was vigorously defending Parma, and it was a question of his life and all his fortunes), nevertheless he refuted the tale of Paul Jovius about the disease which they call the "French evil." "It is only fair," said he, "to clear the French name from this brand of infamy, since the Spanish brought this kind of illness into Italy from the western isles." Moreover, his zeal for ferreting out the truth was remarkable. He affirmed nothing rashly, but with all needful proofs. He is said to have extracted and interpreted letters, decrees, alliances, and speeches from the sources. And often this expression occurs, "He spoke in these words"; or, if the words are lacking, "He spoke in such sense." Whereby it came about that he was plainly unlike Jovius, who, just as he invented a great part of history, also invented speeches or rather declamations in the manner of the scholastics. For evidence, the speech of Baglioni is clearly contrary to that which Guicciardini transcribed from the original. He was such a diligent investigator of matters, places, and persons, and even of plans and deeds, that he seems to have inspected thoroughly all the towns of Italy, municipia, camps, rivers, and what I think most important, the official records. But he never overlooked a rumor circulating among the common people; for example, in the battle of Marignano, where the French broke the army of the Swiss, he could not know the number of the dead, "because," quoth he, "the majority were influenced by jealousy or enthusiasm or error. Many say fourteen thousand Swiss, some ten, others eight; there were those who report only three thousand." Moreover, when he wrote of the events that had taken place in Italy over a period of almost forty years, he treated the foreign affairs only lightly, or within suitable limits. He wisely omitted also the wars of the Turks and the Persians, which were known to him much better than to Jovius, so that he might not make reckless statements about affairs known to him only slightly. But lest they should be entirely forgotten, thus briefly he commented: "Selim is said to have invaded Syria' and Egypt." Sometimes, however, he seems rather prolix to some people, but to those who wish to study the state of public affairs and human concerns as a whole, he seems only too brief, because no part of the world suffered more events or greater changes of public institutions in those times than Italy. Then it is extremely valuable to learn the truth of so many things from him, who, by the agreement of all Italy, was said to have been endowed with the greatest sagacity, erudition, integrity, and experience of practical affairs. When other men shape history askew, and each practically in accordance with his own wishes, one at least has been found who built it on so high a level that not only does he seem to dim the light of lesser men but even of Jovius and Bembo.

Although Bembo [88] was a famous man, and for a long time was much in the foreground throughout Italy (I do not mention his unusual eloquence), nevertheless, in kindness to his fellow citizens he has written many things otherwise than as they actually happened, or else certainly Guicciardini is often to be charged with deceit. Of this matter one proof may be that when the French overwhelmed the allied troops of Venice near Fornovo and, as one says, cut their way through with a sword, Bembo wrote that they were neither conquered nor conquerors, and he called their return into France a flight. Guicciardini judged acutely in this manner: "If to conquer is to obtain possession of that thing for the sake of which the war was undertaken, the French won, since they had engaged battle only for the purpose of returning to France with their king unharmed. Since, then, they put the enemy to flight, slaughtered a part, drove the other into the Taro, and betook themselves safely to their native land, who thinks of asking about the victory?" Bembo likewise concealed the truth of the matter in the battle of Ravenna, a famous and well-known victory, which no one ever denied to the French. "More than eighteen thousand infantry and knights," says Bembo, "were killed, and the number on both sides was almost equal, but their fortunes were unequal." When in one passage he called the Venetians

[88] Cardinal Pietro Bembo, 1470–1547, was historiographer of the republic of Venice, and wrote *Historiae Venetae libri xii.*

the leading state of Italy, in another, the recognized ornament of the world, and at one time extolled their equity and faith, at another, their magnificence and riches; then praised the incredible bravery of one Venetian ship opposed to the resources of the Turks; finally stressed constantly the dutifulness of all the citizens, their sobriety, reverence, and sagacity—he conducted himself in a manner worthy, not so much of a good historian, as of a good citizen. But the fact that he inveighed against the French everywhere with scornful words, said that nothing was regarded as sacred by them or safe, reported that the promise made to the Venetians and Alfonso Avalos [89] was broken—this is characteristic, not of a writer praising his own side, but of one persecuting the other side. If, indeed, by military law a man is unworthy who dishonors a nation with scornful words, how much more should this be avoided by a historian? Especially if he is convicted on the very count which he reproaches in others—of reporting false things for true? Guicciardini laid the charge of a violated alliance against the Venetians not only on account of overwhelming suspicion of their perfidy against the French but also because they received into the city Alviano, the bitterest foe of the French. They received him when he was triumphing over the French and even tried to include him within the terms of the alliance, although the king of France was unwilling. Therefore what Bembo wrote oratorically about the perfidy of the French is about as true as that in Apulia during the Venetian war the crows and the vultures fought from the air with such violence and in such multitudes that twelve carts were filled with their bodies. Bembo did not hesitate at all about this matter, but openly affirmed it. Yet, since he betook himself to writing unwillingly, as he himself averred, and at sixty years of age, he greatly disliked the labor demanded for writing history. "It bores me," said he, in the fourth book, "to follow the trifles of this war. For who would read the details without disgust?" These things were clearly written for effect. Of the same nature is the speech of Loredano against Minius; nothing can be more flowery. He strained so for purity of diction that he was unwilling to use words not actually Latin, yet necessary to the sense. He called the emperor of the Turks the king of Thrace, although Thrace is hardly the hundredth part of his empire, and the duke of Milan, king also. This, indeed, is Latin, but I do not think it sufficiently close to the sense of the passage.

[89] Alfonso Avalos was the general of the imperial armies.

A man entirely unlike Bembo was Procopius, who apparently did not know the ornaments of history and the purity of Greek speech, or else neglected them; he did, however, commemorate the details pertaining to the subject, and with great zeal he pursued the most trifling matters. Since he was the perpetual companion of Belisarius in managing affairs and shared the whole public counsel, he also undertook embassies for the state rather often; finally, he was moderately informed on the theoretic side, so that I should not hesitate to count him among the chosen few. But because he described the separate letters, decrees, alliances, and speeches in various types and styles of speaking, he afforded good evidence of a most truthful writer, except that he overwhelmed Belisarius oftener than is fitting with praises for the most part stupid. Even more stupidly did he excuse the murder of Constantian, who had been Justinian's master of horse—a murder which was committed at the command of Belisarius. He said it was destiny that Constantian should die thus. I except also the absurd ideas about the thirty pigs and a statue of Theodoric and the fact that he made Thule ten times greater than Britain, although it really is so much smaller. But this exceeds the belief of all —that the ashes of Mount Vesuvius, which is situated this side of Naples, were carried even to Byzantium by the wind and the people were so terrified that they placated God by annual supplications; these prodigies smack of Greek vanity and often destroy confidence not only in profane but even in ecclesiastic historians.

Nicephorus Callistus was full of such stories, in which even Zonaras, otherwise an approved historian, and Nicephorus Gregoras [90] often delighted—at times even Eusebius of Caesarea. Similar is the prodigy which by every oath he affirmed he had seen—a plant springing up on the pedestal on which rested the brass statue of Christ (which 300 years earlier a woman cured of a hemorrhage had dedicated to the Savior). This plant cured all kinds of diseases when it touched the edge of the clothing of the statue. With such trifles the books of Antonine, Ado, [91]

[90] Nicephorus Gregoras, c.1295–1360, was keeper of the archives in Constantinople and author of *Romanae hoc est Byzantinae historiae libri xi*, and of a treatise *De astrolabo*, first printed in Italy in 1498. He suggested calendar reforms very like those achieved by Gregory XIII two hundred years later.

[91] Ado, Frankish bishop of Vienne (in Lorraine) in the ninth century, who was later canonized. He was author of a *Breviarium chronicorum ab origine mundi ad sua usque tempora, id est, ad regnum Ludovici, Francorum regis, cognomento Simplicis*, which he based on Bede. For him the unity of the Roman Empire extended into the Carolingian period.

Saxo Grammaticus,[92] Sigebert,[93] Freculph,[94] Naucler,[95] Marianus,[96] Merlin,[97] the abbot of Ursperg, Aimoin, Turpin,[98] Gaguin,[99] and the old annals are filled. We cannot get along without them altogether, yet in this respect some far exceed others. Gregory of Tours, Antonine of Florence, William, bishop of Tyre, and the abbot of Ursperg wrote useful and informative histories, however full of portents and miracles, especially for those periods in which savagery overwhelmed everything. They were also thoroughly experienced for a long time in managing the state and public counsels.

We ought to collect the remnants of other works just as gems from mud, if better are lacking. With the exception of Marco Polo [100] and Hayton,[101] we have almost no one who has written the deeds of the Tartars, and even these reports are rather meager and mixed with legends. Hayton is more truthful. Let us therefore reject in Marco Polo the statements that the Caspian Sea is always empty of fishes except in Lent; that the circumference of the city Quinsay exceeded seventy milestones; that this same town had twelve thousand bridges of such height that freight ships easily passed with sails unfurled; that for protection against hostile weapons the Zipangi wear rings whose virtue makes them inviolable. These things having been eliminated, we may to some extent understand the deeds of the Tartars, their customs, laws, and an outline of their religion.

[92] Saxo Grammaticus, c.1150–c.1200, was born in Zeeland and wrote *Gesta Danorum*.

[93] Sigebert of Gembloux died in 1112. Although a monk, he supported Emperor Henry IV against Gregory VII. He was the author of *Chronographia*.

[94] Freculph, d.850, was a Benedictine monk and bishop of Lisieux. He had the favor of Louis the Pious and dedicated to the Empress Judith his chronicle, which covered history from the Creation to the kingdom of the Lombards. In contrast to Ado he recognized the end of the Roman Empire.

[95] Johannes Nauclerus (Vergenhanns), c.1430–c.1500, was a member of the lesser Suabian nobility and doctor of both laws. His *Chronica . . . ab initio mundi usque ad annum Christi nati 1500* is an important source for medieval history.

[96] Marianus Scotus, 1028–1082, was a monk of Fulda, Irish by birth. He wrote *Chronica*, which attempted to cover universal history.

[97] Merlin Caledonius, c.540–612, was a bard and a prophet.

[98] Turpin, archbishop of Rheims in the eighth century, was the supposed author of a life of Charlemagne. The name may be Tilpin.

[99] Robert Gaguin, 1425–1502, was dean of the faculty of canon law at Paris. He was sent on embassies to England and the Empire, and wrote *De origine et gestis Francorum*.

[100] This is given as Paulus Venetus, but the context seems to indicate Marco Polo, rather than the other Venetian.

[101] Hayton of Armenia flourished 1310. He was a nephew of the king of Armenia and a Praemonstratensian monk in Cyprus. He wrote *Liber historiarum partium orientium, sive passagium terrae sanctae* reprinted as *Historia orientalis quae de Tartaris inscribitur*.

Francis Alvarez, however, with much greater faith and diligence, first wrote the affairs of the Ethiopians, which now are approved by foreigners and the best writers and are not read without great pleasure. Ziegler,[102] Cromer,[103] Krantz,[104] and Olaus [105] have likewise published the histories of the Goths, Saxons, Nervii, Sarmatians or Poles, and Danes, formerly unknown. Most of these are indeed very credible, but Olaus often tells unbelievable things. Yet there are some matters which in a certain way become accepted because of the number of writers who agree about them. The tales about the change and the metempsychosis of the Nervii into wolves (they are now called Livones) which once upon a time were spread abroad by Herodotus, Pomponius Mela, and other historians, have been approved by more recent writers. Indeed, Gaspar Peucer,[106] a man of great erudition and not at all trifling, as well as Languet,[107] famous no less for his education than for his long wanderings over all Europe, affirmed to me that they had learned this from the inhabitants. Whether it might happen through some occult force of powerful nature, as is reported in the case of Parrhasius, or by divine revenge, as with Nabuchodonosor, is not yet clear to me.

Leo the African follows Alvarez. These men, along with Pomponius, Strabo, and Pausanias, I usually call geographistorians on account of their method of writing, because they treat history along with geography. Strabo, of course, touched lightly upon the states and empires of the world; Pausanias described the provinces of the Greek world, the condition of public affairs, the changes, peoples, towns, camps, rivers, mountains, whirlpools, fountains, temples, and statues so carefully that

---

[102] Jacob Ziegler, 1470–1549, was a German astronomer and geographer. He wrote a commentary on Pliny's second book and *Schondia*, a history of Scandinavia, which was the first to recognize the north and south axis of that peninsula.

[103] Martin Cromer, 1512–1589, was a Polish scholar, bishop of Ermeland. He was sent on important diplomatic missions, attending the Council of Trent. He wrote a geographical work, *Polonia*, as well as *De origine et rebus gestis Polonorum libri xxx*.

[104] Albert Krantz, 1448–1517, had an appointment in connection with Hamburg cathedral and wrote *Historia de Vandalorum vera origine, variis gentibus, crebris e patria migrationibus*, and *Regnorum aquilonarium chronicon*.

[105] Magnus Olaus (Olaf Månson), 1490–1557, was archbishop of Upsala, as well as historian and cartographer who performed various diplomatic missions for Gustavus Vasa. He wrote *Carta marina et descriptio septentrionalium terrarum*.

[106] Gaspar Peucer, 1526–1602, contributed a section to continue the chronicle of Johann Carion of Lübeck, which was edited by his father-in-law, Melanchthon. He wrote also *Commentarius de praecipiis generibus divinationum*.

[107] Hubert Languet, 1518–1581, was a Protestant humanist and diplomat, who studied law at Poitiers and at Padua. He was a friend of Melanchthon and the ambassador of the German princes to the court of Charles IX. *Vindiciae contra tyrannos* is probably his work.

in this kind of writing he surpassed the expectation of all. The same thing is true of Leo the African, by race a Moor, by nation Spanish, by religion Mohammedan and later Christian. After he had wandered over almost all Africa and Asia Minor on long journeys, and a good part of Europe also, he was captured by pirates. He was presented as a gift to Pope Leo, at whose residence, with incredible zeal and diligence, he translated into Italian what he had composed in Arabic about Africa— customs, laws, and institutes of the people of Africa and the situation and limits of the whole region. He touched lightly upon military train- ing, but he commemorated briefly the defeats and the victories of the generals without any speeches or ornament, not as a historian, but as a geographer. He holds the unwilling reader by the unceasing delight of new things. He narrated nothing entirely incredible except the aston- ishing docility of the Egyptian ass, or rather the golden ass. When he affirmed that he had seen tails of Egyptian sheep which weighed fifty pounds and that they sometimes equaled one hundred and twenty, he wrote in accord with Bellonius [108] and Jerome Cardan. I suppose he is the only one who after a thousand years discovered Africa, buried in miserable brutishness and forgotten by us, and revealed it to the atten- tion of everyone.

I add to these F. Leander [109] and Munster,[110] one of whom placed all Italy, the other, Germany as in a picture before the eyes and com- bined the history of the peoples with the geography. But although Mun- ster entitled his Germanography a cosmography, yet the whole dealt with the regions of Germany and of Switzerland—towns, site, origin, and description of the peoples. When this has been taken into account, almost no space is left for the world in general. But it is worthy of

[108] Bellonius (Pierre Belon), 1517–1564, studied medicine and botany, visited Greece, the Aegean islands, and the Asiatic mainland and wrote *Histoire naturelle des étranges poissons marins*, among which were included sturgeon, tuna, dolphin, and hippopotamus. His book contains anatomical comparisons, and suggestions of embryology. It is the basis of modern ichthyology. There is another work, *Portraits d'oyseaux, animaux, serpents, herbes . . . d'Arabie et d'Egypte.*

[109] Frater Leander Alberti, 1479–c.1553, was born in Bologna. He was a Dominican, historian, and geographer. He traveled about Italy and France with the general of the Order and wrote *Descrittione di tutta Italia*, which resembles the book of Biondo, and is the author also of *De viris illustribus ordinis praedicatorum.*

[110] Sebastian Munster, 1489–1552, was a German theologian and cosmographer, mem- ber of the Franciscan order. He became a Lutheran, taught Hebrew at Heidelberg and mathematics at Basel. He wrote *Cosmographiae universalis libri vi, Organum uranicum,* and *La Declaration de l'instrument . . . pour coignoistre le cours du ciel jusques à l'an MDLXXX.*

notice that all—not only historians but also geographers—whom I have happened to read (except Polybius and Ptolemy) give the size of islands and regions in circumference. Those whose perimeter is the same or unequal they consider equal or unequal. Nothing is more stupid than this. Yet it seemed inevitable to many people and often to me until I noticed by a geometrical demonstration that it very often happens that the circuit of an island may be three times greater than the circuit of another, yet its size may be ten times less. Moreover, as geographistorians mingle regions with history, so the philosophistorians weave into the narration of deeds precepts of wisdom. In this respect Xenophon wins great praise, the greater since he had no one to imitate, as Velleius writes about Homer; nor was there afterwards anyone who could imitate him.

Plutarch follows him; then Laertius; [111] afterwards Philo the Jew, between whom and Plato, I suppose, the ancients certainly had not only a preliminary bias, but obviously a preference. Josephus, the contemporary of this man, seems inferior in renown for more recondite philosophy, yet far superior in his knowledge of antiquity. Jerome indeed wondered that so much of Greek antiquity was known to a Jewish writer. His knowledge can be estimated from his books against Apion the Grammarian. In these he so confirmed the writings of Moses (although for winning confidence they are self-sufficient) by evidence from Greeks, Persians, Egyptians, and Chaldeans, that nothing more useful for understanding origins seems to have been written. It is true that statements were made by Moses about the ages of men which he confirmed by the authority of twelve historians, lest they should seem incredible to anyone. But he placed the Hebrew people superior to all others in antiquity, faith, religion, doctrine, and integrity—not so much that he might reclaim from oblivion the faded glory of his compatriots as to assert the truth of the matter. From his writings the legends of Herodotus, Diodorus, and Justinian can easily be refuted. After his time Hegesippus [112] the Jew covered the Jewish War in five books, which Ambrose [113] is said to have made into Latin. Yet Josephus wrote more truly and better

[111] Diogenes Laertius flourished in the middle of the third century, but we have little information about him. He left *De vita et moribus philosophorum libri x.*

[112] Hegesippus flourished in the fourth century A.D. He translated and paraphrased the *Wars of the Jews*, by Josephus.

[113] Ambrose, c.330–397, was born of a Roman family and took up public office. He became bishop of Milan before he had even been baptized. He left a great number of exegetical treatises on the Old Testament, inspired to some extent by the ideas of Philo and Origen.

because he was not only present but also in charge, and after he had been taken prisoner by Vespasian and Titus he won the right of citizenship, the name of the Flavian family, and a statue. In this man certainly were embodied those virtues of a historian which we have mentioned before —the highest erudition, unusual integrity, and the greatest experience in managing affairs. With what honesty and reliability he wrote is quite plain from the fact that although he was in religion a Jew he advanced extremely weighty and praiseworthy testimony about Christ. In contrast, almost all ecclesiastical writers are animated with such hatred when they write about the adversaries of our religion that not only do they try to tone down their virtues but even rend them with scorn. A case in point is Julian Augustus, who is usually called the Apostate. Even if he deserved the greatest scorn and every kind of punishment, yet in writing history an author cannot fittingly overlook his excellent deeds, as our men have done.

In this, certainly, they should have imitated the candor of Ammianus Marcellinus and his zeal for seeking the truth. He, like every good writer, noted the virtues and the vices of princes with the utmost fidelity. He blamed Julian for confusing the Christian religion, complete and simple (for so Ammianus says), with an old woman's superstition; because he cruelly took away education from the Christians; and because he ordered the counts palatine of Constantius to be killed. Yet the unusual virtues of the same man he commended in remarkable language —highest sobriety, courage, self-restraint, enthusiasm for wisdom, and justice greater than any mere opinion. These things he confirmed with important illustrations and testimony. An example is the incident when Delphinius, an extremely brilliant French orator, violently attacked Numerius, the president of Gallia Narbonensis, before Julian, who was then at Paris, and embarrassed by want of witnesses. Delphinius cried out, "Oh, most glorious Caesar, is there anyone who will ever be guilty if it is sufficient to deny?" To this Julian replied, "Is there anyone who will ever be innocent if it is enough to accuse?" Ammianus, moreover, was by nation a Greek and, as he himself confessed, a soldier, the perpetual companion of Ursicinus, the master of horse. He was actually engaged in almost all the wars waged by the Romans in Europe and in Asia in his time, and information on all these has been preserved, comprised within eighteen books, extending from the thirtieth year of the rule of Constantius to the death of Valens. The earlier thirteen books can easily be supplied from other writers. Then, too, he started from

Nerva, where Tacitus left off. This man, of all others, Ammianus seems to have proposed to contemplate and imitate. Yet he differed from him in this—that Tacitus maintained the dignity of the Roman speech, as the times demanded, but Ammianus wrote Greek in Latin words and too often not even in Latin. He often wandered far from the matter in hand. With this fault, however, the greatest men are afflicted, and Posidonius gravely noted it in Cicero himself. But Ammianus met this reproach, if not in Latin, yet appropriately enough for his purpose, in this manner: "Moreover," he says, "the fact that the style is a trifle prolix will be an advantage to complete knowledge. Whoever affects too great brevity when recounting new material does not ponder what he may explain more clearly, but what he ought to omit."

From this great variety of historians it is necessary for each reader to make individual choice according to his judgment, lest in the brief course of this life we should be overwhelmed by the multitude of writers. If we consider the well-known Polydore Vergil to have written most truthfully on English affairs (although, of course, he is suspect to the Scots and the French), Rhenanus [114] on the German, Aemilius on the French, we shall not need to worry very much about Bede, Gaguin, Gazus, Saxo, and such writers, who have written on the same subjects confusedly. But I do not know by what freak of nature it has happened that although at some periods a great abundance of historians existed contemporaneously they began to disappear almost at the same time. Plutarch wrote that three hundred historians described the battle of Marathon. Likewise, almost thirty writers reported in writing the Italian affairs of the recent period. Yet I think that Guicciardini alone, whose authority is accepted by general consent, ought to be put before all the others. Now almost all Europe abounds in numerous historians, who detail all the most trifling affairs, although many centuries ago it had almost no one.

But lest tracing all the commentaries should take too long, we shall select the best one by these criteria which we have indicated or by even better ones. Readers who approach writers of history ought also to be warned that many authors, in a continuous series, have written the same book. Of this nature are the books of Judges and the books of Kings; and this is done rather often under the name of one writer. Such is the

---

[114] Beatus Rhenanus (Bild von Rheinau), 1485–1547, was born in Schlettstadt, became a critic and an editor, was a friend of Erasmus and an author. Among other works he wrote *Libri iii rerum Germanicarum*.

book of Samuel; yet it is plain that the last fifteen chapters were written after the death of Samuel. The last section of Deuteronomy is another instance. The book of Joshua is thought to be by another writer, because the book Jasher [115] is cited about the immobility of the sun. However, it appears from the first chapter of the first book of Kings that this book was written five hundred years later, unless we may say that the book of Jasher is by many writers and was started before Joshua. By the same reasoning the account by Haemo, who is called Aimoin incorrectly by our men, has been put together from many writers, since it commemorates the affairs of three hundred years supposedly surveyed by him. The same classification holds for the works of Regino [116] and Carion.[117] So much about the choice of historians. I should like to have written so that an impartial judgment may be left to each reader.

[115] Bodin quotes this as "Recti," but the *Jewish Encyclopedia* prefers Jasher. See also Joshua 10:13.

[116] Regino of Spires (or Prüm), d. 915, at Trier. He was abbot of Prüm and wrote a chronicle from Christ to 906, as well as *De harmonica institutione* and *De synodalibus causis.*

[117] The major portion of this paragraph, from "Readers" through "Carion," is lacking in the first edition.

CHAPTER V

THE CORRECT EVALUATION OF HISTORIES

AT THIS POINT it seems necessary to speak about the correct evaluation of histories. There would be no reason to impugn history, or to withhold agreement, if those who ought to have had the highest standards had had regard for truth and trustworthiness. Since, however, the disagreement among historians is such that some not only disagree with others but even contradict themselves, either from zeal or anger or error, we must make some generalizations as to the nature of all peoples or at least of the better known, so that we can test the truth of histories by just standards and make correct decisions about individual instances. We ought to proceed a little differently from Diodorus, Volaterranus,[1] Caelius,[2] Sabellicus, and Boemus, who have written very meagerly about the various laws, religions, sacrifices, public banquets, and institutions of peoples. About these no generalizations can be made, because they vary infinitely and change within a brief period through natural growth or at the will of a prince. Since that is so, let us seek characteristics drawn, not from the institutions of men, but from nature, which are stable and are never changed unless by great force or long training, and even if they have been altered, nevertheless eventually they return to their pristine character. About this body of knowledge the ancients could write nothing, since they were ignorant of regions and places which not so long ago were opened up; instead, each man advanced as far as he could by inference of probabilities.

At first, therefore, we shall explain the nature of peoples who dwell to the north and to the south, then of those who live to the east and to the west. Next, we notice the characteristics of special places, that is, mountains, marshes, windy and placid regions. Following this, we shall consider what efficacy lies in training to alter the nature of men. Afterwards we shall refute the errors of Ptolemy and the ancients, who thought the customs of peoples could be traced to the parts of the zodiac they apportioned to each region. When we have grasped and understood these things, I trust that a great part of history will have been

---

[1] Volaterranus (Raphael Maffei), 1451?-1522, author of *Commentariorum rerum urbanarum libri xxviii* and *De Romanorum Graecorumque magistratibus*.

[2] L. Caelius Antipater was a Roman jurist and historian, a contemporary of the Gracchi, living about 123 B.C. He was the author of *Annales*.

grasped and understood. I do not know any discussion more necessary for a general knowledge of history and for the impartial judgment thereof.

I have, however, a firm conviction that [astrological?] regions and celestial bodies do not have power to exercise ultimate control (a belief wrong even to entertain), yet men are so much influenced by them that they cannot overcome the law of nature except through divine aid or their own continued self-discipline. What Galen and Polybius affirm is false—that a moderation of the air necessarily affects us. Anacharsis [3] the Scythian was proof that it has indeed great influence for changing character, yet does not have final control. To topographical diversity we must relate the opinion which Plato expresses in Book v of the *Laws*, where he says some people are made better than others and some worse from the very difference of site; [4] on account of this it is necessary to restrain these peoples by laws often contradictory and varying from one district to another. This difference proceeds also from the waters and the air and even from the variety of foods. The ancients report, therefore, almost unanimously that the men living to the north are larger and stronger in body; to the south, on the other hand, they are weaker, yet they exceed the others in ability. Of course this was learned by long-continued experience, because observation of the fact is easy; but how far the power of the north and of the south goes, what defines the east and the west, or what ought to be thought about the traits and the innate nature of each, it is difficult to say, the more so because there is no one who offers a torch in such darkness. Hippocrates, who represents the highest authority, reported that men in the north were slender and swarthy. Aristotle, in *Questions*, declared that the men who were handicapped by excessive heat or cold were equally uncivilized. These statements seem clearly to contradict the preceding. For how can the southerners be both clever and uncivilized? Yet each one spoke truly.

In order that this may be understood more easily, let us establish four quarters of this hemisphere: the southern in the circle of the equator, the northern on the vertex of the pole, the eastern in the Moluccas, the western in the isles of the Hesperides. Strabo made a different division: the Indians in the east, Celts in the west, Scythians in the north, Ethiopians in the south. Ptolemy did not depart very far from this arrangement. Not so long ago, however, it was found that the ancients

[3] Anacharsis was a legendary Scythian prince who traveled widely in the days of Solon.
[4] Plato *Laws* v. 747 D.

had made a serious error in this regard, for the mathematicians deny that there is any separation of east and west—how truly, we shall say in its place. For the present it suffices to place the meeting of the east and the west in America, because this region is removed by boundless distances from India and Africa. Then the dividing line between the north and the south is the equator which reaches around the world. In turn, the middle of the hemisphere on this side of the equator is marked by the forty-fifth parallel of latitude, so that whatever lies above towards the pole is classified as northern, the rest, lying below, as southern. Since the ancients, except Posidonius and Avicenna, believed that men lived between the tropics and the polar circles and thought nothing else was safe or habitable, we must eradicate this error.

It has actually been found by frequent explorations that the region of the equator is very healthful, while the areas beneath the tropics burn with an incredible heat, and the reason is, of course, manifest. For the sun rises higher at the equator and, on account of the size of the circle, is carried much more swiftly than on the tropics. Indeed, Alvarez wrote that in the month of June the waters on the equator stiffen into ice, even when the south wind blows. Other features are a heavy rainfall, lofty mountains, and thick woods. Lastly, the color of men's faces is not black, but olive. Under the tropics, on the other hand, are burning heat, no rain, no woods, few rivers, and perpetual flatness of the sands, except in Arabia Felix and certain areas of India, where the difference is due to the mountainous region and its eastward position. Finally, the inhabitants have black skin not only among the Ethiopians, but also among the Indians, as Ctesias discovered a long time ago and our men recently. I can hardly be persuaded that men are made black from the curse of Chus,[5] as a certain learned man reports. For a long time they have ridiculed the opinion of Herodotus, who thought that the seed of the Ethiopians was black. He argued that the Ethiopians would be born black in Scythia and the Scythians white in Ethiopia, although all peoples for a long time have been fused in repeated waves of migration.

Yet we see men as well as plants degenerate little by little when the soil has been changed, and it is for the same reason that fire and sun color men black, as Aristotle reported. Moreover, Pliny wrote that in Ethiopia the lions are sable, such as Oppian the poet,[6] in his book *On Hunting,* claimed to have seen. After I had set forth these books in

[5] Chus was the son of Ham, the son of Noah.

[6] Oppian of Apamea in Syria wrote *Cynegetica,* a treatise on hunting in four books,

Latin verses and commentaries, a certain grammarian, in prose, taking as much as he pleased from my work, again published these same books. In order, then, that we may avoid the error of the ancients, we shall divide into three equal parts the region from the equator to the pole, which contains ninety degrees, in such a way that we shall give thirty degrees to the heat, the same number to the cold. There will remain thirty of the temperate zone, in which one can live comfortably and happily, except in rugged and precipitous highlands, or sunken swamps, or areas desert through aridity, or dangerous and sterile because of injurious qualities of water or soil. Such is the fertility of the earth in certain regions of the tropics that the inhabitants feel less seriously the hardships of the climate. Once more, we shall divide in two the thirty degrees of heat and of cold and of the moderate area, so that fifteen on this side of the equator are more equable, while fifteen around the tropic are warmer; and in the temperate region the first fifteen are more moderate on account of the mildness of the climate; the following, from the forty-fifth degree to the sixtieth, somewhat colder. Again, out of thirty degrees of the coldest zone, fifteen are inhabited; further, there are no cities, no towns, no means at all of giving protection to men.

Nature itself and expediency taught me that I should make this division. From the equator the thirtieth parallel, like a frontier, cuts the Atlas Mountains, which run from the distant African shores as far as Egypt and, facing the heat of the sun, water the nearer [Mediterranean] shore of Africa with innumerable rivers. The same frontier divides the crests of Arabia and the farthest parts of all the Persian and the Indian coast. The sixtieth parallel from the equator in its turn touches the boundary of the Goths, Livonia, Muscovy, the Orkneys, and the ends of the Imaeus range.[7] From this line habitation can take place even to the seventy-fifth parallel, but only with difficulty and beyond not at all, if we have confidence in geographers and historians. I divide each thirty-degree unit in half because the tropics and the polar circles cut respectively fifteen degrees in one direction and seven in the other, if anyone admits this division of which I have spoken.[8]

---

and dedicated it to the Emperor Caracalla. Bodin published a Latin translation of the Greek original in 1555.

[7] The Imaeus mountains are shown on the map of Henricus Martellus Germanus (1489) and on the map of Diego Ribero (1529). The Pamirs may be the modern equivalent.

[8] The Latin reads: "ob id etiam, triginta quasque partes bifariam divido, quod tropici et Polares circuli quindecim gradus hinc inde septem secant."

Since the maximum of cold or heat is under the tropics [9] and each pole, there will be under the equator the same moderation of climate as in those areas situated under the thirtieth parallel. Indeed the Leuko-Ethiopians are reported to be in both places. Under the tropics they are unusually black; under the pole, for the opposite reason, they are tawny in color. After that, down to the sixtieth parallel, they become ruddy; thence to the forty-fifth they are white; after that to the thirtieth they become yellow, and when the yellow bile is mingled with the black [melancholy], they grow greenish, until they become swarthy and deeply black under the tropics. So the statement of Hippocrates that men in the northland are ugly because they are pale and thin would be absurd unless we were referring to the furthest places of the north. Likewise, when the ancients say that they were robust and tall, we must apply this to places nearer us. When I was in doubt, my supposition was corroborated by Gaspar Holster, a Swede from the metropolitan town of Stockholm, sprung from the depths of Gothia, who unites the glory of learning and a command of languages with the reputation of a soldier. His face and his hair are reddish, and he is plainly red-nosed,[10] without any flaw of skin, medium in stature, broad shouldered, his eyes rather bluish, with poor vision, for he always suffers from myopia. Languet, a Frenchman equally well known for his learning and his wanderings throughout Europe, has often told me this same thing—beyond Gothia the men are tawny and gradually grow thinner. In Gothia and in Sweden itself they grow ruddier and yet are not to be compared with the Germans in size. It greatly troubled Galen also that Hippocrates and Aristotle wrote that all in the north have carroty fine hair, as if they were blond, although many from the extreme north seem auburn. I have learned from the inhabitants that the men in Britain and in Germany who have red hair take their origin from Danes and Norwegians who seized the neighboring territories. They maintain an uneasy attitude toward the latter. There are many in France also, especially in Westria or Normandy, which succumbed to the Danes. But the Germans and the Britons are almost all blond. About them the saying of Lucan can be understood—"The blond Suabians come down from the home of the north wind" [11]—for old Suabia and the Suabian Sea extend to the

[9] Each of two parallels of latitude on the earth's surface, distant about 23° 28′ N. and S. of the equator, being the boundaries of the torrid zone. The arctic circle is at 66° 32′ N.

[10] φοινικορύγκος is used in Aristotle *Historia animalium* IX. 24.

[11] Lucan *Pharsalia* II. 51.

fifty-fifth parallel. They used to think that beyond this there was no land.

Furthermore, this question of physical type will help us greatly both for the customs of the people and for the knowledge and appraisal of history. Let us consider other evidence. Scythians differ very much from the southerners in that the latter have black eyes, the former grey and blue; those who dwell midway have yellowish [*caprinos*] eyes. Amyot, a man of the highest erudition, in Plutarch's "Marius" translated ὀμμάτων χαροπότητα as "chestnut eyes" and "eyes of a reddish color." I should rather say "ferocity of eyes." Tacitus said of the Germans, "fierce blue eyes, reddish hair, great bodies," [12] and Juvenal, "Who does not know the caerulean eyes of the German, and his blond headdress twining the moist ringlets into knots?" [13] "Caerulean," however, has nothing in common with "red," for χαροπότητος is an ambiguous word, signifying both cruelty and color of eyes,[14] as Eustathius [15] wrote about that line of Homer, which I should render thus: "Wild boars and bears and snarling lions." [16]

Catullus translated it "bluish grey," and each way is correct. As Oppian called the sea χαροπήν, so Seneca called it "caerulean." Amyot has as authority Gaza,[17] who rendered χαροπὸς sometimes "red," sometimes "tawny." Scaliger [18] said "greyish yellow"; Hesychius [19] wrote that χαροπὸς signifies bluish grey and yellow, as Aristotle in one place called the eyes of goats ὄμματα χαροπά. They are actually yellow. The beginning of this confusion and error is in a false understanding of Homer. Because he called lions χαροπούς, referring to the eyes, like the expression γλαυκῶπις Ἀθήνη, *glaucopis Athene*, many thought it applied to the hide.

[12] Tacitus *Germania*, paragraph 4.   [13] Juvenal *Satires* XIII. 164.

[14] Liddell and Scott's *Greek-English Lexicon* defines χαροπός as expressing, originally, the glare of the eyes in beasts of prey.

[15] Eustathius, archbishop of Thessalonica, d.1192? He wrote *Commentarii ad Homeri Iliadem*, *Commentarii ad Homeri Odysseam*, and *De capta Thessalonica liber*.

[16] *Odyssey* XI. 611.

[17] Theodore Gaza, professor of Greek at Ferrara, d.1478. He had the patronage of Panormitanus, secretary of the king of Naples, and of Cardinal Bessarion at Rome. He produced *Grammaticae Graecae libri iv*.

[18] Julius Caesar Scaliger, 1484–1558, was an Italian exponent of Aristotelian physics and metaphysics who later moved to France. He wrote commentaries on Aristotle's *Historia animalium* and *Exercitationes* on Cardan's *De subtilitate*.

Joseph Scaliger, 1540–1609, was the son of the foregoing. He became a Protestant and started a new school of historical criticism. He was the author of *Conjectanea in Varronem* and *De emendatione temporum*.

[19] Hesychius was a fourth-century Alexandrian, who wrote a Greek lexicon.

This, Aristotle reported, was invariably tawny. Lions are therefore called "tawny" by the Latins. The eyes of a lion do gleam, moreover, by the testimony of Homer and more emphatically of Oppian. So Simon Portius [20] has fallen into a like error, in that he interprets χαροπὸς as "yellowish grey" and thinks it is the color of ashes from the fact that Horace called a wolf "yellowish grey." It really relates to the eyes, which Varro would make yellowish grey [*ravus*] in a rustic cock, or rather yellow [*flavus*], as in Festus [21] the grain is yellow [*ravus*]. They are really lighter, like the eyes of hawks and eagles which gaze into the sun. Things are called "yellowish grey" in color, said Festus, when they are between *flavus* and *caesius*. These Plautus called *ravistelli*. Recently, in the last Debates, a certain man interpreted "yellow grain" in Festus as "dry grain." Then he submitted as his reason that the voice becomes hoarse from a dry throat; in this can be seen a poor grammarian and a bad physician. For grain is yellow, and a hoarse voice comes from a damp throat.[22]

Therefore, as Aristotle allotted dark eyes to the Ethiopians and blue-grey to the Scythians, so he gave to the middle region goat eyes, that is, yellow or yellowish grey, which Pliny called "red." And yet the middle region has an infinite variety blended from the extremes; the extremes have no variety. There is, then, in a Scythian face an obvious characteristic whereby it differs from the others—to wit, the bluish color of the eyes. That is, as Plato would have it, blue turning to white, like the eyes of the night owls, which on that account are called "silvery." They grow dim in the light. Such the Cimbri also have, on the evidence of Plutarch. This I have noticed in many Danes. The Germans and the Britons, on the other hand, do not have this bluish-grey with a lighter gleam, but blue of a distinctly unusual darkness. This color is even called *aquilus*, from water. Now, bluish-grey color in eyes is a marked indication of heat, as Aristotle wrote in *Questions*, while black, such as southerners have, signifies want of heat. Those who are in the middle region have goat's eyes, or yellowish-grey, and they have the most accurate vision of all. (Indeed Pliny reported that goats never have bleary eyes.) Furthermore, they denote the best habits, in the opinion of Aristotle. But bluish-grey eyes are cruel, and Pliny and Plutarch declared that the eyes of Sulla, Cato, and Augustus were of this sort. Plutarch sig-

[20] Simone Porzio, 1497?–1554, author of *De humana mente disputatio*, *An homo bonus vel malus volens fiat*, and *De rerum naturalibus principiis*.

[21] Sextus Pompeius Festus was a lexicographer of uncertain date between Martial and Macrobius. He wrote *De verborum significatione*.

[22] *Raucus*, hoarse, and *ravus*, yellow, are etymologically connected.

nified by the ambiguous word χαροπότητος both the color and the cruelty of the Cimbri, since he used "grim" and "gleaming." Three principal colors of eyes appear, therefore, in the three peoples: black, bluish grey, and yellowish grey, from which an infinite variety is produced. Vitruvius confirmed these things in part: "Up in the north," he said, "are bred races with huge bodies, fair complexions, straight red hair, grey-eyed, and full-blooded; but those who are along the southern axis are made over by force of the sun to a shorter stature, swarthy color, curly hair, black eyes, weak limbs, and scanty blood." [23] This is his explanation. The blood of the Scythians is full of fibers, as in boars and bulls, whence they say strength and audacity are engendered. The southerners are thin-blooded, like hares and deer, whereby it comes about that they are more timid and more feeble.

Let us therefore adopt this theory, that all who inhabit the area from the forty-fifth parallel to the seventy-fifth toward the north grow increasingly warmer within, while the southerners, since they have more warmth from the sun, have less from themselves. In winter the heat is collected within, but in summer it flows out. Whereby it happens that in winter we are more animated and robust, in summer more languid. The same reason usually makes us hungrier in winter so that we eat more than in summer, especially when the north wind blows. The south wind has the opposite effect, that is to say, living things are less hungry, as Aristotle wrote. So it comes to pass that when the Germans visit Italy, or the French, Spain, we observe that they eat more frugally or suffocate. This accident happened to Philip, duke of Austria, when he dined according to his usual custom in Spain. But the Spanish, who live frugally in their fatherland, in France are more voracious than the French. Let it serve as evidence that the shepherds commonly say that when the herds and the flocks go down to the south they are wasted with fasting; they are more active in the north. Nor is it remarkable that Leo the African wrote he had seen almost no herds of oxen or horses and only a few flocks of sheep in Africa; the ewes gave only a little milk. In contrast, the flocks of the Germans and the Scythians are praised by almost all writers. This ought not to be attributed to the fact that they have better pastures than the southerners, as Pliny thought, but to the climate. For the strength of inward heat brings it about that those who live in northerly lands are more active and robust than the southerners.

---

[23] Vitruvius *Ten Books on Architecture* VI. 1, paragraphs 3–4. Morgan's translation differs from that of Bodin in having "strong" instead of "weak."

Even in the opposite area, beyond Capricorn's circle, the same thing happens: the further men move from the equator, the larger they grow, as in the land of the Patagonians, who are called giants, in the very same latitude as the Germans. This, then, is the reason why Scythians have always made violent attacks southward; and what seems incredible, but is nevertheless true, the greatest empires always have spread southward —rarely from the south toward the north. The Assyrians defeated the Chaldeans; the Medes, the Assyrians; the Greeks, the Persians; the Parthians, the Greeks; the Romans, the Carthaginians; the Goths, the Romans; the Turks, the Arabs; and the Tartars, the Turks. The Romans, on the contrary, were unwilling to advance beyond the Danube. After Trajan had built a stone bridge of remarkable size across the Danube (for it is said that it had twenty pylons, of which the fragments even now remain), he did indeed conquer the Dacians completely. But when Hadrian understood that these tribes were not easily kept in subjection and did not submit to defeat, he ordered the bridge to be destroyed. Let us, however, cite more recent examples.

The French often suffered serious defeat at the hands of the English in France itself and almost lost their territory; they could never have penetrated into England, had they not been invited by the inhabitants. The English, on the other hand, were frequently overwhelmed by the Scots, and although they fought for control for more than 1,200 years, yet they could not drive the Scots from a small part of the island, even when in resources and numbers they were as much superior to the Scots as they were inferior to the French. It is not a fact, as the English complain, that the contest was unequal because of French hostility, for when the Roman Empire was tottering the South Britons were forced to call the Anglo-Saxons for protection, lest they should fall into servitude under the Scots. Yet the men who withstood the onslaughts of the Scots were not willing to attack at home.[24] I omit the serious incursions into Europe and Asia of the Scythians, Parthians, Turks, Tartars, Muscovites, Goths, Huns, and Suessiones, since the list is endless. Unless I err, this is what Ezekiel, Jeremiah, Isaiah, and the remaining Prophets threaten so many times: wars from the north, soldiers, horsemen, and the coming downfall of empires.

All these things pertain more truly to the region I have mentioned, which extends from the forty-fifth to the seventy-fifth parallel, where

---

[24] The Latin reads: "Anglosaxones ad praesidium evocare qui Scotorum impetus cohibuerunt lacessere domi noluerunt."

Biarmia [25] is situated. The inhabitants of the farther regions, who, more-over, are either few or none, according to Hippocrates, are burned by the cold as much as those who live near the tropics [are burned by the heat]. Not, as Aristotle thought, in *Meteorologica*, Book IV, on account of the strength of internal heat resulting from excessive reaction [26] (for the same thing happens to plants—they are burned by the cold in the same way as by the heat), but because the cold penetrates to the innermost regions and consumes the humor, whence it is called by Pompey [27] the "hoarfrost." Hippocrates, however, thought this information applied to the people who live beneath the Bear, because in his time the northern regions were unknown. Caesar, on the other hand, was not uninformed about the area, yet he alleged a false cause when he wrote that the Germans grow taller and stronger since they enjoy liberty of will and are not shaped by a lib-eral education from boyhood; their growth really ought to be attributed to heat and humor. The same heat brings about a counteraction—they drink rather often. They call thirst the appetite for wet and cold. This form of carousing, which the Germans, especially the Saxons, use, as well as the dwellers near the Baltic Sea, can never be changed at any time or by any laws. "To devote day and night to drink," says Tacitus, "is a disgrace to no man; numerous brawls are usual between the intoxi-cated." [28] But Athenaeus, charging the Scythians with "drinking of un-mixed wine," from the old proverb, said that the Laconians "whenever they wish to drink a stronger mixture, call it drinking Scythian fashion. Chamaeleon of Heracleia, in the book about drunkenness, said, 'Right it were to celebrate in Scythian fashion.' " [29] For instead of ἐπίχυσαν, that is, pour water, the Spartans used to say ἐπισκύθισον, that is, pour plenty of wine.

They likewise overflow with humor. From this, hunger is created by the desire for hot and dry; yet they are pleased less by food than by drink, since they have more heat themselves. This is the reason why Hippocrates thought that it was impossible for the same man to take

[25] The region around the White Sea.

[26] Aristotle *Meteorologica* I. 12. 348b: "Now we see that warm and cold react upon one another by recoil. Hence in warm weather the lower parts of the earth are cold and in a frost they are warm." Book IV. 5. 382b has similar content.

[27] Pompey must be a misprint for Pliny, who in *Natural History* II. 61, says in indirect discourse: "grandinem conglaciato imbre gigni et nivem eodem umore mollius coacto, pruinam autem ex rore gelido."

[28] Tacitus *Germania*, paragraph 22.

[29] Athenaeus *Deipnosophists* X, paragraph 427. Bodin has quoted several disconnected sentences from this paragraph.

both food and drink copiously. When Tacitus noticed this fact among the Germans, he did not understand the cause. "Fasting and cold they bear," says he, "inured to the nature of the sky and the soil," [30] because the climate is cold and the soil sterile. Nay, rather the internal heat resists more vigorously the surrounding cold. Energizing humor wards off hunger. An abundance of humor is evidenced in the growth by which marine animals, on account of excess of water, excel the remaining animal life. From this also comes a gruff and severe voice, although among the Spanish, Carthaginians, and Ethiopians it is unusually thin and clear. In the three latter this proves cold and dryness; in the Germans, dampness and heat. Too much moisture produces in lead and green wood a heavy sound. Heat also opens the interior passages [of the body], while cold closes them. Hence women, by nature colder, speak in a higher tone than men. In a moderate temperature the voice becomes sweet and melodious, as in the Asiatics, the Italians, and the French. Excessive dampness causes the northerners to dissolve in perspiration when they make their way to the south or wage wars in the warm regions.

"The Germans," said Tacitus, "have a curious inconsistency of nature, since the same men love doing nothing, and hate quiet. Either they wage wars, or when they abstain from wars, they abandon themselves to sleep and to food." [31] The inner warmth drives them to action, as may be seen in boys, whom heat does not permit to rest, but moisture brings softness and goes out in sweat. So Plutarch confirmed these things in the life of Marius, where he wrote that the damp bodies of the Cimbri are usually softened by heat and sweat. Wherefore the Spanish and the Italians, if they sustain the first attacks of the French and the Germans, easily break them, as Polybius first noticed and Marius and Caesar then established in famous victories. About the French Caesar said that at the beginning of the fight they were more than men—afterwards weaker than women. Tacitus made the same comment about the Germans: "Great bodies have the Germans, and powerful only for the first attack. Impatient at the same time of work and of drudgery, they do not endure thirst and heat at all. Cold, on the other hand, they bear easily." As Pomponius Mela wrote, up to the age of puberty they go about naked. Galen, however, marveled at the story that they are plunged into cold water by their parents as soon as they are born. But Julian Augustus explained this in his "Discourse at Antioch, The Beardhater." He said that the bastard children of the Germans are drowned in the Rhine; the

[30] Tacitus *op. cit.* paragraph 4.   [31] *Ibid.*, paragraph 15.

legitimate swim. He wrote this extravagantly, however, and without authority.

The Africans, with dry, cold, and very hard bodies, bear work and heat patiently, as Aphrodisaeus [32] wrote in *Questions*. Yet they cannot bear the cold, since they have no internal heat, unlike the Scythians, who endure external heat with difficulty, since they are abundantly supplied within. In the same way horses, by their very nature warm and wet, live with difficulty in Ethiopia, but more easily in Scythia. On the other hand, asses, dry and cold, are lively in Africa, tired in Europe, nonexistent in Scythia.

Those who occupy the middle region are impatient of both cold and heat, since the mean contends with each extreme; both, however, they endure equally well. I do not call the mean between the pole and the equator the middle region, but that space halfway between the tropic and the pole, because heat is not [33] violent under the equator, as we have made plain, although it is under the tropic. So the most temperate region will not be that which runs from the thirtieth parallel to the fortieth, but that from the fortieth to the fiftieth; and the more moderate, the more it slopes to the east. In this tract lie Further Spain, France, Italy, Upper Germany to the Main, both Pannonias, Illyricum, both Mysias, Dacia, Moldavia, Macedonia, Thrace, and the best part of Asia Minor, Armenia, Parthia, Sogdiana, and a large part of Greater Asia. The nearer to the east the regions lie, however, the more temperate they are, although they seem to incline more to the south, as Lydia, Cilicia, Asia, and Media. However, we shall speak of the east in its proper place. The southerners nearer to us, then, are the Spanish, Sicilians, Peloponnesians, Cretans, Syrians, Arabs, Persians, Susians, Gedrosians, Indians, Egyptians, Cyrenaeians, Phoenicians, Numidians, Libyans, Moors, and the Americans who inhabit Florida, but they are such that those who dwell in the same latitude further west are of a colder temperament. The northerners, in turn, are those who inhabit the land from the fiftieth parallel to the sixtieth. They are, however, more temperate than their neighbors who have their homes near the seventieth. In the former tract are Britain, Ireland, Denmark, part of Gothland, Lower Germany from the Main and the Bug River even to farthest Scythia and Tartary, which cover a good part of Europe and Greater Asia.

[32] Alexander Aphrodisaeus flourished in the third century A.D. He was a celebrated commentator on Aristotle. Bodin refers apparently to *Quaestiones naturales et morales*.

[33] The edition of 1583 omits the negative. The editions of 1566, 1572, and 1595 have it.

There remain the people who have made their homes hither and thither under the fifteen degrees of the tropic, but since they are enervated by extreme heat, we must speak about them in a separate place. The others who live below the thirtieth parallel, on this side and beyond the equator, experience almost the same moderation as those who are placed under the thirtieth parallel, as we shall make plain from the very reason of heat and our knowledge of history.

The chief discussion is about the peoples who dwell from the thirtieth parallel to the sixtieth, because we know their history, about which we must form an opinion. We have almost no material for other peoples, but by this illustration we shall learn what must be believed about all. The Mediterranean peoples, then, as far as concerns the form of the body, are cold, dry, hard, bald, weak, swarthy, small in body, crisp of hair, black-eyed, and clear-voiced. The Baltic peoples, on the other hand, are warm, wet, hairy, robust, white, large-bodied, soft-fleshed, with scanty beards, bluish grey eyes, and deep voices. Those who live between the two show moderation in all respects. But this one thing is open to question: that the southerners, weak by the consent of all, are yet hard; the northerners, indeed, are robust, but soft. In opposition to this, Hippocrates and almost all the other writers said that Scythians and mountaineers who resemble the type of the Scythians were hard, wild, and born to endure labor. Among these conflicting opinions of historians and philosophers, however, we shall judge correctly about history, as well as reconcile with Hippocrates and Alexander, Livy, Tacitus, Polybius, Plutarch, and Caesar, who reported that the French and the Germans were impatient of work, if we grant that the northerners in a cold region patiently bear labor, but in a warm region dissolve in sweat and languish. With this the account of Agathias about the Germans and of Krantz about the Scandinavians agree—that they wage war willingly in the winter, but rarely in the summer.

In contrast, the southerners easily endure heat suited to their nature, although they become more energetic in a cold region, languid in a warm one. And so, as I hear, in their language the Spanish women usually call the Germans "soft fish." But the Celts and the Belgae, when they come into Italy or Provence, are tortured by the mosquitoes and vermin to an unusual extent because of the softness of their skin. The natives, due to their toughness, are not annoyed so much.

We have given enough about the form of body from which the habits of mind are inferred and a correct judgment of history is developed.

Since the body and the mind are swayed in opposite directions, the more strength the latter has, the less has the former; and the more effective a man is intellectually, the less strength of body he has, provided the senses are functioning. It is plain, therefore, that the southerners excel in intellect, the Scythians in body. Aristotle intimates this in Book VII of the *Politics*; [34] robust and spirited men have less talent, and their public affairs are not properly directed. Africans, however, have more than enough wisdom, but not enough strength. Yet this is necessary, both for repelling enemies and also for protecting the citizens.

The third class is composed of men who possess the fine arts of obeying and commanding, who can blunt the cunning of the southerners with their strength and withstand the attack of the Scythians through their wisdom. From this type Vitruvius thought that soldiers should be selected, since they excel no less in sagacity than in strength. How rightly, I leave to the opinion of others. The historical problem is left for solution—why Goths, Huns, Heruli, and Vandals invaded Europe, Asia, and Africa, but, lacking wisdom, could not hold it. Those who adopted the plans of wise men have founded nations suited to civil society and have held flourishing empires for a long time; the poets do not inappropriately depict Pallas armed or Achilles protected by her. Since Scythians almost always dislike letters, and southerners arms, they could not found a great empire. In both respects the Romans achieved success with the greatest felicity and sagely combined gymnastics with music, as Plato wished. It is true that they received laws and letters, that is, civil discipline, from the Greeks, just as they received the Palladium; they acquired naval science from the Phoenicians and Sicilians. On the other hand, they obtained military experience through constant warfare: whereas formerly they learned from the custom of the Scythians to strike only with the edge of the sword, afterwards they learned from the Spanish to pierce with the point as well, as is stated in Polybius. So it ought not to seem remarkable that they excelled all peoples in the fame of their deeds, when they joined to discipline the highest gifts of nature. But it came about by a certain divine goodness—or shall I say wisdom? —that the Africans have more wit and the Scythians a more powerful physique, lest, if He had given a foxlike cunning to men wild as bulls or great strength and endurance to Carthaginians keen as foxes, they might use His gifts for destruction. Nothing is more cruel, said Aristotle, than armed injustice. Moreover, he believed that those to whom

[34] Aristotle *Politics* VII. 6. 1327b 23ff.

He allotted moderate strength excelled the remainder in humanity and justice, a trait which in *Questions* he attributed to a temperate climate. "Why," said he, "are people who suffer from too great cold or heat uncivilized?" Is it because the best climate makes the best customs? In that case why do all historians praise so highly the innocence and the justice of the Scythians and execrate the customs of the southerners?

Here I seek a decision in history, in order that we may not have disagreement between philosophers and historians. The matter is not without complexity, for fat men are not at all evil, as Caesar decided rightly about Antony and Dolabella, but Brutus and Cassius, lean men, must be feared. The northerners, however, are heavy, the southerners lean. What Tacitus said of the Germans is therefore true: "The race is not astute or cunning; for the freedom of revelry opens the secrets of the heart, and the frank opinion of all is reconsidered the next day. Due weight is given to both periods." [35] Moreover, this is one reason why kings and tyrants formerly sought for their bodyguard, and in these days also always seek, Thracians, Scythians, Germans, Circassians, and Helvetians at large salaries; not that they distrust the strength of their own men, as many stupidly think, but that they understand that in the vast bodies of the Thracians there lies concealed the minimum of cunning and malice and that they are more pleased with the office of soldier than with that of ruler. In what respect, then, are they called cruel and uncivilized? The reason is obvious, for the farther one is from human culture, that is, from the nature of men, the nearer he approaches to the likeness of beasts, which, since they are lacking in reason, are unable to restrain their wrath and appetites. So it happens that the northerners are carried by impulse into acts of cruelty. Hence Thucydides called the Thracians, when they feared nothing, "The most ruthless race." Tacitus also said about the Germans, "They are accustomed to kill without strict discipline, but on a wrathful impulse, like an enemy." In this way the Hungarians, when they had killed Gritti,[36] dyed their military cloaks and spears in his blood, according to national custom. The Britons,

---

[35] Texts of the *Germania* read sometimes *ioci* and sometimes *loci*. The 1566, 1572, 1583, and 1595 editions of the *Methodus* give *ioci*. The subject of this passage, in paragraph 22, is the drinking bout. The discussion is carried on when the men are too intoxicated to conceal their thoughts; the decision is made after they have become sober.

[36] Luigi Gritti was a natural son of the Venetian doge Andrea Gritti. He was born in Constantinople, 1480, and followed Suleyman to the siege of Vienna. He assisted John Zapolya against Ferdinand I and became the inspirer of Turkish policy in Hungary. The Hungarians murdered him in 1534.

in a civil war, killed twelve out of forty kings, as well as innumerable princes, indeed a hundred in thirty years, after they had a little respite from external wars. If the chronicles of the Poles and Jovius are true, the Transylvanians drove their soldiers into a frenzy of cruelty by a three-day fast. This was done so that the men might use great severity in their treatment of George, the leader of the rioters (he had transfixed on stakes some Hungarian magnates). As a result the soldiers tore apart with their teeth the limbs of the still-breathing leader and swallowed them; then, cutting the disemboweled man into bits, they served them cooked on spits to the captives. I pass over the savagery of Dracula, the prince of Transylvania, universally conceded to be excessive. I omit also the formerly unheard-of cruelties of the Goths and the Huns, practiced not only against men but also against animals, towns, fortresses, grave-stones, and sepulchers of the Romans, which they overturned from their foundations. They could not restrain their wrath any more than their other appetites. Tacitus said about the Germans: "When sober they play dice in the midst of serious things; so great is their recklessness of gain or of loss that when all else fails, they will stake personal liberty on the last throw." Hence comes that lust of possession among the Germans and the French, reproached by Procopius, which is so great that they abandon life for gold and war for money.

The southerners are not so avaricious as they are parsimonious and stingy; the Scythians, on the other hand, are extravagant and rapacious. Since they know that they are at a disadvantage, they are unusually suspicious. This trait our men formerly knew well enough. Holster related to me the additional fact that spies and listeners in Gothland hide in public inns, for suspicion arises from want of knowledge. They do not have intercourse with southerners unless they are sober, and when they feel themselves deceived, they draw back, or often anticipate by deceiving the strangers, or as a last resort use force. Whereby it happens that by universal consent they are supposed to be as perfidious as the southern-ers. (Of this fact the old historians were entirely ignorant, because they had no intercourse with the Scythians.) Later, when they left their homes, they revealed their character. Since the Franks came from Ger-many into France (for the Germans boast that the French are of Teu-tonic origin), it is in keeping that Procopius, in speaking of the Franks, commented: "This race is the most likely of all to betray their faith." And Vopiscus said: "It is customary for the Franks to break their faith laughingly." Hence, Alciati wrote that a scorpion's tail was tossed at

the Germans. This proverb we retain in France in the vulgar tongue—
with due apologies, may it be said, lest our discourse should seem to
harm the name of any race. I am not discussing this particular characteristic, but the inborn nature of each race. In this trait, however, the
Germans are exceeded to a considerable degree by the Danes and the
Norwegians, from whom they differ widely. Certainly greater perfidy
or cruelty of people toward princes or of princes among themselves was
never engendered than between Christian and Gustavus, between Danes
and Swedes. From these races originate also the Normans, who, the
common people believe, are unreliable.

But if from want of reasoning and wisdom the northerners cannot
control their appetites and furthermore are regarded as intemperate,
suspicious, perfidious, and cruel why are the southerners much more
cruel and perfidious even than these? Here again I seek the decision in
history. It is evident that by nature the southerners have the greatest
gifts of ability; thus Columella, in Book i, chapter iii, declared: "It is
well known that the Carthaginians, a very acute race, said 'the field must
be weaker than the plowman.'" [37] Concerning the Egyptians who
fought against Caesar, Hirtius said: "These very clever men shrewdly
constructed the things they saw made by us, so that our men seemed to
imitate their work." A little later the same author added, "The race of
Egyptians is much given to treachery." Moreover, who does not know
how artfully and how long the Carthaginians eluded the power of the
Romans? Nevertheless, they always practiced incredible cruelty against
the enemy, as may be seen in the Punic War and also in that combat
which the Spendii and the Carthaginians, both Phoenicians, waged
against each other. As Polybius said, "It far exceeded all wars of which
we have heard in cruelty and all kinds of crimes." Yet the things related by Polybius about the cruelty of the Carthaginians would seem
ludicrous if anyone compared them with the history of Leo the African,
or even with the unheard-of cruelty of Muley-Hasan and his sons, which
not so long ago they practiced against the citizens and then against each
other. For Muley-Hasan, driven from the kingdom whence he had
driven his father, came as a suppliant to Emperor Charles, suffering
from the loss of his eyes, which had been burnt out through the brutal
violence of his brother.

Thus from the Carthaginians, we can trace the gouging of eyes, tearing of limbs, skinning, cutting, slow burning, and impaling. But the

[37] Columella was born in Cadiz in the first century A.D. He wrote *De re rustica*.

breaking of the whole body on a wheel originated with the Germans, as may be seen in Munster's description of Cologne. From these punishments Italians, French, Spanish, Greeks, and Asiatics have always turned in horror or unwillingly have learned them from others. Before the Portian Law (which even then forbade rods on the body of citizens) for capital punishment the Romans executed criminals with an axe or by breaking their necks; later the method was starvation; at length exile was permitted. Among the Greeks the use of hemlock was customary. This the Chiians even tempered with water, as Theophrastus said, so that they might invite death without distress. They judged that in death itself more than enough bitterness lay, unless, indeed, a man were guilty of some new and horrible crime. Lest anyone should believe that such cruelty spreads from vicious training, as Polybius maintains, let him consider the nature of the South Americans, who plunge boys into the blood of slain enemies, then suck the blood, and feast on the broken limbs.

The cruelty of the southerners and of the Scythians is therefore very different, because the latter are driven to wrath by impulse alone and to revenge by a certain magnanimous valor of the soul; after they have been irritated, they can easily be mollified. The southerners are not easily angered, but when once angry they can with difficulty be softened: they attack the enemy with a foxlike cunning, not with open violence, and they inflict horribly painful torture upon the conquered. This savagery comes partly from that despotism which a vicious system of training and undisciplined appetites have created in a man, but much more from a lack of proportion in the mixing of humors. This, in its turn, comes from elements affected unequally by external forces. The elements are disturbed by the power of the celestial bodies, while the human body is encompassed in the elements, the blood in the body, the spirit in the blood, the soul in the spirit, the mind in the soul. Although this last is free from all materiality, yet it is very much influenced by the closeness of the association. So it happens that those who are in the furthest regions are more inclined to vices. As black bile is removed from the blood [with difficulty], in the same way as dregs from wine, so disturbances of the intellect which proceed from black bile are difficult to eradicate.

Now the southerners abound in black bile, which subsides like lees to the bottom when the humors have been drawn out by the heat of the sun and increases more and more through emotions, so that those who are mentally constituted in this manner are plainly implacable. Such, they say, were Ajax and Marcius Coriolanus. The latter could not be mollified before he had destroyed by fire and sword the frontiers of his fatherland and allied cities. The other, when he could not take vengeance on the enemy, turned about in rage and slew flocks and herds.

It is easy to form an opinion about history when we have learned the cause of madness. On the one hand, it is evident that the southerners are seized by frenzy more easily than are the northerners, since men become mad more easily than animals. Leo the African wrote that there was a great multitude of raving men in Africa and that everywhere public buildings were set apart for the unbalanced. There are also many in southern Spain. In Lower Germany there are almost none who are mad from black bile, but rather from blood; this type of lunacy the common man calls the disease of St. Vitus, which impels them to exultation and senseless dancing. Musicians imitate this on the lyre; afterwards they make use of more serious rhythms and modes, doing this gradually until by the gravity of the mode and the rhythm the madmen are clearly soothed. On the other hand, those who inhabit the middle regions are driven into frenzy when yellow bile starts to burn them. This breaks out in wounding and killing. Those who live beneath the Bear, since they abound in rheum, must struggle with the madness of old men, that is, with drowsiness, a kind of mental weakness which brings stupor and forgetfulness. But insanity is encountered everywhere. I call it insanity when reason cannot conquer the appetite, which happens chiefly to the northerners. Fury can fall upon a wise man, as Cicero said, but insanity cannot. Our authors explain this matter rather stupidly when they say that rude and simple men are incurable. All these things are general statements. Of course there are everywhere raving, melancholy, frenzied, and drowsy men; everywhere wise, strong, and moderate men. Yet in one place there are many more; in another fewer. The statements made by physicians about eliminating melancholy and by Aristotle concerning melancholy people fit the southerners fairly well, and in the light of this information our judgment of history ought to be formulated.

These things we pass by, explaining more clearly only what has been omitted or not sufficiently emphasized. In that class is this fact: the southerners are especially given to all carnal pleasures and lust, whereas Hippocrates said that the Scythians were not fitted for love, on account of the excessive coldness and dampness of their bellies, as he himself wrote, and also on account of riding; therefore they were unfruitful.

Since they vainly made trial of love, they hated it and castrated themselves. "Castration" he called elsewhere the cutting of the vein of the head which lies under the ears; we have learned that certain people still practice this now-a-days. These allegations, however, are denied by almost all historians.

Let us apply that correct standard of value for history which we sought and eliminate the disagreement among philosophers and historians. Actually the fecundity of the Goths, Scythians, and Germans is such that not only do they embellish the vast solitudes and forests of the north with great cities but also they have sent colonies into all Europe. Germans live beyond the Danube, and Scandinavians dwell even in the extremest confines of Scythia. Thence Methodius [38] and Paul the Deacon reported that armies used to come forth like swarms of bees. Indeed Jordanes [39] and Olaus called the north a factory of men, because there Goths, Gepidae, Huns, Cimbri, Lombards, Alani, Burgundians, Normans, Picts, Herulians, Suabians, Slavs, Suiceri, and Rugi originated. Moreover, since the Scythians are warm and wet, whence fecundity is generated, there is no doubt that of all peoples they are the most fecund. I do not know why Hippocrates thought the Scythians were cold ventrally. Nature itself demonstrates that that is false. The same cause which produces greater heat in the viscera in winter than in summer (the warm breath from the smoking mouth shows this) affects also people who inhabit the north. In winter, therefore, men are more capable of begetting, not more lustful, as Aristotle would have it. Men are more lustful in summer (on account of irritation of yellow bile, which at that time is more bountiful), yet less capable. This came about through the highest wisdom of God, because to those who have sufficient ability to beget, passion is not very necessary; but to those who have less humor and heat, the best parent, Nature, gave the greater stimuli of desire. Otherwise they would not wish to propagate their kind or to establish societies. The same Nature brought it about that in winter men, in summer women, are more inclined to lust, as the physicians say; not to seek lust for itself, than which nothing is more shameful, not for procreation alone, a common motive among other living things, but so that there is an abiding desire of enjoying union, to which we are born. Passion could maintain the union for a short interval, as it does in the other living

[38] Methodius, 825–885, was the apostle to the Slavs.

[39] Jordanes, living in the sixth century A.D., was the author of *De origine actuque Getarum liber*.

things, but no longer; and it could not preserve the mutual love. I cannot sanction the reasoning of Hippocrates as to why the Scythians are less capable of love—that they wear breeches and ride constantly, since by the testimony of Aristotle, and indeed for most definite reasons, which he adduced in *Questions*, people accustomed to riding are more lustful.

From these facts we can understand what to decide about Caesar, Volaterranus, and Tacitus, who so highly praised the continence of the Germans. Tacitus said, "Very late do the young men try love, and on that account their youth is not over-strained, nor do the maidens hasten." Yet this can in no way be attributed to self-control, since we have already shown that the northerners, by their own nature, are most intemperate in drinking, food, wrath, gaming, and stealing. It is the temperate man who is also continent, not the opposite. Moreover, there is no cause for restraint when there are no lusts and passions which tempt; as no one can be said to be brave when no danger or toil has been confronted. But the southerners, who have more wisdom and reasoning power, have through their special gift brought it to pass that they might sin more freely for the sake of pleasure. Because self-control was difficult, particularly when plunging into lust, they gave themselves over to horrible excesses. Promiscuous coition of men and animals took place, wherefore the regions of Africa produce for us so many monsters. Hence is derived that unbelievable jealousy of the southerners and of the Carthaginians referred to in Leo, from which the Germans are entirely free. About the latter Caesar wrote thus: "To have knowledge of woman before the twenty-fifth year they consider among the basest things; of this there is no concealment." [40] Althamer [41] also, Poggio,[42] and Munster in the description of Baden reported that Germans as well as foreigners bathe promiscuously with their wives without suspicion. The word "jealousy," said Munster, has no place among them. Irenicus,[43] a German, added: "That custom in our time is observed everywhere in bathing places." Caesar also wrote that the Britons have twelve wives in common and that brothers cohabit with sisters, parents with children. The Italians could never endure this way of living, much less the Spanish, who often go mad with love and jealousy. Indeed the Carthaginians and the Amer-

[40] Caesar *De bello Gallico* VI. 21.
[41] Andreas Althamer, d.1564, was the author of a commentary on the *Germania* of Tacitus.
[42] Poggio, 1380–1459, wrote a *Historia Florentina*.
[43] Irenicus (Franz Friedlieb), 1495–1559, was the author of *Exegesis Germaniae*.

icans think that death is preferable. On this account it is not remarkable if the kings of the Persians, Carthaginians, and Hebrews have always had a great multitude of wives. So said Diodorus, Book II, Herodotus, Book III, and Josephus, Book IV, chapter XVII. The Scythians, in contrast, have their wives either in common or as individuals; with them, however, they live in such a way that we hear of the most incredible examples of continence, even of the very kings from whom the customs of the people are acquired. Tacitus writes that of all the barbarians the Germans almost alone have individual wives; Volaterranus averred that Casimir of Poland and Wenceslaus, king of Bohemia, always lived chaste and celibate. The Emperor Henry II not only abstained from the wives of others but even remained apart forever from his own.

The sources of generation are, then, heat and dampness; of lust, both biles. In the case of yellow bile, lust is probably due to irritation, but in the black, lust is caused by froth and gaseous matter, very abundant in this kind of bile. I think Aristotle meant to say so in that passage in *Questions* where he debated why melancholy people are the most sensuous. It serves as evidence that those who use acid and gaseous foods become lustful, the more so if the bile becomes sour and salt from inflammation. Perhaps it is for this reason that the poets imagine Venus to have been born from the foam of the sea. Of the whole race of beasts, none except the hare practices male love. Moreover, on the authority of Varro and Aelian [44] it conceives and produces; but the female alone, of all living things, can conceive when already pregnant.[45] The hare has this trait, I believe, because it has a greater supply of black bile than any other animal. Therefore it is not remarkable that the southerners, who are full of this bile, are said to be more inclined to passion. Ptolemy reported that on account of southern sensuality Venus chiefly is worshiped in Africa and that the constellation of Scorpion, which pertains to the pudenda, dominates that continent.

It is due to black bile, again, that the southerners are afflicted with leprosy, which for that reason is called by the ancients the Punic [46] sickness; not because of ruddiness, since the southern leprosy, in the judgment of Moses and Pliny, is not red, but because it originates in the Carthaginian area. Thence also the illness of the Arabians, which is

[44] Claudius Aelian lived in the third century A.D. and wrote *Varia historia* and *De animalium natura*.

[45] Herodotus III. 108.

[46] *Puniceus* means "Carthaginian" as well as "reddish."

called *alphus* by some, by others *leuce* and *vitiligo*. Indeed, before the time of Pompey the Great, on the testimony of Pliny, Italy had seen no lepers. This disease, he reported, was peculiar to Egypt. It serves as evidence that Moses, the most ancient writer of all, made a great number of laws about lepers, while the Greeks and the Romans made none. In this respect, of course, Leo the African and Alvarez agreed, for the one alleged numerous houses in both Mauritanias for lepers, the other wrote that in Abyssinia they mingled with the people, so that it seemed to be a common ailment. Our men, however, have left witness that America abounds with lepers or, as they say, with men afflicted with the Neapolitan disease.[47] This sickness Scaliger called "the Indian"; the Indians call it "Pua." It was carried into all Europe and Africa from those islands, and little by little it penetrated at last into Syria and Scythia. That it is actually generated by black bile is plain from the fact that those who have more of the melancholy humor are with difficulty cured of this illness. The black bile likewise makes the southerners sad, with downcast face, slow step, and thoughtful; the northerners, on the other hand, are happy and quick on account of their supply of blood.

From these things it is clear why all historians report that southerners are inclined to the greatest vices of body and mind. The reason is obvious—they are badly [48] disposed by black bile. Yet if that melancholy called "wasting" (although there are many kinds) has been well tempered, they achieve remarkable strength of mind and body. First, they are free from numerous kinds of illnesses derived from overeating, fluxes, and bad blood. In Africa fevers are very rare and light, on account of the lack of internal dampness and heat. But the quartan fever peculiar to a melancholy state, once cured, never recurs, said Hippocrates. In the north the farther one recedes from the middle region, the more frequently languishing fevers occur, tumors and edemata, epilepsy, convulsions, and blindness; one reason is the amount of thick humor and excretions, which are scanty in the southerners.

In the temperate region pests lie in wait, due to frequent changes of air. Although in the extremes it is perpetually winter or summer, in the middle portion there are rapid alterations of spring and of autumn.

[47] The age of the Renaissance used leprosy as a general term for skin affections. See the *Shorter Oxford English Dictionary* under "leprosy." The *New English Dictionary* under "leprosy" gives a quotation from the *Colloquies* of Erasmus, "The new Leprosie . . . which some . . . do call the Neapolitan scab."

[48] The editions of 1566, 1572, and 1583, give *male*; that of 1595, *mala*.

Hence come articular ailments, tertian fever, skin diseases, and gangrene, which our men stupidly, or rather impiously, derive from St. Anthony. He is worshiped by many in Italy and in Gallia Narbonensis with more burning vows, certainly with greater fear, than is God Himself. They are mistaken who think that the men of the temperate region, because they are further away from the extremes, have better health or longer life. The nature of the southerners is suited to the heat; that of the Scythians to the cold. Those who are in the mean area, although they seem more moderate than the rest, nevertheless are assailed by heat and cold, and they have frequent changes of air, creating diseases and premature old age. Hence the divergent opinions of historians about the duration of life. Aristotle thought that it was longer in the south; Pliny, toward the north; Galen, in the middle region, which he himself placed in Asia Minor, where he thought that men had the best tempering. Indeed the Gauls, the Scythians, the Egyptians, and the Arabs did not attain a disposition of this sort even through dreams. The same Hippocrates reported that all the larger, better, and more beautiful forms of life were found in Asia,[49] which seems to me partly true and partly false. For those to the north are greater, as we have shown before, and indeed of nobler shape. Josephus, Caesar, and Tacitus testify to the remarkable size of the Germans, and the ancients considered the beauty of the Gauls proverbial (from their white color the Asiatics themselves called them *lacteos*, milky, or *Galactas*.) Tertullian regarded the Gallic features in the same light; in this respect, however, they seem inferior to the Britons. But Galen did not know Gaul, and he could not be induced to see it when M. Aurelius urged him to go.

Moreover, since longevity is sustained by warmth and dampness, it would be fitting that life should be longer in the north. For this reason, perhaps, Pliny thought that the Hyperboreans protract their life to a very old age. Indeed, in Britain men have been known to live more than one hundred years, nor do I doubt that the life of the Scythians would be far longer if they did not surfeit themselves with drink and food. The writings of the ancients and of more recent authors bear witness that the southerners also live a long time, even though they do not have abundant warmth and dampness and the amount of excretion is also scanty. By consent of all, these traits are thought to hasten old age and death. The less plants increase in size, however, the longer do they

---

[49] Hippocrates *Airs, Waters, and Places*, paragraph 12.

thrive, as Theophrastus tells us. Others think that life is prolonged under more moderate skies. Italy nourishes many who in these days have surpassed their hundredth year. From the census Pliny reported that some of the Romans lived 140 years.

But the man who compares the modern historians with the ancients and the ancients with each other and adds physical considerations also, will make the most certain judgment about history: for instance, the southerners enjoy a longer life, more especially the Numidians. This is credible, since old crows, who have almost no heat and even less moisture, are said to round out four human life-spans. Furthermore, elephants, who by the testimony of Aristotle and of Juba outlive all living things, are found only in the south. Likewise the palm tree, said to flourish for a thousand years, cannot grow except in the southern area. Moreover, gold and adamant, which are indestructible, are best in the south; there is almost none in the north. It is not true, then, as Galen thought, that life is made longer by the best tempering. If this were so, rocks would be more temperate than plants, plants than living things, the elephant and the deer than man, which would be absurd, since he thought also that outstanding talent is determined by a proper tempering.

Now, since the mind does excel the body and greater force of genius exists in the south than in the north, there is no doubt that the more able part of the world extends to the south and that greater virtues are in the southerners than among the Scythians. The greater vices likewise are found wherever the former migrate. Hence we shall easily understand a judgment from the history of Livy. After he had commemorated the virtues of Hannibal, he said, "The many great virtues of the man were equaled by monstrous vices: inhuman cruelty, perfidy more than Punic, no truthfulness, no respect for holiness, no fear of the gods, no regard for oaths, no reverence." [50] What Machiavelli wrote is false —that men at the last cannot be extremely wicked, quoting the example of Paul Baglioni, the tyrant of Perugia, who although he could easily have killed Pope Julius along with his escort, preferred to lose control rather than perpetrate such a crime. Hannibal would not have acted in this way. The same Machiavelli called the Italians, the Spanish, and the French the wickedest of all races. In one passage he extolled the justice and sagacity of the Germans in a most remarkable way. Elsewhere he

[50] Livy *De urbe condita* XXI. iv. 9.

attacked their perfidy, avarice, and haughtiness. These contradictions have developed from ignorance of the customs and nature of each people. Stupid and uncouth men cannot be really infamous, but, as Plato said, in great talents great virtues or vices are usually present; as the fecund earth produces a large supply of noxious weeds unless it is cultivated and when worked in a proper manner becomes really fruitful. But sterile earth, on the other hand, produces neither healthful nor noxious weeds, nor anything at all except with the greatest effort. So also I judge to be the case with the talents of the southerners and of the Scythians. For this reason it is not remarkable that almost all historians and poets—from Aeschylus to the present—praise the great integrity of the Scythians and attack the cunning of the southerners. "The good customs among the Germans," said Tacitus, "have more force than good laws elsewhere." In those days, however, the Germans lacked any kind of training, so they did not differ much from beasts, as they themselves confess. Since they lived in the utmost ignorance, I do not see why their integrity is worthy of so much encomium, for they could not really be either very good or very evil. On the other hand, the man who when he has the chance to be unjust advisedly cultivates virtues whose value he has appreciated is worthy of the highest praise, either because there is only one approach to virtue, like a straight line, around which, here and there, are many oblique lines, or because men, even if they have been shown the extremes of good and of evil, are inclined more to wickedness, from which they cannot be deterred by cruel punishments alone or by the threat of eternal death. Not even the reward of immortality impels them to justice, so that many think that men would live in the highest integrity and be much happier if they had never tasted the fruits of evil (without which, however, the nature of good cannot be understood), but, like other animate beings, had lived in accordance with their own nature. We have seen, indeed, that the Scythians and the mountaineers, trained by no discipline, approach more nearly to this type.

Out of this difficulty remains the question, what judgment must be formed of the historians who attack the superstition, impiety, magic, infamous lusts, and cruelties of the Greeks, Egyptians, Arabs, and Chaldeans, yet omit the qualities which are praiseworthy? From these people letters, useful arts, virtues, training, philosophy, religion, and lastly *humanitas* itself flowed upon earth as from a fountain. The Scythians, however, do not lack industry, nor do those who hold the middle region, but the southerners attained the most outstanding gifts from immortal God, which cannot be understood better or be judged more certainly for historical purposes than if we use the analogy of the human body, or the well-constituted state, or the world and the celestial constellations.

For the sake of theory let us imagine, therefore, that certain planets preside over these three peoples set up in that order in which we have given them; let us attribute Saturn to the southerners, Jupiter to the next group, and Mars to the northerners. Returning the round again, Venus to the southerners (the sun like a fountain of light, will be common to all), Mercury to the next, and the moon to the northerners. From this distribution, as it were, of three peoples, we shall understand more plainly the precise power of all nature. For the Chaldeans say that the power of Saturn controls the understanding, that of Jupiter guides action, that of Mars directs production. This, moreover, is understood by the best Hebrew expounders of nature. They called Saturn quiet, than which nothing can be of greater importance for contemplation. Jupiter they called just. The Greeks took this idea, as they did all good things, from the Hebrews. They imagined that justice was sitting on the side of Jupiter. But Mars they called strong and brave. On this account the Chaldeans and the Greeks thought he ruled over war. Saturn, of course, is said to be cold, Mars warm, Jupiter more moderate than either. The first presides over knowledge and those things which find their realization in solitary contemplation of the truth; the second,[51] wisdom, which is embodied in action, embracing all virtues; the third, arts and fabrication, which depend upon skill and strength. The first pertains to the mind, the second to reason, the last to imagination. For the southern people, through continued zeal for contemplation, befitting black bile, have been promoters and leaders of the highest learning. They have revealed the secrets of nature; they have discovered the mathematical disciplines; finally, they first observed the nature and the power of religion and the celestial bodies. Because the Scythians are less suited to contemplation, on account of the supply of blood and humor (by which the mind is so weighed down that it hardly ever emerges), they voluntarily began to take an interest in those things which fall under the senses, that is, in the exercise of the arts and fabrication.

[51] Bodin obviously is giving the attributes of Jupiter although he put him in third place in the preceding sentence.

Hence from the northerners come those objects called "mechanical"—
engines of war, the art of founding, printing, and whatever belongs to
the working of metals, which George Agricola,[52] a German, has discussed so exhaustively that Aristotle and Pliny in this respect appear to
have understood nothing. It should not seem remarkable that Italians
and Spanish are accustomed to seek aid from Germans and Britons because by some celestial gift they know how to find the hidden veins of
earth, and, when found, to open them. Likewise the same sons of Mars
in former times always cultivated military discipline, and still do with
incredible enthusiasm. They practice arms, level mountains, draw off
waters, and usually devote themselves to hunting, farming, cattle rais-
ing, or to the arts of construction, so that their talent seems to be placed
in their hands. This fact is made clear enough by every kind of household utensil and implement, which is made so skillfully and ingeniously
by these men that other peoples marvel at the products, but cannot re-
produce them. This is, perhaps, what Plato meant when he said that
Mars and Vulcan had discovered the arts. If, then, we are to have faith
in the astrologers, those who have Mars in the ascendant at their birth
will be either soldiers or skilled workers.

On the other hand, men of the middle region are not designed for
the secret sciences as are the southerners or dedicated to manual crafts
like the northerners, but are the best fitted for managing affairs. If anyone reads all the writings of the historians he will judge that from men
of this type institutions, laws, and customs first came, and the best
method of directing the state; then, also, commerce, government, rhetoric, dialectic, and finally the training of a general. Moreover, the masters of these disciplines are said to be Jupiter and Mercury; whoever
has Jupiter or Mercury or both in the ascendant at his inception is said
to be suited by his very nature to such pursuits. Indeed, it is evident
from the reading of histories that great empires have always flourished
in Asia, Greece, Assyria, Italy, Gaul, and Upper Germany, which lie
between the pole and the equator from the fortieth to the fiftieth degree; and from those regions the greatest rulers, the best legislators, the
most equitable judges, the sagest jurisconsults, the most versatile orators, the cleverest merchants, finally, the most famous players and dra-
matic actors have had their origin. No jurisconsults come from Africa,

[52] Agricola (George Bauer), 1490–1556, was physician, chemist, and mineralogist.
He wrote *De re metallica, sive Bermannus,* and *Dominatores Saxonici a prima origine ad
hanc aetatem.*

much less from Scythia; no orators, few poets, fewer historians, very few who ply an abundant and profitable commerce, such as Italians, Greeks, Spanish, and Asiatics. Let us then compare these facts with history, that we may judge more correctly concerning the entire matter.

Galen complained that no philosopher ever came from Scythia except Anacharsis, although many were from Greece. Where he discussed the Gauls, whose nature he had, of course, discovered and known through continued contacts, the Emperor Julian wrote, "The Celts bestowed no pains on philosophy or on mathematical discipline; but they are interested in dialectics and rhetoric." Hence Juvenal's "Eloquent France taught the British lawyers." [53] Indeed, the very religion which they used makes this plain. "The Gauls worship especially the god Mercury," said Caesar. "There are many images of him; they consider him inventor of the arts; they think that he has great power in seeking riches and pursuing trade." A lasting experience has approved these historical passages. For nowhere in the world are there more advocates, nowhere is civil law cultivated with greater zeal. Occult knowledge and mathematical discipline are, however, really neglected.

On the contrary, the southerners, since the innate humor of black bile causes prolonged meditation, betake themselves voluntarily from the conduct of affairs and seek the desert solitudes. The power of contemplation and meditation (which is called by the Hebrews and Academicians a precious death) consists, in fact, in this: it sharpens the wits and divides man from man. When he has attained this, he not only sees the secrets of natural things but also, with a purified mind, is borne to the heavens on swift pinions, and is filled with the knowledge of things divine. Afterwards, through the assistance of immortal God, he reveals difficult and wonderful matters to unlearned men. For this reason it should not seem strange to those who have read history that the ablest philosophers, mathematicians, prophets, and finally all religions in the world have poured forth from those regions as from the most plenteous spring. Not that the divine mind is unwilling to breathe upon man elsewhere its heavenly spirit. That would be wicked to say, since God flourishes everywhere, like the splendor of the sun. Yet as that same splendor shows itself more in very limpid water than in turbid, so also the divinity shines more clearly in a purified mind than in one looking downward, influenced by contact with the body and disturbed by warring perturbations within itself. Those who have a greater abundance

[53] Juvenal *Satires* XV. 111.

of blood and humor with more difficulty separate themselves from these earthly dregs, so that not without justice did Heraclitus call wise men "dry souls." What Jerome Cardan said is absurd and not at all worthy of a philosopher—that a man is very wise because he is very wet and warm, for we see that those beasts which are the colder are the more sagacious, as Aristotle wrote in Book II *De partibus animalium*.[54] Let us take as illustration the very wise elephant, whose blood, Pliny recounted, was the coldest of all.[55]

Since these things are so, it is easy to judge the truth of what the historians report about the religion of the southerners. In particular, Leo the African said with reference to the foundations of the temples, "There are in the city of Fez seven hundred temples. The greatest has a circuit of one thousand paces and thirty-one doors; nine hundred torches are burning day and night." We may also believe what Alvarez reported in the history of the Abyssinians about the unheard-of size of the temples, about the infinite number of monks, who walk around, not only in isolated areas but also in the countryside, in crowds, in the market place, and in the camps; from them even the armies are conscripted, since the princes themselves follow this way of life. Moreover, the king, who is called Negus and Jochan Belul, that is, very precious jewel, acts like a priest, proceeds like a priest in vestment and ornament, with priests leading and bearing religious symbols before him. In addition, he told of fasts of the whole people that are plainly incredible if anyone compares them with ours. If, however, you should exercise historical judgment, you will pronounce them really credible. Many sustain life without bread on raw lentils or vegetables cooked in plain water and, of course, tasteless. Others wear an iron band like a belt on their bare flesh. In the time of fasts, that is, a third of the year, many pass the nights without rest. Some of them sleep in water up to the neck. There are some who stand for twenty-four hours and gaze into the heavens. On stated days all flagellate themselves repeatedly with rods and whips. Those who sin against the faith only a little or refuse to kiss a wooden cross (as some do) are burned in avenging flames. They think that fortunate as well as unfortunate experiences flow equally from the will of one all-powerful God, a belief very useful for the protection of the state and for a happy life.[56] Yet how stupid they are in managing

---

[54] Aristotle *De partibus animalium* II. 2. 648a 5.   [55] Pliny *Natural History* VIII. 12.

[56] "A belief . . . life" appears in the edition of 1566 and 1595, but not in those of 1572 and 1583.

affairs and governing the country is made plain by the fact that they do not cease lashing a man who has committed a fault before the victim has paid the fine stipulated by the person who is beating. Moreover, a chief justice, who like the chancellor directs the most important affairs, often is flogged to death by order of the king. A murderer is delivered for crucifixion to the relatives of the dead. All judgments, however, are handed down without any documents or writing. Debtors, unless they can make payment, are given into servitude to their creditors. No wages are paid to the soldier, no leaves given, but each one is required to carry barley or some similar thing. There are no towns, no camps, no fortresses. The people roam about the country hither and thither, the leader lives in tents, although he has valuable household goods and considerable wealth. They do not use paper, but entrust the public accounts to vellum. Such proceedings prove that men of this type are little suited to manage affairs.

Even less adapted are the Scythians, who accomplish everything by force of arms like slaves and in the way of wild beasts. As Tacitus wrote about the ancient Germans, "The official does nothing either public or private without arms." To this Boemus, a German, and Munster also agree today in these words: "Injuries suffered they rarely avenge by law, but by sword and pillage; nor are they ashamed to plunder." Moreover, what is more iniquitous or more barbarous than what customarily happens at Clagenfurt? If anyone is suspected of theft, he is killed. Then they hold a trial. This custom, they say, is taken from the Huns and the Goths. From them also the laws of dueling are taken. Of all kinds of injustice, none can be greater or more base than that a weak and helpless man, when he has been insulted, should be scornfully treated unless he tries the issue at arms and exposes his life to perils, no matter how strong the adversary may be. By this system even the Scythians would be justly scorned if they were matched with beasts which outdo them in strength. In general it has been so arranged by nature that Scythians, who have less reason, but more strength, should place the height of all virtues in military glory; southerners in piety and reverence; but those of the middle region in wisdom. Although all defend the state by every means, nevertheless some habitually use force, some awe of the divine; the rest more often rely upon law and legal decisions.

So it should not seem strange that the majesty of the caliphs, or priests of the Ismaelite faith, was so great that they had ultimate control not only of laws and of religions but also of empire and arms and all possessions, then of liberty and servitude, finally the right of life and death over everyone. But the Turks, the progeny of the Scythians, and the Mamelukes, by race Circassians, first broke away from their domination and drove them out from their ancient holdings.

Perhaps this is why we are told by the poets that Saturn was driven from power by Jupiter, which means that in early times wise and pious men were created kings for the sake of dispensing justice. Although men thought that through the performance of duty alone they could continue in office, nevertheless they could not succeed in this way, since of course very many were influenced neither by awe of the divine nor by any other scruple. So the more sagacious, taking over power, began to rule the state, while the religious and philosophic gave attention to sacrifices and contemplation, and the plebs took up military training, farming, and manual arts. From this it happens that wise men maintain the state with prayers and warnings; the prudent by rule and command; the strong by power and activity. By these three divisions—principles, ordinances, and actions—I say, the state is supported.

Priests and wise men give warning; officials issue orders; agents carry them out. Thus Anaxagoras influenced Pericles; Plato, Dion; Isocrates, Nicocles; Plutarch, Trajan; Polybius, Scipio. And constantly, with sensible precepts of wisdom or some religious teaching, the Magi advised the Persians; the Brahmins, the Indians; the seers, the Greeks; and the pontiffs, the Romans. Yet they were incapable of managing affairs, a fact which Plato, although a very wise man, exemplified when he took over the state committed to his care. In the same way Aristotle wrote that Anaxagoras, a very learned man, lacked prudence because he suffered himself to die of hunger and want through neglecting his finances, a thing which happened also to Theodore Gaza in extreme old age. So Philo commended Moses with high praise, because alone among all mortals he was at the same time a very brave general, a prudent legislator, and a most holy prophet.

It remains, then, to apply to the republic of the world the same analysis that has been made about one state, so that when the functions of the various peoples have been meted out wisdom may in a way belong to the southerners, strength to the Scythians, and prudence to the intervening races. This idea may be seen even in the parts of the soul. For the mind itself warns, reason commands, and then the senses, like agents, are employed for carrying out orders, and in the threefold power of the soul—animal, vital, and natural—the first, of course, brings motion and sensation from the brain, the second the vital spirit from the heart, the third quickening power from the liver. I think that there is no better way of understanding the inborn nature of each people or of obtaining a truer and more definite opinion about the history of each than if this microcosm be compared with the great man, that is, with the world. Therefore, what Plato did in his *Republic* we shall do for the republic of the world, but a trifle differently. He wished control to be in the possession of guardians, whom he placed in the mind, like Pallas in the citadel. In this he seemed to wish to restore the reign of Saturn; hence that sentence of his praised by all—yet understood by few—"Either kings should be philosophers, or philosophers should reign." Philosophy, however, the perpetual contemplation of the most beautiful things, as all Academicians would have it, has nothing in common with military or civil affairs. Furthermore, he armed soldiers and stationed them in the heart, because there is placed the seat of anger. Finally he assigned farmers and manual workers to the liver, so that they might supply food and necessaries for the state. Nevertheless, these arrangements could not be carried through without great disturbance, as we shall explain in its place.

Now let us consider this only as far as it concerns the republic of the world, and the nature of peoples; if it can be done, let us set up this world like a man, in its proper position. On this matter also writers differ greatly among themselves. Homer, Aristotle, Plato, Galen, Pythagoras, and Averroës placed the right side of this world—which they call "animal"—to the east; the left to the west. Pliny and Varro, on the contrary, placed the left to the east and the right to the west, following the ancient custom of the Latins. "The left hand," said Varro, "is in temples on the east; the right on the west." [57] He called temples the regions of the sky divided by the augurs' wand. Thus the Mohammedans pray. Augurs, however, used to turn toward the east, as Livy wrote in his first book—"The augur toward the south the right-hand parts, the left to the north." With him the eighty-ninth Psalm of David, verse thirteen, seems of course to be in agreement, "The north wind and thy right hand, thou has created them," whereas all the interpreters read "the southern quarter" for "the right hand." Thus said the Chaldean interpreter. To this may be added the fact that they call the Orient "face"; the inference then being that the south is attributed to the

[57] Varro *On the Latin Language* VII. 7.

right side when the face is turned toward the east, a custom which we use in taking oaths. But since they advanced no support for their statement, we shall follow Philo, with whom Empedocles,[58] Lucan, Cleomedes,[59] and Solinus also agreed. Moses turned the left side of the sanctuary to the south; the right to the north. This was for the best of reasons—because motion is rapid from the east toward the west, but the tread of man is forward, not backward or sideways.[60] Hence Lucan said, "Wondering that the shadows of the grove do not fall to the left." [61] To the Greeks, of course, the right was of better omen than the left, while among the Latins in auguries the left was thought really lucky, as Plutarch and Pliny reported, not because the sun rises at the left, as Pliny would have it, but because the left part lies toward the south. This section of the world excels the rest in the value of its plants, metals, gems, men, minds, and celestial bodies, and the Hebrews thought that the wanderings of Abraham were directed toward the south on that account. On the other hand, evil, said Ezekiel, comes from the north. Moreover, Arabs and Moors, as we find in Pico della Mirandola, say evil demons are rare or non-existent in the south, either on account of the abundance of light, from which they are thought to flee, or on account of the rarity of the air which cannot sustain them. Nowhere is there a greater number of demons and witches than toward the north, if we have faith in Saxo Grammaticus and Olaus.

Now we have assumed that the northerners were more robust, the southerners weaker. But the left hand of man is the weaker, the right hand the stronger, as Macrobius [62] wrote in Book VII, chapter 4, of the *Saturnalia*. Pliny stated that in the uterus males move to the right, females to the left,[63] in agreement with Varro, Aristotle, and Hippocrates. Artemidorus,[64] in his interpretation of dreams, explained that the right eye signified a son, the left a daughter, and he interpreted the teeth on

---

[58] Empedocles flourished 444 B.C. We have *Fragments* on cosmology.

[59] Cleomedes flourished in the first century B.C. and wrote the *Circular Theory of the Heavenly Bodies*.

[60] Cf. Jean Bodin *Theatre de la nature* V. x. 902.

[61] Lucan *Pharsalia* III. 248.

[62] Macrobius lived at the beginning of the fifth century A.D. Probably he was a Greek. His most famous work is a commentary on Cicero's *The Dream of Scipio*. He wrote also *Saturnaliorum Conviviorum libri vii*. The reference to Macrobius does not appear in the *Methodus* of 1566.

[63] Pliny *op. cit.* VII. 4.

[64] Artemidorus Daldianus, a physician of Ephesus in the time of the Antonines. He wrote *Oneirocritica*.

the right as male friends, on the left as female friends. In general in Book xxvII he said that the right-hand parts must apply to men or to young people, the left-hand to women or older people. Aristotle, Book iv, chapters 3 and 9,[65] Book iv, chapter 1,[66] and Book i, chapter 15, of *The History of Animals*, called the part on the right masculine, on the left feminine.[67] In addition, the right foot and the right arm are greater (which shoemakers even now understand) and more energetic than the left.

Then we have made plain that the Scythians are reddish in coloring and abound in blood, while the southerners are bloodless and full of black bile. Now on the right side is the liver; on the left, the spleen. The latter is the receptacle of black bile, the former of blood. We have shown also that the Scythians are intemperate and wrathful and that they are driven to vengeance by impulse; but the southerners, only after premeditation. The former trait is, of course, suited to the right side; the latter, to the left. Then black bile makes men quiet, the gall bladder wrathful, the liver immoderate. The result is, therefore, that in this republic of the world we should place the Scythians, like soldiers and manual workers, on the right side, the southerners on the left, and men of the middle region in the heart, like officials in the middle of the city. For the heart is between the brain and the liver, as well as between the liver and the spleen. Moreover, Aristotle said, "Nature makes certain people slaves and their bodies strong for necessary uses; others weak, but really useful for human association."

I am not moved by the fact that the Hebrews, as well as other peoples, thought that the right hand excelled the left—as may be seen in Psalms 109, Matthew 22, Mark 12, Matthew 25 and 26, and Acts 7, Colossians 3, Hebrews 1 and 10, Ephesians 1, Hostiensis,[68] John Andrea,[69] Panormitanus,[70] in the chapter "About Sovereignty and Obedi-

---

[65] These references do not fit modern editions.

[66] Aristotle *Generation of Animals* III. i. 763b 30.

[67] The passage "in agreement with Varro . . . feminine" does not appear in the edition of 1566.

[68] Henry of Susa, bishop of Ostia, called Hostiensis, lived from 1210 to 1271. He taught canon law and wrote *Summa aurea* and *Summa super titulis Decretalium*.

[69] Giovanni d'Andrea, 1275–1347, wrote *Additiones ad speculum judiciale G. Duranti* and *Novellae . . . super v libros Decretalium*.

[70] Nicolas Tedeschi Panormitanus, called "Lucerna juris," one of the famous canonists, 1389?–1445. He wrote *In quinque Decretalium libros commentaria, Glossae in Clementinas*, and *De concilio Basilensi tractatus*. The reference is to *Corpus juris canonici decretals* 1. 33. 6.

ence," starting at "usual," Aristotle, Book xxxi, chapters 11, 13, 19, and 25 and Book xxxii, chapter 7, and that Jacob placed his right hand on the head of Ephraim to give a blessing. Baldus [71] gave the same opinion on the law "Concerning holy churches," starting at "we decree," [72] and Curtius senior, in *Consilia* lxxiv, "the more honorable place is at the right hand." Plautus said in *Pseudolus*— "All orders I will bring beneath the signs: my legions with a favorable (*sinistra*) omen, with most certain auspices, and to my liking." [73] Cicero, *Laws* iii, "Such a one, under good omens, was called master of the people." [74] Cicero gave an explanation: "However, I am not unaware that we call *sinistra* the things that are good, even if they are on the right hand; but of course we regard signs on the left as best, the foreigners those on the right." [75] More famous, even, is the statement of M. Varro, Book v, *Letters and Questions:* "From the seat of the gods, when you look toward the south, to the left are the eastern parts of the earth; to the right, the western. I think it was done," said he, "in order that we might associate the better auspices with the left rather than with the right." Nevertheless, many Latins thought that the left is of ill omen. Virgil wrote, "The south wind, unkind (*sinistra*) alike to trees and crops and herds"; [76] and Cicero, "No one reproaches me with unfavorable (*sinistris*) speeches; I myself blame no one but myself."

"Oft from the hollow ilex tree croaked the unlucky raven." [77] The reason they understand right and left in different ways is that the Hebrews, following the custom of all peoples everywhere, placed the right hand to the south, the left, to the north, since all peoples worship the sun with the face turned toward the east. This Moses forbade. However it may be, accepting one opinion or the other, it is evident that the south excels the north, and the right hand of man is toward the north. [78]

---

[71] Baldus de Ubaldi, born 1325, was professor of law of Padua. He lectured on the three books of the *Decretals* and wrote commentaries on the *Old Digest* and the *New Digest,* and on the *Codex.*

[72] *Decernimus de sacrosanctis ecclesiis c.* is from the *Corpus juris civilis codex,* I. 2. 16. See note 71.

[73] Plautus *Pseudolus* II. iv. 72.

[74] Cicero *Laws* III. iii. 9. The quotation should read *esto,* the imperative.

[75] Cicero *De divinatione* II. xxxix. 82. This passage is paraphrased, Cicero's first clause coming last in Bodin.

[76] Virgil *Georgics* I. 444.

[77] Virgil *Eclogues* IX. 15. The line should read "Ante sinistra cava monuisset ab ilice cornix."

[78] This entire paragraph is missing from the edition of 1566.

Then I disagree with Plato in this respect, in that he placed soldiers in the heart, magistrates in the brain, common people in the liver. I should prefer priests and learned men in the brain, officials in the heart, manual workers and soldiers, who are drawn from the people, in the liver. Nor does the vital power of the heart produce strength, which is proper to blood and liver; rather, it impels to activity. Certainly Machiavelli did not mean that the best soldier should be chosen from Italy, but the best general, because he wins by means of greater sagacity, not by greater strength. "Service of the body is demanded from the soldier," said Ammianus, "of the mind, from the general." Indeed, it is not the function of a general, as Plutarch stated in the life of Pelopidas, to fight hand to hand with the enemy. It is not for a magistrate to work as lictor, but to rule and to control. Moreover, when Plato gave the command to philosophers and wise men, who, we have shown from history, were fitted for contemplation, although incapable of action,[79] it was consistent to place the soldiers in the heart. They, however, were best selected from the farmers, as Pliny wrote about the old Roman training, or from manual workers, as in our times, because they had become inured to work. As a matter of fact, Aristotle included operators and manual workers among the plebs. We observe that formerly, and even today, the Scythians, or Germans, have always been sought for military service at high salaries. To reiterate, the best soldiers always are chosen from the farmers and plebs, whose abilities are in manual work. If these things should be considered in relation to the celestial bodies, they will be equally consistent with them.

If we allot Saturn to the spleen, Jupiter to the heart, Mars to the gall bladder, the liver to the moon, the characteristics attributed by the astrologers to each part of the body correspond. For Mars with the moon is like combining the gall bladder with the liver, nourishing and animating the whole body, as the elemental earth is nourished by the moon. As its light waxes, it strengthens the plants, waters, and animals considerably. In truth, those who have the moon in their horoscope are said to be exceedingly strong and healthy—all of which is most appropriate to the Scythians. In addition, there is a passage which Caesar wrote about the Germans: "All life," said he, "consists in hunting and in the activities of military matters." What, then, could be more appropriate to Diana or to Mars? Pliny's comment is also worthy of attention— "Thunder and lightning is created in the middle region; none in Ethi-

[79] The word is *actiones* in editions of 1566, 1572, and 1583; *lectiones* in that of 1595.

opia and Scythia." [80] This we have found out from the inhabitants. Now thunder and lightning are the properties of Jupiter, in the opinion not only of the poets, but also of the naturalists. But I should not object if anyone should allot to the heart the sun, which we have made common to all, because it is placed in the center of the planets, or as Copernicus placed it, in the center of the world, because it signifies the most lasting life of all and has moderate heat, not burning like Mars. It may be that it is common to all and at the same time peculiar to some particular portion. Yet all these traits apply, not to men of the extreme zones, but to those of the temperate regions.

Again, this division of peoples into three groups can be referred to the threefold universe: that is, the intellectual, consisting of the minds; the celestial, the stars; the elemental, where the origin and destruction of things occurs. Here, in turn, belongs a threefold order of souls (except that which is beyond classification, which is contaminated by no worldly stain). The first seems to turn purified intellects of men to God; the second, to direct states; the last is occupied with matter and form. Since these things are so, the race of man in its three varieties, Scythians, I say, southerners, and men of the middle regions, can be related to the triple activities of the soul, wisdom, prudence, and creative ability, which abide in contemplation, action, and production. I believe they [three races?] can be easily related to the intellectual, the courageous, and the lustful, from the action of brain, heart, and liver and of the celestial stars, and they can be applied to the most certain judgment of all history.

As they say that in six thousand years the period of the elemental world will be complete, from the prophecy of Elia, a certain Rabbi, so for two thousand years men excelled in religion and wisdom and studied zealously the motion of the celestial stars and the universal power of nature. Likewise, in the next two thousand years they were occupied in establishing states, in enacting laws, and in leading forth colonies. In that period dominion was transferred from Saturn to Jove, from the southerners to the men of the middle region. In the following thousand of years, that is, from the death of Christ, various arts and handicrafts, formerly unknown, have come to light. Then came also the great disturbance of wars throughout the world, when of course pagan faith in Jupiter died, and empires, so to speak, were overthrown and fell

[80] Pliny *op. cit.* II. 51.

to the Scythians, sons of Mars. Hence suddenly legions of Goths, Burgundians, Herulians, Franks, Lombards, Angles, Britons, Huns, Vandals, Gepidi, Normans, Turks, Tartars, and Muscovites filled Europe and Asia. Either there is some power of the celestial bodies over these lower beings, as even now the theologians confess, or there is none, as many think. Nevertheless, through sensation we perceive being itself, as they say, and that it exists, even if the causes are more obscure. Hence we may understand many works, not only of historians but also of philosophers and astrologers. Whether or not the histories are false is indeed very easily detected, as in this remark of Ptolemy, "The southern Asiatics are superlative in designs and counsels, strong, and warlike; the northerners, wise magicians, skilled in divine affairs and very just." These things plainly are false or badly confused. What Pliny wrote is also incorrect—that the size of bodies in south and north is the same, because the latter have greater nourishment of humor, the former have greater strength of fire. He erred not only in the light of history but even in his very reasoning. There are innumerable things of this sort in Aristotle, Hippocrates, Galen, Diodorus, Herodotus, Volaterranus, and Sabellicus. It would be endless to follow them in detail. To indicate the sources is enough, so that we may understand better and more accurately what should be our judgment about the universal history of all peoples.

Although some differ from others and often contradict themselves, yet all, except Jerome, agree on this point—the Gauls are fickle. This was written by Caesar, confirmed by Tacitus and Trebellius, and repeated often by the Italians and the Germans, especially by Sleidan in the speech of Emperor Charles. Others, however, call other races trifling; "Syrians," said Livy, "Asiatics, and Greeks are the most unreliable races of all." About the Scythians, with whom they had no commerce, they said nothing. Well, if they call levity of mind that alacrity and celerity which makes the men of the middle regions the most able of all for affairs, then, indeed, the French, Italians, Pannonians, Asiatics, Chaldeans, and Parthians, who are noted by writers for this vice, are fickle. To be sure, Julius Scaliger, a Veronese, wrote about the French in this manner—"We see the French versatile in training and adaptable to all trends of events. They have a fiery vigor of soul and an effective rapidity which is given to no other nation. In whatsoever they interest themselves, they exert themselves successfully and make swift progress. Zealously they ply their trade, follow letters, arms, learning, honesty, and eloquence, yet of all races and nations they are the most outstanding in loyalty, integrity, and constancy." This is his testimony.

The Scythians, however, are handicapped by thick humors as though by a weight, so that the force of the intellect does not shine through. The southerners are held fast by black bile in the most serene contemplation of the greatest things. Therefore it happens that the rapid pace of their soul is retarded. We see this not only in the Moors and the Carthaginians but also in the Spanish, when they live in more southerly latitudes. Such is the slowness in their speech, motion, walk, and all actions that they seem to languish from inertia. The French, on the other hand, do all things so rapidly that they have finished the matter before the Spanish can begin planning. Indeed, they are said to walk so quickly that the Spanish think that they are running, not walking. They show rapidity and ease no less in learning than in other actions, and the things which the southerners discover by prolonged investigation they make very quickly or imitate, so that not without justice did Caesar wonder at their aptness. These are marked indications of yellow bile. When Galen applied the forces of the humors from the body to the soul, he attributed prudence to yellow bile, constancy to black bile, gladness to the blood, and mildness to the phlegm. From these blended together there is produced an infinite variety. If these same humors begin to overflow, or burn, or deteriorate, they incline to the opposite vices. Thereby it happens that too abundant yellow bile drives men into recklessness and burning leads to frenzy. Hence their headlong and too great rapidity in action, which prevents planning, brings it about that the French are called fickle. But when fickleness becomes nothing else than a certain inconstancy in sayings and deeds, I suppose it ought to be called daring, not levity. Or if we are to be judged trifling, the Scythians easily outdo us in this respect.

Then contraries have opposite traits. So if the southerner is black, the northerner must be white; if the latter is large, the former must be small; the latter robust, the former weak; the latter warm and wet, the former cold and dry; the latter hairy, the former bald; here a raucous voice, there a clear one; here they fear warmth, there they fear the cold; the latter happy, the former sad; the latter gregarious, the former solitary; the latter reckless, the former timid; the latter given to drinking, the former moderate; the latter careless about himself and others, the former guarded and given to ceremony; the latter uncouthly insolent, the former lofty in mind; the latter too extravagant, the former parsimonious; the latter not at all lustful, the former extremely so; the latter filthy, the former spruce; the latter straightforward, the former deceitful; the latter a soldier, the former a priest; the latter a manual worker, the former a philosopher; the latter uses his hands, the former his mind; the latter seeks out the veins of the earth, the former investigates the heavens. If, then, the Carthaginians are very tenacious, as Plutarch wrote, what about the Scythians? We have shown that both are cruel and perfidious when they fall into vice, but we have adduced contrary causes. However, if the vices denote extremes and the southerner is obstinate, while the Scythian is fickle, it follows that the mean is constant. Certainly the barbarians and those who have less reasoning power are more like the beasts, which are as easily irritated as they are easily placated and are carried hither and thither causelessly within a short time. Likewise, boys and women make and cast off friends, but men having judgment do not. In the human race, the more talented each man, the less is he usually drawn to friendships or hatred or extreme opinions; but when he is enticed in this way, he is with difficulty distracted. When I look more closely, the southerners, the intermediates, and the Scythians seem in a certain measure to have the customs and the humors of old men, of men, and of youths, expressed neatly in an ancient line: Prayers of the old, deeds of youth, and plans of grown men. I call them old men who are not yet decrepit. The Scythians, of course, are warm and wet in the fashion of young men. The southerners are cold and dry, as befitting old men. Those who have attained middle life have achieved the proper blending.

Indeed, if we are to believe Aristotle, writing to Theodectes, young men struggle unduly with desires and lust, which we have shown is characteristic of the liver and the multitude. Aristotle added, "since they are fickle and changeable, disgust and desire for new things seizes them suddenly." And a little later: "They have sudden wishes, but not long-lasting, are ambitious, reckless, wrathful, gay, wasteful, not wicked, but well-intentioned and straightforward, because they have not seen much evil." He attributed this to ignorance, not to virtue; furthermore, he said, they are credulous and delude themselves with empty hope. The old men are the opposite. Those who are of middle years, however, possess everything in moderation. These matters, however, are given more fully in Aristotle. They apply very well to the three kinds of people, not only theoretically but also by actual illustration. For the northern Germans, who are either Scythians or close to the Scythians, always offer the most conspicuous proofs of that levity with which they reproach the Gauls. About the ancient [Germans] Tacitus wrote thus: "The race," said he, "is not astute or cunning; the freedom of revelry opens the secrets of the heart, and the frank opinion of all is reconsidered the following day. Due weight is given to both periods. They deliberate when they do not know how to pretend, they decide when they cannot err." This is his opinion.

Although there are innumerable examples of Scythian fickleness, none is more conspicuous—and in a field where constancy should shine most clearly—than in the religion they have adopted. The Ostrogoths and the Visigoths, driven from their homes by Attila, implored Valens to grant them lands, promising that they would conform to the laws of the empire and the Christian religion. After they had obtained their request, with incredible perfidy they overpowered Valens and burned him alive. When the Goths came into Italy, they at first became Christians, then deserted to the Arian faith. The Greenlanders, who dwell near the pole, said Munster, since they are changeable in disposition, readily accepted the Christian religion, yet afterwards they relapsed into idolatry. The Turks, a branch of the Scythians, as soon as they invaded Asia were converted to the Arabian faith. The Tartars accepted Christianity under no compulsion and soon afterwards changed to Mohammedanism. The Normans, still rude and wild, although they had subdued a great part of France, nevertheless immediately rejected their tribal beliefs and followed the faith of the conquered. Then the Icelanders were at one time idolaters, yet later they became Christian at the wish of foreigners, as Ziegler and Munster reported. Bohemians and Saxons were the first to desert the Roman rites, how wisely I do not dispute, nor is it relevant to our subject. Although they had particularly worthy and erudite men, who exposed the chief frauds of the popes, yet after a conference had been held and the matter deliberated profoundly for a long time, they took the most difficult way of all. But I am speaking about the plebs and the farmers, who although they did not understand the matter, at once accepted the opinion of their leaders. Immediately all Saxony fell away, the Baltic cities, Denmark, Norway, Gothic Sweden, and those who trace their origin from Swedish Goths—the Helvetians—soon even Britain and Scotland. For a long time there was resistance in Upper Germany, which is not so far to the north, and has not yet clearly abandoned the old rites. France decided with much more difficulty. In truth

Sleidan, who in imitation of others complained of French fickleness, confessed that during the nine years in which he lived in France he witnessed very cruel executions of Frenchmen at the stake. For forty years we have unfortunately inflicted and executed these penalties. Some, indeed, influenced by religious motives, thought that in doing this they were showing allegiance to God; others, again, because they preferred the worship of one God before all joys, riches, honors, even life itself. No deaths at the stake in Germany are recalled, except that of Caesar Leo, a native of Bavaria. Italy can with difficulty be wrested from her ancient opinions. If the Germans had constantly adhered to their religion, they would have carried the rest along with them much more easily. But swayed in a brief interval to this side or to that, they have accepted an innumerable variety of opinions. They not only followed the teachings of Huss or of Luther, but also of the Anabaptists, of von Leyden, Zwingli, Karlstadt,[81] Osiander, Westphal, David, Stancar, the Adamites, the Waldensians, the Interimists, and almost countless others.

The southerners, however, Asiatics and Africans, unless indeed by miracles from heaven or by force of arms, do not abandon the religion they once adopted. This admirable constancy, not only in men, but also in women and boys, almost drove King Antiochus to frenzy. He tortured seven Hebrew boys most cruelly by every sort of punishment and yet could not force them to eat swine's flesh. Moreover, their mother voluntarily urged her sons to a most noble death. Certainly that race could never by any reward or punishment be enticed from its doctrines and, dispersed over the whole world, alone it has vigorously maintained its religion, received three thousand years ago. When Mohammed himself could not impose his doctrine either by miracles or speeches, he finally turned to arms, and having offered liberty to the slaves he accomplished by violence what he could not do by reasoning. Just as the English complain about their fortune because, although they are superior to the French in strength (as Comines stated), yet they are far inferior in wisdom; as the Italians for their part easily outwit the relatively uncivilized French and Germans (as Cardan wrote), but inveigh against the cunning of the Greeks; the Greeks of the Cretans, and these latter of the Egyptians and the Carthaginians; so likewise the Hebrews and the Egyptians complain that the Greeks are fickle; the Italians, the French; and the French, the Germans.

My own opinion is that there is in the deeds and sayings of men, as,

[81] Selestadt in the editions of 1566, 1572, and 1583.

in all things, a certain golden mean which is called "constancy." This maintains the mean between fickleness and stubbornness. Perpetual persistence in one opinion has never been praiseworthy for wise men. As in sailing, it is an art to yield to the tempest, even if you cannot make port. At such a time it is regarded as the highest prudence to turn the helm to every quarter of the sky, and to change the arrangement of the sails rather often; thus, in human affairs (I except divine), which are diverse and contradictory, the really wise man thinks it honest to alter his opinion. In public affairs, it is said, endeavor as forcefully as possible to convince your citizens. But those who defend their opinions stubbornly to the end and think it base to be refuted and shameful to be defeated, or those who prefer to depart from life rather than to abandon their deliberately formulated opinion—such men are not useful to themselves or to their fellow citizens, and they frequently bring ruin to the state. Men whom the world deems most wise, Plato and Xenophon, permit magistrates to lie for the sake of the state.

Since these vices are, as it were, innate in each race, history must be judged according to the customs and nature of each people before we can make unfavorable comments. For the moderation of the southerners is not praiseworthy, nor is the drunkenness of the Scythians, which is so much criticized, really to be scorned, because the southerners, through lack of inward heat, are at once satiated with food and drink; the Scythians, on the other hand, could not easily restrain themselves even if they wished, for they are impelled by internal warmth and lack the resources of genius.

In view of this the luxurious living of the southerners is to be reproached more than the bestiality of the Scythians at banquets, although it is not very different from the feeding of beasts. Tacitus said about the early Germans, "Without elaboration and condiments they drive off hunger." And a little later, "In each home, naked and filthy, they grow into that girth of limb and body which we admire. Among the very flocks, on the same mud floor, they spend their time." But when hunger comes upon the Scythians, they cut the veins of horses under the ears, suck the blood, and feast on the flesh, as tradition reports about the army of Tamerlane. The southerners, however, are neat and elegant and cannot endure filth. This can easily be understood from the basins and baths they use in sacrifices as well as in private life. It is made plain not only by the ancients and Xenophon but also by Alvarez; the former wrote that, among the Persians it is base to expectorate, the latter, that among the Abyssinians to expectorate in the temple is regarded as a flagrant sin. Athenaeus said, in turn, that there were incredible delicacies among the Asiatics and the Egyptians. When Mark Antony, a famous spendthrift,[82] was easily outdone by Cleopatra in this respect, he laughed at himself and at the Romans as stupid and uncouth. I pass over the rewards of the Persians decreed by law to those who have discovered new delights, as Theophrastus wrote. A similar elegance of manner is found in the Persian posture and action. They also accomplish dulcet harmonies and use the Lydian mode on the lyre. The Scythians, however, dislike mellifluent speech and charming diction, as we understand from their language and their consonants striking together harshly without vowels. They cannot endure the Lydian mode, but they cultivate roughness of voice; as Tacitus wrote, with a battle cry they kindle their spirits, making a noise with their shields brought up to their lips so that the voice may swell to a fuller and heavier note.[83] They listen gladly to trumpets and drums, but care nothing for the lyre. Strangely enough, the Scythians also like associations and assemblies of men; hence they are called by the ancients "nomads," and in these days also "hordes," as the Tartars say, when they roam the plains in countless numbers.

The southerners seek the solitude and prefer to hide away in the woods rather than to move about in plain sight. Men of the middle region there is no need to describe, if one understands the extremes, since from these the means are easily understood. For instance, Scythians use the Phrygian mode more often; southerners, the Lydian; those in the intervening region become fiercer to the sound of the Dorian and stir up Mars with song, as the poet says.[84] The Lydian makes the southerners even more languorous. The Dorian, in harmony with nature, directs the strivings of souls toward valor and honor. This mode is therefore praised by Plato and vigorously approved by Aristotle in his books about the commonwealth.[85] When the Christian religion was accepted by the Romans, the Dorian form was adopted with so much enthusiasm that a warning was issued lest anyone should use any other mode than the Dorian in the rites. On the other hand, the Spartans used the flute, the Cretans the lute in warfare—not to restrain their wrath, as Thucydides and Plutarch wrote (for in the opinion of Plato and Aristotle

---

[82] The word is *decoctor* in the first three editions, but *decoctos* in 1595.
[83] Tacitus *Germania*, paragraph 3.   [84] Virgil *Aeneid* VI. 165.
[85] Aristotle *Politics* VIII. 7. 1342b 15.

it was given to men as helpful for purposes of revenge), but to suit their own nature, since in Europe there is no race more southerly than the Cretans and the Spartans.[86] So much may be said in general about the customs of peoples from the actual character of the north and the south and the middle region.

About the Orient and the Occident in flat and level places (for with these we have to deal) it is difficult to judge, since in truth there is no rising (*oriatur*) and no setting (*occidat*). Yet not only physicians but also farmers and builders have learned through most convincing proofs that in hilly country there is a great dissimilarity between the eastern and western aspects. For instance, the plain of Turin is east, due to the fact that the Alps rise to the west, yet Palestine is westerly, because Hermon and Lebanon look down from the east, even if the sun on the equator rises earlier in Palestine than in Turin by almost an hour and a half. Since the rising light by its moderate heat purifies the harmful thick heaviness of the air, it makes the region much more temperate. Moreover, when the sun burns with its greatest heat, that is, in the afternoon, it sets for the eastern region and rises for the western. Hence the great difference between the Allobroges and the Turini, who are in the same latitude and longitude of the heavens. This stands to reason, but with reference to level places no definite cause is apparent why Galatia of Asia Minor differs from Campania of Italy, since they are in the same latitude. It is, however, confirmed by lasting experience, with the unanimous consent of the Hebrews, Greeks, and Latins, that the eastern quarter is more temperate and better than the west. On this account Ezekiel wrote that the chosen worshiped with their faces turned toward the east. Isaiah, too, said that justice comes from the east. In the same way another warned, "Look to the east and watch joy coming from God to thee." I use these witnesses willingly, the more willingly because I understand that they have been most truthful interpreters of natural and divine things. Among the Latins, Pliny, Book VII, commented that by long observation it was found that the pest was carried from east to west. This I noticed in Gallia Narbonensis. So that if the opposite trend should set in (it did happen in the year of Christ 1557), they predicted that the epidemic would spread everywhere. Ammianus,[87] among the Greeks, gave evidence that when Seleucia was devastated and

---

[86] In the passage referred to above, Aristotle states that the flute is better suited to express the Bacchic frenzy, which required also the Phrygian mode. According to Bodin the Phrygian mode is the most stimulating to southerners.

[87] Ammianus Marcellinus *Roman History* XXIII. vi. 24.

they opened the sanctuary of a temple closed by the mystic science of the Chaldeans, a plague of incurable diseases developed. In the time of Marcus and Verus these maladies spread contagion and resulted in a high mortality in the whole area from the very borders of Persia to the Rhine and the Gauls. Not long thereafter the pest, advancing northward from Ethiopia, is said to have ravaged almost the whole world. The reason for this is clear, since the south wind blew upon damp regions of the north, the warmth increasing the corruption.

The next influence, then, is attributed to differences in the winds. The winds flowing from the south are warm and damp; from the north, cold and dry. But since winds blowing along the north-to-south axis and the east-to-west axis usually blow gently, they do not create the change of air brought by those coming in obliquely. When the sun is far distant from the north-to-south axis, it cannot stir powerful exhalations, while in the east-to-west axis the more violent heat of the sun agitates the wind, but restrains its violence.[88] Therefore the force of winds is much greater in spring and autumn than in winter and summer. The most violent of all are the southwest (*Africus*) and northwest (*Corus*) winds. Next, opposite to them, are the east-southeast (*Vulturnus*) and the north (*Aquilo*) winds. Corus, of course, is cold and very wet; Vulturnus is warm and very dry; Africus is wet and warm; Aquilo is dry and cold. Along the north-to-south axis the winds are observed to be very cold and very warm. Two in the east-to-west axis are very moderate: that from the exact west, the zephyr (*Favonius*), but this is very gentle and rarely blows, or almost never except at sunset. The wind from the east (*Subsolanus*) is very healthful and somewhat more boisterous than zephyr, especially when the sun is leaving the equator. Yet the more distant and secret cause for the superiority of the eastern region over the western is wholly hidden from me, since nothing actually rises and sets. The effects which follow, however, are obvious and wonderful. The end of the eastern region seems to me to be, as I have said before, in the isles of the Moluccas, but the west is in the isles of the Hesperides. This, then, is half of the whole earth, for the meridians of these islands are distant from one another by 180 degrees. Another part of the earth remains, in which is situated America, separated by an infinite space of sea from each extreme, so that it seems to contain the dividing line between east and west. I pass over the many problems

[88] Apparently his theory is that the sun in winter is distant from the north-to-south line, so it does not give rise to gales, whereas in the summer the sun is near the east and west axis, and creates winds, although the heat checks their force.

disputed by the magi about the nature of the demons of each region.

Now I touch upon only the things which strike the senses. The most serious and learned men of the Greeks, that is, Aristotle, Hippocrates, Galen, and Ctesias, in many passages asserted and confirmed by appropriate examples that all the more beautiful and better things are found in Asia rather than in Europe. Even if they often fell into error because they did not know the latitudes of the regions, nevertheless, now that the latitudes have become known it has been discovered that in one and the same quarter of the heavens the people who dwell in the west are pre-eminent for strength of body; the easterners, for talent. The Celts often led vast armies into Italy, Greece, and Asia, but the Italians dared not attack France until they had brought their power to its zenith under the leadership of Caesar, when the Gauls were harassed by civil war. Cicero and Agrippa therefore praised Caesar, because he had overwhelmed peoples whose attack the Romans could barely withstand; they did not dare provoke them. The Italians, however, conquered the Greeks so readily that they suffered no hardship. The Greeks, in turn, who penetrated the innermost recesses of Asia with their armies, hardly ever went into Italy except under King Pyrrhus. When he had been defeated, however, he sought safety in cowardly flight, like Xerxes, who led so many troops into Greece that the rivers were nearly dried up; he was, nevertheless, halted by a handful of Greeks and driven back, to his great shame. So Cato reproached Murena, and Caesar, the shades of Pompey, that the wars which they had waged in Asia had been waged against mere women. Hence this remark of Emperor Julian: "Celts and Germans are daring; Greeks and Romans sometimes warlike, sometimes pacific; Egyptians are more industrious and shrewd, although weak and soft; the Syrians, with quick and supple minds, are suited for training." [89] A little later the same author said: "Why should I mention how eager for liberty and impatient of slavery are the Germans, how tractable and quiet the Syrians, the Persians, the Parthians, and lastly all people living in the east and the south?" He wrote these things in his books against the Christians, where he revealed clearly the power of the east and the west. Similarly, Tacitus wrote that the Batavians who occupied the westernmost part of Germany were the most ferocious of all and pre-eminent for valor. This Plutarch confirmed in the life of Marius. Indeed, they are conspicuous for their size, like all who inhabit cold swampy places. In the same way, the most westerly peoples are

[89] Julian, *Against the Galileans*, p. 347.

reckoned as most warlike of all Gaul. Caesar himself first noticed this. "Men of the best kind," said he, "come from the Aquitanians and Rhutenians." Moreover, of all the races of Europe the most western are the Britons and the Spanish, and they are the most active.

The west has a great affinity with the north; the east with the south. One may see it not only in the nature of living things but also in the shrubs, the stones, and the metals. There is a fixed tradition that the finest gold and precious stones are found in the east and the south, but the other precious metals toward the west and the north. It is true that Cardan was censured by Scaliger on this account, since he had written on the authority of others, without proof. Before Cardan wrote, Agricola, a master of the metallurgic art, had supported this statement with his most weighty testimony. "The most highly valued gold metal of all Europe is produced in Hispanic Betica, which is the most southerly part of all Europe," he said, "but of Africa, in Ethiopia." The same author a little later asserted, "The east and all Africa lacks red lead and quicksilver; iron also is rare in Africa, yet frequent in Cantabria (the most northerly part of all Spain and the furthest west of Europe). It is very common in France and in Germany." And the same: "The most excellent iron of all is among the Swedes and the Ostrogoths. They call it *osemutum*." Moreover, he wrote that among the Ligii near Sagau iron was mined in the meadows at the depth of two feet; when it grows again, after ten years, it is dug up. They cannot go deeper on account of the water. Nowhere on earth is there a greater supply of sulphur than in the island of Thule, called Iceland. From there it is carried into all Europe. The same author reports that it is found nowhere in Germany except in Goldkronach and the Carpathian Mountains, which abound in all metals. It is true that they are the boundary of Germany to the east, as well as extending to the south.

Each year the Turks are said to take out from Siderocapsa two hundred thousand gold pieces. Iron is more difficult to find, so in sacking towns the Turks seek it much more than bronze or tin. As in the north iron lies almost on the surface of the ground, so in the south gold is found in the fields and clean sands. Indeed, they report that in the kingdom of Damutus, adjoining the mountains of Bet, beyond Capricorn, gold has been found after a heavy rain. As the other metals are melted by the strength of fire in the north, in the mountains of the Pyrenees, the Juras, the Cevennes, the Alps, the Carpathians, the Thracian range, Mount Pangaeus, Mount Laurius, Mount Tmolus, and the Caucasus, so in the south gold is collected, not by the heat of fire, but by the force of the celestial stars and the heat of the sun, even on the surface of the earth and in sand. Similarly, the southerners and the easterners are sustained by the celestial heat and the strength of the stars, but the westerners and the northerners by the fiery heat held within them.

So, returning from details to the general, I understand that in the north the interiors are warm and damp, the exteriors dry and cold. On the other hand, the interiors in the south are dry and cold, the exteriors warm and damp. The east and the west, however, are more moderate. This, indeed, is evident in the purer natures and elements more free from materiality. When the air in summer has grown warm above and below, so much cold is gathered in the middle regions that at this time hailstones take on their greatest weight, although in winter they are unable to do so. In a similar way, the earth burnt by the ardor of the sun retains the cold; yet when all things are stiff with cold, the earth holds the heat within. This may be seen in wells, which give forth retained heat in winter; in summer they seem very cold. Inasmuch as in the north there is practically perpetual cold, so perpetual heat exists in the interior, not only of the earth itself, but also of living things and plants. As Empedocles says, nature seems to have placed heat in cold, and cold in heat. Since the food of plants and animals grows out of warmth and dampness, so there is a great abundance of woods and living things in the north. Hence Pliny reported that Germany was full of marvelously deep forests. Moreover, Vitruvius wrote that the loftiest trees in the Apennines grew on the northern side. That area under the pole called Greenland has its name from the verdure and the number of its forests. In Africa there are no woods, except in the mountains, which have the nature of the north, as we shall explain later. Little by little the lofty trees, as well as the men, seem to become smaller as one goes southward. There are in Gallia Narbonensis oak trees two feet high which bear fruit and do not grow any taller.

In addition, the greatest abundance of all metals, except gold, is in the north; there is almost none in the south, except in the loftiest mountains. But eruptions of fire and great conflagrations are reported in northerly lands. Chimaera, Gazeuale, Vesuvius, Etna, the Peak of Teneriffe, Carpathus, and Thule, that last of lands (for it is situated on the seventieth degree and throughout almost its entire extent glows with volcanoes), as well as most places which Olaus names in the description of Gothia, are blazing with perpetual flames. The Pyrenees take their name from fire. On the other side of the thirtieth degree from the equator no volcanoes are recorded. There are no springs of hot water, such as are in Italy, Gaul, Germany, and farthest Gothland. I suppose that is what Pico della Mirandola signified somewhat obscurely in these words, "He who knows the characteristics of the north wind understands why God will judge the world by fire." This opinion is old, enunciated not only by Pico but also by Heraclitus, as Plutarch said, and by the Hebrews, who believe that the world sometime will burn. Fires will not fall from the sky, as Maggi [90] thought, but will burst forth from the inner vitals of the earth. Moreover, this fire must be kindled in the north, not in the south, since here the waters, there the concentration of earth-masses extends, nourishing the fires held within. Although to a man gazing at the world of earth and water, as much of earth is hidden as revealed, and the size of the lands and of the whole sea seem to be equal; nevertheless, that entire part which is free from water extends northward, if we define the limits of the south and the north by the equator, which in general is usually done. There remains a certain small portion of Africa and of America. The land called southern is depicted of enormous size for elaboration, not for the truth of the matter.

And so we must interpret the words of Esdras [91] in some other way than the ancients did or what he wrote will be absurd—God has revealed seven parts of earth; he had collected the waters in the seventh. What the ancient Peripatetics thought is even more preposterous, that the land was ten times less than the water. For it would be necessary that the land (so that nothing else than its surface may touch the center of the earth) be immersed altogether in the waters, if the globe [92] of waters were even seven times greater than the land, as we are taught from the ratio of the circle to the diameter. How much more if the center of land were placed in the center of the earth? Yet the former position must be the correct one, [93] since near the straits of Magellan, not far from the other pole, the sphere of earth projects a little. It is remarkable, yet confirmed by voyages and the experience of many men, that the weight of the sea and the waters is borne from the north south-

---

[90] Jerome Maggi died in 1572. He wrote *De mundi exustione et de die judicii*, supporting the principles of the Stoic philosophy, and commentaries on Justinian.

[91] *The Apocrypha and Pseudepigrapha of the Old Testament*, IV Ezra 6:42.

[92] I follow here the editions of 1566 and 1572, reading *globus* rather than *globo*, and giving a more logical interpretation. See also Bodin's *Theatre de la nature*, II. vi. 259.

[93] That is, the eccentric position.

ward with great momentum. When crossing to Britain and Ireland Cardan learned this from the sailors and reported it, but because he inquired into neither the causes of the matter nor the effects, he has been justly reproached by Julius Scaliger, as if he had introduced this as an invention of his own.

Since it pertains to a thorough understanding of the general nature of the elemental world and of men, as well as to confirmation of these facts which we have stated (that is, that the lands lie northward, the waters southward; here the outside is warm and damp, there cold and dry; here the inside is cold and dry; there warm and damp), let us compare observations of the ancients with our own. First let us notice that the Chaldeans attributed the fiery triplicity to Europe, the watery triplicity to Africa; then that the south wind is called by the Greeks "from the damp, or southerly," Notus, as if from dampness. That wind is warm and damp. Boreas is cold and dry. There is also the fact that, by common agreement, the current of the waters is carried from the Baltic through the Skagerrak to the Channel, hence to the French and the Spanish shores. But the Caspian Sea, through inner and secret approaches, comes out as the Sea of Azov in Pontus and thence is carried through the Hellespont into the Mediterranean. Farther on, a great rush of waters bursts forth near the Straits of Hercules, so that it is carried back to the south.

These things sailors and traders have averred, and geography and hydrography also lead us to the same conclusion. Pliny did not without good reason relate that greater waves were put into motion by the south wind than by the north, although he adduced a stupid reason, since it is plain that the south wind presses forward against the flow of the sea. We have also as proof that once upon a time Diodorus, not so long ago Alvarez, and even more recently our men who have sailed to Africa unanimously testify that incessant rain inundates the regions beyond the equator, whence come the Nile floods. Pliny, Book II,[94] averred that everlasting dews water Africa, even in a burning summer. He advanced no reason for this. The last consideration is that toward the south, where the hypogaeum [95] is located, the sun is nearer the earth than in the north by the whole width of the ecliptic. On this account it can apparently drag the weight of the waters thither. This supporting evidence

[94] Pliny *Natural History* II. 63.
[95] The word *hypogaeum* is used by Vettius Valens in the sense of "nadir."

for our opinion is not only credible but also, I think, makes agreement inevitable.

But it can be objected, according to Aristotle, that fevers are more acute toward the north and that the force of heat in summer is greater than toward the south. As for fever, the reason is obvious, for when the pores are closed the result is that in winter everywhere illnesses are more serious than in summer; but it may seem absurd that in a European summer men suffer more from the heat than in Africa. Yet Aristotle stated this as if well known. Indeed, Alvarez wrote that an Abyssinian from Ethiopia died from the heat on the day when he reached Portugal with the ambassador of Prester John. Of course the Spanish in France complain that they feel the summer heat more than in Spain. Moreover, I have learned from Purquer, a German, when he was living in Toulouse, that in the middle of summer the heat was greater in the region of Danzig, that is, near the Baltic, than at Toulouse. I suppose this is the reason why the Germans, on the authority of Tacitus, divide their year into winter, spring, and summer; the bounties of autumn, like the name, they do not know. The Danes, in turn, have only winter and summer, like the Carthaginians, who do not consider spring and autumn, as Leo the African wrote.

The cause of the northern heat we shall trace to the sluggishness and heaviness of the air. Europe and Scythia are full of rivers, flowing from the internal dampness, which create muddy and swampy places. From these a dense vapor rises in summer. This, enveloping the warmth, produces a more stifling heat than the African air, rarefied from lack of rivers. Therefore, as the fire kindled in metal burns more ardently than in wood, and in this than in straw, so in thick air it burns more violently than in thin. For this reason those who wish to heat warm baths at less expense, sprinkle the soil with water, so that the steam lifts and the air, made thicker, can support the heat. It also serves as evidence that on a rainy day in summer we perspire and feel the heat much more than on a clear day. Yet, we shall not go on to say that the external portions of the north are warmer than the south. In accordance with their nature they are dry and cold. But when the south wind is blowing and the vapors rise up, the air holds and maintains the warmth better.

On the other hand, in Africa the earth, the stones, and waters when warmed grow hot with much more violence than in Scythia, on account of the strength of the rays. So it could have been said more appropriately by Aristotle that in summer in the north, even up to the sixtieth degree, greater heating of the air occurs than in the south. These things may be adduced in general about the customs of the peoples who inhabit flat level places.

Now let us consider the different characteristics of areas either mountainous, swampy, desert, windy, or tranquil. There is the same difference between the natures of men from plain and from mountain as between those from the south and the north, and almost the same difference in temperament, if the plains are not swamps. As the greatest cold in the north extends universally over the plains; so in the south, over the mountains. And in the middle region of the air such is the strength of the cold from the reaction to the heat that the Hyperboraei, if there are any, do not stiffen with the cold to a greater degree than the Mountains of the Moon or the Peak of Teneriffe, the loftiest of all. This is easily deduced if one considers the process in summer by which hail is firmly compressed in the middle region of the air. In winter we hardly ever see this happen. Since the cold is distributed, it has less strength. Hence, what Averroës thought is false—that plants and living things are more vigorous in the mountains because they are nearer to heaven. If that were true the mountaineers would be more godlike and more talented, nevertheless they are considered by everyone to be very rough and uncouth.

What Hippocrates wrote is also false [96]—that the changes of seasons in the mountains produce ferocity and gigantic stature in men. Since we know very well that the northern regions are exceedingly well watered, while the mountains are dry, the mountaineers, then, must be tougher, hardier, and longer-lived and superior in appearance, as mountain birds and flocks excel those from the marshes and mountain trees the others. Since almost no crests are inhabited, but only the slopes of the mountains, that part which faces north is more temperate and more healthful beyond the forty-fifth degree from the pole. Yet on this side of that parallel the slope to the south is more healthful. There is a great difference between the two, which men who have journeyed through the mountains understand well enough.

What we have said, then, about the middle region and the customs of the people does not extend to those who dwell on the Alps, the Pyrenees, the Cevennes, the Acroceraunians, the Great Balkans, the

[96] Hippocrates, *op. cit.*, paragraph 24.

Carpathians, Mount Olympus, the Taurus range, Mount Stella,[97] the Caucasus range, the Pamirs, and the mountains of Auvergne, and yet this climatic belt is the most temperate of all. From the southerners, likewise, must be excepted the inhabitants of Atlas, the Arabian highlands, the Mountains of Bet, Mount Angaeus,[98] the Peak of Teneriffe and Sierra Leone, a mountain called by Pliny, "Chariot of the Gods." For mountaineers are tough, uncouth, warlike, accustomed to hard work, and not at all cunning. Not only in the mountains of the north, but even in that very Atlas near the tropic great sturdy men are said to grow, of the sort we have often seen. From these the Mauritanian and the Numidian rulers were wont to recruit their legions. It surely is remarkable that those who dwell in the mountains of Arabia never could abandon their ferocity and steadfast courage, but relying either on the powers of nature or on the protection of the area, have lived always in the greatest freedom. Even the ruler of the Turks, as I hear, gave to them sixty thousand gold coins that he might freely enjoy the plain of Damascus and Palestine. Again, the ancient Marsi, inhabitants of the Apennines, are reported to have been the most ferocious of all the peoples of Italy. It was commonly reported that without the Marsi no one could triumph. Where did Gustavus recruit legions to invade the kingdom of Sweden, if not from the Dalecarlians who lived in the Swedish mountains? What of the Swiss? Since they trace their origin from the Swedes, they obtained liberty not only for themselves but also for the neighboring peoples, crushed by tyranny. Often they defeated the princes of Austria. They inflicted great slaughter upon the Germans. They took by force no small part of the German Empire. Finally, they accomplished so much by strength of arms that they are called masters and censors of princes.

From this we may understand what Cicero said, "The mountaineers of Liguria, in accordance with their nature, are rugged and wild; those on the coast are very cunning." I omit how the mountaineers of Cilicia and the Balkans waged endless wars with the Turks, how long they sustained and repulsed their forces under their leaders, the Caramani. Their nature is altogether contrary to those who live in swampy places, who on account of the abundant moisture are taller even in the same

[97] Bodin seems to be moving from west to east, which would place Mount Stella somewhere in Asia Minor, but I cannot identify it.

[98] Angaeus must be a misprint for Pangaeus, a mountain in Thrace. Bodin refers to Pangaeus on p. 133, above.

latitude; as the Batavians and Friesians, who control the mouths of the Rhine, are greater than the other Germans in this area. On account of marshes and flat places the Belgae are taller than the Britons, whose country is flat, they say, and not at all marshy, but sandy. Worst are those who live in marshy warm places, as in Egypt and Gallia Narbonensis, which is covered with swamps. There pest, hydrocele, skin eruptions, and leprosy are endemic. Here, also, are to be seen feeble men and ugly pale faces. A florid color is the chief proof of a temperate climate. But the arid regions, no matter how warm, are nevertheless healthful. Spain, Numidia, Persia, Chaldea, and Arabia Felix have active and sinewy men, stronger than the others in the same area. When Egypt, Cyrenaica, Mauritania, and Gallia Narbonensis were infested with white leprosy, lepers were still very unusual in Spain and Numidia, as Leo the African wrote.

Even the barrier of one river sometimes produces divergent natures of men, when it has a long course (as the rivers Danube, Niger, Po, Tagus, Asopus), because it divides northerners from southerners, so that they do not so easily form associations and engage in trade. On this account they often have very serious feuds. The southerners who dwell by the River Niger are small, weak, and ashen colored; those to the north, on the other hand, are larger and stronger and very black. It is not remarkable that Plato rendered thanks to the gods that he was an Athenian, not a Theban; yet Athens and Thebes are divided only by the Asopus River and are about twenty thousand paces apart, but the Athenians face toward the south, the Thebans toward the north. Those who live in southerly valleys are subjected to greater heat than those facing north in the same region, so that the latter attain approximately the nature of the Scythians, the former, of the southerners. On this account it happens that those who dwell near the Carpathians on the south are tanned; those on the opposite side are white. For the same cause Galen sent men who were wasting away to the region of Tabianus, between Sorrento and Naples, where a valley facing south has in winter the climate of spring.

Thence, also, arise the divergencies and differences in the nature of those who inhabit Rhetia, Carinthia, and Croatia, from that of the Istrians and the Illyrians; and of the Lombards from Ligurians and Tuscans. There are also people who are surrounded on all sides by valleys who stand very intense heat, beyond the forty-fifth parallel from the pole, on account of the concentration of the rays and the protected char-

acter of the areas everywhere. Moreover, since springs and rains from
the mountains are muddy, the maximum fertility is generated. What
the ancients reported about Mauretania and the valley of both Atlases
—that the one hundredth harvest was reaped—does not seem to me fictitious because even in modern times Leo the African confessed that
he had seen the fiftieth. Certainly Pliny wrote that the procurator of
Mauritania sent to Augustus an ear of wheat which had almost four hundred grains. More unbelievable is the tale of Strabo about the valleys
of the Taurus Mountains—that grape clusters of two cubits are grown and
that from one fig tree seventy pecks are gathered. Almost the same things
are noted about the Damascene fields in the valleys of the Lebanon
Mountains. As illustrations we have the Limagne of the Arverni, the
countryside of Turin, the golden valley of the Pyrenees, Thessalian
Tempe, the valley of Sitten, and the Carpathian valleys, which luxuri-
ate in such fertility that the richness of the valleys compensates abundantly for the sterility of the mountains. Therefore, because of this abundance of produce the inhabitants must devote themselves to agriculture,
neglect military matters, cultivate peace, and languish in pleasure.

Athenaeus, in Book XII, wrote that Lydians and Umbrians were no-
torious for their shameful delights. Both regions are situated in level
lowlands, and so Propertius said that Mevania was situated in a flat and
hollow place.[99] Such is said to have been the home of the Sybarites, who
saw neither the rising nor the setting sun, and whose pleasures and luxury Athenaeus described. But Alciati stupidly read the word *parcos* in
Plautus and Catullus, where they called the Umbrians *porcos*. It is even
more absurd that in Plutarch, Book II, chapter 10, *Symposiaca,* he should
think ὀμβρικὰς διαιτάς pertains to the Umbrians, whereas there the discussion is about wild beasts. For ὀμβρίκια and ὀμβρίκαλα [100] are said to be
whelps of beasts by Aelian and Aeschylus, while creatures born from a
sheep and a moufflon are called umbrians by the Latins.

Those who dwell in fertile valleys of this kind are devoted to luxury,
in contrast to the disposition of those who inhabit sterile places. The
latter are valiant soldiers in war, clever workers in peace, or diligently
engage in trade. It was for this reason that the sterile Attic plain made
the Athenians inventors of the arts. It is recorded that leisure was considered a capital sin among them, as it was by the Genoese among the

[99] Propertius *Elegies* IV. i. 123.

[100] The Greek ὀβρίκαλα, the young of animals, is employed by Aeschines, and Aelian
gives ὄβρια also, according to Liddell and Scott, *Greek-English Lexicon.* Stephanus,
Thesaurus, gives ὀμβρίκαλα as an occasional spelling.

Italians, the Limousins among us, and the Nurembergers among the Germans. The valley dwellers are happier because of the abundance of supplies but the others on account of their talent. Since the icy waters melted from the snows run down into the hollows, it very often happens that scrofula or hydrocele are contracted, especially if the outlook is west and north. All those who inhabit the Valedoca valley in the region of Turin have scrofula or tumors of the throat or tonsillitis. They are also unbalanced and unable to speak, like the Labdani people in Aquitania, on account of *labdacismus*. These illnesses their bodies derive from the waters. From these bodies they are transferred to the soul. How great is the strength and the power of the waters to change customs is understood clearly from Hippocrates; there is no need of more. Yet what Pliny wrote is worthy of notice—that by the Vistritza River in Greece sheep are made white; by the Axius, black; by the Xanthus, yellow. This also Vitruvius confirmed.

From the air, by which chiefly we live, no lesser defects arise, sometimes even greater. Although we have mentioned this fact in general, yet in detail we find that windy places render men more fierce and more changeable; quiet places, on the other hand, kinder and more steadfast. The reason is clear: the mind cannot be tranquil in a place where it is tossed hither and thither. A proof of this is that no one can meditate in motion and tumult, but only with a mind purified and free from emotion and likewise with a motionless body. The wiser each man is, the slower the movements of his body and mind. The insane, indeed, are forever dashing about in body, as well as in soul. So I think the perpetual tossing of wind and waves makes sailors barbarous and inhuman. However it may be, it is known that Thrace, France, Britain, Circassia, the Libyan desert, Lusitania, Persia, Norway, Noricum, and Pannonia, which are said to be more disturbed by the force of the winds, have inhabitants fiercer and more easily moved than have those regions within the same zone that are quiet, like Assyria, Asia Minor, Italy, except Liguria, and Egypt, where the climate is reported to be golden. It is true that the Circassians who inhabit the Tauric Chersonese have a really mild climatic zone, yet they are said to be astonishingly savage, faithless, and cruel; but nowhere have the winds a greater force. It is evident also that no people in France are more spirited than the men of Narbonne, Aquitaine, and Provence, yet they are more southerly than the rest. So that I should think this ferocity and unquiet stirring of the mind is engendered partly by the south-southwest wind (*Atlanis*, for this name is applied by Pliny, and commonly, to Vulturnus, which constantly sweeps across Gallia Narbonensis), partly by the northwest wind (*Corus*), or by the west-northwest wind (*Circius*), called by the inhabitants *serra* [the saw?], which blows most violently of all.

The fusion of peoples changes the customs and the nature of men not a little. It is not true that all the Scythians in the same quarter are alike because in each quarter of the world there is one specific temperament. This was the belief of Hippocrates. The opinion of Empedocles and the Stoics would be nearer to the truth. As Plutarch reported, they thought that facial differences are produced by the image received from the soul. Some are born like wild beasts, because they are affected not by their thoughts, but by their senses alone, as Pliny said. So the Scythians, who like simple delights in accordance with nature and are distracted less by the variety of their thoughts, are wont to produce children more like their parents. I am inclined, however, to a different line of reasoning.

In Ethiopia, where, we have said, the race of men is very keen and lustful, no one varies markedly from the uniform type. They are all small, curly-haired, black, flat-nosed, blubber-lipped, and bald, with white teeth and black eyes. Among the Scythians there are no differences. Hippocrates himself wrote, and Tacitus made the same comment about the Germans. We have discovered, in reality, that the farther one moves from the middle region, the more the faces resemble each other, while within that zone we see an infinite divergence among men. Although in the moderate area the eyes of everyone ought to be reddish-yellow (for all eyes of that variety are blended from black, blue, and yellow eyes), yet we see in addition to reddish-yellow, greyish (*glaucus*), bluish-grey (*caesius*), black, greyish-yellow (*ravus*), and countless blendings of these. There are large-nosed men and flat-nosed; curly-haired, black, white, and reddish; red-bearded; florid, and wan; dwarfish and gigantic. This state of affairs ought, then, to be attributed to the blending of peoples, who are wont to move from the extremes to the middle region, as though to the region of most equable climate. The countless hordes of Scythians, Goths, Turks, and Tartars settled in central areas. None except the Vandals crossed into Africa, from which they were driven out somewhat later. Since Arabs and Carthaginians, whom men of old called Saracens, brought colonies from Africa into Europe and Asia, they also settled down in the middle region. None penetrated into Scythia, for although they invaded Spain, Italy, and Greece, they were defeated and overwhelmed in Gaul. Afterwards the French liberated

Italy and a great part of Spain from servitude. In the same way the ancient Celtic and Roman colonists sought their homes in the middle regions; none was led into Scythia or Ethiopia.

Therefore, as we see diverse forms develop from the diverse kinds of living beings and plants, as in the mule, panther, hyena, wolf-dog, and giraffe, which are unlike their parents, so we must make a similar judgment about variations in human beings. The wolf-dog, conceived from a wolf, differs in almost no respect from a dog, since a wolf is nothing but a woodland dog, on the authority of Varro himself. But the mule differs very much from the horse and the ass; the giraffe, from the camel and the panther. Thus if the Scythians were crossed with the Ethiopians, there is no doubt but that a varied and different kind of man would be produced. Athenaeus wrote that Ptolemy Philadelphus showed a man on the stage who was of two colors in face and body; one side was black, the other white. In this way, then, it came about, I think, that Danes, Saxons, and English mingled with Britons, making them more ferocious, while they themselves became more kindly. Indeed, when the Britons, driven from their homes, entered Gaul, they renounced with difficulty their wild courage and redeemed themselves gradually from servitude to the Gauls. I think we must make the same inference about the colony of Saxons which Charles the Great led among the Belgae, for they always fought very bravely for their liberty. Then, unlike plants, which when transplanted elsewhere quickly lose their identity and adapt themselves to the nature of the soil whence they take their nourishment, men do not change the innate characteristics of their own nature easily, but after a long period of time. The Gallic Tectosages, who had seized some of the most fertile places of Germany, as Caesar wrote, in the course of time so altered their customs and nature that in the days of Caesar they were living in the same poverty and hardship as the Germans; they had the same food and habits of living. So when L. Memmius, consul, was going to fight the Galatians, who had a great reputation for warlike prowess, he encouraged the Roman legions, terrified by the Gallic name, into the hope of victory by saying that the Galatians had long ago ceased to be Gauls. They had become effeminate through the delights of Asia and had lost their ferocity through the mildness of the climate, so that there was nothing more to fear from them. Rightly Cyrus said, in the pages of Herodotus, "Unmanly men are born of a mild sky"; indeed the Turks gradually cast aside the wild character of the Scythians and, except when they were cultivating military training with great zeal, were easily defeated by the strength of the Muscovites and the Sarmatians.

Then it remains to consider how much training can accomplish in changing the nature of men. Now training is twofold, divine and human; the latter may be wrong or right. Each, of course, has power sufficient to overcome nature fairly often. If Hippocrates truly thought that all species of plants can be domesticated,[101] how much more is this true for human kind? Was there ever a race so huge and savage which, when it had found leaders, was not carried forward along the path of civilization? What race once instructed in the most refined arts, but ceasing to cultivate the humanities, did not sink sometime into barbarity and savagery? Although innumerable examples of this exist, yet none is more illustrious than that of the Germans, who as they themselves confess were once not very far from the level of wild beasts. Then they wandered in marshes and forests like animals and by some rooted dislike they avoided letters. Nevertheless, they have now so far advanced that in the humanities they seem superior to the Asiatics; in military matters, to the Romans; in religion, to the Hebrews; in philosophy, to the Greeks; in geometry, to the Egyptians; in arithmetic, to the Phoenicians; in astrology, to the Chaldeans; and in various crafts they seem to be superior to all peoples. Indeed, Machiavelli urbanely chided the Italians of his age that while they thought themselves rather clever, yet they invited Germans to measure the boundaries of their lands. Furthermore, Pope Leo, when he wished to make corrections upon the course of the sun and the moon, sent his emissaries into Germany, as once Caesar had sent them into Egypt. When the Arabians and the Carthaginians, according to their nature soft and effeminate, commenced to cultivate military science, their training resulted in their seizing control of Asia and Africa. Likewise the Marseillais developed civil skills with such success that they were thought to be of all peoples the wisest and most just, by the plainest testimony of Cicero. Concerning the education of the Spartans the historians tell plainly incredible things, which, however, are the more certain in that they come from a hostile source. There can be no greater example of neglected discipline than that of the Romans. Although they formerly excelled all peoples in their reputation for justice and in military glory, yet now they are outdone in both respects by almost everyone. Therefore I think that the innate character of the Romans, and indeed of the Italians, is highly praiseworthy; but there is no

---

[101] The text reads ἐφημερώσται which should be ἐξημερῶσθαι.

natural goodness so unbounded that it may not be corrupted by a perverse training.

I will not dwell longer on matters discussed in common talk, which each man can obtain from the same sources that I use. I will take instead familiar examples. Since our forefathers thought long faces more beautiful, the midwives gradually arranged that they should seem very long indeed. These may be seen in old statues and pictures. In western India the forehead [102] is very wide and the nose of immense size; we read that this is due to obstetricians. Then Synesius [103] reported that he saw a woman in Africa artificially shaped like an ant, so that she afforded pleasure to spectators. Of course it is regrettable that the style of clothing which women now use to make the contour of the body more alluring results in carrying the young in a narrower space. Due to the change in form they become consumptive. But if the influence of custom and training is so great in natural and human affairs that gradually they develop into mores and take on the force of nature, how much more true is this in divine matters? We see that the power and influence of religions is such as to change profoundly the habits and corrupt character of men, although it can hardly happen that the traces of our earlier dispositions can be altogether obliterated. While the Germans have with infinite labor achieved a knowledge of all the great arts, yet in the judgment of many they lack decorum, beauty, order, and system such as we see revealed in the writings of Greeks and Italians. As their bodies develop great size, so do their books. Musculus [104] wrote more, Martin and Erasmus wrote more, than anyone can read in the course of a long lifetime. The southerners are very different. In a few lines they embrace the secrets of all divine and natural things. As they compensate for the weakness of their bodies by the strength of their minds, so for the scantiness of their books, by the maximum of usefulness.

The last thing is to refute the errors of Ptolemy and of those who apportion to each region the parts of the zodiac and the triplicities, as they are called, from which they think the nature of peoples can be adjudged. They say that Europe, placed between the west and the

[102] The edition of 1583 gives *fons*, while the editions of 1572 and 1595 give *frons*. The entire sentence is omitted from the edition of 1566.

[103] Synesius of Cyrene lived in the early fifth century in Alexandria. He was a Platonist and wrote *Aegyptius sive de providentia* and various other works, none particularly suitable for the anecdote in question.

[104] Wolfgang Mäusslin (Musculus), 1497–1563, was a convert to Lutheranism. He lived in Switzerland and wrote Biblical commentaries.

north, is under the sway of the first triplicity, that is, the fiery one, Leo, Aries, and Sagittarius, Jupiter and Mars being the dominating forces. Asiatic Scythia, between the north and the east, belongs to the aerial triplicity, that is, the Gemini, Libra, and Aquarius, when the rays of Jupiter and Saturn have met. Africa, between west and south, is under the watery triplicity, that is, Cancer, Scorpion, and Pisces, with Mars, Venus, and Mercury. Southern Asia, between south and east, is subject to the earthly triplicity, that is, Taurus, Virgo, and Capricorn, along with Venus and Saturn. These things are clearly at variance not only with previous statements but even with nature itself and history. The beginning of the error is traced to ignorance of places and of geography, which was so great that some ancients thought that the ocean was a river and Spain, a town. How many mistakes were made by Ptolemy himself, who guided the others, is understood well enough by men only moderately versed in this sort of thing. The ignorance of celestial motions increased the error, for the Chaldeans could hardly have spent fifteen hundred years in this study, as can be understood from sacred history and their observations, which Ptolemy used. They could not even grasp the motion of the eighth circle, and Ptolemy could not observe the course of the trepidation.[105] However, these things have become known little by little through the studies of the Arabs, the Spaniards, and the Germans. As for the fact that the Chaldeans boast, as Cicero says, that they spent 470,000 years in taking the horoscope of every child and testing it by results,[106] this is false. The levity of this fancy, which is self-refuting, does not require discussion; for had this been true they would not have been unaware of those things which in course of time we have observed and comprehended. Moreover, what they have given us about the signs of the zodiac is altogether indefensible, since all parts of the zodiac and whole signs have changed place since the time of their observations. For the first star of Aries, which occupied the first part of this constellation for six hundred years before Ptolemy, has arrived at the twenty-eighth

[105] Johnson, *Astronomical Thought in Renaissance England*, pp. 54–55, says, "When . . . Arabian observers found that Ptolemy's figure for the rate of precession was too small, this oscillatory motion was combined with the theory of uniform precession, and the idea of variable precession, or trepidation, obtained a foothold among astronomers. To represent this imaginary phenomenon of trepidation the Arabs added a tenth sphere to the system. This extra sphere accounted for the progressive motion of the equinoxes around the heavens, while the sphere of the fixed stars had its poles moving about small circles located on the surface of the ninth sphere, thereby producing the supposed periodic inequality of precession."

[106] Cicero *De divinatione* II. 46.

part. Hence, since the observations of the Chaldeans it has run through a whole sign and much more. The Pleiades, which in those times composed the head of Taurus, now are in the Twins. The star of Regulus, which then was in Cancer, now has passed the twentieth part of Leo. But what is common to Aries and Pisces, Leo and Virgo, Taurus and the Gemini? What is common to fire and water? Yet fiery stars have passed over into a watery sign. If we invent a ninth circle, which is needed, there would be no star in it. This doctrine of triplicities, therefore, can in no way stand.

But let us investigate the examples of Ptolemy. What is more absurd and more unworthy of a great man (if indeed he is the author of this book) than to call the Phoenicians and the Chaldeans simple, humane, and observers of the stars, because they were under the sway of Leo and the sun? Yet the same man subjected Babylon, Assyria, and Mesopotamia to Virgo and Mercury, and therefore he confessed that the Chaldeans were lovers of the sciences. Moreover, he called the Jews, the Syrians, and the Idumaeans bold and impious, because they were subservient to Aries, Scorpion, and Mars. By unanimous agreement of all historians the Syrians are tractable to the point of servility; the Jews seem born for religion. Nothing can be more pliant than the Idumaeans (except the mountaineers), a consideration which Cicero cast at the ashes of Pompey. "He thought," said he, "that he had to do with the Syrians and the king of the Nabathians." These theories belong to ideas of relation, since Syrians and Idumaeans are northerly in respect to the Egyptians, such as Ptolemy. Some of them are even mountaineers. Yet Cardan, the commentator of this book, because he knew that the constellations had changed their places from the age of Ptolemy to the present, ridiculously reported that the Spanish, the Britons, and the Normans had become rapacious and cunning and thought that they were now subject to the heart of Scorpion, although he wrote that once, when they were under the sway of Sagittarius, they were loyal and true. I answer him what Appian wrote about Cassius. When the army of the Romans was decimated by the arrows of the Parthians and Cassius tried to save the remainder, who were fleeing to him, a Chaldean warned him that he might delay a little while until the moon should reach Sagittarius and Scorpion should have set; then said he, "I fear the Archer more than the Scorpion." [107] So also the arrows of the Britons and the Normans,

[107] Plutarch *Lives*, "Crassus," paragraph 29. The work which Bodin quotes is a forgery.

not the scorpions, harmed us, when they invaded almost all France, devastated by civil wars, and slew our army with their darts.

If, then, these teachings of Cardan should be seriously accepted, it would be necessary to reverse and to defy the actual nature of things. Then the region of the north must be turned into the south, and instead of daring Germans, mild Egyptians must be born; Africans must be born warlike, instead of timid men. But if Cardan thought that the stars have altered their influence because the positions of the constellations have been changed, what should be done to Ptolemy, whose decisions about the stars he so greatly admired? What to Cardan himself, who elsewhere always confirmed the pronouncements of the ancients by his own authority? Moreover, to bring forward one example from many, Sleidan wrote in *The Ecclesiastical History* that Emperor Charles V was made emperor in the same calends in which he was born, captured Francis, king of the French, and triumphed over Germany. Yet he had in his horoscope the constellation of Capricorn, as Cardan confessed. Under this sign Augustus was born, who on that account struck a coin with the fortunate constellation Capricorn. Horace referred to this when he called Capricorn the tyrant of the west. In this passage all interpreters have erred. Cardan wrote that under this same star were born Charles of Bourbon, Cosimo de' Medici, and Selim, prince of the Turks, who on the seventh day before the calends of September, in the same month in which Augustus conquered M. Antony, that is, in August, defeated King Ishmael of the Persians in the Calderan fields. Two years later, in the same calends, he drove Sultan Gampso from his empire. Now it is indeed evident that from the time of Augustus to that of Selim and Charles V all the constellations had changed their places, having passed through seventeen degrees. Yet Capricorn has retained the same strength, for Augustus, Charles V, and Cosimo de' Medici attained supremacy in their nineteenth year. Who, therefore, thinks that the strength of the celestial bodies and the habits of the peoples are controlled by the system of triplicities, inasmuch as their nature is not altered even when the stars have been altered?

Although we have already made this plain, it will be still plainer and better understood, if the greatest conjunctions of the planets (I omit the inferior) are compared from the time of Ptolemy, or even from Caesar, with historical events. Nothing is better known in history than the disturbances of wars. As for the fact that they say that Mars dominates

Scorpion, the superior planets came together in that constellation when civil wars between Pompey and Caesar blazed over all the world; but the change of empire and commonwealth took place in Europe, which Ptolemy had placed beneath the control of Aries, Leo, and Sagittarius, while Africa was under Scorpion, Pisces, and Cancer. The same conjunction in Scorpion occurred in the year 630, when the Arabs launched forth from the deserts of Asia, conquered almost the entire world with their armies, brought new laws, overthrew religions, and destroyed the empire of the Persians. Afterwards they caused the disappearance of the Greek, the Latin, and the Persian languages in Asia and Africa. This revolution, moreover, took place in southern Asia, which Ptolemy thought was subject to Taurus, Virgo, and Capricorn. The same conjunction happened in the year 1484 [*sic*] when suddenly Italy, which had lain quiet in a long peace, was overwhelmed first by its own armies, then by those of the French and the Spanish. This calamity of wars spread to the Western Isles and the New World. But then an unheard-of plague of illness, brought by the Spanish, commenced to devastate all Europe. So, the greatest alterations concerning Africa actually occurred in Europe and in America.

Again, in A.D. 73, the same planets met in Sagittarius, when Otho, Galba, Vitellius, and Vespasian harassed the Roman Empire. Yet there were nowhere more serious wars than in Palestine or greater slaughter than of the Jews, whom Ptolemy placed beneath Scorpion. When in A.D. 430 the planets met in Aquarius, suddenly the legions of the Goths, pouring into Europe from the extreme northern region, overwhelmed the Roman Empire. Eastern Asia lay quiet, although Ptolemy had bound it to Aquarius. Again, in the same constellation of Aquarius, in the year 1373, they came together. At this time Germany was shaken by a great earthquake; Apulia by war; and a cursed pestilence started to move from east to west and to harass all Europe. Europe, however, had nothing in common with Aquarius, as these very men maintained. This same meeting of the planets occurs in the year 312, in the constellation of Capricorn, which they give to southern Asia. There ensued the wholesale slaughter of three emperors and their Roman legions, when the Emperor Constantine seized the empire by force of arms against the wish of the Senate and the Roman people. He overthrew the laws of the whole Roman Empire and the state in a short while, yet all this occurred in Europe, which, if we believe Ptolemy, is not affected by Capricorn or by the Pisces. In this sign, however, a great conjunction took

place in A.D. 1464; at this time tyrannies and civil wars spread throughout all Europe. Edward III [*sic*] killed Henry, king of England.
Zadamachus, prince of the Tartars, driven from his kingdom by his
people, fled to the Lithuanians. A conspiracy was formed in the Pru-
tenic [108] cities; Emperor Frederick was besieged by his own people in
Vienna; Louis XI, king of France, was gravely threatened by a conspiracy of princes; there were great uprisings in Florence; the towns of
Saxony waged war with the dukes of Brunswick; Scanderbeg, the duke
of Albania, broke away from the Turks and defeated them with great
slaughter. Yet I see nothing happening in Africa. In the same sign
[Pisces] a conjunction occurred in the year 1524, when France was troubled with civil wars and all Germany was terribly shaken by the clashing arms of nobles and plebs. The king of the French himself was captured at Pavia, and a little later Rome was taken by the Spanish, Rhodes
by the Turks. Then came great floods of water, by which they predicted
the world would be submerged. Yet I have not heard that anything
happened in Africa. But it would be endless to follow all instances.

Although these great crossings signify a change in affairs and various
warlike movements, yet, since it is not known to anybody's observation
or by science perceived what fixed signs do affect each region more, nothing certain can be decided about a matter of this sort from the principles
[of the authors mentioned?] although I do not doubt that by long-continued observation a more certain system could be established, if anyone
should wish to collect the histories of earlier times and the conjunctions
by going back to the beginning. For instance, it can be understood from
Polybius that in the 140th Olympiad a definite change of all things took
place. In that period the younger Philip succeeded to the rule of Macedonia; Antiochus, of Asia Minor; Ptolemy Philopator, of Egypt; Hannibal, of the Carthaginians; Antiochus, of Syria; Lycurgus the Younger,
of the Spartans. Very serious wars took place then between the Romans
and the Carthaginians, Antiochus and Ptolemy, the Achaeans and Philip
against the Spartans and Aetolians. Likewise in Diodorus and Justin we
shall read that servile wars occurred in those same times in Sicily,
Greece, and Asia. Spartacus, a robber, invaded Italy with an army of
runaways at the same time that pirates seized control of the Mediterranean Sea. Again, when Mohammed had promised liberty to serfs, the
Christians also gave freedom to theirs, so that a little later almost no
vestige of serfdom remained. On the other hand, tyrannies infested the

[108] The Prussian Union of 1454?

whole earth at almost the same time, when Mohammed the Great defeated two emperors and four kings. Louis XI, king of the French, first of all drove his subjects into servitude. Christian imposed upon the Swedes a wretched tyranny; Zadamachus, upon the Tartars; Edward III, when the king had been killed, upon the English; Circassian Mamelukes, upon the Egyptians; Ussumcassan, the Persians; Pandolfo, the people of Sienna; Francis Valori, the Florentines; Ludovico Sforza, the Milanese; John Bentivoglio, the Bolognese; Baglioni, the Perugians.

It remains for us to form an opinion about letters and disciplines also. At one and the same time there lived a great number of learned men. Then, when the memory of letters had become almost extinct, once again others brought it back to the light of day. Plato, Aristotle, Xenocrates, Timaeus, Archytas, Isocrates, and an infinite number of orators and poets flourished at the same time. After a long interval Chrysippus, Carneades, Diogenes the Stoic, and Arcecilas appeared. Again, Varro, Cicero, Livy, and Sallust were contemporaries; then Virgil, Horace, Ovid, and Vitruvius grew famous. And not long ago, Valla, Trapezuntius, Ficino, Gaza, Bessarion, and Mirandola flourished contemporaneously. If anyone, then, having collected passages of memorable affairs, should compare with them these great trajections and ascertain the regions affected or the states changed, he will achieve fuller knowledge about the customs and the nature of peoples; then, also, he will make much more effective and reliable judgments about every kind of history.

CHAPTER VI

THE TYPE OF GOVERNMENT
IN STATES

SINCE HISTORY for the most part deals with the state and with the changes taking place within it, to achieve an understanding of the subject we must explain briefly the origins, developed form, and ends of principalities, especially since there is nothing more fruitful and beneficial in all history. Other things, indeed, seem very valuable for a knowledge of the nature of the soul and really admirable for shaping the morals of each man, but the things gathered from the reading of historians about the beginnings of cities, their growth, matured form, decline, and fall are so very necessary, not only to individuals but to everyone, that Aristotle thought nothing was more effective in establishing and maintaining societies of men than to be informed in the science of governing a state. Yet, about this matter the opinions of great men are so varied and divergent that it is noteworthy that in so many centuries no one until now has explained what is the best kind of state.

Since Plato thought that no science of managing a state is so difficult to understand that no one could grasp it, he advocated this method of formulating laws and establishing the government on a firm foundation; if sage men, having collected all the customs and all the laws of all countries, should compare them, they might compound from them the best kind of state.[1] Aristotle seems to have followed this plan as far as he could, yet he did not carry it out. Following Aristotle, Polybius, Dionysius of Halicarnassus, Plutarch, Dio, and Tacitus (I omit those whose writings have perished) left many excellent and important ideas about the state scattered throughout their books.

Machiavelli also wrote many things about government—the first, I think, for about 1,200 years after barbarism had overwhelmed everything. [His sayings] are on the lips of everyone, and there is no doubt but that he would have written more fully and more effectively and with a greater regard for truth, if he had combined a knowledge of the writings of ancient philosophers and historians with experience. Jovius reports that he lacked this qualification, and the work speaks for itself. Following

[1] Plato *Laws* III. 681 D.

him, Patrizzi,[2] Robert Breton,[3] and Garimberto[4] composed serious and lengthy treatises about developing customs, curbing the people, educating a prince, and founding laws, but made only slight reference to the development of the state. There is nothing about changes of government, and they do not even touch upon those things which Aristotle called the devices or secrets of princes, and Tacitus, the secrets of empire. Others place before the eyes as though historical some ideal types of government, with no underlying system. I except Contarini,[5] who not only held up for admiration the type of the Venetian Republic, which he himself thought was most excellent, but even proposed it for imitation. These men are almost the only ones whose writings we have about the state. Even if they had written as accurately on this subject as they ought, I should nevertheless in this short *Method* have considered it necessary to devote attention to the matter. How much more so if the treatment of many writers is so inadequate!

On that account it seemed to me useful, for this *Method* which I am planning, to study the disputations of the philosophers and historians about the state and to compare the empires of our ancestors with our own. When all have been duly noted, the general history of principalities may be more plainly understood. We shall carry away from the discussion this benefit, that we may easily understand what laws are needed in a monarchy, and likewise what are necessary in a popular and in an aristocratic state (for of these laws there are as many varieties as of the government).

But lest in disputation more importance is attached to weight of authority than to cogency of reasoning, we must refute, with necessary proofs, the definitions of Aristotle about the citizen, the city, the state, the supreme authority, and the magistrate, which are the fundamentals of this discussion. Then we shall explain our opinion about each point and reject the rooted error about the mixed state. We shall speak in its turn about the three types of rule, later about the changes in empires, and finally about the best form of government.

WHAT IS A CITIZEN?

Aristotle defined a citizen as one who may share in the administration of justice, may hold office, or act in a deliberative capacity.[6] This defini-

---

[2] Francesco Patrizzi, 1529–1597, was the author of *Dieci dialoghi della historia* and *Discussionum peripateticorum libri xv.*

[3] Robert Breton wrote *De optimo statu reipublicae liber,* Paris, 1543.

[4] Jerome Garimberto, bishop of Gallese, wrote *De' regimenti publici de la città* and *Fatti memorabili d'alcuni Papi.*

[5] Gaspar Contarini, 1483–1542, cardinal and diplomat, was conciliatory to reform. He wrote *De magistratibus et republica Venetorum.*

[6] Aristotle *Politics* III. 1. 1275a 23 and 1275b 19.

tion, he confessed, is suited to a popular rule only. But since a definition ought to deal with universals, no one will be a citizen according to the idea of Aristotle, unless born at Athens and in the time of Pericles. The others will be exiles or strangers in their own cities, debarred from honors, judicial matters, and public counsels. What, then, is to be done in the case of Emperor Antonine, who in a proclamation ordered that all free men included within the limits of the Roman monarchy should be Roman citizens? If we are to believe Aristotle, they were aliens because they had been denied popular rights. Since these opinions are absurd and dangerous for governments, then the conclusions which follow from them must seem absurd also. This definition of Aristotle caused Contarini, Sigonius, Garimberto and many others to err. There is no doubt that in many countries it offered an excellent pretext for civil war. But what if this description of a citizen brought forward by Aristotle were not suited even to a popular state? At Athens, where the rule is reputed to have been most democratic of all, a fourth class, the weakest and the poorest, that is, by far the largest part of the population, according to the law of Solon had been kept away from honors, from the senate, and from the sortition of office, as Plutarch wrote.

The same man defined a magistrate as one who has power, jurisdiction, and the deliberative capacity.[7] From this he intimated that the man who has actually rendered those services, which a citizen is eligible to give, is called a magistrate, whereas a citizen is such only by qualification and capacity. But, not to argue too subtly, who then in the state could be called a magistrate by this system, when so few officials are admitted to the council? Almost everywhere the senate of the nation lacks sovereignty and jurisdiction, and those things which it decrees will not take effect before they are ratified by the people or the optimates or the prince, as we shall make clear later. But why discuss the matter, when Aristotle himself in his last book listed many kinds of magistrates who have neither power nor jurisdiction nor any right of sharing counsel? Indeed, when he called a state the aggregation of magistrates and the citizen body, he clearly made the citizenry earlier in time than the state, so that the citizenry would be a group of men without officials or powers, whereas the government would be the aggregate of citizens and magistrates. But if many come together in one place without laws and controls, if no one protects public interests, which are practically nonexistent, but each one his private affairs, if there are no punishments decreed for the wicked, no rewards for the good, wherein lies the resemblance to a city? Under such

[7] *Ibid.* IV. 15. 1299a 25.

conditions this collected multitude ought not to be called a city-state, but anarchy, or by any other name than that of *civitas*, since men of this kind are without a country, and as Homer said, without law.[8]

Indeed, he never defined the supreme authority, which he himself called the supreme government and the supreme power,[9] in which consists the majesty and the determining condition of the Republic. Unless we are to think that he meant to do this when he specified [10] three functions of government and no more: one taking counsel; another, appointing officials; the last, giving justice. But that power which is called the highest ought to be of such a sort that it is attributed to no magistrate; otherwise, it is not the highest (unless the people, or the prince, divests itself entirely of control). Moreover, the man to whom sovereignty is given, unless it is given temporarily, will no longer be an official, but a prince. As a matter of fact the right of deliberation about the state is conceded even to private citizens, and the administration of justice to the humblest man. These, then, do not pertain to sovereignty.[11] So there is no one of these three in which the highest majesty of power can be reflected, except in the creation of magistrates, which belongs to the prince alone or to the people or to the optimates, according to the type of each state. It is much more typical of the supreme power to decree and to annul laws, to make war and peace, to have the final right of appeal and, finally, the power of life [and death] and of rewards. But if we grant that Aristotle did not wish to signify sovereignty, but merely the administration of the state, we must also admit that he never defined sovereignty or the type of rule at all, since the form of government is determined by the location of sovereignty, while the actual governance of the state, which extends far and wide, perhaps will be defined more briefly and concisely in decisions, orders, and execution. There is no fourth thing, and in these three all functions of the state, military and civil offices, and honors are comprised.[12] For instance, the senate decides upon war, the prince proclaims it, the soldiers carry it out. In trials, private justices and arbitrators also make decisions, the officials give orders, the public servants carry them out. These things are often done by one and the same man. Then, since magistrates decree and proclaim edicts, those proclamations, which the Latins called "orders" and "commands," cannot indicate the supreme

---

[8] Homer *Odyssey* IX. 106.   [9] Aristotle *op. cit.* III. 6. 1278b 11–13.

[10] *Ibid.* IV. 14. 1297b 41.

[11] "Summum imperium" has been translated as sovereignty. See the section of this chapter headed "What Is Sovereignty."

[12] Cicero *De Amicitia* XVII. 63.

government, much less the decisions or executions in which the administration of justice consists.

This being the case, let us seek more definite principles, if only we can do this—principles better established than those which have been suggested hitherto. So I hold that the family or fraternity is the true image of the state, and since the family cannot come into existence in the solitude of one man, so the state cannot develop in one family or in one guild. But if more than one should come together under the same roof, and one did not command or the other obey, or one command all (or a few, the separate individuals, or the whole group, the separate individuals), the family or fraternity could not stand together, because it is held together only by domestic rule. On the other hand, if several are held together by private authority or domestic rule of the same person—for example, a man, his wife, children, and serfs, or several colleagues—they make a family or a guild. Only, there should be three persons in a guild, as Neratius [13] would have it in the passage "Neratius" under the title "About the meaning of terms." [14] In a family three persons with the mother should be subjected to the rule of the father of the family, as Ulpian defined it in the passage "Renunciation," under the title "About the meaning of terms," [15] if we combine his words with the discourse of Apuleius. The latter wrote that fifteen persons constitute a populace [16] —that is, five fraternities or three families, for a family includes five persons, a fraternity three. Then three or more families or five or more fraternities form a state, if they are joined together at a given moment by the legitimate power of authority. If, on the other hand, families or colleges are separated from each other and cannot be controlled by any common rule, the group should be called an anarchy, not a state.

It is of no importance whether the families come together in the same place or live in separate homes and areas. It is said to be no other than the same family even if the father lives apart from children and serfs, or these in their turn apart from each other by an interval of space, provided that they are joined together by the legitimate and limited rule of the father. I have said "limited," since this fact chiefly distinguishes the family from the state—that the latter has the final and public authority,

---

[13] Neratius Priscus lived under Trajan and Hadrian. He was an eminent jurist, whose decisions are freely quoted in the *Digest*.

[14] The Latin reads *Neratius de significatione verborum*, referring to *Dig.* 50. 16. 85.

[15] *Detestatio de significatione verborum*, referring to *Dig.* 50. 16. 40.

[16] Apuleius was born in Africa about 125 A.D. The reference may be found in *De Magia* chapter 47.

the former limited and private rule. So, also, it is still the same government, made up of many families, even if the territories and the settlements are far apart, provided only that they are in the guardianship of the same sovereign power: either one rules all; or all, the individuals; or a few, all. From this it comes about that the state is nothing else than a group of families or fraternities subjected to one and the same rule.

A citizen is one who enjoys the common liberty and the protection of authority. Cicero's definition of the state as a group of men associated for the sake of living well [17] indicates the best objective, indeed, but not the power and the nature of the institution. This definition applies equally well to the assemblies of the Pythagoreans and of men who also come together for the sake of living well, yet they cannot be called states without great confusion of state and association. Furthermore, there are families of villains, no less than of good men, since a villain is no less a man than a good man is. A similar observation must be made about the governments. Who doubts but that every very great empire was established through violence by robbers? The definition of a state offered by us applies to villages, towns, cities, and principalities, however scattered their lands may be, provided that they are controlled by the same authority. The concept is not conditioned by the limited size of the region or by its great expanse, as the elephant is no more an animal than the ant, since each has the power of movement and perception. So Ragusa or Geneva, whose rule is comprised almost within its walls, ought to be called a state no less than the empire of the Tartars, which was bounded by the same limits as the course of the sun.[18]

What Aristotle said is absurd—that too great a group of men, such as Babylon was, is a race, not a state. But there is no empire common to races, nor any one law; moreover, Babylon was not only controlled by the same authority, officials, and laws but also circumscribed within the same walls. What, then, is a state if not this? The definition of the word which Cicero gave elsewhere seems furthermore rather obscure—the union of several associations under an approved law for a common advantage.[19] If we accept this, then it will not be enough that citizens acknowledge the same authority unless at the same time they are bound by the same laws. But it would be absurd to say that the empire of the Turks, which includes peoples living together under no common system

[17] Cicero *Republic* I. 4.

[18] "An empire upon which the sun never sets"?

[19] Bodin used *coetum multitudinis societatum*, but Cicero *Republic* I. 25 and VI. 13, used *sociatus* and *sociati*, respectively.

of law, is not a state, since all are kept together by the same officials and authority. It will have to be either a government or an anarchy; it is not the latter, therefore the former.

From this it follows that a state is defined by one and the same rule; a city-state, by government and law, but it is a town when it encompasses its citizens not only by government and laws but also within its very walls. So a town includes villages; a city-state, the countryside, sometimes also cities and walled towns joined only by common law; principalities, or, more suitably, hereditary lands include several city-states; finally the state, like a class, includes all these variations. Thus Caesar said, "The entire Helvetian *civitas* is divided into four cantons." Cicero reported that the Tusculan municipality was comprised within the Roman *civitas*. Bartolus [20] differed, since in the passage "the name town" under the title "Concerning the meaning of matters and terms," [21] he limited a city-state by its walls. Under the heading municipal law [22] he called a *municeps* a kind of citizen, without advancing any reason or authority. Yet Censorinus, in Appian's "Libyan War," answered the ambassadors of the Carthaginians that he would indeed destroy the town of Carthage, but that he would spare the city-state and the citizens enjoying its laws,[23] as the Romans had promised: the city-state itself did not consist of walls or land.

Then, since the association of those who belong to the same village is closer than that of the town, so is propinquity closer for those who are of the same town than for those of the city-state, because not only government, justice, laws, and institutions are common to the citizens but also the very town, its protection, market place, temples, halls, streets, amphitheaters, sacrifices, and many friendships and interests. So that after the Roman Republic had developed from an initial three thousand Albans in one narrow valley, it first took into the same city-state Antemnates, Camerinians, Crustiminians, and Sabines; afterwards it received the conquered Albans, some within the same city-state, the rest within the municipal fields and town walls. Moreover, when they had defeated in war Tusculanians, Aequians, Volsci, and Hernicians, they did not admit them into the town or the Roman plain, for lack of room, but still they received them into the state, and while they allowed them to keep their

---

[20] Bartolus, 1314–1357, a prominent jurist of the school known as post-glossators. He wrote commentaries on the *Corpus Iuris Civilis*. See Introduction, page 1.

[21] *Appellatio urbis de significatione rerum et verborum*, or *Dig.* 50. 16. 2.

[22] *Dig.* 50. 1. is headed *Ad municipalem et de incolis*.

[23] Appian *Roman History*, "Punic Wars" XII. 81.

own laws, permitted them to accept the honors of office. These men were citizens under the same name as the others, burgesses in their own right, but the inhabitants of the Roman fields, whose status was higher, were more accurately called Quirites.

Hence the well-known remark of M. Scaurus to the uncle of Cicero, who preferred to live at Arpinum rather than at Rome: "M. Cicero, would that you had chosen to live in the greatest state with the same courage and valor as in the municipality." His nephew the orator not only acquired a residence in the city but even a home worth 50,000 gold crowns. Nevertheless he was still called a *novus homo* and "a foreigner" by his adversaries. He was, indeed, a new man, because first in his family he had attained honors. His son was *nobilis*,[24] since he had a father who was *novus*. The latter was scornfully called "a foreigner," because he had been born at Arpinum, not in the Roman countryside.

From this it happened that citizens were given different names by the Latins, and urban citizens got better terms than citizens of the colonies; for although they had the same laws, customs, and privileges, yet they did not inhabit the same fields or the town which had the prestige of authority and granted exemptions. But the municipalities themselves were at one time on a lower status than the colonies, on account of the importance of race and of Roman blood. As a special grace the legal rights of colonies were given to municipalities up to the time of Tiberius, when they voluntarily repudiated these rights and preferred to use their own laws and customs rather than the Roman, as Gellius reported. So in truth they were citizens of the same state, yet not of the same city; in this sense, then, we ought to interpret the Julian Law, whereby the Romans in the Social War extended citizenship to all allies. Not that they were not citizens before, since they were all controlled by the same government, but that they were denied the seeking of honors. Afterwards this right was extended gradually to all Italians. Then the colonies which Ulpian treated in the chapter on taxation received the rights of the Italians. The remaining population was in part tributary, as Pliny listed them, although at intervals some concession might be made to some group. Another group was free, maintaining the dignity of its own government, as among us Albii, Meldi, Bituriges, Santones, Tarbelli, Arverni, Nervii, Verunni, and Ulbanectectes;[25] among the Greeks, Atheni-

---

[24] Those families, whether patrician or plebeian, whose members had held curule office were *nobiles*. If a man outside of these families became a curule official, he was called a *novus homo*.

[25] The edition of 1566 gives *Ulbanectes*.

ans, Spartans, Thessalonians, and afterwards even all Achaea, by grace of Nero. Still another part was free and federated, enjoying the honorary right of citizenship, as Massillians, Aeduans, Rhemi, and Carnutani, yet they were not really citizens, since they were not living under Roman authority, although of course they enjoyed the unhampered right of freedom and exemption. "To the Achaeans," said Seneca, "to the Rhodians, and to many famous towns Rome restored their laws intact and their liberty, with immunity, yet that same city paid tribute to the eunuchs of M. Antony." [26] Pliny, Book x, epistola vi, asked citizenship of both Alexandria and Rome for his Egyptian friend. Then Livy, Book xxiv, wrote "colonists were drawn off to Puteoli, Salerno, and Buxentum." [27] When they claimed citizenship, they were adjudged by the senate not to be citizens. This decision was based on the right of suffrage and of seeking honors, than which nothing more valuable or more significant can be given to a citizen. It did not mean precisely that they were not citizens, otherwise it must be confessed that they would have been foreigners. Even Boethius [28] reported that according to Cicero, Roman citizens suffered a moderate lowering of status when they were led into Latin colonies and lost their citizenship in these particulars—the right of suffrage, residence, sacred rites, and membership in a tribe. However, the municipals and colonials obtained the right of holding honors, offices, class distinctions, legal obligations, domain, formal ownership, wills, and intermarriage, but some groups gained more than others. If all were to enjoy the same rights, however, no one would be regarded as a citizen except a man born a freeman at Rome, and throughout in Livy and in other writers men are called citizens who enjoyed the right of Quirites, which was less than the Roman: or who enjoyed municipal rights, or the rights of Latium, or the rights of the Latin colonies, which were inferior to that of the Roman colonies; or the Italian rights, which likewise were of two types, in Italy and the provinces, as is plain in the heading "About the census." [29]

But if the title "citizen" is valid for all, the definition is false which measures all citizens by honors, suffrage, counsel, juridical decisions, and exemption from tribute, especially when the Julian Law about the citizen-

[26] Seneca *De beneficiis* v. xvi. 6. This is paraphrased. The passage in the original reads *ut . . . penderet,* whereas Bodin ignores the purpose clause and quotes an indicative.

[27] *Livy* xxxiv. xlv. The edition of the *Methodus* of 1583 skips a line in the quotation, from Puteoli to Salerno.

[28] Boethius wrote on the *Topica* of Cicero.

[29] *De censibus* refers to *Dig.* 50. 15.

ship gave that status to all allies. In addition, the law of Antoninus Pius about the status of individuals was conceived in these words: "Those who are in the Roman world, let them be Roman citizens." Not only to the allies but also to all the provinces he granted citizenship; yet he did not equate the provincials to the Italians or the prefectures of Italy to the *municipia*, or the Italian *municipia* to the Latin, or the Latin *municipia* to the Latin colonies, or the Latin colonies to the Roman colonies, or the Roman colonies to the Quirites, or the Quirites to the Romans, as many falsely think. Why, otherwise, would the jurisconsults interpret so painstakingly the Roman rights, the Italian, and the municipal? Scaevola, Papinian, Paul, Hermogenian, Marcellus, and Modestinus [30] flourished later than Antoninus Pius, who promulgated this law; Panvinio was mistaken in thinking that it was decreed by Antoninus Caracalla, as *Authentics* lxxviii [31] makes plain. Furthermore, what Dio wrote would be false—that Severus allowed Alexandrians to become senators. Why, then, someone will say, was citizenship granted by the Julian Law to the allies, if they already enjoyed liberty and the protection of authority? Why in order to attain citizenship did they wage wars for so long? The reason is, of course, that they might seek honors and vote in the assemblies. This they called the highest right of Roman citizenship. To some it was permitted to seek honors, yet not to vote; to others neither, although they enjoyed the private law of the Romans, which still others lacked, even though they were free from tribute. Different rights of different groups are explained by the jurisconsults. It would take too long to recount them.

But by the law of Antoninus all those of Roman race, even provincials, attained *nobilitas*,[32] for thus Justinian wrote, so that afterwards officials had the same jurisdiction over them, while formerly a citizen's free appeal took away cognizance from the governor. When St. Paul, whose father had bought the right of citizenship, appealed to the emperor in a capital case, then Felix, governor of Syria, said, "This man could have been acquitted if he had not appealed to Caesar." [33] Pliny the Younger, writing to Trajan about the Christians, reported: "Those who were citizens I have designated to be sent to the city." [34] Not only in the Roman Republic, but everywhere else we shall find this difference in citizens. At

[30] Roman jurists ranging from the time of Antoninus Pius to Alexander Severus.

[31] A collection of the constitutions of Justinian, issued A.D. 554 in part, and subdivided by the later Glossators into 9 collations and 98 titles.

[32] See note 18.   [33] Acts 26:32, "Agrippa says unto Festus . . ."

[34] Pliny *Letters* X. 96. *Qui* should read *quia*.

Rome within the same walls there were patricians, knights, and plebs; among the ancient Egyptians, priests, soldiers, and workmen, as Diodorus wrote; among our ancestors, Druids, knights, and farmers; today, clergy, nobles, and plebs; among the Venetians, nobles, citizens, and plebs; formerly among the Florentines, nobles, people, and plebs, and three classes of the people—the more powerful, the ordinary, and the lowest. Plato also provided for guardians, soldiers, and farmers. Everywhere each group in turn was divided from the other by rights, laws, offices, votes, honors, privileges, status, exemption, or by some other means. Yet all are citizens of the republic, like the members of the same body. Rightly St. Paul said, "Will the foot say, I am not the eye, therefore I am not of the body?"

Then, of course, it ought to seem absurd, with due respect to Aristotle, that citizens of this kind should be partly citizens, partly foreigners.[35] The definition of the thing and its name ought to agree. But what Cicero said is more obscure—that no one could be citizen both of his own state and of the Roman state, yet among the Greeks it was permitted.[36] I should think that all had the same system, and the saying of Cicero about citizens of two states concerns honorary citizens. For in his speech in behalf of Cornelius Balbus he said, "Many Roman citizens of former days, unsentenced and safe, left their possessions of their own volition and betook themselves into other cities."[37] And a little later, "Oh excellent laws, lest any one of us could be of more than one citizenship: lest anyone unwillingly should be deprived of citizenship or should remain unwillingly in the citizenship."[38] Hermogenian interpreted this in the passage *municipes*, under "municipal law," in the sense that he must be an actual citizen of one city-state, honorary of the second.[39] Otherwise it must be confessed that the same citizen would be bound at one and the same time to diverse rules and orders, which would be absurd. For what would be done if one commanded, the other forbade? What Ulpian reported, then, under "municipal law"—that a freedman can become a citizen of two governments—is interpreted in this way also. Moreover, in case one state is under the control of another, as when prefectures, colonies, marketplaces, exchanges, *municipia*, and provinces were once held under Roman sway, then every man had to obey the decrees of his fellow citizens, while safeguarding the majesty of the Roman Empire. In the

---

[35] Aristotle *Politics* III. 1. 1275a.   [36] Cicero *Pro Balbo* XII. 29–30.
[37] *Ibid*. XII. 28.   [38] *Ibid*. XII. 31.   [39] *Dig*. 50. 1. 16.

same way, brethren are bound by the statutes of the fraternity, saving the dignity of the state, according to the ancient law of Solon, which is at the end of the title "About fraternities." [40]

Moreover, I see that what was permitted to the Romans has likewise been permitted to all peoples, that when they have renounced their own citizenship, they may without crime take another, provided they are accepted. I except the English, who dare not go away from the country without permission, as I learned from the Earl of Rutland himself, famed not only for the splendor of his race and his riches, but also for valor. To be made a beneficiary or vassal, it is necessary that a man shall be born in this status, or if he wishes to give his homage to another, the consent of the superior and that of the inferior are then needed. So, also, in being made citizen it is enough that he should accept the rule of the man in whose territory he was born (he agrees if he does not openly dissent), or if he would betake himself elsewhere, he must subject himself to the rule of the other and be accepted before he is called a citizen. If this has been accomplished, however, he cannot go back, by virtue of the law of return, since he has been made a foreign subject and a stranger to his state, as I remember was decided in the court of the Parisians. Therefore, in the case of Mancinus,[41] who had been given to the enemy, but had been repulsed by them, judgment was rendered that he had not ceased to be a citizen, although a tribune of the people had ordered that he should be led forth from the senate as a foreigner.

Then we shall distinguish foreigners from citizens chiefly by the criterion that the latter either acquiesce in the authority of the fatherland or subject themselves to an alien rule and are accepted, but the former do not acknowledge the rule of the place of origin and have not submitted to others, or when they have surrendered, have been rejected. The rest are allies or enemies or neutrals. Appian wrote that he had seen messengers of many races come to Rome to surrender themselves and their possessions to the power of the Romans; yet they were refused by the latter. Although justice is granted equally to foreigners and to citizens, on account of the bond of reason which exists among men, and though many things are shared freely, such as residence in the city, religious rites, the market place, the roads, and the theater, nevertheless, there is no authority over these people unless they bind themselves by crime or conspiracy. They cannot be forced to perform duties except in the place where

[40] This sentence does not appear in the edition of 1566. *Ult. de collegiis* is Dig. 47. 22. 4.
[41] Hostilius Mancinus, commander against the Numantians 137 B.C.

they establish the site of their fortunes, as the jurisconsults report. The Venetians demand that a stranger shall inhabit the town for fourteen years before he is made a citizen, nor does he even then partake of honors, but he enjoys the company of his fellows and the protection of authority. Moreover, the fact that men who acknowledge the authority of the place of origin are citizens, even if they are born of foreign parents, becomes plain from all the customs and the institutions of all tribes. The Germans grant even more, since they admit them to honors, unlike the Venetians, the ancient Romans, and the Athenians, who did not unless they were born of citizen parents, as Plutarch reported in his life of Pericles. The latter promulgated a law: "Only those born of two Athenians are Athenians." In the pages of Livy, where he discussed those who were born of Roman citizens and Spanish women he said, "Among us, he who is born of foreign parents is a citizen with equal rights as though born of citizens; and he can enjoy freely the property of his foreign parents," which is appropriated by the treasury not only by our laws but also by those of the Britons and the Turks, unless there are legitimate children in France itself. It is of great weight and importance that by the law of all nations foreigners can be expelled when war is threatening, while citizens are demanded from illegal captors by due process of law.

The kings of the Abyssinians and the Muscovites, however, are said to hold foreigners against their will, contrary to the law of nations, and to assist them liberally. But these things we have discussed more at length in the book *De decretis*.

From this it becomes plain that the definition of "citizen" brought forward by Aristotle and approved by Contarini, Sigonius, Garimberto, and Soderinus [42] can in no way stand. But that all ambiguity may be removed, we may ask whether governments federated among themselves can create one and the same state; for example, the city-states of the Swiss and the towns of the Baltic. This often seemed the case to Leander Mutius [43] and to many others, indeed, because the Swiss are allied together in the closest union, have furthermore the same assemblies, a town in Baden,[44] and many places common to them all where they send common officials. But to have exchange of goods, sanctity of contract, rights of intermarriage and of mutual entertainment, finally a firm bond of friendship does

---

[42] Francesco Soderinus, 1453–1524, a Florentine who became bishop of Verona.

[43] Huldreich Mutius, a professor at the University of Basel in 1539. He wrote a chronicle of the German people from the earliest times to his own.

[44] Vivien de St. Martin, *Nouveau dictionnaire de géographie*, gives this as a town in Switzerland in the canton of Aargau on the Limmat, and an important medieval fortress.

not create one and the same republic, otherwise the kingdom of the French and that of the Spanish, who have these things in common, would be the same. This is not the case, even if they use the same laws, as once upon a time the Romans and the Greeks did, after the Romans had accepted the laws of the Greeks. Finally, it is not true even if they had so close a union among themselves that they attacked the same enemies and welcomed the same friends, as often happens among princes of the greatest loyalty and sympathetic understanding.

There remains, then, this common control and centralization of power to which I referred. Thirteen Swiss city-states, three of the Rhetians, and seventy of the Baltic area sealed a lawful alliance to the effect that they would not injure each other and that in their common peril they would fight their sworn foes with mutual aid. But there is no common authority and no union. The seven Amphictyonic cities used no other type of alliance, nor the three Aetolian, nor the twelve Ionic, which, however, had certain common assemblies that they might defend their possessions and drive off the enemy. Yet each one of these city-states was separated from the others by its sovereign right. Thus the separate city-states of the Helvetians are bound by the decrees of the others only so far as they voluntarily agree, as in private partnerships. On the contrary, in one and the same dominion what pleases the majority binds all.

A different opinion must be given about the forty-seven states of the Latins, twelve of the Achaeans, the same number of the Etruscans, and about the German imperial towns and provinces, which compose a state because they are subordinated to the same empire and the same emperor. Achaeans, Latins, and Etruscans created an executive for each separate year (sometimes, however, they extended the term longer); the Germans, for life. The two Philips and Antigonus, kings of Macedonia, were once elected leaders by the Achaeans, as Plutarch and Polybius reported. Similarly, Servius Tullius and Tarquin the Proud were created rulers of the Latins, and Coriolanus, of the Etruscans, as Dionysius wrote. The Spanish and the French kings were created German emperors in the same way. But the Suabian association, which was formed for forty years, and the alliance of Baltic towns differ from the Helvetic association only in this respect, that the latter was made for all time, the former for only a stated period, saving, however, the majesty of the German Empire.

Sometimes there are associations even more sacred, in which city-states not only cultivate the friendship of princes, but even swear loyalty. They are not held to any other responsibility, nor can any other commands be given them, like the feudal relationship of Utrecht, Liège, Guelders, Constance, and Cambrai to Austrian princes. There are very many others also in Germany that pledge their loyalty to dukes and counts, yet take no other responsibility, like most vassals. This really is only, as the ancient Latins used to say, to maintain the majesty of the Roman people willingly, as Modestinus in the title "About prisoners" starting at "I do not hesitate," [45] and Cicero, "On Behalf of Balbus," explained. "It has this significance," Cicero said, "that the former may be the weaker in the alliance." A city-state can be joined to city-state in friendship, association, covenant, contract, or treaty, as M. Tullius wrote. Moreover, the instances which we have mentioned were approved by the most weighty opinions of emperors and kings. When the allies declared war on the men of Zurich, because they had concluded a treaty with the Austrians, Zurich explained that this action was permissible provided that they were attempting nothing against their allies. Yet no one doubts that the Austrians were the common foes of the Helvetians, and indeed were their chief enemies. For this reason the war against Zurich did not come to an end until the bishops of Basel and Constance had forced them to abandon the Austrian alliance because they were playing false with their covenant. Not that they were bound by the orders of others, but by their own pacts. Of this principle there is no greater proof than in the case of hostile land taken by the Bernese: the allied city-states contended that the booty must be divided equally, but Francis, king of the French, who was chosen arbiter, judged that the things acquired by their own arms, not by those of their allies, should be the property of each state, as Leander Mutius wrote. Finally, when the people of Glarus recently abjured their old religion, a great quarrel arose among their allies. Some denied that it was right to violate the treaty contracted in the holy war, which solemnly forbade abandoning the accepted faith thereafter. The converts denied that this pact could bind them against the divine law, much less their posterity. Indeed, it seemed that the matter would precipitate war, if they had not agreed to the counsels of wise men in accordance with the principle that each one should enjoy his own religion and obey his own government.

This principle holds true also when the greatest princes and kings form so close an accord of friendship and alliance among themselves that they have the same foes and friends and ought to support each other with mutual aid and protection against all comers without exception: it is not permitted to enter into any alliance or friendship unless both consent,

---

[45] *Non dubito de captivis* refers to *Dig.* 49. 15. 7. The commentator is Proculus.

and into these alliances they bind themselves, their people, and posterity. Such are the alliances which Philip Augustus made with Albert, king of the Romans; Louis IX, with Alfonso, king of Castile. Even more holy is that compact which was made between Charles V, king of the French, and Henry, prince of Castile, who by this treaty recognized Charles as his superior lord. This alliance, copied with all the early history of the French from the originals of the treasury, was shown to me by Charles Le Voisin, my colleague, a man famous for erudition and integrity.

Then an alliance of diverse city-states, exchange of goods, common rights, laws, and religions do not make the same state, but union under the same authority does. So the king of Spain has dominion over provinces of considerable extent and separated by wide distances, but the individual provinces contain many city-states, which differ in laws and customs. Each city-state has some villages, cities, walled towns, and camps, which use the same fundamental law; but there is no town which does not have some individual difference (disregarding areas belonging to the community) which is not shared with the others. Yet the laws of the empire are common to all, uniting under the majesty of one and the same prince many peoples who are separated by great differences of language, customs, and religion. The same decision ought to apply to the remaining cases.

Moreover, all kingdoms of all peoples, empires, tyrannies, and states are held together by nothing but the rule of reason and the common law of nations. From this it follows that this world is just like a city-state and that all men are associated, as it were, under the same law, because they understand that they are of one blood and subjected to the same guardianship of reason. But since this dominion of reason constrains no one, one state cannot actually be forged out of all peoples. So princes, by using either their armies, or treaties, or mutual good will, seek to obtain lawful conduct and adjudication of affairs outside the borders of the kingdom.

WHAT IS A MAGISTRATE?

Having explained the definition of "citizen," let us also define "magistrate," for these are the elements of the city-state. This man, then, Aristotle described as a man of authority, jurisdiction, and deliberative capacity, but in the end he includes all functions of the state under the name "magistrate." By this reasoning almost no one could be a magistrate, since men who share the right of counsel, jurisdiction, and authority are few. It may also seem absurd that all those who hold public offices should come under the appellation of "magistrate," for this would mean that scribes, attendants, adjutants, public servants, even executioners may be called magistrates—those who formerly were classed as slaves and might more truly be called "attendants." The word "magistrate," however, signifies authority and power. Thus, a dictator, the greatest magistrate of all, is called "master of the people." This was the subject of a serious controversy between Aeschines and Demosthenes, since Aeschines said that τειχοποιός was a master.[46] Demosthenes denied it, but called this office some public commission or service. Moreover, he defined "magistrate" as a man with authority. But these things are discussed by us more thoroughly in the book *De imperio*.

Then let a magistrate be a man who has part of the public authority. I add "public" that it may be distinguished from the authority of a father and of a slaveowner. Furthermore, the command of a magistrate is nothing more than an ordinance, whereas in a prince, it is law. But an order is given in vain unless action follows the commands. However, since the smallest part of exercising authority against the unruly is vested in arrest, according to the ruling of Varro and of Ulpian, it follows that he who lacks the right to arrest lacks authority. And so in almost all city-states arrest is permitted to the least important magistrates, even to those who do not have the right of summons, like the tribunes of the plebs, although they abused their power too often and summoned to trial. Among the Venetians, triumvirs and advocates may arrest and accuse criminals; they do not have the right of summons. Among us arrest is granted not only to all judges but even to those whom they call "commissaries of the fortress," who nevertheless may not serve as judges. Those who have more authority can also summon and impose penalties, in accordance with their power, for the sake of maintaining jurisdiction, which otherwise would be an empty thing. The right to exact fines is granted even to those judges who have the most limited jurisdiction, which we call mercantile. To the others a greater fine is permitted; to some the power of flogging; even the use of torture, to a few; the final limit is reached when the right of the sword is granted. In the last-mentioned jurisconsults place pure (*merum*) authority, since nothing greater can be given to a magistrate unless he enters upon sovereignty—that is, the power of life and death.

That power of pardon is expressed in the use of the greatest clemency

[46] Aeschines, paragraph 24, uses the participle of the verb "to rule" in connection with this office. The Loeb translation of Aristotle *Politics* VI. 5. 1320b 15, applies the word "magistrate." Bodin, however, uses *magister* rather than *magistratus*.

or severity despite the laws—things which are fitting for those who have the sovereignty of the state. But the authoritative functions of magistrates range from the power of the sword to the power of arrest, which constitute the upper and lower limits; these often are distinct from jurisdiction. The latter is based on laws, but authority is vested in edicts. So we see that private judges and deputies of magistrates decree and judge; the magistrates themselves command and execute, while only occasionally do they judge. Thus, among us the superior courts decree, the prince himself commands. Since Varro attributed to certain magistrates the right to arrest and to summons, to others the right to summons and to attend, to still others, neither, so it seems that he gave the name "magistrate" also to those who lack power to command, such as aediles and quaestors. I think that this is done because of a common, but incorrect, designation.

For who would call a man a magistrate when he lacks an agent and cannot issue a command? He may be endowed with office and honors, indeed, but not with authority as well. Charles Sigonius and Nicolas de Grouchy [47] are mistaken when, following Festus, they think that power is given to such officials, but not authority. Such matters should not be settled by the rules of grammarians, but of jurisconsults, who make power equal to authority and sometimes even greater. The word "power," said Paul the Jurisconsult, signifies authority in a magistrate. But a proconsul is a magistrate who has the widest jurisdiction (for thus Ulpian defined the office), and he alone of all the confidential magistrates, has authority (*imperium*). It is called "power" by jurisconsults, in the title "About jurisdiction," starting at "authority." [48] Thus Emperor Alexander asserts in Lampridius, "I will not suffer traffickers in power." So when a warning was issued in the words of an edict, lest it should be allowed to summon to trial the consul, the praetor, and others who have authority or power, the final words are understood to apply to provincial magistrates. Otherwise, if what they say is true, it would not have been permissible to summon to justice aediles and quaestors, contrary to what Varro wrote and Valerius Maximus proved by examples. For they lacked power and authority, although aediles took a part of the praetorial jurisdiction, [49] as we learn from the *Institutes* of Justinian.

---

[47] Nicholas de Grouchy of Rouen, 1509–1572, professor of Greek and theology at Paris, was author of *De comitiis Romanorum, Jus publicum Romanorum*, and *Ad posteriorem Caroli Sigonii de binis magistratum Romanorum comitiis disputationem, refutatio*.

[48] *Imperium de jurisdictione* refers to *Dig.* 2. 1. 3.

[49] Only the curule (patrician) aedile had the right of promulgating edicts.

It is false, also, that the censors had power, but lacked authority, as Sigonius wrote, for to a man they had the right to summons and therefore the right to arrest, according to Varro's ruling. These things are the insignia of authority. By what right would the censors have promulgated edicts (the Latins called the orders of magistrates edicts), which we see in Livy, Book xl, chapter xliii, and in Zonaras, Book ii? By what right would they have chosen senators and knights into their order or have excluded them when selecting; by what right would they have called the citizens to the census, taken pledges, convened the senate, led all the people to the lustrum, unless they had authority, the right to summons, and the right to arrest? Varro, *On the Latin Language*, Book v, denied that it was permitted to the praetor to summon the army of the capital.[50] It was permitted to the censor, the consul, the interrex, and the dictator. Now, indeed, it seems absurd that the tribunes of the plebs, who are called lesser magistrates, should have had authority, but that the censors, greater magistrates, created under greater omens, should have lacked authority.

Aristotle, also, when he defined the magistrate as one who had the right of pronouncing judgment and of taking counsel, did not refer to authority, for those who preside over the council of state have the right to decree, indeed, but not to command, and private judges and priests can also judge and decree, but they cannot command. They have no right to summons or to arrest, indeed no summoner or attendant. "Priests," said Cicero in a letter to Atticus, "are judges of religion; the senate, of law." But the senate cannot execute what it has decreed, as we shall make plain from Dionysius, nor have priests any authority at all or a summoner. But the praetors used to execute their judgment about incest, vestals, and extinct fires, as may be seen in Livy and Valerius. Similarly, our clergy have neither summoner nor lictor, but they either ask for summoners and lictors from a magistrate, or the magistrates execute their capital decisions —"since it is not permitted to us (for thus they say absurdly) to kill any one." These are the words of the Jews, from whom all authority was taken, and Judea was reduced to the form of a province forty years before the second overthrow of the temple, as the rabbis write. Not that they were prohibited by the law of Moses, as our men falsely think, since it was permitted only to priests and deputies, and to their agnates, to pronounce capital sentence on malefactors, and hold capital trials; so the jurisconsults of the Hebrews report in the books of the Talmud under

---

[50] Varro *On the Latin Language* v, paragraph 80, gives "Praetor dictus, qui praeiret iure et exercitu."

the title "Sanhedrin," chapter 4, and in the commentary on Jeremiah. The Chaldean interpreter thought it worthy of note. Since the municipal magistrates of the Jews had only ordinary power of chastisement against the slaves, as Ulpian wrote in the passage "in the case of magistrates," under the title "About jurisdiction," [51] they publicly answered Publius Pontius, governor of Judea, who wished Christ to be punished only lightly by them, that he had admitted a capital crime according to the law of Moses, yet it was not permitted to them to pronounce death for anyone. From these things it becomes plain that the division of the public functions brought forward by us in chapter iii is no less true than necessary.

WHAT IS SOVEREIGNTY?

Let us come to the definition of sovereignty, in which is involved the type of state. Aristotle calls it τὸ κύριον πολίτευμα or κύρια ἀρχή; the Italians, *signoria;* we, sovereignty; the Latins, *summa rerum* and *summum imperium.* When this is understood, many obscure and difficult questions about the state are explained. Nevertheless, it was overlooked by Aristotle and by those who have written about government. I used to think that the *summum imperium* was defined either as the power of creating magistrates or as the right to give rewards and penalties. But since various penalties and rewards are usually given at the wish and command of the magistrates themselves, it would be necessary that they should be associated with the prince in the sovereignty, which is absurd. Yet it would be more dangerous to grant all power in the state to a magistrate, as Soderini wisely commented in Guicciardini's book; when the Florentines used to do this, it brought ruin to the state. Likewise among the Assyrians and our own ancestors; in olden times mayors of the palace were created by the prince; they controlled all power in the government to a point where they invaded royal authority itself. Therefore the state will not be well constituted in which all authority is attributed to a magistrate.

Then, having compared the arguments of Aristotle, Polybius, Dionysius, and the jurisconsults, and these with the general history of principalities, I see the sovereignty of the state involved in five functions. One, and it is the principal one, is creating the most important magistrates and defining the office of each one; the second, proclaiming and annulling laws; the third, declaring war and peace; the fourth, receiving

---

[51] *Magistratibus, de jurisdictione* refers to *Dig.* 2. 1. 12.

final appeal from all magistrates; the last, the power of life and death when the law itself leaves no room for extenuation or grace. These things are never granted to the magistrates in a well-constituted state, unless because of pressing necessity and out of due order. If a magistrate does make decrees about these things, the sanction should reside with the prince or people, depending upon the type of each state. It is evident that these things are peculiar to the prince in the opinion of the juris-consults, and indeed many other attributes; for example, the power of laying taxes and tribute and of striking coins. This they say belongs to the prince alone, although these things were often granted to magistrates in former times and are even in these days. They have been discussed more fully by us, however, in the book *De jure imperio* [*sic*],[52] in the chapter about the right of majesty. Moreover, when in a democracy or an aris-tocracy the optimates and the people have power equal to that of the king in a monarchy, the result is that these most important points of authority are accordingly attributed to the people. That they may be understood more clearly, the problem must be explained. It has been discussed at length by the jurisconsults, but not precisely decided: that is, whether the magistrate should have *merum imperium,* or whether this is suitable for the prince alone. To settle the problem, Emperor Henry VII at Bologna, when he was elected arbiter between Lothair and Azo, promised justice and decreed that *merum imperium* belongs to the prince alone. From this Lothair was said to be right, but Azo wrong.[53] All others, except Alciati and Du Moulin, have written that they judged the opinion of Azo was the more correct.

But this question ought to be taken from the hypothesis to the thesis that it may be plainly understood. *Merum imperium* lies in the power of the sword alone, as they explain from Ulpian himself. At this point, how-ever, it ought to be asked whether the authority given by the prince to the magistrates, of the sword or of waging war or of concluding peace or of creating magistrates or of proclaiming law or of rewarding or penalizing, is the peculiar property of the prince or is transferred to the magistrate also? All are of the same opinion. Lothair adopts the rule of Papinian about the office of a man to whom jurisdiction has been given, whereby the magistrates are said to have the dispensing of public justice and to be unable to deputize it. Fairly often they are called executors and administrators in justice. In respect to this, Accursius [54] himself wrote

[52] *De jurisdictione?* This sentence is not in the edition of 1566.
[53] See the dissertation of M. P. Gilmore, *The Argument from Roman Law.*
[54] Accursius, 1182–1260, a Florentine who was a pupil of Azo. He composed a Glossa

that justice resides with the prince, but that the exercise of justice, which consists in fulfillment, rests with others. As to the words of the law by which the praetor is said to do anything on the basis of his own authority or the governor to have the greatest authority after the prince, Azo has explained these as referring necessarily to justice alone. Then, even the prefect of Egypt is said to lay aside the authority given to him. This is the most significant evidence which has been brought forward by any interpreter. They do not, indeed, define the question, but make it more and more ambiguous. Not only this problem, but innumerable questions of law are involved in the greatest obscurity, because none of the interpreters up to now has explained what is the difference between the action of the law and the office of judge. In such a multitude of writers no one seems to have revealed what is the statutory process, as I hope in a short time to make plain, and what strength and power there is in each of these concepts.

Now, only this on the question at issue: there are two main types of universal law—law and equity—on which the statutory process and the office of magistrate depend. The relationship of the law to its action is the same as that of equity to the function of the magistrate. Papinian, Ulpian, and the ancient jurisconsults believed this: the magistrate may not commit to another whatever functions are granted by the law. He has only the bare statutory process, because these things do not belong to the magistrate so much as to the law itself. But whatever is granted to him through equity, this of his own right he can entrust to another. For example, the praetors and the judges of public trials (this illustration Papinian proposed) may not pass on this authority to others, or in judging, detract from the sternness or mildness of the law or add anything, but must give sentence in a word, nay, rather in a letter, that is, A., C., N.L., I absolve; I condemn; it doth not appear. This has been done in order that reputation, life, and finally the fortunes of the citizens shall not depend upon the arbitrary will of any man, but upon the will of the law itself.

On the other hand, civil cases, because they are less dangerous, cannot be included entirely within the law, for their number is infinite. They were left to the attention of the urban or the foreign praetor, so that in settling these the praetors were not bound by the statutory process as by chains, but through their own sense of equity and piety they might decree

ordinaria covering the *Code,* the *Digest,* and the *Institutes.* His son Edward lectured on Roman Law at Oxford.

many things beyond the law or sometimes even contrary to law, or judge, or appoint judges; finally they might promulgate edicts in which they could emend, alter, moderate, or make the laws more severe, at their own will. Therefore this is properly the function of the magistrate, which Bartolus called *nobile*, and the statutory process, salaried—better, a servile function, because it serves only the law. Whatever private judges do, or legal arbiters, or delegates, they are said to do by the action of law rather than by the office of judge, for even if the urban praetor were not held by the statutory process, yet he bound the litigants by this. Not that the magistrate who follows out the orders of the laws does not fulfill the function of a magistrate, but he is called so less truly and properly. He who in his own right has authority, or jurisdiction, or anything of this kind has it as peculiarly his own, and this he can pass over to another, as Ulpian wrote in the title "About jurisdiction," starting at the passage "in accordance with the custom of our ancestors." [55] But the man who has a mandate cannot lend to anybody else a thing lent to him, as it were; otherwise he would be held for theft. This is true not only of a private citizen but also in the case of a magistrate who has received jurisdiction mandated from another. In the title "Concerning the office of a man to whom jurisdiction is delegated," starting with "and so," [56] Julian wrote that he has a jurisdiction belonging to someone else.

Since many things are permitted to magistrates outside the law and many things are included within the laws, it becomes plain that whatever they have of their own right when they take office is peculiar to them, the rest pertain to the law or to those who commissioned them. From this it is clear that the praetors did not have unlimited authority over public trials or the power of the sword, but they had the bare execution and action of the law, just like the lictor himself whom Brutus addressed and said, "Lictor, act according to law." It is clear that the man who always has extraordinary cognizance over capital crime has been hampered by no restrictions from moderating or aggravating the penalty at his will, only providing that he does not go beyond accepted custom, as Ulpian wrote in the passage "today," under the title "About punishment." [57] For this reason he has power of the sword. In the same way the Roman consuls, put in charge of the army, had the power of waging war by right of office, since they might freely harass or attack the enemy and volun-

---

[55] *More maiorum de jurisdictione* refers to *Dig.* 2. 1. 5. The commentator is Julian.

[56] *Et si, de officio eius cui jurisdictio mandata est* refers to *Dig.* 1. 21. 3.

[57] *Hodie de poenis* refers to *Dig.* 48. 19. 13.

tarily direct the system of supplies and military discipline. They could not, however, declare war or make peace, for the latter was the right of the plebs, the former the right of the people. Hence came about the surrender of the consuls who had made a treaty with the Samnites and Numantians without orders. So when the army of the Helvetians made a treaty with Tramulius and accepted hostages, they would have paid with their heads if the prince had not ratified. For the prince alone has the right to declare war and to make peace.

So Cato suggested that Caesar ought to be surrendered to the Gauls, because he had declared war upon them without proper authority. When the general is given power of ratifying peace or of declaring war under certain laws or conditions, this commission is extraordinary, and he cannot exceed the delegated power or give it to another, for he does not have it by right of office and authority, but has only the bare statutory process. On the other hand, the dictator had the power of war, peace, life, death, and control of the whole country by right of this office, but still it was only temporary, while he was dictator of the state. He held, not actually an office, but a trusteeship. Even if the magistrate's authority is peculiar to him, nevertheless no one has an office or honors in his own right, but as a trust until the term has elapsed or until he who has given it takes it away. Ulpian meant this when he said, "I have laid down the office which I once took up." This disturbed Alciati. Moreover, when the prince dies, or the man who delegated powers, whatever was entrusted to the magistrate or the private citizen according to his peculiar right or statutory process is recalled if power is still intact, as in a procuratorship, but not so the things appropriate to the office. We shall, however, handle these things more fully in their place; in the book *De imperio* these matters are more accurately discussed by us.

A more difficult question is whether the senate's decrees need the sanction of the prince or of those who have the highest authority in the state. It is less doubtful about the prince, because he is the head of his senate and his council and so all decrees have the sanction of the prince. They do not have force in any way except that the prince himself orders them, since the senate has no authority, no jurisdiction, unless by the concession of prince or people, who seem to approve the acts of the senate which they do not actually disapprove. But if there is anything more serious and pertaining to sovereignty, it is usual to refer it to the prince. We too have this law, but in a popular state and in an aristocracy it is not so obvious, since neither the people nor all the optimates can take part in the councils of the state. If they could, it would be dangerous and full of peril to spread the most secret counsels of the state among the crowd; but they cannot be ratified without being understood. This, however, Dionysius confirmed, Book II. "For the senate of the Romans," said he, "is not supreme arbiter of those things which it has decreed, but the people." Hence these expressions occur frequently in the pages of Livy—"the senate decreed," "the people ordered." And when he described the power of Scipio Africanus he said, "The ruling city-state of the world lies beneath the shadow of Scipio; his mere nod takes the place of the decrees of the senate, of the orders of the people." "But nothing can be sacrosanct," said Cicero, "unless the plebs or the people order it." So *senatus consulta* were only annual, contrary to what Connan thought; the source is again Dionysius, Book VII. It was just the same among the Athenians, as Demosthenes wrote in his speech "Against Aristocrates," and decrees did not bind the people or the plebs. The same system applies to the edicts of the magistrates, who had only the adjudication of the lighter fines after the *Lex Aterina*, whereas the adjudication and penalizing of the heavier fines were made by the judgment of the plebs. This may be seen in the pages of Livy in his twenty-fifth book and frequently in Valerius.

Wherefore, since it is the peculiar responsibility of the people alone to approve legislation, neither the commands of the magistrates nor the decrees of the senate were said to be laws, and they differed in many ways, with respect to punishment, to sanction, and also to strength and power. In sanctioning any law, not only the magistrates, but the entire population swore to it, as Appian wrote,[58] in Book I, "The Civil Wars." So in the twelve tables and the sacred laws it was understood that no one should be released from their effect except by act of the people. As the rules of an assembly cannot derogate from public justice, or the statutes of the colleges from municipal laws, or the municipal laws from the customs of the city-states, or the city-states from the laws of the empire— so private individuals could not derogate from the authority of the magistrates, or the powers of the magistrates from the authority of the senate, or the authority of the senate from the power of the plebs, or the power of the plebs from the majesty of the people, for the final authority of government rested with them. But since it seemed dangerous to spread the counsels of the state among the herd (yet this would have been necessary if all decrees of the senate were to be sanctioned by the

[58] Appian *Roman History*, "The Civil Wars," I. vii. 59, where the emphasis is different.

people), it was granted to the senate by the people that it should administer matters pertaining to the state, except the creation of magistrates, the proclamation of laws and of war and peace, the power of life and death and of final appeal, which on account of the majesty of sovereignty the people reserved to itself. This may be seen in the speech of M. Valerius, consul, in Dionysius, and from the opinion of Polybius. For the rest, in order that the senate might not abuse its power, it was permitted to the tribunes of the plebs to intercede against all *senatus consulta.* So when the senate was deliberating, the tribunes used to stand before the doors, and the *senatus consultum* was not valid before the tribunes superscribed the letter "T" as a sign of approval. In later times they were permitted to enter the senate.

Then the powers which are attributed to the senate or to magistrates have a significance distinct from sovereignty. Otherwise, it must be confessed, the sovereignty would be vested in those who had received it from others. If this seems absurd, what Polybius affirmed ought also to seem absurd—that the sovereignty of the state was partly in the people, partly in the senate, partly in the consuls. Furthermore, he thought that the form of government seemed to be mixed—aristocracy, monarchy, and democracy. This opinion Dionysius and Cicero adopted; then Machiavelli, Contarini, Thomas More, Garimberto, and Manutius [59] vehemently approved it. We must refute them in debate, because this subject is of great importance for the thorough comprehension of the history of states. When the restoration of liberty to the people was mooted with bitter contention among the Florentines and it did not seem sage, and indeed was dangerous, to spread the secrets of empire among the throng, it was decided that after they had segregated the dregs of the plebs, who could not legally hold office, the laws must be ordained and the magistrates must be elected by the people. Other matters were to be regulated through the senate and the popular magistrates. For thus Guicciardini wrote.

From this, also, it is made plain that the right of sovereignty is chiefly displayed in these specified attributes. Therefore, in every state one ought to investigate who can give authority to magistrates, who can take it away, who can make or repeal laws—whether one citizen or a small part of the citizens or a greater part. When this has been ascertained, the type

---

[59] Paul Manutius, 1512–1574, wrote a commentary on Cicero's orations, and other works on Roman antiquities. He was a younger member of the house which founded the Aldine press.

of government is easily understood. There can be no fourth, and indeed none can be conceived, for virtue and viciousness do not create a type of rule. Whether the prince is unjust or worthy, nevertheless the state is still a monarchy. The same thing must be said about oligarchy and the rule of the people, who, while they have no powers but the creation of magistrates, still have the sovereignty, and on them the form of government necessarily depends. We shall then call the form one of optimates, or else popular (let us use these words in order that we may not rather often be forced to use the names aristocracy, oligarchy, democracy, ochlocracy, according to the type of virtue or vice); much more so if in addition to the creation of magistrates there is also power over war and peace, life and death. Moreover, it is evident that these things have always been so, not only in a monarchy but also in a government of optimates or in a popular state. For the frequent statement that there was no right of appeal from the senate and the praetorian prefect refers only to ordinary law, since it was permitted in extraordinary cases to call upon prince or people, an appeal which Arcadius called "supplication" lodged when the unusual character of the case or the importance of the persons affected required. But not to take endless examples from history, we shall use as examples Athenians, Romans, and Venetians, in order to show that what they taught about the mixed type of the Roman state is false.

TYPE OF STATE OF THE ROMANS

Then I think this—that the type of state of the Romans in the age of Polybius, and much more in the time of Dionysius and Cicero, was entirely popular. When they had driven the kings from the city, the first law about the government proposed by Brutus to the people was this, that annual consuls were to be created by the people. This Livy and Dionysius reported. From this it is evident that all consular authority ought to be sought and asked from the people. Then, the fact that they say that the semblance of royalty was in the consuls is as false as if anyone should say that under the Roman emperors the praetorian prefect had the royal power, or the great pasha among the Turks, or even the mayors of the palace under the kings of the French, simply because they themselves unaided managed all the most important affairs in the state. These men, indeed, had power not only greater than the consuls but also perpetual. Wherefore, if it is absurd to vest royal power in the leader of the soldiers, it is much more absurd to place it in the consuls. Later we shall show that the power of the tribune of the plebs was greater than consular power.

I come to the senate, in which they placed a semblance of aristocratic rule, even though it had all right and authority from the people. Indeed, the choice of senators was made at the will or the command of the people. "Our ancestors," said Cicero, "created magistrates each year so that they might offer constant direction to the state. They were chosen for this counsel by the people as a whole, and the approach to this highest rank lay open to the endeavor of all citizens." Afterwards, to lighten its labors, the people by the law *Ovinia tribunitia* ordered the censors to select from every class each best man according to *curia*, as we read in Festus. Furthermore, the censors, like other magistrates, were created by the people. The result, then, is that authority of whatever kind was received from the people. Where, then, is the aristocratic rule of the senate? If there is any, it ought to be the same in a kingdom, where the council is established by the prince and has power equal to that of the Roman senate. But to unite this body in an association of power with the prince is not only stupid but even a capital error. The same decision ought to be made about the senate of the Romans, to which these authors attributed a share of the rule with the people. That is, they united masters with servants and agents in exercise of dominion. But we assert that all powers of the senate and the magistrates had their source in the authority and will of the people, which is sufficient proof that the type of state was altogether popular.

P. Valerius, the colleague of Brutus, however, brought forward a second law, which Livy calls the unique bulwark of Roman liberty. In the first section it was provided that there should be free appeal from all magistrates to the people; in the second section, that no magistrate should execute or scourge a Roman citizen in the face of an appeal or wish to fine him; then, that no one should have any authority unless it had been given to him by the people, a capital penalty being added. On this point, also, Livy, Dionysius, Valerius, Plutarch, and Pomponius all agreed. This law of appeal, because it was often violated, was introduced three times by the same family, by P., L., and M. Valerius. Where, then, is aristocratic rule in the senate? Where the royal power in the consuls, who could not whip the citizens or fine without risk of appeal? The fact that a declaration of war rested with the people is too well known to need examples. This was proclaimed by the Servian Law in the time of the kings, as Dionysius reported, but was applied much more often after their flight. In Book IV Livy said there was a controversy whether war should be declared by popular order or whether it was enough to have a *senatus consultum*. The tribunes carried their point by making a declaration that they would oppose the levy if Quinctius did not offer the *senatus consultum* to the people. All the *centuriae* commanded it. In the same way, by the Acilian Law war against Antiochus was declared. Moreover, it is plain that the right of whipping, liberty, and exile (already we have spoken about death) lay with the people, from the law *Portia tribunitia*, brought forward by Valerius and Apuleius, consuls in the year A.U.C. 454 [60] (for Sigonius was mistaken when he wrote that it was offered by Cato the Censor). By this law it was forbidden to use rods on the body of a citizen. A hundred years later it was solemnly confirmed by the Sempronian Rogation, which added the penalty of treason. Why, then, did Polybius say, "If anyone turns his attention to the powers of the people, he will think that the state is a popular one; but if to the senate, he will judge that authority lies with the optimates; since this body takes the lead in public counsel, has control of the treasury, receives and dismisses ambassadors, has cognizance of conspiracy, treason, and poisonings." In this he was mistaken in many respects, as also in explaining the power of the people, which he (like almost all the Greeks) confused with the plebs, in great error. He omitted the highest powers of the senate, and activities which could not really be carried out without the people he made the special function of the senate. The senate had no power greater than that *senatus consultum* "Let the consuls take care," and so forth, which like a sword it exercised in crises of the state against Spurius Melius, the Gracchi, Saturninus, and Caesar. It had also power to create a dictator, but only under extraordinary circumstances. For the interrex was usually created by the consul, and the dictator by the interrex, on the decision of the senate when affairs demanded it. By this system, said Dionysius, the senate deceived the plebs. But this secret of empire the tribunes of the plebs easily discovered, and for a long time, by an excellent law, they did not permit this official to be created, that is, without appeal. So Festus called the law providing for a dictator excellent. Moreover, although all the magistrates abdicated at his appointment, the tribunes of the plebs retained their power, said Plutarch, and they assisted the citizens by exercising the right of intercession against him. In opposition to Fabius Maximus, the dictator, when he wished to demand a penalty from Minutius, the leader of the soldiers, the tribunes arranged that

[60] Livy X. v, vi, ix.

Minutius should not be liable to penalty and should be equal to the dictator in power.

What Polybius reported about capital trials we have shown to be false in the Portian, Valerian, and Sempronian laws.[61] Livy quoted a senator as follows, "When the people are unwilling, I do not see that action can be taken by the senate on the Campanians, since they are Roman citizens." But because the Campanians had favored Hannibal for a long time, they were accused of the great crime of treason.

Why then, some one will say, were so many citizens executed by the senate, more even by the magistrates, although the people were unwilling? While examples of this are countless, yet there is none more famous than that about the army which elected a scribe when Jubellius the general[62] died near Reggio. The senate, said Valerius, took the deed so badly that it recalled the soldiers into the city and condemned them to death. Each day it beheaded fifty, after they had been scourged, and it also forbade them burial or mourning. M. Fulvius, the tribune of the plebs, cried out in vain that the customs of their ancestors were being violated and that the sacred laws were dishonored by the senate. On another occasion Appius, the consul, attacking the army as disobedient to military discipline,[63] had the centurions, sign bearers, and even men rewarded with double-pay beaten to death, not in camp, where it was permitted to the general, but in the midst of the city. Of the remaining multitude, he ordered that each tenth man should pay the penalty. The senate similarly released many from the regulations, contrary to the sacred laws and before the Cornelian Law. To this objection a certain jurisconsult answers: we must consider, not what is done at Rome, but what legitimately ought to be done. For we must judge about the type of state, not from abuse of institutions, but from the actual institutions. The superintendents of public prisons, whose jurisdiction was limited to slaves and foreigners of the lowest class, condemned to the extreme penalty not only citizens but also the magistrates themselves and even curule officials after they had been incarcerated, as may be seen in the pages of Valerius Maximus. Yet anyone was permitted to accuse them of *crimen majestatis*[64] as Clodius before the plebs charged Cicero with treason, because he had inflicted extreme punishment on conspirators without the consent of the people. But this accusation against Cicero was

---

[61] *De capite civium*, 123 B.C. Caput was the status of a Roman citizen, which by this law could not be affected without trial by the people.

[62] Valerius Maximus *Factorum et dictorum memorabilium libri ix* II. vii. 15.

[63] *Livy* II. lix.   [64] Crime against the people.

withdrawn, since he could not be judged except by the people. From these differences arose the struggles of the plebs against the patricians and of the magistrates against each other, when they used their powers contrary to law.

Great, but yet limited, authority, then, has rested in the magistrates; in the senate, greater authority than in the magistrates; in the plebs, the greatest power of all. But no one in considering this matter profoundly can doubt that the majesty and sovereignty of the state itself lay with the people, both from that which we have said and also because the people, like a judge and a moderator, arbitrated controversies between the patricians and the plebs. When the senate tried to oppress the plebs or the plebs to rise against the senate, there was no means of stilling the sedition unless the consuls themselves or a dictator who was created should ask the people what they pleased. This may be seen in the three secessions of the plebs, but chiefly in that long-drawn-out contention in which the patricians persistently scorned the plebiscites, and the plebs, the *senatus consulta*. L. Valerius and M. Horatius, consuls, calling the people together, as we may read in Dionysius, brought a law before the *comitia centuriata* that plebiscites should bind the senate. Suddenly the trouble quieted down. But little by little the senate began to ignore the plebiscites. The tribunes stormed; they interceded with the senate. Again, one hundred and ten years later, Q. Philo was made dictator; he brought the same measure before the people, that the plebiscites should have the strength of law, just as if the people had given the order. It is true that there was in one section a provision that laws should not be presented to the people in the *comitia centuriata* until the senate had been consulted. But they were brought before the plebs without consulting the senate, and on this account the patricians unwillingly renounced frequent violations of the plebiscites until the dictator Q. Hortensius, fifty years later, brought before the people the same proposal.

Hence came the disgrace of the Roman Empire—that the plebs, that is, the lowliest throngs, were enabled to order what should be law, whereby citizens were held just as if the people themselves had ordered it. The plebs even obtained the right to create all magistrates and priests, except consuls, praetors, and censors. Furthermore, they obtained control of public trials, except capital crimes, and the right to bring to a close a war declared by the people and to extend authority granted by the people. In the end the plebs seized other rights at the instigation of the tribunes. They declared war fairly often, for example, by the Sulpician,

Manilian, and Gabinian rogations, which the tribunes brought before the plebs contrary to the customs of their ancestors; and they sent into exile the best men contrary to the sacred laws. From this it happened that the supreme control descended from the people to the plebs—from democracy to ochlocracy and the dregs of the population—chiefly in the periods when the Gracchi, then Livius Drusus, afterwards Saturninus and P. Sulpitius, tribunes of the plebs, stained the city with their own blood and that of their co-citizens.

If, then, we may assign the highest authority of the empire to the people, that is, to the five classes (for the sixth had no ranking in the greater *comitia*), or to the plebs, that is, to all the citizens except the patricians, divided promiscuously into thirty-five tribes, it becomes clear that a state of this type is popular. Actually the senate had all its authority from the people and could do nothing without their command or assent. It ordered whatsoever it should order in their name. But what difference does it make in judging the type of state, whether the people themselves order, or whether orders are given in their name?

Yet it seems even more absurd to want to attribute a characteristic of one person, that is, power of a king, to the two consuls, when actually the tribunes were more powerful. What Charles Sigonius wrote in the chapter about magistrates is not true either—that consuls could detach an assembly from any magistrate, but no one could summon an assembly away from the consuls—since nothing happened more frequently than the intercession of the tribunes in opposition to the consuls. Livy wrote in Book xliv that the property of Tiberius Gracchus, a man who had been both consul and censor, was confiscated by the tribune of the plebs because he had not obeyed the intercession of the tribune with respect to fines and the taking of pledges.

The same man impeached Claudius Censorius because he had summoned an assembly away from him. L. Flavius, also a tribune of the plebs, ordered Metellus, the consul, to be led away in chains, another ordered Appius, the censor, as may be read in Livy, Book ix.[65] The same author said, in Book ii, "The tribune sent his attendant to the consul; the consul sent his lictor to the tribune, crying out that the latter was a private citizen without power and without office." Yet Drusus, a tribune of the plebs, because Philip, the consul, questioned him in the assembly, had an attendant twist his neck and throw him into prison, as Florus wrote, chapter 45. On the other hand, it was a capital crime to touch in violence the

[65] This should be Livy iii. xxxiv. 107.

sacrosanct body of a tribune. Furthermore, Vectius was killed with impunity because he had not risen in the presence of the tribune. Finally, such was their power that one might by his intervention block not only acts of the senate but also acts of the magistrates and their colleagues and of the plebs itself. No further progress could be made until the plebs in a solemnly executed right of suffrage had taken away his authority. For proof, there is M. Octavius, a tribune of the plebs, who, as we may read in Plutarch, single-handed opposed all his colleagues and Tiberius Gracchus when the latter was introducing the Agrarian Law. The law could not be enacted before authority was taken from Octavius by the vote of the plebs. Finally, when a dictator had been created, the tribunes alone retained their powers, although the other magistrates abdicated. Thus, if there was royal power in the consuls, certainly it was much greater in the tribunes, unless one argues those facts of which Contarini makes so much —that they lacked royal trappings. Since they always had to move about in the capital and among common men, they were without fasces, without lictors, without the curule chair, without right of summons, and without jurisdiction. So on this account Plutarch, in *Questions*,[66] and Livy, Book II, denied that they were magistrates. But omitting these things, since the property of all citizens, fortunes, liberty, life, death, the condition of the entire state, dominion, justice, laws, wars, alliances, finally the authority of the magistrates, of the priests, and of the senate itself depended upon the will of the people, who then will continue to doubt that the state was popular? The Athenians, indeed, were more popular than the Romans; yet both were nevertheless popular.

These things have been discussed very fully by us, that we might refute the opinion of Polybius, Cicero, and Dionysius about the mixed type of state and might maintain our own. I will not insist upon its truth or falsity, but it seems more likely than the other view. Now it is easy to refute the arguments of Machiavelli, Contarini, Sigonius, Manutius, and others who have been of the same belief. For they assume from the opinion of Polybius himself and Dionysius that the state of the Spartans, as well as of the Romans, and even the Venetian Republic, was mixed and tempered by combining the three types which I have mentioned. As far as concerns the Spartans, Aristotle seems to have offered an opportunity for error to men who thought that the type of state was mixed, because he reported the opinion of others, who said that it was partly popular, partly royal, partly aristocratic. These he did not refute. But since after

[66] Plutarch *Questions* LXXXI.

he had started the discussion he postulated three kinds of state only, no further inquiry, it seems, should be made as to what he thought of the whole matter, when what he has written is clear. If, however, anyone wishes to understand thoroughly the type of this state, one must read neither Aristotle, whom Plutarch tacitly refuted, nor Xenophon, who expressed a judgment only about customs, but Plutarch himself, who went to Sparta and investigated the most ancient authors on Spartan affairs so that he might write more truly and better.

GOVERNMENT OF THE SPARTANS

He wrote, then, that when the royal power was taken away, Lycurgus created a senate of twenty-eight men, to whom he added two kings, Charilaus, his nephew, and Archelaus, who traced their descent from Hercules. A law was passed that this senate of thirty men should make decisions on all matters which pertained to the state, then the people should ratify the decisions of the senate. Lycurgus created no further institutions for the state, nor did he create any magistrates except the leader of young men. However, he gave to the kings as generals the duty of waging war. Dionysius, also, in Book II, confirmed the fact that Lycurgus permitted the people to order the laws, create magistrates, declare war, and make peace. From this it becomes plain that the state of Lycurgus was altogether popular. But since the people were unwilling to ratify the decisions of the senate for the most part, as Plutarch reported, Theopompus and Polydorus, kings in the one hundred and thirtieth year after Lycurgus, transferred that sovereignty of the people to the senate, under pretense of obeying an oracle, in order that the people might not regret that the power had been taken from them. They willed, then, that five ephors with tenure for one year should be created by the senate, like inspectors of the kings and the senate, so that a tyranny might not develop. The kings had no power beyond the name. Machiavelli and many others were mistaken when they affirmed that there was only one king. If the royal power, which ought to be peculiar to one man, is made common to two, it will belong to many. Because of this fact, then, came the change from popular rule to that of the optimates, for no place in the government was left to the people. There was just this much, that on the death of an optimate candidates used to come forward. Each one received applause according to his popularity. Then the judges, who were concealed under cover, chose as senator the man who had received the greatest applause. But there were no ballots, no votes, and, finally, no

one time. Contarini denied that there was any distinction between patricians and plebs, since all were counted as citizens on an equal basis and shared in the same popular government. In the pages of Guicciardini Vespucius quoted the example of the city of Venice in that speech which he delivered at Florence in behalf of the aristocratic form (for there was a discussion about changing the government of the Florentines). Soderinus, however, defended the popular rule and asserted that those who directed the state at Venice were falsely called "patricians," since they were nothing but citizens, while the others were foreigners. For this there is additional support in Donato Giannotti, a citizen of Venice, in that careful book which he wrote about the Venetian state. He reported that the word "gentleman" was never used in documents of the Venetians before the time of Sebastian Ciani, that is, before the year 1175. Indeed, if the Venetians confess this, obviously the state was popular, since the community of all citizens, excluding foreigners, had the highest right of appeal, gave all offices and authority, finally, ordered what was to be law, as Contarini wrote. Besides, they had even the power of war and peace, life and death, as may be seen in the pages of Bembo with reference to the wars undertaken against Pope Julius and Louis, king of the French, which were not waged until the people by their votes had ordered them. It is no objection that sometimes wars were undertaken by the decision of the senate without the consent of the people, since this was done very often among the Romans and the Athenians also. Although appeals from the decemvirs and the forty men were rare, lest the granting of a free appeal too often might eventually mean that crime would go unpunished, nevertheless capital cases sometimes were carried before the people because of the importance of the citizens or on account of the atrocity of the crime. This may be observed in that passage of Bembo concerning the case of Antonio Grimani, who because of the splendor and power of his race was judged by the people and condemned to exile. If judges inflict punishment on criminals without appeal, they do not for this reason have the right of life and death, since they are bound by the laws and may not liberate those deserving death. This power of pardon is a prerogative of the king or of the people or of the optimates, with whom clemency contrary to the laws is rightfully placed. So Cicero, pleading grace for Ligarius from Caesar, said: "Before the judges never have I acted in this way: 'Oh, judges, forgive him, he has erred, acted rashly, if ever henceforth'; to a parent one usually conducts himself in this way. Before the judges, 'he did not do this, he did not plan it, the witnesses are false, the charge is invented.'" But if the decemvirs or forty men evade their duty, they can be accused when their office has expired.

Therefore we see that attributes of the majesty of empire are the property of the Venetian people, that is, of all the citizens. Almost all other matters are managed by the Ten: but if the affair is of considerable importance, they usually summon the Seven to them. If they disagree among themselves, they employ the Sixteen also as consultants; if even then they cannot agree, or if the matter seems of even graver moment, they take it to the senate. If it cannot be transacted in the senate or belongs to the majesty of empire, it is carried to the people, as was wont to be done among the Carthaginians (whose rule Aristotle reported was popular). But now, since there are sixteen kinds of magistrates to be created, and this by lot or election or by both methods (to which must be added two kinds of royal power, when all officials, or a few, are appointed by one man) yet no greater evidence of popular rule is seen by Aristotle than that all the magistrates are created by all the citizens, as among the Venetians. In that multitude of all the citizens which I have mentioned (since Contarini and Sigonius regard the rest as foreigners, not citizens) all attain power from all, and indeed without any regard for property, nobility, erudition, or worth, although among the Athenians, who are said to have had the most popular state of all, great importance was attached to wealth and the fourth class, which far exceeded the other classes in numbers, had no opportunity to attain honors by the law of Solon, until Aristides repealed it. Moreover, by lot, which itself makes no concession to excellence or to prestige, combined with voting, all the great offices are distributed among the Venetians. Nothing, however, seemed to Aristotle more popular than to permit the creation of magistrates by lot. But the contrary was true among the Spartans, whose state Contarini made similar to his own. They had absolutely no use for the lot.

Since these things are so, I do not see why Contarini thought that the Venetian Republic was a blend of the three kinds. "There is," said he, "in the great assembly a democratic strain; in the senate, an aristocratic; in the doge, the royal power." But whence the grant of tenure for one year to the senate, to the doge, to the magistrates, if not from the people? Moreover, the doge has not even the right of appeal or arrest. It is not enough to deprive him of arms and authority; they also employed the Ten as investigators and guardians of liberty, whereby they inflicted capital punishment upon the Doge Faliero. But the likeness of the doge is on the coins; he gives names to the holidays, so that Contarini said that everywhere you may see the semblance of a king, but never the power. The same things may be said also of the Roman consuls and the Athenian archon. By the same line of reasoning we shall say that at Athens the royal power was tempered by popular authority. We must make the same comment upon the statue, the purple vestment and glorious golden crown, as well as scepter and diadem, which the ruler of the Venetians is forbidden to wear. This permitted one to gaze at the likeness and the semblance of a king, never at his power. If the latter seems absurd, the former also will be. I suppose they committed an error, as do unlearned artists when they adorn the Virgin Mary with a golden vestment and a splendid diadem, although they are depicting her in labor in a dilapidated stable. Since Contarini thought that only those whom he called "patricians" were citizens and reckoned all others as having the status of foreigners, following Aristotle's definition of "citizen," we must by that reasoning call the Venetian state popular, as Soderinus argued. Contarini himself confessed that in the great council of citizens the principle of popular rule inhered. For a large number of citizens does not determine the type of state; we must observe whether all citizens share in power. Otherwise not even the Athenian state could have been called popular, not even in the time of Pericles, when it was most powerful, since not more than 14,040 [70] citizens through both parents were included in the Periclean census after five thousand who had crept into the status of citizens had been publicly sold, for thus Plutarch wrote in the life of Pericles.[71] Afterwards, when the number had increased, the census gave twenty thousand citizens, ten thousand foreigners, and four hundred thousand serfs, as Athenaeus [72] reported. Demosthenes, in his speech "Against Aristogeiton," wrote that twenty thousand citizens in his time were counted at Athens; he did not mention the foreigners. But Dinarchus against Demosthenes said that the suffrage of legal clients was granted to fifteen hundred citizens. From this it can be understood that relatively few in such a multitude had a share in authority. Demosthenes in his speech "About the Organization of the State" wrote that the orators are the leaders of the state; to these the generals were subordinated. About three hundred citizens exercised the suffrage.[73] The rest were followers of the three

[70] The Greek gives ten thousand and four thousand and forty. Bodin in the edition of 1572 gives 14,400; in the edition of 1595 he gives 414,000. This is obviously an error as the following sentence reveals. The edition of 1566 gives *xiii millibus*.

[71] Plutarch *Pericles* 37.   [72] Athenaeus *Deipnosophists* VI. 272 c.

[73] Demosthenes *On Organization* 20.

hundred. Although in so great a number of foreigners and slaves very few citizens had authority, yet this by the consent of all was called a popular state. Who would deny that by this line of reasoning the Venetian state is popular, since it has about five thousand citizens, or a little less, who are qualified to attain honors? It is true that Aristotle denied that a city-state can embrace more than ten thousand citizens. Plato imposed a limit of 5,040,[74] and on account of the factorability of the number, which has 49 [75] divisors, he preferred that abortions should take place and that they should kill not only deformed children but even normal children rather than admit more people.

But let us compare, if it please you, the forms of government of the Athenians, the Venetians, and the Romans, so that we may recognize more readily that they were popular (for they have nothing in common with the Spartans). When I speak about the form of the Roman state, I always mean the popular one, when the people had actual, not fictitious, power, as in the early days under the kings, who referred to the people the highest rights of war, peace, magistracy, and appeal, as may be read in Dionysius, Book IV, although in truth the kings themselves decided these matters arbitrarily. Augustus, also, when he had taken over the power, maintained the semblance of the *comitia* and brought before the people the laws of which he himself was actual arbiter. There was a factor common to all—that the assembly of the people had the sovereignty. Yet there is this difference, that the Venetian people control only those things which we have said pertain to the highest power; the rest are entrusted to the senate and the magistrates. Rarely is an appeal made to the people; more rarely is there a discussion about war; even more rarely, about making or repealing laws. When they do convene, it is almost always for the sake of creating magistrates. The Roman plebs, however, were the final authority even in public trials, which really did not pertain to the majesty of empire, for almost everywhere they are assigned to the magistrates. On the other hand, the Athenian people, in addition to laws, alliances, wars, and public trials, about which they held discussions very often, handled religion, embassies, plans, decisions of the senate, and even trifling things oftener than was suitable. In early days, indeed, citizens were compelled under penalty of fine to attend the assemblies, as may be read in Pollux.[76] After Pericles had decreased the

---

[74] Plato *Laws* V. 738 B.   [75] Plato gives 59.

[76] Julius Pollux flourished A.D. 183, and wrote a chronicle, *Historia sacra ab orbe condito*, and *Onomastikon*.

power of the Areopagites, he increased the popular power and offered a reward to the people if they would attend the assemblies. What was even worse, they indicated their votes by a show of hands (as now the Helvetian mountaineers do) by which the weak are compelled to vote by the stronger fists of the more forceful, except in ostracism and co-optation of the citizens, as Demosthenes wrote in his speech "Against Neaera"; worst of all, the people alone proposed rewards and granted citizenship, immunity, largess, crowns, front seats, statues, and food in the town hall; for thus Demosthenes reported in his speech "Against Leptines." These were obtained by all the most shameless, but denied to the most honorable. It was even more absurd that in creating magistrates everything was staked on the lot, so that this state was more truly a lottery than a democracy, since power was granted in accordance with the favor of the lot, not of the people.

The Roman way was better, for they chose all magistrates by vote of ballots, according to the law of Cassius and Papirius, which I marvel was repudiated by Cicero, although open suffrage is subject to so much hatred and strife. The people, however, used to give rewards, although we see that among the Romans almost no reward was offered except that of glory. This is true also among the Venetians, who grant citizenship to foreigners deserving well of the state; to the citizens, honors, offices, and statues. Moreover, the senate of the Romans differed from the senate of the Venetians, the Athenians, the Carthaginians, the Genoans, the Ragusans, and almost all the German city-states, which are controlled by the rule of optimates, in this respect, that the latter have annual power, the former, perpetual power. Plato's senate also was annual. Among the Venetians the senate has very great power; among the Romans, only moderate; among the Athenians, least, for the more authority is given to the people, the more the power of the senate is diminished. Once upon a time the power of the senate could be blocked by the speech of one protesting tribune. Most interpreters of Roman law are mistaken when they give to the senate the power of drawing up legislation. This was not granted to the senate before Tiberius transferred from the people to the senate that function of the *comitia* which Augustus at his death had left to the people, before whom he used to bring the laws of which he was arbiter. He also allowed half the offices and half the provinces to be appropriated by the people, although he himself introduced the candidates. What Tacitus, Book II, and Dio, Book LIII, reported—that the *comitia* was transferred to the senate—means that those things which in pretense had been left to the people were then granted to the senate. From this time the *senatus consulta* had the force of law. The laws, however, really were made by the princes and ratified; this may be seen in the speeches of the emperors Marcus, Hadrian, and Severus, which we have in the Pandects.

But here we are discussing the democratic period and the power of the tribunes. There is no tribune among the Venetians, and so no shameless orator who dares to sway the popular will and thence obtain what he wishes. But the senate orders all things freely except those in which the majesty of empire is involved. It is common to both, however, that nothing could be brought to the people of Athens or of Rome without the advice of the senate, as Plutarch wrote, and Demosthenes in his speech "Against Androtion." Demosthenes accused him because he had brought a law before the people without the approval of the senate. Against this charge Androtion opposed the accepted custom, that is to say, the procedure was usually different. Worse still, by permission of the law they were allowed to bring some measures before the Roman plebs without the advice of the senate. The Venetians very prudently provided that there should be no proposal of any matter whatsoever to the people, not even to the senate without the advice of the Sixteen, who correspond to the wise men of Aristotle. Likewise, it is common to both, that as long as the state was free neither the Athenian nor the Roman senate touched upon litigation; unless, perhaps, the unusual character of the matter or the atrocity of the crime demanded punishment beyond the ordinary. But when the Athenian senate took extraordinary cognizance, it could not demand a greater fine than five hundred drachmas, as Demosthenes wrote in his speech "Against Euergos." If there was anything more serious, it was brought to the people. Among the Venetians the Ten and the Forty have special cognizance of public trials, which the Greeks call εἰσ ἀγγελείας, yet the Athenian senate had this additional function that it could remove a senator from the order, expel him, and hand over the defendants to the people. Among the Romans the censor had this power; among the Venetians, it was attributed to the functions of the Ten.

There were magistrates among the Venetians and the Athenians who have great similarity, but do not at all resemble those of the Romans. It is known that there were very few magistrates in Rome, but the Athenians had a great many. Besides the senate of five hundred there was the court of the Areopagites, with power equal to that of the Council of Ten among the Venetians. Yet there is the difference that the latter have authority for a short time, the former for life. They were first instituted under the kings for capital cases; then by Solon they were made investigators of all matters and guardians of the laws, as Plutarch wrote. But as Pericles destroyed the power of the Areopagites, so to no small degree the power of the Ten was decreased by the creation of the Forty, then of the Seven and the Sixteen.

Next comes the college of nine archons, which is somewhat analogous to the Seven of the Venetians. Again there is the college of Forty, who had cognizance of injurious violence, and the fifty ephetae, who can be compared with the forty criminal judges of the Venetians, but the ephetae had jurisdiction only in cases of accidental homicide, as we read in Suidas, Pollux, and Pausanias, in his description of Attica, where the types of trial are fully explained. Trial was held not only for citizens and foreigners but even for brute beasts and inanimate things.[77] This was customary among the Greeks. Plutarch wrote in the life of Timoleon that after Dionysius the Younger and Icetes had been driven from the city along with the Carthaginians, capital punishment was exacted from the statues of the tyrants, as though from the tyrants themselves. There were also 220 arbiters taken yearly by lot from each tribe. They were above sixty years of age, according to Pollux, or above the fiftieth year, as Suidas reported. To these can be compared the eighty men for civil cases among the Venetians, of whom forty were for cases between citizens, and the same number for cases between citizens and foreigners. The archon headed the arbiters of the citizens; the polemarch, the arbiter of the foreigners. Two praetors fulfilled this office among the Romans, the urban and the foreign praetor, along with a hundred men. At the head of these were ten men to judge litigation in behalf of the praetor. The praetors presided at the public trials of the criminal courts along with the senatorial and knightly appointees. By the Aurelian Law the tribunes of the treasury were added to these. Yet it is worth our attention to note (something which misled Budé and many others) that although the senate determined no cases, either by law or by proclamation, nevertheless, from the expulsion of the kings until the time of the Sempronian Law [78] they selected judges of the criminal courts and quaestors of parricide from the senatorial order alone. But it is one thing that the senate should judge;

[77] Pausanias *Description of Greece* XXVIII. 8–11.

[78] This deprived the senate of the power of supplying the judges from their own number.

it is a different thing that men of senatorial rank should be selected by lot by the praetors for the trials.

Among the Athenians the ten phylarchs, or chiefs of the tribes established by Cleisthenes, were clearly much like the six men, heads of the tribes among the Venetians; and the phratriarchs of the Athenians were like the prefects of guilds among the Venetians or the priests of the *curiae* among the Romans. Such officials are found almost everywhere. Again, the demarchs of the Athenians resemble the tribunes of the plebs only in name, not at all in power. Presidents, archons, and superintendents of the senate, of the assembly, and of the trials—the Venetians have their like in various guilds. Among the Romans the consuls presided over the senate; one of the greater magistrates,[79] over the people; the tribune, over the plebs, or the aedile (though rarely), or a greater magistrate; the praetors, over the trials. Among the Athenians, however, were eleven men who were called "guardians of the law" by Pollux; they were almost the same as the triumvirs for capital cases among the Romans. There are many lesser judges among the Venetians such as the Romans and the Athenians did not have, although the epagogues were like judges of commercial cases. These matters, however, may be traced in Contarini.

There is a kind of magistrate among the Venetians called triumvir-advocator. They have the right to arrest and to accuse criminals, so that no one may be accused with impunity, as among the Romans and the Greeks. In our country the summoning of three men in all classes of judges is similar. *Logistae* [80] of the Athenians also compare roughly with the syndics of the Venetians, because each demands an account of the office performed; but the former had an investigation of the candidate's habits before he entered office; the latter inquire only about provincial magistrates; decemvirs and triumvirs inquire about the municipal magistrates. Other magistrates, who take care of the treasury, were almost the same among the Athenians as among the Venetians. The latter have prefects of taxes and tribute as many and as varied as the many kinds of tribute and taxes: prefects of loans, tribunes of the treasury, who receive public funds, and urban quaestors, to whom the money is turned over. Among the Athenians were the receivers, *hellenotamiae*, treasurers of Pallas, municipal treasurers or collectors, investigators, syndics, who demanded sacred money under penalty of fine, treasurers of games, military treasurers, treasurers of goods for sale, registrars of goods, and con-

---

[79] Either the consul, praetor, or censor.
[80] A board of auditors, to whom outgoing magistrates submitted their accounts.

trollers. But the most important of all was the treasurer of the people. The magistrates of food supplies also were more numerous among the Venetians or the Romans. The latter had one prefect of the food supply, or at the most two aediles. To the former, besides the clerk of the market, were added fifteen inspectors of weights and measures, as many inspectors of grain, and, furthermore, an overseer of shops. There are in addition among the Venetians the wardens of public health, the supervisors of the currency, road commissioners, the commander of the fleet, and the procurators of St. Mark, who have the care of orphans and widows. Among the Athenians an almost infinite number used to care for the safety of the citizens and the dignity of the city, Aristotle called them "city guardians," such as commissioners of the water supply, walls, and public works. Furthermore, the guardians of law supervised ceremonies; the superintendents, the customs; the *gynecocosmi*, the women; the wine inspectors, the banquets; the training masters, the wrestling school; the *choragi*, the chorus. Special public officials had special administrative tasks. The recruiting officers separated foreigners from citizens. The overseers investigated the acts of the magistrates. Orators defended public cases. Ambassadors were sent to allies or foreign peoples. I omit the military officials, taxiarchs, cavalry generals, captains or donors of triremes, and commanders in chief. I omit pontiffs and priests, who became more numerous among the Romans when they began to cultivate religion and military matters more intensively. I observe no provincial officials among the Athenians, since their allies had their own magistrates; but the right of appeal was lodged with the Athenian magistrates, as we read in Xenophon.

So it was also among the Venetians and the Romans. Yet they had provincial magistrates as well. The Romans had three: governor, deputy, and treasurer (Ulpian included proconsuls, praetors, and *proquaestores* under the name "governor"). If a province were of great extent, more deputies were added. The Venetians are wont to create four: the praetor of urban training, the military prefect, the guardian of the citadel, and the treasurer. Such was the structure of the most famous states of the democratic type, with the exception of the Carthaginian, traces of which are faintly discernible in the pages of Aristotle, Polybius, and Livy.

From these facts it becomes plain that the Venetian state formerly was popular, but little by little began to be changed into an aristocracy. Since most of the citizens and the plebs were occupied with handicraft, they willingly gave up the management of affairs; the foreigners and resident aliens were not admitted, and the right of sharing in the government was not granted to anyone unless he had merited well of the state, and then only grudgingly. Little by little the old families began to disappear, and they would have been much fewer in number, if thirty foreigners had not bought the right of citizenship during the Genoese War, when the city was hard pressed by want. The very same thing would have happened to the Romans and the Athenians if they had used the same system as the Venetians. Cleisthenes increased the number of citizens among the Athenians when he received all sojourners and freedmen into the citizenship. The Romans, for their part, accepted all freedmen with the exception of a very few, and on this account the Latins were wont to sell their children to the Romans for slaves, on the authority of Dionysius, so that when they were freed they might attain the right of honors. Afterwards, forced by the Social War, the Romans granted citizenship to all Italy, later to foreign peoples also, finally to all who lived within the Roman Empire. *Citadini* and *plebei* are, then, among the Venetians as much citizens as the nobles, as a private person is as much a citizen as any magistrate, but they are barred from honors and a share in the government.

We ought now to come back to the point where we started the entire discussion. Because the Venetian citizen can be chancellor (although it is granted by votes, not by lot) or even secretary, he is not therefore reckoned as a citizen, since in such a paucity of offices which are held in perpetuity only a few can be citizens in this manner. The rest would be foreigners. Among the Athenians, if we follow the writings of Athenaeus, when twenty thousand citizens held a share of power, ten thousand foreigners, born of foreigners, although they were barred from honors and voting, nevertheless must have been citizens. Since they enjoyed liberty, the protection of the government, equality of the law, a permanent residence, and finally the fatherland in which they were born, they could not rightly be claimed by other states or princes. Therefore there were actually thirty thousand citizens, of whom twenty thousand formed the basis of the popular government. It is not necessary in a state of this type that all citizens share in the government, but only the greater part; because it is said that what pleases most, pleases all.

On the other hand, when a small part of the citizens rule, and what pleases a few citizens is regarded as legal, the power is aristocratic. Unless, indeed we should base everything on a nice precision of words, so that the governments are not aristocratic unless the best men are at the head. By this reasoning, however, not only will no aristocracy be found among the Venetians, the Ragusans, the Genoese, the people of Lucca, and the Germans, where very few have control, but nowhere else will any aristocracy be found to have existed. Corruption will appear to exist in states in which nobles or rich people alone have political power, without any regard for virtue or erudition, while sometimes the best and most sagacious are cast aside on account of poverty or obscurity of birth. This conception leads to an absurdity. Therefore let us use the popular parlance and define the rule of optimates as rule by a few, and define a few as the lesser part of the citizens: [81] either two (for more than that number are understood, as jurisconsults report) or three, as when Augustus, Antony, and Lepidus, triumvirs for establishing the state, ruled it arbitrarily. Nevertheless, this government gave place to three monarchies at once and a little later to two, and finally to one. Or if more than three ruled, yet they were very few and remarkable for virtue, as among the Hebrews before the kings, or among the Spartans after the kingdom had been overturned, or among the Pharsalians before the time of Alexander. There have been cases in which the rulers were very few and very sinful, as among the Megarians and the Athenians under the Thirty Tyrants, among the Romans under the decemvirs, among the Perugians under the Oddi, among the Sienese after the patricians had been ejected. Or if the noblest ruled in considerable numbers, as among the Romans the patricians actually held the power before the creation of the tribunes, the popular label was a fiction. It was so among Cnidians, Venetians, Ragusans, men of Lucca, and men of Nuremberg. Or the rulers may be a few rich citizens, as among Rhodians, Thebans, and Genoese, when power had been taken from the people. But the number varies infinitely: among the Pharsalians twenty, among the Spartans thirty, among the Hebrews seventy-one, among the Germans two hundred, or at the most three hundred, almost the same number in Ragusa and in Lucca. The ancient Massilians had six hundred, as Valerius Maximus gave evidence. Among the Genoese there are today about fifteen hundred. In Venice the number of optimates is three times greater, but in that case it is difficult to be precise, since the optimates are taken according to family.

If, however, they are to be drawn by election or by lot, it is better that each hundredth man be co-opted according to the geometric ratio, which is best suited to the rule of optimates, since the harmonic ratio is for a kingdom, the arithmetic ratio for the popular state. Therefore, if we as-

[81] The editions of 1583 and 1595 read "optimatum imperia civium paucitatem minore civium parte definiamus," but the edition of 1572 inserts *paucitate* before *paucitatem*.

sume ten thousand citizens, a hundred optimates ought to be selected. This is the result according to geometric ratio, for this number is the mean proportional between one to ten thousand. Likewise, for twenty thousand, two hundred complete the number of optimates. Lycurgus chose almost the thousandth man, that is, from five thousand Spartans and thirty thousand Lacedaemonians he took only thirty. In co-opting the senate, far fewer are desired than in choosing the optimates. Plato wanted the other extreme when he selected each thirtieth man for the annual senate, that is, from 5,040,[82] 180 which I think was done in accordance with former practice. Romulus chose each thirtieth man, that is, one hundred senators from three thousand citizens, whom he had brought to establish his town. But in the subsequent colonies each tenth man was taken, as the jurisconsult wrote in the passage "a ward," under the title "Concerning the Meaning of Terms."[83] Moses, however, seems to have drawn from ten thousand only one by divine lot. For although 622,000 men above twenty and below fifty-five years[84] were counted who could bear arms, he put seventy-one in charge of the senate. This ratio will fit if we grant that there were a hundred thousand minors. I do not count the slaves, old men, and women, whose number must have been twice as great, since almost everywhere there are as many women as men, and more than one gave a name to the town of Athens.[85] But I marvel that this system of choosing the senate and the optimates was neglected by Plato and Aristotle, although they limited the number of citizens, which always varies, diminishing and increasing. Dionysius reported that by the first census, that of Romulus, there were three thousand citizens; by the second, that of Servius, eighty; by the fifth, one hundred and thirty; by the seventh, one hundred and ten; by the eighth, one hundred and three thousand, except slaves, women, workmen, and tradesmen. Of these latter he affirmed that the number was three times as great. Moreover, it was easily estimated in the separate years, because when anyone was born a coin was hung to Juno Lucina; when anyone died, to Venus Libitina, according to the Servian Law. But in an aristocracy of a very few, the same men are both optimates and senators, as happened among Spartans, Pharsalians, and Hebrews. So much about the popular and the aristocratic state.

[82] The Greek gives 5,040, but Bodin seems to think it is 5,400.
[83] *Pupillus de significatione verborum* refers to *Dig.* 50. 16. 239.
[84] The edition of 1595 gives 50.
[85] Possibly because the name is plural, Athenae?

THE FORM OF MONARCHY

We must now discuss monarchy; although there is but one kind, yet several variations are included. Five are defined by Aristotle. Not to be too long in refuting him, I leave this matter to be decided by each reader. I call [a state] a monarchy, when the sovereignty is vested in one man, who commands either lawfully or unlawfully. The latter is called tyrant; the former, king. The aim of the one is honor, of the other, selfish pleasure. What Aristotle said—that the king becomes a tyrant when he governs even to a minor degree contrary to the wishes of the people—is not true, for by this system there would be no kings. Moses himself, a most just and wise leader, would be judged the greatest tyrant of all, because he ordered and forbade almost all things contrary to the will of the people. Anyway, it is popular power, not royal, when the state is governed by the king according to the will of the people, since in this case the government depends upon the people. Therefore, when Aristotle upheld this definition, he was forced to confess that there never were any kings.

Then, one tyrant may be more unjust than another, yet all are united by crime and violence. Of the kings who command lawfully, there are two kinds: those restrained by no law at all; and others who are bound by them. Of the first kind are the kings who once upon a time without any laws governed empires most justly by prerogative. Such the kings of the ancient Greeks are said to have been before Lycurgus and Draco, that is, before any laws had been made binding. Such, also, the ancients remember the rule of the kings in Italy. At that time no laws were promulgated by kings or by private citizens, but the whole state and the rights of citizens depended upon the will of the prince. The Latins were governed by the royal power, as Pomponius wrote, without any definite system of laws. Josephus inferred that Moses was the most ancient legislator, because Homer, in his long work, never used the word "law." Although afterwards statutes were introduced, yet they were brought forward by private citizens, not by kings; until somewhat late the princes were not willing to be bound by these regulations. Indeed, not even when the kings were driven from the city did the consuls allow their own authority and power to be limited legally.

There is and always has been that long-abiding and serious controversy between the powerful and the weak which has brought great empires to truly calamitous ruin; the powerful want to rule arbitrarily and unrestrained by laws, the weak want everyone to be bound by the same law.

Terentius Arsa, tribune of the plebs, proposed to the people that laws should be written down for the use of the consuls so that the plebs might not depend upon their caprice. This bill, said Dionysius, was opposed by the consuls for six years, but finally carried. Hence decemvirs were created for the codification. But it is one thing to hold the magistrate by law, an entirely different matter to hold the king, since the latter has his authority from himself, the former from the prince or the people. No proof of the coming downfall of a state seemed greater to Plato than that the magistrate was supreme over the law, not the law over the magistrate. It is really dangerous for a king to be created so that there are no legal restrictions whatever upon his power and he directs all things by his nod and will. This problem was given serious consideration by Aristotle in the passage where he inquired whether it was more excellent to grant authority to a man than to the law. Although he said that it is better that a good man should command [86] if only such a one can be found in the state, he later commented, "power is given to God, when it is given to the law, but when it is given to a man, a monster is added," [87] because men are wont to be diverted from justice by all sorts of emotions. While the law needs interpretation and in view of the changing circumstances of place, time, and cause cannot comprehend all possible cases, he thought it necessary that whatever could be included within the compass of the laws ought to be. The rest we must leave to the equity and conscience of mankind. If this is true, it seems to apply, not to princes or to those who have the highest power in the state, but to the magistrates. For those who decree law ought to be above it, that they may repeal it, take from it, invalidate it, or add to it, or even if circumstances demand, allow it to become obsolete. These things cannot be done if the man who makes legislation is held by it.

On this account Demosthenes rejected the law of Leptines, because it would have overthrown the form of government. Leptines brought to the people a rogation making it illegal to give anyone immunity from the people; anyone who should seek immunity should suffer capital punishment. But when the Romans had decreed by a sacred law that it should be illegal for anyone to propose immunities, they added, "except to the *comitia centuriata*," otherwise the people would not have had the power of repealing their own measure, which is absurd, since no one can proclaim a law for himself without being permitted to recede from it—in the title "About the Law," starting "If any one at first" and in the

---

[86] Aristotle *Politics* III. 13. 1284b 30-35.　　　[87] *Ibid.*, III. 16. 1287a.

title "About the Term Pledge," starting "By Titius." [88] This seems to have been one reason why first Augustus and then Vespasian, having received dominion over the empire, was released from the laws by the senate; but in this respect, however, deception was often practiced upon the empire.

Indeed, it is a fine sentiment that the man who decrees law ought to be above the laws, for the reasons we have given; but once the measure has been passed and approved by the common consent of everyone, why should not the prince be held by the law which he has made? On this account the tribunitian law of Cornelius was promulgated, whereby it was provided that praetors were bound by their own edicts and that they could not reorder regulations already made or change them, although they had been accustomed to decree arbitrarily and ostentatiously contrary to what they had once pronounced, as Asconius wrote. The same reasoning, therefore, that applies to the praetor with reference to his edict applies also to the prince or the people with reference to the law. If it is just that a man shall be held by whatever he decrees for another, how much more just is it that the prince or the people shall be held by their own laws? For that reason the Roman people used to swear to the legislation which they had ordered, as may be read in Appian, Book 1. On this account Metellus Numidicus, because he did not approve the Agrarian [89] Laws and did not wish to swear to them, was sent into exile. Then, since the people were held by their own law until it was more equitable to repeal it, it follows that the princes also were held. But the princes use sophistry against the people when they say that they themselves are released from the laws so that not only are they superior to the laws but also in no way bound by them and, what is even more base, that whatever pleases them shall have the force of law. This opinion Pomponius and Ulpian favored somewhat more than is fitting for jurisconsults. Paul made the significant statement, "It is shameful for the prince to appropriate anything from an imperfect testament; and it befits the majesty of princes to protect those laws from which they seem to be released." In the same period Alexander Severus first confirmed this in his own rescript. Afterwards Theodosius and Valentinian, in a royal speech, clearly acknowledged that they were bound by the laws. "It is a decision worthy of royal majesty," they said, "to confess that the prince himself is bound by the laws. Indeed,

---

[88] *Si quis in princip. de leg.* refers to *Dig.* 32. 3. 22. and *a Titio, de verb. obligat.* refers to *Dig.* 45. 1. 108.

[89] Text gives Appian laws, but the original passage in Appian reads Agrarian.

on the force of justice our own authority depends, and in truth it is of importance for the government to subordinate the crown to the laws. By the language of the present edict we do not consider that it is permitted to us to do what we forbid to others." Few princes consider that this law was passed for them—not the kings of the Turks, or the Persians, or the Scythians, or the Britons, or the Abyssinians. Nay, not even the Roman pontiffs were willing to be held by any laws, and to use their own words, they never tied their own hands. Therefore, when they say that they are masters of the laws and of all things, they resemble those kings whom Aristotle calls lords, who, like fathers of families, protect the state as if it were their own property. It is not contrary to nature or to the law of nations that the prince should be master of all things and of laws in the state, only he must duly defend the empire with his arms and his child with his blood, since the father of a family by the law of nations is owner not only of the goods won by him but also of those won by his servants, as well as of his servants. This, then, is the first kind of prince.

A second kind belongs to that class which binds by law not only officials and private citizens but also themselves, like the Christian princes, with few exceptions, and the Carthaginians, who take a solemn oath when they start the sacred rites, repeating the words formulated by the priest and the notables of the kingdom. They bind themselves to govern the state in accordance with the laws of the country and the public good. The coronation oath of our kings seems to me very moving indeed, not only in the unusual beauty of words and of antiquity but also in weight and dignity of thought. It is significant in this respect especially, that before the priests the prince swears by immortal God that he will give rightful law and justice to all classes and so far as in him lies will judge with integrity and religious scruple. Having sworn, he cannot easily violate his faith; or if he could, yet he would be unwilling to do so, for the same justice exists for him as for any private citizen, and he is held by the same laws. Moreover, he cannot destroy the laws peculiar to the entire kingdom or alter any of the customs of the cities or ancient ways without the consent of the three estates. Hence that serious and lasting controversy between the king and the people of Narbonne concerning their claim based on prescription. They said that it was unfair and unjust according to their own customs and those of the Romans themselves that they should be forced to prove this possession. The investigation was adjourned many times and finally was abandoned by the king, or rather by flatterers and chicaners.

From these things it becomes plain, I think, that Aristotle was wrong when he wrote that the kings who were bound by the laws were not kings. For if they have the sovereignty, of course they are kings, or else not even the Roman people had the sovereignty in the state, since they were bound by the laws under oath. Yet the interpreters of the jurisconsults did more harm when they affirmed that the sayings of Ulpian and Pomponius about the Roman princes (whom they not only freed from the laws, but even said that their will was law) applied to all princes. Even more base is the fact that Jason,[90] when interpreting in the presence of King Louis XII a chapter of law well explained by Azo,[91] affirmed recklessly that all things are the property of the prince. This interpretation violates not only the customs and laws of this kingdom but also all the edicts and advices of all the emperors and jurisconsults. All civil actions would be impossible if no one were owner of anything. "To the kings," said Seneca, "power over all things belongs; to individual citizens, property." And a little later he added, "While under the best king the king holds all within his authority, at the same time the individual men hold possessions as private property."[92] All things in the state belong to Caesar by right of authority, but property is acquired by inheritance.[93]

Therefore let this be the distinction between kings ruling justly—that some are bound by certain laws of the realm, others are altogether free. Another distinction occurs when they are created or are born from a race of kings. The latter kind of kingdom Aristotle calls a foreign type, and the rulers, of course, follow in unbroken succession. Of those who are chosen, some are chosen for life, others for a short time. Thus a dictator with supreme power used to be named by the Latins, an *archus* by the Thessalians, an *aesymnetes* by the Mitylenians, a harmost by the Spartans, an archon by the Athenians before the state was democratic, a *balia* by the Florentines, which, however, consisted of many persons. Such men had without appeal the supreme control over war and peace and penalties and rewards. If they received perpetual power from the optimates or from the plebs, they were called kings by Aristotle. "Men of this sort," he wrote, "lived in heroic times, when the most just and sagacious man was chosen by common consent to be perpetual leader in warfare, interpreter of justice and sacred things." Such men the ancient Romans also

[90] Jason of Mayno, 1435–1519, was an Italian jurist, who wrote *Commentaria in digestum et codicem.*

[91] The text gives *a Zenone*, but see reference cited in note 53.

[92] Seneca *De beneficiis* VII. iv. 2.   [93] *Ibid.*, VII. v. 1.

chose, and our ancestors the Franks, the Arabians, the Scythians, the Danes, the Norwegians, the Poles, and the Hungarians. Pyastus, an uncouth man, was created king of Poland in the year of our Lord 800; from him were descended the other kings down to the Jagellons, from whose stock comes this Sigismund now ruling. But not so long ago Matthias Corvinus was elected king of Hungary and Gustavus was elected king of Sweden from private life. The Huns call an election *cari*. It takes place in the fields of Pesth, where the army is collected.[94] The rulers of the Egyptians used to be elected by the Mamelukes, that is, by the praetorian guards, in the same way as are the kings of the Carthaginians and the Moors, unless they were brought into expectation of power by adoption by preceding kings, as the Caesars once were wont to be appointed to power by the Augusti. Aristotle supposed a fifth kind of king in a military leader. He suggested an example in the kings of the Spartans, but it is not sufficiently apt, since these kings had no power at all; they could neither declare war nor end it, as we have said previously. But Aristotle was misled, I think, by the mere name which Lycurgus preserved when he took away the power, lest the kings should disturb the state. And the leaders of the soldiers had much more importance in the kingdom, like the hereditary banner bearers among the old Genoese, who, however, were not included in the list of kings. There are also the leaders of Thebans, Achaeans, Phocians, men of Lucca, Ragusans, and the ancient Gauls, whom Caesar reported were annual officers.

TYPE OF GOVERNMENT OF THE GERMANS

There is some doubt about the emperors of the Germans. At the very beginning, that is, when the race of Charlemagne was dying, as soon as the elective system was inaugurated, they had, of course, royal power, as in the case of Henry the Fowler, the Ottos, and the rest, with only a few exceptions up to Rudolph. He, however, lost completely what royal power remained, since new leaders, more eager for honor than for control, had allowed themselves to be bound by regulations of the electors. The third Otto wished to be created leader by election, not by inheritance. In this way a change to aristocracy was effected, because the sovereignty of the empire was yielded entirely to the princes and the optimates. This may be seen in the Golden Bull of Charles IV. For the emperor, who, it is true, is the leader in war, as was true once upon a time among the Hebrews, cannot make law, declare war, create magistrates, or

---

[94] These two sentences are not in the edition of 1566.

demand tribute. He himself has in truth the imperial dignity and something also from the taxes and customs; other than these, nothing. The creation of chief justices, members of the imperial court, which consists of twenty-four men and one justice, is shared by the emperor with the other princes. He cannot make anyone prince; but while among us princes are usually created by the king, so among them the emperor is created by the princes, and the princes also. Finally, authority can be taken from him, as not so long ago Wenceslaus, the son of Charles IV, was deposed.

It is the complaint of Julius Pflug,[95] a German bishop, that the emperors who ought to command the princes and the people bow to the commands and orders of these men. Moreover, the princes have more power over the citizens than the emperor himself has. In these words he clearly sketches an aristocratic state. In addition, an assembly of princes and optimates is made up of electors, dukes, landgraves, margraves, counts, barons, bishops, and representatives of the allied towns. There the laws of the empire are proclaimed and repealed. Taxes and tributes are ordered, wars declared, armies assigned, embassies admitted, and treaties ratified. But the system of votes is based on a threefold arrangement of estates. The first estate consists of seven electors; the second, of the princes of the empire; the third, of the delegates of the towns. So if two estates—for example, electors and princes, or princes and towns—agree, the third estate has no power. It is worthy of attention, because this system of estates is not taken into account anywhere.[96] Yet this institution is not so old, as may be seen in the grant of the county of Burgundy made to Philip, duke of Burgundy by Charles IV, emperor, on the vote of the electors alone. In a matter of such importance this could not have been done without the consent of the princes and towns of the empire if at that time they had had the right to vote. It is no argument that the princes have control over their own peoples (although the control is limited by imperial law), since they receive from the orders their life, fortunes, lands, and all rightful power. It serves, however, as evidence that serious controversies of princes and city-states, and trials of capital cases are heard either in the estates or by the imperial court, and also private cases of appeal, if the matter exceeds twenty crowns. Everything else is obvious and easily understood from the Golden Bull. Because the government approaches closer to the form of aristocracy, the most important church

---

[95] Julius von Pflug, 1499–1564, bishop of Naumburg, wrote *De republica Germaniae, seu imperio constituendo.*

[96] "Nusquam ea ratio comitiorum habetur."

offices are allotted to the nobility; almost nothing to the plebs, as Julius Pflug wrote. The imperial cities themselves are partly free (of this sort there are about seventy), partly subject to the princes in a certain way, yet using their own laws and governed by the optimates. This can be understood from the state of Nuremberg, which is considered greatest of all and is famous for its internal organization.

THE STATE OF NUREMBERG

It has about three hundred optimates (the number is not fixed) who, as Conrad Celtes [97] wrote, are taken from twenty-eight patrician families. Craftsmen and merchants, while admitted to the suffrage, do not receive any share in the government, contrary to what is usual in the other German cities. In these men, then, the sovereignty of the state is placed. For from these are chosen censors, or electors, for the senate. When these have been selected, the other magistrates abdicate. But the senate consists of twenty-six men, who usually co-opt eight former members. And there are other officials; for example, thirteen men from the senatorial ranks, who are called "squires," and seven men, burgomasters, who have power almost equal to the decemvirs of the Venetians. There are created also five chief men, who have jurisdiction over thefts and the damage caused by violence; likewise, twelve men for civil cases, along with the assessing jurisconsults; other matters rest with the senate. Next come seven men, captains of military training, the judge for rural inhabitants, two treasurers of the highest authority among the citizens; the commissioner of the food supply, the guardian triumvirs, of the same functions and power as the procurators of St. Mark among the Venetians; finally the commissioners of colleges and corporations. This is the form of this republic, which other states of the Germans have copied closely, although some have a popular state.

From this it can be understood that men are making a serious error when they think that the emperors of the Germans have the sovereignty because Charles IV in the Golden Bull (which, however, is in part repealed) calls princes and electors his cupbearer, butlers, cooks, shield-bearers, and hostlers; they really have all the power, Caesar none at all. There is no greater proof than that the emperor is proclaimed only after plighting his faith to the electors. He has no power over the public funds,

---

[97] Conrad Celtes, 1459–1508, wrote *Germania illustrata* and *Libellus de origine, situ, moribus et institutis Norimbergae.*

but there are altogether three treasuries—one at Strasburg, the second at Lübeck, the third at Augsburg—where they guard the revenues.

THE GOVERNMENT OF THE ACHAEANS

This form of dominion is like the government of the Achaeans, which consisted of twelve cities at first. Although they had lived under a royal government from Orestes to Siges [98] the tyrant, after the tyrant was killed they established a government of optimates. Then, their common friendship having been disrupted by the various stratagems of Demetrius and Antigonus, they slipped back under the control of tyrants. Again they won their way to liberty when Pyrrhus took his army across into Italy. Then Iseas, the tyrant of the Ceraunians, fearing for his own safety, voluntarily abandoned the city to the Achaeans. Afterwards Carinia, Leontia, and Pellene were added; finally the neighboring cities, when they had exiled their tyrants, also came into this association: that is, Argives, Sicyonians, Arcadians, Corinthians, Lacedaemonians, and all the Peloponnese, on account of the reputation for valor and justice which the Achaeans had acquired in controlling the quarrels of the Greeks. When the clubs of the Pythagoreans had been suppressed in Italy, so great a disturbance of the states followed that after all the wisest and ablest leaders had been killed the cities of Italy unanimously surrendered themselves to the control of the Achaeans, although in arms and resources the Athenians and the Lacedaemonians were much more wealthy and powerful. At last, through alliance and agreement they obtained so many advantages and so many towns were drawn into friendship with them that although it seems incredible it is nevertheless true that the whole Peloponnesus used the same laws (for thus Polybius reported), the same customs, the same weights, the same measures, the same coins, the same judges, the same council, the same religion, and the same rule. Since this good will, diffused far and wide, embraced and favored so many peoples and city-states, the only thing lacking was enclosure within the same walls. It is even more admirable that by their valor they had accomplished so much that they not only offered an invincible front to the enemy but also were called censurers and masters of tyrants (which is reported likewise about the Swiss). They could not be conquered by the Romans until their mutual friendship had been destroyed by the wiles of that people. Like the Germans, they held annual assemblies; but while they

---

[98] Polybius IV. i. 5, says Ogyges.

had generals for a year, the Germans elected them for life. From this it is understood that these military leaders are erroneously called kings by Aristotle, for a man is called king when the power of promulgating laws, appointing magistrates, declaring war and peace, and receiving appeals resides in him. If these things are lacking, the name king is an empty one. The other things which we have observed in the popular and aristocratic forms of government are the same in a monarchy.

THE HIERARCHY OF A MONARCHY

After the prince, the highest power is the senate, which among us usually is called the privy council, the royal council among the Spanish, the divan among the Turks. In addition to this there is everywhere another senate, which the Spanish call the secret, and we the inner council: it consists of either four or five men, on friendly terms with the prince, who deal with the secrets of empire. Such among the Venetians is the college of decemvirs. Among the Spanish the royal council usually consists of twelve men, who with the prince decide about the laws, about war and peace and the condition of the entire state, as Alfonso Ulloa [99] writes. Another council is for Indian affairs; a fourth, of five men, who usually discuss the order of nobles, campaigns, and crusades. A fifth is for the Inquisition, where matters of religion are taken into consideration. The sixth, which usually meets with the generals and nobles of the realm, is confined to military matters. Among the Poles there are two: one the more exclusive, the other larger. To these are admitted all bishops or guardians of fortresses or those who have held some major office, as Sarius [100] the Pole wrote. Among the English a senate of about fifteen men was established by Edward II from those who seemed to be of the highest prestige and sagacity, and this was done at the instance of Archbishop Robert of Canterbury to restrain the tyranny of princes.[101] Among the Turks they say the senate of the prince is made up of four pashas, two cadileskers, and eight bellerbeys. Among us, princes of the blood royal are admitted to the council and then the greater magistrates: for example, chancellor, constable, chamberlain, keepers of the books, marshals, admiral, and great sword bearer. The rest are chosen by the

[99] Alfonso Ulloa died at Venice in 1570. He wrote *Vita dell' invitissimo e sacratissimo imperator Carlo V*.

[100] Jean Sarius Zamoyski, 1541–1605, chancellor of Poland and ambassador to France was the author of *De senatu Romano*.

[101] Is this a reference to the Lords Ordainers of 1322? The archbishop of Canterbury of that date was Walter Reynolds.

will of the prince, for example, cardinals, bishops, certain officials of the treasury, and presidents of the Parlement or other people, in consideration of their record in international negotiations and experience of managing affairs.

After the council, there are two officials of the next grade of importance, the constable and the chancellor, who in almost all monarchies fulfill the same function. Formerly, under the Roman kings, indeed, the tribune of the patricians was said to be the moderator of laws as well as of arms; under the dictators, the master of the soldiers; under the emperors, the prefect of the imperial guard. Then the same man was a good senator, a brave general, and a fluent orator, as the times required. Such was Themistocles, Aristides, Pericles, Demetrius Phalereus, Demosthenes, Cato, Caesar, Brutus, Antony, and innumerable others. After a multitude of laws developed in the states, the system of military and urban administration was divided, and everywhere a double system of offices began to be established—one for peace, the other for war. The same man who in our country and among the Spanish and Britons was once called mayor of the palace, but now leader of the soldiers or constable, among the Carthaginians was called *munafidus;* Jovius calls him *niphates* incorrectly, as Edegnarus [102] (thus Leo the African) calls him *diadarius* among the sultans. Among the Turks he is known as pasha vizier, that is, the leader of the council; among the Abyssinians, *betudeta,* that is, servant. The authority of these men has always been greater, indeed, and more honored than that of the peacetime officials, because the safety of the state and the domestic order depends upon the support of the military arm. Although the former issues decrees and orders, it is the military administration which carries out the orders.

The function of the chancellor, also, is almost the same everywhere— to be interpreter of justice and the laws and custodian of the sacred seal. Machiavelli absurdly attributes to the chancellor of the French the unlimited power of life and death over the citizens. The same official is called chief justice among the Abyssinians, as Alvarez reported; among the Turks, cadilesker, or leader of the judges. There is one for Asia, another for Europe. They take precedence over the pashas themselves. They have supervision over the judges and final decision in the trials. The

[102] Leo the African was born in Granada and is called Eliberatanus. He wrote *Descrizione dell'Africa.* The passage in the *Methodus* reads: "nam qui apud nos, Hispanos, Britannos, magister militum sive Conestabilis, olim magister palatis, idem apud Poenos Munafidus, quem male Jovius Niphatem, ut apud Sultanos Edegnarus (sic enim Leo Afer) ipse Diadarium vocat."

man who is mufti, or chief priest, is indeed regarded as interpreter of the divine law to this extent, that no one may introduce legislation which violates religion. The other military or peacetime officials are inferior to them, for example, the marshals, under consular authority like military tribunes. The same men who were called satraps among the Persians, governors among the Romans, bellerbeys among the Turks, neguses among the Abyssinians, among the Germans, French, Britons, and Spanish were once called dukes and counts, but are now governors of the provinces. Those whom the Turks call *sangiachi* differ somewhat from our seneschals.

We have given a definition of citizen, of republic, of city-state, of magistrates, of sovereignty; we have spoken of the form of the state and have said that there are no more than three. Now let us consider changes within the republic.

CHANGES IN STATES

In progressing, then, from the origins of society to that which now extends far and wide among all men, we shall find almost infinite degrees of difference and change. For the first companionship, that of man and wife, is thought to be the most ancient of all, because there is a certain community of soul, body, and all fortunes. Then the addition of children causes a little difference from the first community. Then comes the relationship of brothers; later of agnates and members of the same race, who, since they cannot all live under the same roof, go out to other homes, where they have other possessions and interests. There follow new relationships and new marriages, from which result more relatives separated from the agnates according to family. When you leave the association based on intermarriage, the next grouping is that of friends, based on excellence; then of neighbors, who, having had offspring, meet in many communities and build their homes near one another; hence phratries and cantons (*pagi*), because they used to drink from the same well or *paga*, that is, spring.

Later the villages were increased in size, so that they might be safer from strangers, who, wandering around in considerable numbers, as we read in the pages of Thucydides, began to occupy the cultivated fields and buildings when they had driven out the owners. At first, then, they surrounded themselves with a wall,[103] whence the names *oppidum* and

[103] Thucydides *Peloponnesian Wars* I. 8, where the translation is "wall" rather than "moat."

polis, because there they placed their food and wealth (*opes*), or they hoped for help in obtaining them or that they might live more comfortably. *Polein* and *poleuein* [104] mean to inhabit, nourish, or govern. Moreover, since a ditch did not furnish sufficient protection, at first they enclosed the town with *varris,* as we believe. Hence came the name walls (*vallis*) by an early change of letters. Then they constructed fortifications around the towns, which on this account were called *urbes* by the Latins, either from *urbus,* as Festus reported, or from orbis, according to Varro, because a circle for the outline of the walls was made by a furrow inside. The Greeks called it *astu purgos,* the Germans *purgum;* both come from "safer citadel." [105] But then when the number of citizens was increased, it was necessary to extend the city limits. On the authority of Tacitus, this was not right for anyone among the Romans unless he had taken land from the enemy and increased the Roman holdings. Otherwise colonies must be sent elsewhere; since they used the same customs as the older cities, the colony originally was considered one and the same as the mother city. A citizen (*civis*), I think, is just the same as *quivis* (the ancients lacked the letter q), because each one (*quivis*) enjoyed the same law as all the others.

Thus, little by little friendship, the tie of human association, has been extended from one home into several families, into villages, towns, cities, and nations, and has spread until, embracing all human kind, it maintains them. Either these or some other principles have been the basis of social groupings, for man by his own volition (since his own nature is gregarious) or from some cogent necessity betakes himself to a meeting place with others, through whom he sees provided for him the necessary means of making life pleasanter and more comfortable. It is evident that contiguity and common interest is lessened more and more the further one goes from the original relationship of man and woman. Thus, nature has arranged that what each one loves the more this he wishes the more to be his own, and verily all his own, and he does not wish to share it with others. So not for long does nature permit the common use of things. Yet the ties of friendship and those of possessions are different, because goods are diminished in quantity the more people share them, but friendship like a light shines the more brightly, the more people there are to enjoy it. For this reason nature forbids that brothers should be joined to sisters in marriage, or parents to children, or rather the common law of all races forbids it. Among the wildest Americans this is said to have been observed

[104] πόλις; πολεῖν; πολεύειν.   [105] *ab arce tutiori.*

without violation. So domestic society has expanded into political society, and friendship which used to be comprised within the same homes has expanded far and wide to all neighboring regions, as Augustine wrote. He is nearer the truth than Pope Innocent, who (in the penultimate chapter "about relationship") [106] defined the marriage of relatives to the fourth degree, because in the body there are four humors. This ought not to seem remarkable, since not even Plato himself appears to have understood the significance of extending this relationship, when in Book v [107] of the Republic, he forbids only the marriage of parents and children, but permits the other types.

But that charm of life which men derived from their mutual society soon was spoiled by quarrels when, of course, the weak were oppressed by the strong, a tendency attributed by Varro to universal nature:

> He who can, demands the more,
> As the great fish eats the lesser and the hawks
> Kill the birds.

To escape, some of the weak and feeble flee to the robust and strong, but others flee to the most just to save themselves from the threatened injury. Hence two kinds of state have arisen—the one established by force, the other by equity. From the second group come the kingdom, the aristocracy, and the democracy; from the former, tyranny, oligarchy, and ochlocracy, which Cicero, when he lacked a Latin word, called tyranny also. But since empires won by crime cannot be retained without justice, the tyrants themselves are forced to cultivate this virtue, not for itself, but for themselves. For this reason the reputation of justice was enhanced. Thereupon men fled to each most just and sagacious citizen, guarding him by interposing their own bodies, lest he should be harmed. Then he ruled the citizens equitably. From this it becomes plain, even if we were not guided by history, that the full liberty of everyone, that is, the power of living as you wish, without laws or authority, has been handed over by the separate citizens to one; and the first kind of state was set up under the rule of one man, who was called judge because he was created so that men might enjoy justice (as Demosthenes wrote was done at the beginning among the Athenians, and Herodotus, among the Medes). For further evidence, in the pages of Homer and Hesiod, the judges are oftener called kings, lords, rulers, or even better, shepherds or pastors

---

[106] The passage in parentheses is omitted in the edition of 1595. *De consanguinitate* refers to *Decretals* 4. 14. 8.   [107] Plato *Republic* v. 9.

of the people. These words signify neither authority, nor domination, but care, solicitude, governing, and equity in judging. It is because of this that Ammianus Marcellinus, Book xxix,[108] reports dominion is nothing but care for the safety of others. Plato wrote, in Book v of the Republic, "Justice and the just way are literally the other fellow's good, the advantage of the stronger and the ruler." [109] Many ages before Homer, Minos and Aeacus, who governed great empires, are called simply judges. Likewise, the seventy men who guided the public affairs of the Hebrews were called judges. When the kings had been expelled, the consuls, in turn, were said to be judges. This may be observed in the pages of Livy and of Varro, who introduced the chosen attendant of each consul elect, saying, "All citizens, come ye hither to the judges to a meeting by invitation." [110] It ought not to seem strange that Augustus rendered justice so assiduously that even when ill he gave decisions from his litter, and the other Caesars had cognizance of trifling matters; even now when our kings are consecrated they swear first that they will give impartial justice, so that this seems to be the chief cause of their creation.

The earliest organization of public affairs, then, was monarchical. It was either equitable without laws, established on the justice of the king alone, or inequitable when some very powerful man accompanied by a band of robbers reduced the weak to slavery, as Moses writes about the giants and Nimrod, who they say first forced men into servitude. Then in order that they might retain the power which had been obtained through crime, it was necessary to secure it by equity. All writers of history agree on this one point, that in the beginning no attempt was made to establish governments of the optimates, much less of the people. Kings, moreover, were selected from one family because those who had most power left the rule to their children. Those who had been esteemed for their justice were worshiped, not only living but also dead, and their children were made kings by the people, because it was thought that they would be like their parents, as Polybius wrote. But when dominion started to be measured by greed and personal advantage, not by justice, the change from kingdoms into tyrannies followed. Hence developed the quarrels of the powerful, afterwards even of the weak, since they were horribly exploited and tormented by those who ought to have protected them. So

---

[108] Ammianus *Roman Wars* XXIX. 18.

[109] Plato *Republic* I. 16. Compare Everyman edition, p. 20, "Both justice and just are . . . a foreign good, the advantage of the more powerful and of the governor."

[110] Varro *On the Latin Language* VI. 88 gives *visite* where Bodin gives *vos ite*.

it has often come about that the more powerful form a conspiracy and overthrow the autocrat, on account of either cruelty, or lust, or both. Because of cruelty Phalaris, Alexander of Phera, Caligula, Nero, Domitian, Vitellius, Commodus, Eccelino of Padua, and John Maria, the tyrant of the Milanese, were overthrown. But more despots were ruined by lust than by cruelty; since the latter holds citizens to their duty and produces fear, the former produces contempt, for the man who cannot control his own desires seems unworthy to rule. Alexander de' Medici, the tyrant of the Florentines, was killed when he tried to commit adultery with the wife of another, and Peisistratus was killed by Harmodius, whose sister he had seduced. For this reason, also, power was snatched from Aloysius, the tyrant of Piacenza, Galeazzo Maria, Roderick, the king of Spain, Tarquin, Sardanapalus, Heliogabalus, Appius Claudius, and innumerable others. Due to hatred of despots, the reward of authority has been given to the leader of the conspirators. Thus Arbaces, having done away with Sardanapalus, seized the kingdom of the Assyrians; each Brutus took the consulship and the army; Louis Gonzaga, the command of the Mantuans, after he had killed Bonacolsi the tyrant. Moreover, experience teaches us that a very just prince follows a most wicked despot. Their fate terrifies others, and they think it base and dangerous to imitate their lives. So Galba, a very good prince, followed Nero; Nerva, Domitian; Alexander, Heliogabalus; Pertinax, Commodus; Gordian, Maximinus. But little by little altering habits turn them from the path, until another prince returns to the extremities of vice.

This ceaseless change is characteristic of all monarchies which have ever existed. What first Plato, then Polybius and Cicero, have written about the necessary change to the democratic form and to that of the optimates is false, since the Scythians are reported never to have had an aristocratic or popular form of government, or the southerners, or the Asiatics beyond the Euphrates, or even the Americans. In the middle region only, toward the west, I see democracies and aristocracies. They occur somewhat late, and they have not flourished long. In the end they have developed into legitimate monarchies resembling all nature, except in a very few places. At first the Cretans, then the Carthaginians, afterwards the Athenians and the Spartans brought into all Greece the form of democratic or of aristocratic government. The Sicilians followed them; then Italians, French, and Spanish, finally Germans and Swiss. And this seems to me to be the one reason: since the men of the middle region are born to the management of affairs, as in a former chapter we have pointed out, all think themselves worthy of rule; yet more especially the westerners, who cannot endure a tyrant easily, because they excel the easterners in independence of spirit. For that reason either they force the kings themselves to obey their laws (nothing more divine can be desired) or they drive tyrants from power and establish governments of the people or of the optimates. This is so plain from the reading of histories that it does not need illustration.

TWO KINDS OF CHANGE IN AN EMPIRE

Changes of government are external or internal; it is necessary to make this distinction. External changes are made by foes or by friends. The latter form occurs when the state willingly yields to the rule of another, though no compulsion exists, as when the Milanese, freed from German rule, called Eriprando, of an Angeran family, to be their leader [111] and submitted to his power, although he had not aspired to the position. Likewise, the Mamelukes, having killed several sultans, put in control of Egypt, Gampso, prince of Caramania, a reluctant foreigner. The Thebans, also, and the Phocians, having sent off a colony, yielded to Plato the city they had founded, so that he might determine its form by laws according to his plans. But this rarely happens, since the rule of strangers is endured with difficulty. It often happens, however, that the conquered must submit to the rule of the victor. Thus the popular government of the Athenians was forcibly changed into an aristocracy by the Spartan leader Lysander. The same judgment holds for all.

Similarly, an internal change may be one of two sorts; one without any violence at all, the other by force. The former deflects from the right to the wrong without any effort, because the nature of men is such that they are wont to slip downward into vices. For what is more excellent than the first five years of Nero? What more divine than the youth of Solomon? What more famous than the early period of Caligula? But on the other hand, what end baser? When they have reached the extreme limit of vice, they cannot be recalled thence without the greatest effort. Therefore it happens that a kingdom has almost always been changed without force into a tyranny; aristocracy into oligarchy; democracy into ochlocracy. But the change from a tyranny into a popular form of government always has been violent, that is, the tyrant has been slain. If this man dies without children, which often happens, the optimates usually take over control, fearing lest they should again relapse into tyranny. At first, then,

[111] From a mythical genealogy of the Visconti family.

they direct the state with the greatest equity and justice, since the beginnings of their rule are wont to be excellent. But among the optimates, those who have the advantage in friends, or favor, or riches, or glory for brave deeds try to be superior even to magistrates and commands. From this comes an oligarchy, which Cicero translates as faction, since a few encroach by evil arts upon the wealth and honors of the many. Under these circumstances conspiracies arise among the powerful, and they plot murder until the plebs, sickened by the rule of the wicked, easily attack, despoil, and kill those who are disunited among themselves. Thus, when the government of the factions has at last been overthrown, a popular state follows. For the people, having recovered their liberty, allow themselves to be easily persuaded by the speeches of men of their own class that they should enjoy the liberty which they have won.

It generally happens that the plebs are carried instinctively from the slaughter of tyrants to the other extreme, that is, to popular power. To a certain extent it is inborn in nature that no one obeys contrary to his will, not even when the orders are just, but he wishes to be led according to his own wishes or else to command and obey in turn. Therefore a new form of the state is set up; the people desire that authority should be asked from them, so that the individual men, first as private citizens and then as magistrates, should yield to the wishes of the entire group. Moreover, it almost always happens that after a victory won from the enemy, factions and aristocratic forms of government disappear into popular forms, or these in turn into ochlocracies. In opposition to these, when reverses have been met, power returns from the people to the optimates. For instance, when the Romans won the war against Tarentum, they began to share all the offices with the plebs. But during the Punic War, when Hannibal terrified Italy with his might, the tribunes were without power. When he had been defeated, as well as Antiochus the Great, the tribunes fulminated and the plebs rose up to demand land. Likewise, the Athenians did not establish a popular government before the Persians had been conquered at Salamis, but on the other hand, at the very time when they themselves were defeated at Syracuse the power returned to the four hundred [112] optimates. In contrast, the Syracusans wrested from this same victory a democratic state, as Diodorus wrote. The reason is obvious. For the plebs, like an untamed beast, rejoice in prosperity; by adverse fortunes they are suddenly cast down and adjust their plans to the events. But the optimates who are nearer to the danger, take the helm as in a tempest.

[112] The edition of 1595 gives "40."

Then, when the people, rash and without foresight, are brought to the management of affairs, it is easy for orators to drive the thoughts of the inexperienced plebs whither they wish and to lead them away from objectives not acceptable to the orators. According to the ability and ambition of each man (for not in languishing spirits does the lust for power arise, but in active minds and in those of considerable ability), he feeds the plebs with banquets, largess, and the delights of spectacles, so that he attains honors and power through no merit of his own. If anyone attempts to intervene, he is corrupted with gifts or through the accusations of false crimes is forced to abandon his opinion or die. Thus the Ephesians cast forth Hermodorus; the Athenians, Aristides and Thucydides; the Romans, Camillus, Rutilius, Metellus, and Cicero. When these men had been driven out, the people, like a conquering hero, held a triumph for valor. They extended honors and offices to the accusers, who after they had for a long time enjoyed the pleasure of authority set up their power with so many guards and such great wealth that they could never in any way be divested of authority. But it almost always happened in popular governments that the plebs acquired as tyrants the men to whom they had entrusted themselves and the state.

In this manner the Corinthians suffered Cypselus the tyrant; the Syracusans, Dionysius; the Athenians, Peisistratus; the Leontinians, Panaetius; the Argives, Phido; the Agrigentians, Phalaris; the Romans, Caesar; the men of Lucca, Castruccio; the Pisans, Della Faggiuola; the Milanese, Napo della Torre; the Sienese, Pandolfo; and the Florentines, the duke of Athens. In order that they may more easily retain the power taken from the people, they devise the detestable arts of tyranny. Although these are understood by many, yet it is useful that they should be understood by more, so that in some way people can be on guard.

First they employ satellites and even foreigners and strangers as bodyguards; they throw up defense works; they seize citadels; they kill the bolder men; they cut down the more powerful like tall poppies; on strangers they bestow honors and rewards; they abolish associations and clubs; they destroy completely friendship among the citizens; they secretly foment discords between nobles and plebs; then they fill the treasury from crimes and assassinations on both sides. Everywhere they place listeners and spies; they declare war on honorable crafts and disciplines; they keep the plebs busy with work and building fortifications, lest they should have leisure for loftier flights of the mind; they undertake wars for the sake of exacting money, and use foreign soldiers; they pretend to have offered an armistice or overtures of peace; they devise new offices and honors and offer them at a price such that they may have more people bound to them. Thieves and wicked men they put in charge of public offices and tax collecting, so that by their activities they suck the wealth and blood of the people. After the thieves have drained them for a long time, orders are issued to drag the thieves to capital punishment. Nothing is more melancholy to observe than the unsuspecting plebs watching the punishment with great delight and applauding the justice of the tyrant. This is more unworthy and wicked because he conceals impiety under the pretense of piety and feigns to reverence the temples of the gods, so that by his very expression and bearing he seems to hold before him the model of virtue. All these things are completely included within two secrets of state. The first is that he shall take from the people all power of harming him; the second, that he shall snatch away even the desire to do so. He takes away power by taking away their riches, their weapons and protection; but the power of the tyrant is not increased without diminishing the resources and comforts of the people—without starvation of the other members, as Hadrian used to say about the treasury. When spleen begins to rise, he snatches away the will to harm by secretly sowing hostility and discord, so that when the citizens distrust each other they cannot form any conspiracy. Finally he brings it about that they learn to do absolutely nothing else than obey the lusts of a tyrant. But fear is an evil guardian of lasting power, said Cicero. Thus no tyranny can be permanent, for it can easily be overthrown by domestic violence, since all fear and hate the one man, and he, in turn, fears and hates everyone. But whoever kills him gains the greatest favor and glory.

Even more easily is he driven forth by violence from without, for good citizens in whom the greatest loyalty ought to abide surprisingly plot with the enemy for the overthrow of one tyrant. So in a short time Aratus and Timoleon destroyed innumerable despots, while the tyranny which Dionysius boasted that he had secured with adamantine chains was wrecked a little later by Dio his attendant. Not long ago Ludovico Sforza was betrayed by the very people whom he most trusted and was driven from power in disgrace.

But it is of the utmost importance whether the state falls through internal weakness or external force. For as certain things are so molded by nature that it seems they can never perish, but others cohere so badly that they can be dispersed in a single breath, so it is in the case of the state—the better it is tempered from its earliest origins, the more easily does it repel external force; indeed, only with great difficulty can it be overthrown from within. Yet those who are engaged in the administration of public affairs must be warned that the abolition of ancient slavery from the state, and in recent years the new religions, as well as the rights of vassalage and feudalism, have produced unbelievable opportunities for revolts unknown to the ancients. Once upon a time, indeed, there used to be fear lest the slaves might be freed and threaten the state, as they had brought great destruction to city-states among Tyrians, Sicilians, and Romans. After tyrannies started to grow, the liberty of slaves appeared to increase, and the power of the masters to diminish, especially in the time of Tiberius, who proposed a monument as sanctuary for the slaves, such as the temple of Diana among the Ephesians, the sepulcher of Theseus among the Athenians, the statue of Ptolemy among the Cyrenians. Afterwards the right of capital punishment was taken from owners, in the time of Hadrian, and when a tyranny prevailed, the owners began to fear lest their slaves should accuse them of treason before the tyrant. After Christian liberty was introduced, it was not thought humane to burden the slaves like wild beasts with chains and services. This was partly due to the fact that the Christians, fearing the slaves of their own religion might fall back into the power of the pagans, constantly used to free them. These things, because they are obvious, need no further proof.

What follows must be gleaned from the haziest antiquity, for although there is no slavery now, we cannot easily know when it ceased to exist so that changes in empire could be attributed to this cause. The laws of Charlemagne about slaves are extant, and of Louis the Pious, and of Lothair, in the book of laws of Charlemagne and in the books of laws of the Lombards. There are also legal codes about slaves and fugitive servants of William, king of Sicily and Naples, and of Emperor Frederick II in his *Placita* of the kingdom of Naples. Frederick lived in the year 1212. There are decrees of the popes Alexander III, Urban III, and Innocent III about the marriage of serfs. Alexander was created pope in the year 1158, Urban in 1185, and Innocent in 1198. Therefore servitude did not exist after Frederick's time, for Bartolus, on the title "Concerning prisoners," starting "The enemy" [113] wrote that in his time there were no serfs and that for a long time there had been none. Men

[113] *Hostes de captivis* refers to *Dig.* 49. 15. 24.

were never sold under Christian customs. But he flourished in the year 1309.[114] Panormitanus wrote that this is worth mentioning. Again we must not overlook what I have read in the records of the court, that by a decree of the senate the bishop of Châlons was forbidden to own a fief or to free serfs even with the consent of his chapter. The decree is of the year 1272. Long ago it is true a servile war gravely harassed the Spanish under Aurelius, the son of King Alfonso, in the year of grace 781. To me it seems probable that the Christians, following the example of the Arabs, abolished slavery, because Mohammed, or rather Omar, freed all slaves of his own religion, an act which stirred serious riots in the empires of the Christians, as may be seen in the laws of Charlemagne about revolts of slaves, Book II, chapter 7. When emancipation had been granted, there followed deplorable poverty, which is wont to overthrow states. From this developed robberies, thefts, slaughter, and the trade of public beggars.

Governments and associations have been greatly vexed by variety in religion, whereas formerly the cult was the same for all except the Jews. Hence came countless changes of government. Many people on the sole pretext of religion have invaded great empires: the Arabs, for instance, the Persians, the Moors, and the Roman pontiffs. The race of Joseph took control of the empire of Mauritania from the Moors in the same way in which Ishmael recovered the kingdom of the Persians, by harangues and the pretense of religion. Charles V tried this in Germany, as recently a certain man among us. The Roman pontiffs themselves subdued to their rule not only the city but also Latium, the Picenian provinces, Umbria, Flaminia, and Aemylia, with a great part of Etruria; not only these but also the kingdoms of Sicily, Naples, Aragon, and England; whereupon they demanded tribute. I have read, not without wonder have I read, of the extent and character of the estates of the Roman Church: what benefices or fiefs it held, what tributes were demanded from kings, and what promises made to the popes by those very kings whom I have mentioned. Charles de la Mothe, my colleague, a zealous antiquarian and an excellent expounder, showed me this important material copied from the originals of the Vatican. Furthermore, Godfrey of Bouillon received both Syrias, conquered by his forces, as benefices of the Roman pontiffs. In this respect he seems to follow the example of the princes of Africa, who acquired kingdoms, empires, life, and all their fortunes from the high priests of the Ishmaelites.

[114] Compare note 17 on Bartolus. The Latin here reads *vixit*, which may mean "died."

CHANGES IN STATES CORRELATED WITH NUMBERS

Having explained these things, let us see whether changes in empires can be calculated from the Pythagorean numbers. The fact that Plato measures the vicissitudes and the collapse of states by mathematical sequences alone seems to me clearly absurd. For although immortal God arranged all things in numbers, order, and marvelous measure, yet this ought not to be attributed to the influence of numbers, much less to fate, but to the Divine Majesty, which itself, as Augustine wrote, is destiny or such a thing does not exist at all. So when Aristotle attributed all things to secondary causes, he laughed at Plato's numbers in Book v of the *Politics*.[115] Nothing in the entire discussion is better than this or more accurately treated by Aristotle.

He brought forward many causes for the changes which seem to me to be included entirely under a few heads. They are, then, injury, honor, fear, scorn, the excessive wealth of a few, or the excessive poverty of the many. I pass over these things, because they have been fully discussed by him. But since Plato, in that *Republic* which he attributed to Socrates as his own, imagined that he had provided by all possible ways lest anyone bring harm to another, or anyone fear or scorn another or disturb the state for the sake of money or honor, and finally removed from his state those ancient blights of governments, wealth and poverty—the matters mentioned by Aristotle could not bring ruin to the state if we assume that one exists such that no better can be imagined.[116] Yet even that one will sense an end from its very age, said Socrates, since this is the common nature of all things. I have wondered, however, why Plato, who thought the world would be everlasting on account of divine goodness, but elsewhere thought it would fall by its own weakness and decay, did not make the same decision about the best type of state.

The interpreters of Plato record that the fall of the state would occur at the point where the harmony of numbers fails. In that case, if the state were going to fall by an internal weakness or loss of equilibrium, it would not be that best form of government which Socrates had in mind. That this should have a mathematical origin would seem absurd, for even if numbers which fit together badly do create a disagreeable discord, because the sounds produced from these cannot mingle and, striking each

[115] Aristotle *Politics* v. 12. 1316a.

[116] If we assume Plato's premises, then the dangers mentioned by Aristotle are non-existent.

other with some jangling, try to enter the ear, yet when the symphony of sounds is mingled harmoniously, that is, when they are arranged properly in numbers according to proportion, there can be no discord. A state thus tempered and blended in constantly pleasing concord, where there is no disagreement, no clashing of sounds, and from hypothesis cannot be—I do not see in what way it can totter. Therefore Forester [117] is wrong when he avers Plato meant to say that his states, though well established at the beginning, especially the one which he proposed to us for imitation, in the course of time little by little grow discordant, just like numbers which were in proportion at the start. He thinks this comes about when they abandon the four to three ratio. But he makes so many mistakes that one cannot say which is the worst. In the first place, there is the fact that he links harmonic means by a three to four ratio, whereas they ought to be joined to odd and even numbers by a two to three ratio, as the very nature of the marriage number shows.[118] So the first harmony of all, and the most dulcet, when you depart from unity, is that called sesquialtera, of two and three, which are joined with no intervening mean. Afterwards, four and nine give a violent discord, since without a mean they cannot blend, but six will join both in equal ratio and with each will pleasantly harmonize. Likewise, 8 is joined to 27 in the same ratio in which the former are joined, if two means intervene, that is, 12 and 18.[119] If you progress ad infinitum in this way, there will be no discord.

It is the same in the sesquitertia ratio of three and four. This is not really harmonious as he would have it, since neither the ancients nor our men can endure this interval without a third or a fifth. Yet this interval also will preserve its attractiveness if, as with the foregoing, we seek intermediate numbers. What is more inept than to make the ratio of three to four the same as that of 27 to 64? Let us therefore give the true means between both, 36 and 48. The relation of each nearest number to the other will be the same as that of three to four. Moreover, this harmony will be perpetual concord, even if you progress to infinity. If we take 243 and 1024, which in the nuptial number are in two to three ratio,[120] they make a discord in association, just as 27 and 64. But if you

---

[117] I cannot identify Foresterus with certainty. There was a German Valentin Forster, 1530–1608, who was a follower of Melanchthon. He studied law and mathematics at Padua and taught at various French universities, where he associated with jurists like Duaren and may have known Bodin also.

[118] The Pythagorean marriage number is six.

[119] See the *Dialogues of Plato* (Jowett translation), "Timaeus," p. 454, and especially the note. See also Jean Bodin *Theatre de la Nature* II. iii. 192.

[120] "Qui in numero nuptiali dupla triplaque ratione sunt quadrati."

insert terms as means, that is, 324, 432, 576, 768, each nearest one will fit and harmonize as well with its neighbor as three to four, since in all respects the ratio is sesquitertian. Forester errs badly also in that he follows the opinion of others and makes the great number of Plato the cube of twelve. If this were indeed the case, why did Plato want one part to be longer than the other? [121] Many have suffered shipwreck on this reef. But since nothing seems more obscure and difficult than the numbers of Plato, I will affirm nothing recklessly; only this, which concerns changes in empires: Plato would have it that states, however well constituted, show signs of weakness in a certain length of time, either from domestic imperfections or by external force. So adamant and gold are constituted of such force and excellence of nature that in themselves apparently they can in no way be damaged, yet by themselves they can be. This is apparent from first principles. Then, also, they may yield to external force, since by the continued application of fire or of chrysulca water little by little they flow away and disintegrate. But it is remarkable that up to now, from all the Academicians, both Greek and Latin, no one has shown by the example of any state, that power and significance of numbers which relates to the type of empires. It is especially remarkable, since this concerns not only the type of government but also the growth, changes, and overthrow of states; it would even force the Epicureans to confess that human things are governed not recklessly and by chance, but by the majesty and providence of Almighty God.

Let us, then, briefly cover what has been omitted by others and perhaps advisedly overlooked. We may be permitted to observe this first: six, the perfect number, affects women; seven, men. Very dangerous for both are those illnesss which occur on the seventh and the ninth periods. Throughout all nature such numbers have great power. Each seventh year, said Seneca, imprints its mark upon the age. However, he ought to have applied this to men. Also I have noted, not without wonder in various cases, that changes happen in states in multiples of either seven or nine, or in the squares of seven or nine multiplied together, or in perfect numbers, or spherical numbers. No one considering this matter attentively doubts that the death of men occurs in multiples of seven and nine: as 14, 18, 21, 27, 28, 35, 36, 42, 45, 49, 56. But if the seventh concurs with the ninth, all antiquity agreed that it was a most perilous year. Hence Augustus, in one of his letters, congratulates his friends because he has safely passed the sixty-third year, which he himself calls fatal for all old men. The next is seventy, when Petrarch died on his natal day. At seventy-two occurred the death of Epicurus, who took such good care of his health. Seventy-seven follows this, which Augustus almost reached; Frederick III completed this. The latter ruled for fifty-three years, the former fifty-six; each died on the nineteenth day of August. Next is the square of nine, 81, on which Plato died, on the same day of the year on which he saw the light. David does not go beyond this number when he describes the life of man. Few attain to the eighty-fourth year, which is made up of twelve times seven, but Theophrastus completed it. When dying he complained that nature had given to him a brief span of life, but to the crows a long one. So in this year also the popes Paul III and Paul IV died. Yet there are those who have completed the ninetieth, that is, ten times nine, such as Francesco Filelfo; John the Apostle lived ninety-nine years, as history testifies. St. Jerome lived to be ninety-one, that is, 13 sevens. Moreover, those very people who have lived a long time, as in our books and letters we have witness, almost all completed multiples of seven or nine. Lamech lived 777 years. Methusala attained 970 [sic], Abraham 175 (that is, he completed 25 seven year periods); Jacob, 147 (that is, twenty-one sevens); Isaac, 180 (that is, twenty nine-year periods); and although a violent death may perhaps sometimes occur on account of the violent conjunctions and trajections of rays, yet oftener it runs into groups of seven or of nine, unless nature is checked by the divine will. For innumerable people die in the sixty-third year: Aristotle, Chrysippus, Boccaccio, St. Bernard, Erasmus, Luther, Melanchthon, Silvius, Aleander, Jacob Sturm, Nicolas of Cusa, and Thomas Linacre. All of them were stricken with illness; in the same year Cicero was killed. At seventy-two Pope Alexander drank poison. Isocrates killed himself by starvation in his ninety-ninth year when he learned of the Battle of Chaeronea. Pliny suffocated at fifty-six; Caesar was killed; Oecolampadius wasted from grief in his forty-ninth year; Atticus died of starvation at seventy-seven.

Now let us use the same guide for the changes of states, but in such a way that we seek the squares and the cubes of seven or of nine, or let us multiply the cube or the square of the one into the root of the other, or even use a perfect number, or at length try spherical and solid cubes included within the great number. There is finally the square and the cube of twelve, which is called the great number of Plato by the Academicians. The square of seven and that of nine, of course, are 49 and 81; the cubes, 343 and 729. The square of seven multiplied by the base nine gives 441, and the square of nine by the base seven, 567. A perfect number is 496; 6 and 28 are smaller perfect numbers; the rest of the perfect numbers exceed 8,100,[122] and they are too large to be suited to states. The square of 12 is 144, and the cube is 1,728. No empire has exceeded this sum of years, and therefore the greater numbers are to be rejected. The spherical numbers included within the great number are four; that is, 125, 216, 625, 1,296. By means of these few numbers in so many which are not perfect, not squares, not cubes—or if cubes or squares or perfect, then made up of even digits, not from odd; or even from odd, but not from sevens or nines, which in this endless sequence are relatively few—we are permitted to study the marvelous changes of almost all states.

First, to make a beginning with the cube of twelve, which some Academicians say is the great and fatal number of Plato, we shall find that the monarchy of the Assyrians from King Ninus to Alexander the Great completed this number to a nicety, in the opinion of Philo himself. Melanchthon, Funck, and indeed all the learned men follow him. But we must go no farther back than Ninus, from whom Diodorus, Herodotus, Ctesias, Trogus, and Justin began their accounts, because he first stabilized the form of government and founded Babylon. It is more accurate to say that there was one monarchy of the Assyrians and of the Persians than that there were two distinct monarchies; or else we must separate the kingdoms of the Chaldeans, the Medes, and the Parthians from those of the Assyrians and the Persians, who nevertheless are inhabitants and citizens of the same region. But Alexander actually made a new monarchy when as a foreigner, of course, he transplanted a new race of men from Europe to Asia, destroyed the troops of Darius, and finally changed the customs and the laws. But these things in their proper place. From the floods until the overthrow of the temple and the Hebrew state Philo counted 1,717 years. Josephus gave two hundred more; others covered considerably less. I should think, both from the truth of history and from the excellence of the great number itself, that eleven years ought to be added to the calculations of Philo, so that the result should be no less and no greater than the cube of twelve. In this same time Egypt broke away from the kings of Assyria; the Scythians invaded Asia Minor; the sons of Peisistratus were driven out by the Athenians; the Tarquinians by the Romans.

The "seven days" of Daniel are chiefly illustrated in this light also.

[122] The text might mean 108,000 but this is not true arithmetically and does not fit in with the context.

Although there is the greatest divergence among all writers about the birth of Christ, yet Philo, who is regarded as the most accurate of all the ancients, counts 3,993 years. From this Lucidus takes three. Joseph Maria adds six, for many reasons which I rather approve, because that number, 3,999,[123] is the product of the squares of seven and nine befitting in a remarkable way the changes in the most important matters which afterwards followed. By this system the death of Christ falls in the year 4,000 from the Creation. Here, of course, belong the seventy hebdomades of Daniel, which took 490 years. If we begin with the seventh year of Darius Longimanus, because Esdras then was sent to Jerusalem to establish the state, that is, in the sixth year before the time of the Hebdomades—that six, the only perfect digit, with seventy hebdomades, that is, seven times seventy years (for the Scriptures take the day for the year) makes another perfect number, 496, which coincides strangely with changes in governments. To make this plain, so that we may not be led astray by any uncertain guesses, let us bring forward examples from the consular *fasti* of the Romans, for nothing can be more reliable. From the founding of the city until that year when Julius Octavian conquered Antony at Actium, was hailed the first Augustus by the senate and was offered the rule of the world, the years are 729, the cube of nine. From Augustus to Augustulus, who is called the last Roman emperor in the *fasti* (for he was driven out by Odoacer, the king of the Goths) the years are 496, a perfect number. From the founding of the city until the destruction of the empire the number of years is a square, that is, 1,225, consisting of whole sevens. In Censorinus, M. Varro is quoted as saying that he had heard Vectius, distinguished as an augur, foretell that since the Roman state had safely passed through 120 years it would reach 1,200 years. I find precisely the same number of years from Ninus to Arbaces, the first king of the Medes. Funck covered three more years; others fewer. But this seems remarkable, that not only from Augustus to Augustulus but also from the time the kings were driven from the city to the dictatorship of Caesar the same number of years, 496, recurs. Not only this but also from Constantine the Great to Charles the Great, in the year when he first was created emperor at Rome, 496 years were counted by Panvinio, a most zealous student of Roman antiquity, who, although he had a great interest in history, yet had none at all in numbers. Not only this but also from the founding of Alba until its overthrow by Tullus Hostilius, there are exactly 496 years. In addition, the fact is that from Saul,

[123] This should be 3969.

the first king of the Hebrews, up to the captivity, 496 years were counted. While Genebrard [124] added three, and Garcaeus [125] even ten, the Talmudists took away almost one hundred; but their pronouncements follow no necessary arguments. From the return of the people and the second construction of the temple, under Zorobable, up to the year when Herod was appointed king by the senate, there were 496 years. Between Arbaces, the first king of the Medes, and Alexander the Great the same period elapsed. Indeed, the kingdom of Macedonia lasted the same number of years from Caranus, the first king, to the death of Alexander. Funck took away eight years; others added twelve. I should think that one ought to strike a mean.

We shall bring forward still more proofs of the changes due to this number with reference to the French state. It consists of the number of Daniel, which becomes a perfect number by the addition of the perfect number six. Furthermore, it alone within the great number is formed from nines and sevens, if unity is taken from both factors. [126] This quantity is the one which the ancients meant to indicate when they said that the cycle of empires is five hundred years. But they had no skill in these matters, for five hundred is inapplicable to cycles in human or in natural affairs. In truth, it is neither perfect, nor square, nor cube, nor spherical, nor made up of nines and sevens, nor developed from the roots or squares of these.

If anyone should observe rather carefully the civil wars of the Romans, the secessions of the plebs, and the domestic strife, he would find that the numbers of years consists in sevens, or in nines, or in both. From the founding of the city to the flight of the kings, the years are 243; from the flight to the parricide, 468; from the flight to the secession of the plebs to the Sacred Mount, 18 years; to the second, 63; to the third, 225; to the sedition of the Gracchi, 378; from this to the Marian Civil War, forty-five; hence to the Caesarian War, seven; [127] from the parricide to

<hr>

[124] Genebrard, 1535–1597, was a celebrated Hebraicist of Bodin's own time, professor at the College de France, wrote *Chronographia in duos libros distincta* and edited the works of Origen. He became bishop of Aix, and a fervent supporter of the Holy League.

[125] Johannes Gartze, 1530–1574, a German astrologer who wrote *Methodus astrologiae*[?].

[126] According to Bodin's practice in the preceding pages this should mean that 9 and 7 are factors of 496, and that 496 is either a factor of 1728, or else is the only number smaller than 1728 which satisfies the given conditions. What he actually meant is not clear to me, possibly $[(7 \times 9) - 1][9 - 1] = 496$, but a similar juggling of figures could be applied to many numbers less than 1728.

[127] Compare p. 237, below, where Bodin may be counting thirty-six years.

the civil war in Sicily, seven; hence to the last civil war, of Actium, seven. All these quantities are developed from whole nines or sevens or from both. Moreover, the town itself was captured 364 years after its founding, which is likewise formed from whole sevens; from the founding of the city until the defeat at Cannae, the years are 539, which is developed by taking 77 seven times. At that time the Roman Empire was nearly destroyed. From the disaster at Cannae to that of Barus, the years are 224. Both numbers are from whole sevens and both defeats occurred the second day of August. Likewise, Lysander leveled the walls of Athens to the ground in the seventy-seventh year after the victory of Salamis. Plutarch added in the life of Lysander [128] that each happened on the sixth day of the month of *Munichion*. So also in the year of our Lord 707, in the seventh year of King Roderick, the Moors invaded Spain; in the seven hundred and seventieth year thereafter they were driven forth, as may be read in Tarafa [129] himself, a Spanish writer.

About the cube of seven there are also many examples. For that number is selected by Moses [130] in establishing the great Jubilee. So from the victory of the Jews over Haman with the aid of Esther, to the victory over Antiochus, the years are 343, and each victory happened on the thirteenth day of March, which the Hebrews called Adar. On this account the Hebrews hold the day in great honor. The same number of years elapsed from the time when Augustus alone obtained control until Constantine the Great alone received the dominion. The kingdom of the Persians, from Cyrus to Alexander, stood 210 years, a number which is formed from thirty whole sevens. The Lombards ruled for the same length of time. Paul the Deacon took away the three years which remain up to the murder of Desiderius. Just so long the English held Calais. The kings of Syria and Asia Minor, from Nicanor, the first king, to Philip, the last, ruled the same number of years. From the Exodus of the Hebrews out of Egypt to the overthrow of the temple and the state 900 years are counted; this number is developed from the two squares nine and one hundred multiplied together. It was no longer from Eurysthenes, the first king of the Spartans, to the tyrant Nabis, whom Philopoemen drove from power before he completely changed the type of government of Laconia. The laws of Lycurgus were abrogated 567 years after they had been proclaimed by Lycurgus, and the Spartans were forced to accept the cus-

---

[128] Plutarch *Lysander* 15.

[129] Francis Tarafa was a sixteenth century Catalan, who wrote *De origine et rebus gestis regum Hispaniae.*   [130] Leviticus 25: 8.

toms of the Achaeans; the number is obtained by multiplying the square of nine by seven. But the Ptolemies, from Lagus to Augustus, who reduced Egypt to the form of a province, ruled for 294 years, which consists of whole sevens. The state of the Hebrews was in decay for seventy years; the same number of years the Athenians held control of Greece, as Appian wrote. The Goths, from Theodoric their first king to Totila, reigned 77 years, as Panvinio wrote in his *fasti*. The Spartans for twelve years commanded all the Greeks; Appian is the authority. Alexander the Great completed this number also, the root of the great number, for he commanded six years before the death of Darius and the same number after Darius had been killed. Afterwards his empire disintegrated as suddenly as a lightning flash.

Not to confine ourselves to ancient history, let us use domestic examples and make the most accurate comparison of the time periods of Jean du Tillet with the *fasti*. France obeyed the Romans from the final victory of Caesar over the Gauls to Marcomer, leader of the Franks (relying upon the strength of her warriors she refused tribute to the ruler Valentinian) in the year 441, a number which is formed from the square of seven multiplied by nine; hence to Waramund nine years; to the end of his reign, three nines, but from the time when he was called duke, to Pepin, who as mayor of the palace usurped authority and drove off King Hilderich, the years are 343, the cube of seven. From the murder of Syagrius, the last of the Romans to rule over Gaul, to Capet, French in race, although the Germans deny it, and Angevin by birth, who took away the dominion from the Franks, the years are that perfect number 496. From Waramund to Capet there were 567 years. This number is obtained from the square of nine multiplied by seven. Again from Waramund to Hugh the Great and the abandonment of Louis IV by the nobles and his captivity, the years are 512, a solid cube. Hence to that other case of treason, of Charles of Bourbon to Francis and his captivity, the time elapsed is the square of twice twelve, that is, 576. The same number of years also is counted from Capet to that accursed and appalling war which recently was waged in the blood of citizens. Nor are there more or fewer from the captivity of Charles, duke of Lorraine (by Capet forced from the legitimate line of succession into a prison at Orléans) to Charles that other Lorrainer, who, when he attained the royal power, incarcerated the scion of the Capets at Orléans; and on both occasions Orléans was of evil portent for the race of Lorrainers. Likewise, from Charles the Simple, whom Count Hebert detained as a captive when he was advancing in good faith to Peronne, even to Louis, the least simple of all, who, however, voluntarily, or rather recklessly, betook himself to Peronne and was held captive by Count Charles, we have 540 years, a number consisting of whole nines. Again from Capet to the memorable expedition of Charles VIII into Italy that perfect number 496 is completed. From the overthrow of the empire of the Lombards and the conquest of the area by Charles the Great to the similar expedition and capture of Lombardy by Louis XII is plainly the cube of nine, that is 729 years. At this time the Venetian state suffered a grievous defeat. We have shown that before Charles the Great the Venetians did not have a stable government, but received their liberty by agreements between Nicephorus and Charles the Great. Therefore the Venetian state had stood for 729 years, when it was nearly overthrown. At this same time Emperor Maximilian, Louis XII, King Ferdinand, and Pope Julius II planned the ruin of this state. Moreover, the sultan of the Turks and fortune itself seemed to conspire with so many and such great enemies. For the town, accidentally set on fire with sulphurous powder, was greatly damaged, and an infinite store of gold was lost in a shipwreck. Indeed, in that time the Venetians showed the extent of their ability and of their wisdom.

This, too, is worthy of notice, that from Godfrey, who in a famous victory broke the power of the Persians and freed Syria from servitude, to the last Baldwin, who was taken by Saladin, the years are 90, a number consisting of whole nines. Then, too, the French controlled the empire of the Greeks for 56 years, from Baldwin, that is, to the Palaeologi. The papacy, however, they directed for 70 years. Each number is from whole sevens. I should be endless, however, if I were to follow all significant indications of change. Yet, by the examples which have been given those who have the leisure are enabled to derive the changes of all governments from unbiased and accurate information of historians, and to prophesy more truly and better those to come (although known to God alone), than by the trifling and erroneous guesses of Cardan. He thought that every great empire depended upon the tail star of Helice, or the Great Bear. When it was vertical to rising Rome, it brought power there; then to Byzantium; afterwards to France; then it moved over to Germany. These things are as true as what he wrote about himself in his biography. He averred that he had never lied, and this seemed to him remarkable. However, a good man ought to excel in this very respect, that he himself does not lie, that is, as Nigidius [131] explains, knowingly say untruths; whereas

---

[131] Nigidius Figulus was a Pythagorean philosopher and astrologer of the first century B.C. He wrote De auguriis, no longer extant.

the prudent man should take care that no lie may escape him, that is, as the same author believed, that he may not against his will repeat what is false. But to a man even moderately skilled in that art which Cardan himself professed, what else is lying if not this? Although he understood that that star had been vertical to countless peoples and towns and always would be, he added that the sun also ought to be in the zenith in conjunction with that star, for the rise of a city. While he maintained that power was extended to all peoples of the same parallel, yet he said dominion ought to be in one place. In this way he thought that he could deceive the most wary. But since that star is distant 54 degrees from the equator and is limited to the Arctic circle, so that no matter how much it deviates because of the motion of trepidation, it inclines twelve degrees from the vertical to the town; it is plain that it cannot be vertical. Let us show not only that it could not have been in the zenith but also that it could not have been in conjunction with the sun, because it is necessary that [a definite correction] should be made with respect to longitude and the meridian time. Moreover, the error can be inferred from Varro, who, as Plutarch wrote, ordered L. Tarutius Firmanus,[132] a well-known astrologer, to fix the natal day and hour of the capital and its founder, if possible. Then, by a diligent investigation of the stars he found that the foundations of the capital were laid in the third year of the sixth Olympiad, to which Dionysius and Varro agreed, on the fifth day before the ides of the month of Pharmuthi, or on the eleventh day before the calends of May, which is called the day of Palilia [133] in the month of April, about three o'clock in the afternoon, Jupiter in Pisces, Saturn, Venus, and Mars in Scorpion, the sun traversing Taurus, and the moon in Libra, in the eighteenth year of Romulus. Plutarch also learned this from Antimachus Lyrius. They never mentioned the Great Bear. At that time this star was in the constellation Leo, 18 degrees, 56 minutes, as becomes plain from the tables of Copernicus himself, and his most accurate principle of motion. But today it is in Virgo, 20 degrees, 50 minutes. Since these are the facts, how could it happen that it was vertical to rising Rome, when the twelfth part of the Gemini was in the zenith? From this point the eighteenth part of Leo is 54 degrees distant.[134] How much less could it (ex-

[132] Firmanus was an astrologer and contemporary of Cicero. See Plutarch *Romulus* 12.

[133] Palilia was a shepherd festival held on April 21.

[134] Each division of the zodiac contains 30 degrees, and the order is Taurus, Gemini, Cancer, and Leo. It is not clear to me why Bodin gave 54 degrees as the distance between Gemini 12° and Leo 18°, when two sentences further on he gave approximately ninety degrees as the distance between Taurus and Leo. Does he place the star at Gemini 12° by measuring clockwise, and at Leo 18° by measuring counter-clockwise?

trema cauda) be in conjunction with the sun, which was traversing Taurus, while the last star of the Bear was traversing Leo? [135] It was therefore distant 90 degrees in longitude and 45 in latitude from any conjunction with the sun.

But it was even more inept for Cardan to say that the tail star was vertical to Byzantium when command was taken over to that city from the Romans, since Byzantium actually was founded before Romulus was born, as is evident from Polybius. Much more absurdly, he leaped from the Greeks to the furthest point of Gaul, thence into Germany, contrary to the nature of the motion and inclination of this star. But such conclusions seem more worthy of a smile than of refutation. Why did the Scandinavians and the Livonians, who alone have not only the tail but also the whole Bear perpendicular to them—why did they never obtain any power from this, but on the contrary, lie open to the attacks and demands of their neighbors? Or if perpendicular stars give dominion, why not those which are said by the ancients to have been brilliant and royal? Regulus, I say, the Hyades, the Pleiades, Antare? Why not those fifteen which Cardan himself called royal? Why do not Spica,[136] the Lyre, Arcturus, and indeed all the planets, which almost alone are perpendicular to Africa, take power thither? Yet the Africans always have submitted to the legions of Europe and Asia.

Copernicus had a different theory, since he decided that the changes of empire were related to the center of a small eccentric circle and to its motion, as his disciples have written. Moreover, the small circle does not belong to the sun, which he judged to be motionless, but to the earth itself, which he thought is in motion. Yet no one was ever so lacking in knowledge as to think that any force was exerted from the centers of the celestial circles, much less the terrestrial, and Copernicus did not dare to write this down; but his followers reported that dream as a definite investigated fact. Since these matters are found false from history, and since neither the motion of eccentric circles nor of the sun is in any way significant in the changes of empire, it must be confessed that this whole thing depends upon immortal God. Or if we should assign the revolution within each dominion to secondary causes, we shall have to judge that it pertains to those well-known conjunctions of the stars, of which we have written in an earlier chapter, God using the stars as his instruments.

---

[135] The editions of 1566, 1572, and 1583 give a question mark after Leo, whereas 1595 puts it after Taurus.

[136] The brightest star in the constellation Virgo.

Although the ancients could not observe this on account of the unknown motion of the celestial bodies, their descendants, on the other hand, have overlooked it altogether.

No system seems to me to be easier than to base the cycle in some way upon numbers, taking the beginning from the origin of each empire (which Ptolemy called "epoch" and Alfonso "era," that is, "root" in Spanish), as in a fever we are accustomed to predict health or the crisis from decisive days, so that if several fall ill at different times, one and the same day may be healthful to some, while to others it may indicate the end (yet sometimes such is the strength of the stars and of their baneful trajection that without distinction of days it affects several at one and the same time). So empires struggle with their own ailments, as Polybius wrote, and as they sometimes have violent ends so they have ends suited to their nature, decreed by certain definite and decisive numbers. Nor am I disturbed by what Aristotle thought in Book v of the *Politics* and at the end of the *Metaphysics*—that there is no importance at all in numbers. Why then does the seventh male heal scrofula? Why does the child born in the seventh and the ninth month live, that born in the eighth, never? Why seven planets, nine spheres? Why has the abdomen the ratio seven to the length of men? Ambrose Paré, the royal surgeon, affirmed this fact to me. Why is the seventh day of starvation fatal? Pliny wrote that this was known by long experience. Why do the marvelous changes of the moon consist altogether of sevens? Why seven sets of strings? Why does the nightingale for seven days and as many nights ceaselessly repeat nine changes of song? Of this marvel I was advised by Jacques Boyer, president of the parlement of Brittany, a man of noble nature, very widely informed in the liberal arts. Why, at length, did the sevenfold flood and reflux of the Euripus drive Aristotle to madness, as some report, or to plunge in it headlong, according to others? Since Aristotle had not grasped the Euripus, the Euripus is said to have grasped Aristotle. Moses, that very wise man, and the Prophets cast almost all prophecies within some multiple of seven. They proclaimed festal celebrations on the seventh day, the seventh week, and the seventh month; on the seventh year the fallow of the fields and the manumission of slaves, but after the year seven times seven a great jubilee and the liberation of all debtors and the reversion of the fields to their former owners. Hence the number seven is called sacred by the Hebrews.

These things show that human affairs do not occur accidentally and haphazard, as the Epicureans boast, or according to an inexorable fate, as the Stoics say, but by divine wisdom. Even if this wisdom arranges all things in an admirable order, motion, number, harmony, and shape, nevertheless it changes these at will, and sometimes arbitrarily; as Isaiah [137] wrote about Hezekiah, God prolonged his life when he prayed and showed him the sun going backwards. But sometimes time is said to hasten, in the sacred Scriptures, on account of the punishment of sins or their forgiveness, as Paul wrote about the prophecy of Elia. For proofs let there be the floods, which at the command of the Deity gathered sooner than in the order of nature the great number could have been properly completed, that is, in the year of the creation 1656. To this number, if eight nines are added, that is, 72, there results that cube of the great twelve. So men may understand that God is bound by no number, by no necessity, but is released from the laws of nature, not by the senate or by the people, but by Himself alone. For since He himself ordains the laws of nature and has received dominion from no other than Himself, it is fitting that He should be released from His laws, and at different times should make different decisions about the same things. Thus Ambrose wrote: not always are the crimes of the wicked punished on earth, lest they may think that there is no punishment for them in the hereafter and no reward for the good; nor yet do all sinful people live without punishment, lest they may boast that mortal things are not cared for by God. So we must reach the same decision about a state of good and evil men, lest we may be forced to attribute something to the fates or to fortune.

I discuss these things about the changes of governments briefly from the innermost philosophy, both to stir the learned to contemplation of these most beautiful things, and also that we may not ourselves be downcast by the changes in empires, a fate which often comes to great men. When Pompey escaped from the Pharsalian defeat, bitterly mourning the fall of the Republic, he could be appeased in no other way than by the speech of Secundus the philosopher. This convinced him that the precise duration of empires was determined by immortal God.

CHANGES OF THE ROMAN EMPIRE

Now from history we shall compare with our own the alteration and decline of states which once upon a time were more famous, in order that from both the truth may shine forth the more. The most famous of all is said to have been that of the Romans, which for a time flourished

[137] Isaiah 38: 8.

under kings, then lapsed into tyranny under the Tarquins. When these rulers had been driven out, it fell into the power of the optimates and patricians, often against the wishes of the plebs, afterwards to the faction of the decemvirs. When they had been overwhelmed and killed, the people for a time ruled lawfully and moderately, until the state fell into the hands of men desirous of revolution. Hence ensued ochlocracy, or rather anarchy of the turbulent plebs, from the sedition of the Gracchi until the time of Marius and Sulla, who befouled the city horribly with the blood of its citizens. Finally, in the thirty-sixth year following the state was miserably harassed by Caesar and Pompey, leaders of parties, until it was brought into control by the lawful dominion of Augustus alone. After him it was governed by various excellent princes. Soon, however, it was captured by tyrants, and finally it lost all prestige when the Emperor Constantine transferred to Byzantium a great part of the senate and his seat of empire. In the end it came under the power of Goths, Greeks, French, Germans, and Spanish and obeyed a foreign rule or the desires of the popes even to these times.

CHANGES IN THE ATHENIAN EMPIRE

The Athenians were troubled by the same storms. When Cecrops bravely defended the twelve towns of Attica from the attack of the enemy, he is said to have attained royal power and from him there was a monarchy for about eight hundred years until the time of Aeschylus. After the death of Aeschylus, who had reigned for life, the optimates created magistrates like decennial dictators, but when this magistrate exceeded his authority, they shortened his term to a year. First Creon was elected a yearly magistrate, called "archon" by the Greeks and "judge" by the Latins; they kept this office until Peisistrastus, in the same way as Dionysius, obtained a guard for the protection of his life against the Alcmaeonidae and seized permanent power. Then Hipparchus and Hippias, the sons of Peisistratus, maintained their rule by force for seventy years, as Aristotle wrote, until one was killed. The other having died, popular power was first established by Solon, but still the government was lawful and just, for the fifth class, that is, the lowest plebs and by far the largest part of the people, was kept from honors and a share in political power by the Solonic legislation. Aristides was the first to abrogate this law. At length Pericles changed a popular state into a turbulent ochlocracy by eliminating, or at least greatly diminishing, the power of the Areopagites, by which the safety and dignity of the state had been upheld. He transferred to the lowest plebs all judgments, counsel, and direction of the entire state by offering payments and gratuities as a bait for dominion. After his death, when Alcibiades had been ejected and Nicias slaughtered with his army, then the control was handed back to four hundred optimates. However, a little later the faction of Thrasyllus restored it to the plebs. Finally, when the fleet was lost at Aegospotami, the Athenians with all their allies came under the control of the Spartans, by whom aristocratic rule was established everywhere, instead of popular. Hence thirty optimates were chosen who governed the state of the Athenians; they immediately became quarrelsome tyrants. Therefore a little later, when they had been overthrown and killed by Thrasybulus, the supreme power returned again to the people and it remained there until Antipater in the Lamian War gave over the popular rule to a few optimates who executed his commands. Their leader was Demetrius Phalereus. But fourteen years later Demetrius Poliorcetes ejected Phalereus and under the semblance of liberty set up a tyranny. When he was captured by his enemies, however, the Athenians again regained liberty up to the time of Sulla. This man besieged the town, because it favored Mithridates, and captured it in so savage a mood and with such slaughter of the inhabitants that rivers of blood are said to have flowed through the whole city. It is true that once they had enjoyed liberty by the favor of the Roman people. Afterwards they recovered it again by the same grace, as Pliny wrote. Yet they had nothing of liberty except the shadow, since they served the lust of tyrants and magistrates. But it is worthy of notice that they held control in Greece only seventy years, as Appian wrote, although Demosthenes, in the third Olynthiac,[138] thought that the Athenians held the leadership for only forty-five years.

CHANGES OF THE SPARTAN EMPIRE

The Spartan Empire started the shift from kings (who reigned about three hundred years from Eurysthenes to Lycurgus) to a tyranny when Lycurgus set up popular power, as Plutarch reported, but this was quite limited, as we have shown earlier. Twenty-four years later Theopompus and Polydorus firmly established the rule of optimates, and in this type of government the Spartans flourished 576 years until the time of the tyrant Nabis, whom the Achaeans under their leader, Philopoemen, drove from his domain; overthrowing the system of Lycurgus, they forced the Spartans to live under the institutions of the Achaeans. At

---

[138] Demosthenes *Olynthiacs* III. 24.

length they in turn were defeated by the Romans, and both yielded to the rule of Rome. Since it is fitting that a man writing of method should not enter into details, but only universals, and should point a finger, as it were, to the sources whence universals are drawn, we shall overlook the more obscure states of Thebans, Corinthians, Messenians, Sicilians, Sicyonians, Argives, Cretans, and Corcyreans, whose changes Pausanias reported carefully, if anyone wishes to investigate them more thoroughly. Now that we have made these matters clear, we shall investigate similar vicissitudes of public affairs in Italy.

CHANGES OF THE WESTERN EMPIRE

After the Lombards had been defeated, Italy was added to the kingdom of the Gauls, and also Germany, Saxony, Pannonia, and a great part of Spain. The rule was divided among the children of Louis the Pious. To Charles the Bald, the eldest, was given France, the chief part of the empire; to Lothair, first Italy, then Lorraine; to Pippin, Aquitania; to Louis, Germany. This was done in such a way that no one was subordinated to the authority of the others. Then by the outcome of various wars Germany and Italy became one realm until, after the race of Charles the Great had become extinct, the kings of Germany were created by the approval of the princes; they used to rule Italy and Switzerland through legates and vicars, while they themselves ruled Germany. But after they had degenerated into tyrants, the Germans, shaking off their servitude, created an aristocratic state; the Helvetians had popular government; the Italians were divided into the parties of the Guelphs and the Ghibellines by the quarrels of popes and emperors, and some found kings, and others tyrants, among the legates of the popes or the emperors. The rest favored popular and aristocratic states. As Pope Urban gave the kingdom of Naples and Sicily to the French, so Emperor Louis presented cities of the Roman Church to his generals as a gift. Others, weary of servitude to foreigners, even preferred to submit to domestic authority. So the counts of a family from Angera [139] seized Milan and a great part of Lombardy; the Della Scala, Verona; the Eccelini, Padua; the Bonacolsi, Mantua, and when these had been driven out, the race of Gonzaga; Bologna, the Bentivoglio; Faenza, the Manfredi; Rimini, the Malatesta; Perugia, the Baglioni, and when these were ejected, the Oddi; Città di Castello, the Vitelli; Ferrara, Reggio, and Modena, the D'Este; Camerino, the Da Varano; Urbino, the Montefeltro; Pesaro, Forlì,

[139] The Visconti. See note 111, below.

and Imola, the Sforza; the popes kept the Picenian province, Umbria, Flaminia, Emilia, Latium, and a great part of Etruria. Meanwhile the Venetians, who had gained their liberty from Charles the Great and Nicephorus, won from others first Istria, then Liburnia (I omit the islands), Treviso, Vicenza, afterwards little by little Padua, Verona, Bergamo, Brescia, Crema, Como, and Ravenna. The Florentines, also, having won their liberty from the Germans, overwhelmed the Pisans, the Volaterranians, the Pistoians, the people of Arezzo and of the neighboring towns. The inhabitants of Lucca, Siena, and Genoa gained independence in the same period. All these walled towns, as well as many more cities divided by political frontiers, changed from kings to tyrants, thence to optimates, soon to factions and popular governments, sometimes even to pure anarchy. No part of the world has had more reversals of government. Finally all states of which we have any record became monarchies again, except the Venetians, the Lucchese, the Genoese, the Ragusans, the Helvetians, and the Germans. We have spoken earlier about the Venetians and the Germans. Let us cover as briefly as possible the governments and changes of government of the others.

FORM AND CHANGES OF GOVERNMENT OF THE HELVETIANS

After the Helvetians had long borne the yoke of imperial legates and vicars and of the counts of Hapsburg, who afterwards became the dukes of Austria, they formed an association in the year 1315 in order to throw off the tyranny. First the men of Schwyz, Uri, and Unterwalden, then of Lucerne, Zug, Zurich, Berne, afterwards even of Basel came in, although for the latter the union was not so essential; later, men from Ticino, the Valais, the Rhetians, the men from Sitten, St. Gall, Muhlhausen, and Rottweil; finally the Genevese. These towns, we have already shown, were divided as to political frontiers, but all have a popular type of government. The five lesser cantons, however, called mountain cantons, have an unusual form, even more popular than that of the Bernese, the men of Zurich, the Basilians, and of those who broke away last from the rule of the Germans. They actually use the old showing of hands in giving their votes, when the people are gathered at one time in one place. Annual election of magistrates is common to all, contrary to what many people think; but sometimes, if the men do well, the office is extended for two or three years. The mountain cantons have one supreme magistrate, who is called "Man." To this official is attached a deputy or chancellor, as well as a treasurer, just like the paymaster, and in addition twelve councillors. These fifteen men together take care of all the civil and military administration. There are, furthermore, provincial officers or magistrates and judges of municipia, from whom appeal may be made to the fifteen men. The Bernese elect a highest magistrate; the people of Basel and almost all the rest choose Burgomasters, except the Genevese, who call the men to whom they have given exceptional power syndics. Many people think that the Bernese, whose rule extends a long distance (for they have about forty towns), as well as the people of Basel, the men of Zurich, the Genevese, and those who broke away from the Germans, are under the rule of optimates because they see a senate of three hundred men, or in other places four hundred, taking counsel for the state. But they are mistaken. The decrees of these bodies, if they concern the type of government, are not ratified unless the people order it. This is done by the summoning of colleges and corporations of workmen, each in its own assembly, commonly called *schaffae*, by the man who is leader of all the colleges. Then the syndic and tribune of each college reports the orders of the people to the greater senate. There are almost everywhere three councils, four, even, in Basel, in which, of course, the safety of the state is an issue. Because they take care of all matters and nothing can be carried to the people when the council is unwilling or to the greater council unless it has been decided upon in the lesser council, nowhere have popular laws greater force. They are not changed according to popular caprice, nor can they be violated with impunity.

As for the five kinds of popular government reported by Aristotle, nothing is more dangerous than that the will of the people be superior to the laws and regarded in place of law, as Xenophon wrote about the Athenians. In the same way nothing can be more temperate and laudable than that the untamed plebs are restrained by legal bonds. It is not remarkable, then, that for two hundred and fifty years the Swiss have been very famous for their deeds. That popular rule has been conserved by two just devices—the equity of the law and the frequency of public gatherings. The nobles, who too often overthrew a popular state among Megarians, Romans, Florentines, Sienese, and Genoese, are nonexistent among the Helvetians, or if any long ago escaped the fury of the plebs, since they are relatively few, they forswear nobility and mingle with the lowest plebs. For the most part they cannot attain the highest offices, which butchers and cobblers enjoy. Not only are quarrels and animosities checked by the banquets, which are very frequent in the guilds, but in addition the citizens are united to one another and to the state in almost unbelievable good will. This is the objective of all their humane laws. Though when the Bernese, the men of Zurich, and those of Basel changed their religion, they tried to abolish these symposia, but they could not. The Genevese, who are less democratic, dislike customs of this sort. They have no public banquets, except sacred ones, which every third month they solemnly celebrate. Indeed, they think that the drinking bouts of the Helvetians are inimical to private and public affairs, as well as to religion and virtue. Both have a probable cause for their opinion, and they do not lack the authority and examples of great men. Yet among the Helvetians there are no dissensions, while the Genevese are said to be harassed with secret private feuds, and they are kept in office more by fear than by love. However, nothing done through fear can be lasting. For proof we have that conspiracy which a few years ago almost wrecked the state. Perhaps the temper of the citizens, disaffected by foreigners, offered opportunity for conspiracy. But with respect to the Genevese there is a praiseworthy custom, if anything in the world is, which makes the state flourishing—if not in riches and greatness of empire, certainly in virtue and piety— censure by the clergy; nothing greater and more nearly divine can be imagined for restraining the greed of mankind and those vices which can in no way be corrected by human laws and judgments. Indeed, this coercion is modeled on the rule of Christ: moderate at first, and in gentle fashion; then a little more stringent; and then, if you do not obey, the solemn and effective interdiction of sacred things follows. Punishment by the magistrates comes after the interdiction. It is ridiculous, as Seneca says, to be good through law. And so it comes about that those things that can never be checked by laws are restrained in that city without violence and tumult by those very censors who have earned the highest respect for their own virtues. Therefore no prostitution, no drunkenness, no dancing, no beggars, and no idle people are found in this city.

FORMS AND CHANGES OF GOVERNMENT OF THE GENOESE

Once the Genoese were famous for seapower and for the glory of their great deeds, since they nearly won from the Venetians the control of their empire and even of their own city. Yet when they had been defeated by the Venetians, they voluntarily surrendered, first to Charles VI, king of the French, and then to the counts of Milan. In those times, when the Fregoso and the Adorno were dividing the state into factions, the plebs, having seized arms, drove out all the patricians. They created eight tribunes of the plebs. They expelled the French guards. They got

back the citadel by force and made a fuller their doge.[140] Afterwards
Louis XII executed him, and having taken the city, punished the citizens
severely. But when Lombardy surrendered to Emperor Charles V,
Andrea Doria, abandoning the French for Charles, like another Aratus
or Lycurgus, formed a state freed from all fear of war and tyranny,
having the best laws and institutions. A government which had been
popular, or rather plebeian, he replaced by an aristocratic regime based
on antiquity of race, wealth, and splendor. He divided it into twenty-
eight tribes, having removed the names of those factions which had
disturbed the state. He did this by making a law that each year ten
optimates should be created from the plebs, from those conspicuous for
virtue or riches. Yet this law became obsolete, as I have learned from the
Genoese, and few were admitted to the enjoyment of honors. He filled
the college of optimates with four hundred citizens, who had supreme
power, so that all the optimates, who are nearly twelve hundred, ruled
in turn. The number of citizens is thought to be eighty thousand, but I
could not learn definitely. Then he gave sovereignty to the optimates,
that is, the right of making laws, war, peace, and highest appeal and of
creating all magistrates, especially the senate, whose tenure is also for
one year.

The power of the doge, which once was perpetual, he limited to two
years, adding a guard of five hundred German soldiers. This man alone
can summon the optimates and the senate. When his term of office has
been completed, he is co-opted into the number of procurators (they have
the highest authority in taking counsel about the state) after the syndics
have given testimony as to his integrity and uprightness. I omit the really
complicated method of selecting the doge; it is, however, such that no
one except those of the highest integrity and nobility of birth can take
this office (although formerly, by the old law, only plebeians were
selected). There is no use of the lot. To this man are attached eight men
for half a year, with the same power as the seven men among the
Venetians, as the five syndics have almost the same authority as the ten
among the Venetians. They take care of the state.

Next is the magistrate at the head of the general jurisdiction, whom
they call "podesta." This man is usually selected from abroad to come
into the city with three legates, for suitable compensation. A capital case
may be appealed from him to the senate. In addition, there are seven
semestrial men, who are called extraordinary because they have the right

---

[140] Paolo di Novi was a dyer according to the *Enciclopedia Italiana*.

of deciding cases arbitrarily and appointing guardians. Furthermore, the five men of civil cases are foreigners, whose term is limited to two years. They are commonly known as the "rota." Finally, there are the censors who supervise the heads of the guilds, lest they should abuse trade, weights, measures, or handicrafts. Military officials are appointed year by year, forty captains whom a single general commands. The care of the treasury is given to the bank of St. George, so much praised by all, which consists of one hundred men and eight paymasters, whence the remarkable wealth and advantages of the city, developed from the customs and taxes of the public domains and pawnshops.

FORM OF GOVERNMENT OF LUCCA

The government of Lucca is also in the hands of the optimates. Although thirty-four thousand men were counted in the city not so long ago, about two thousand in turn head the government. Since the annual college is composed of sixty optimates, the highest power of the state lies in their hands. Ten men with triennial authority are selected by these electors, of whom the greatest is called vexillary [standard-bearer]. It is a capital crime for them to leave the city. There is appointed also a senate of eighteen men, who with the decemvirs take counsel about the state. Next are the lesser officials: the rota of three men, a judge and two assessors, all foreigners; one of the assessors hears public trials, the other private. In addition, nine men with the foreign judge are judges of the merchants. Then there are the commissioners of grain, health,[141] and food supply. Furthermore, eight men watch over foreigners. Finally, there are six treasurers and the same number of captains of the soldiers.[142] But nothing is more famous than the college of censors, who punish with a three-year exile wicked men and those indulging too freely in dissipation, who have been too often censured, according to the opinion of the great council. Yet the men of Lucca and of Genoa are not really free, but obtain their liberty by paying tribute to the king of Spain. The Genoese, to keep possession of the Island of Chios, formerly used also to pay the prince of the Turks thirty thousand golden crowns; the Venetians paid twelve thousand; the Ragusans, thirteen thousand, under the name of tribute, that they might be free from taxes and customs. But recently all the islands, with the exception of a very few, came under the rule of the Turks.

[141] The edition of 1595 gives *salis*, but the editions of 1566, 1572, and 1583 give *salutis*.

[142] The edition of 1583 reads *militum*, while the edition of 1595 reads *milium*.

There is among the Ragusans also a government composed of optimates. Twenty-four families of very ancient nobility still remain, from whom the college of optimates is formed. But, as with the Venetians, all serve at one time. A senate of sixty men is created by them. Next in importance are ten men, over whom the rector, as leader of the city-state, is wont to preside; then five men having almost the same power as the ten of the Venetians. Then six men of consular rank, judges of civilian cases, five men for criminal cases, from whom appeal is made to the curia of thirty men. There are six men for duty at night. The other appointees have no power to command, like the triumvirs who take care of the treasury; four quaestors, two directors of the mint, commissioners of the town, grain supply, and health, and finally the captain of the citadel, who is changed daily. As it was once among the Athenians, the president of the senate used to have the keys to the citadel and the treasury. They have much in common with the Venetians in their system of directing the state. Yet this is really different—that to maintain authority they enlist the executive's bodyguard from the Pannonians, as the Genoese from the Helvetians and the Germans. But of all the states which ever existed, none produced more incredible changes in brief time than did the Republic of the Florentines within 331 years. It seems to me very useful to explain briefly that which I have learned both from Florentines and from their historians—Poggio, I mean, Machiavelli, Antonine, and Guicciardini—so that from this kind of state we may be able to judge more truly and better about the best type of government.

TYPE AND EVOLUTION OF THE FLORENTINE EMPIRE

When the popes and the emperors quarreled about the control of Italy, as we have said before, the Florentines won their way to liberty, in the year 1215, and in an assembly of the citizens they created twelve magistrates whom they called "seniors," as well as two justices, the urban and the foreign, for a term of one year. But when they had bestowed all power upon a few, suddenly dissensions broke out. After authority had been taken from the former officials, the Florentines elected thirty-six men to establish a government, whom they called "reformers"; guilds of craftsmen were founded and for them magistrates like tribunes were appointed. When the more prominent people favored the party of the Ghibellines, the Ghibellines were driven forth and the citizens elected twelve men, whom they called "the goodmen," thinking that if the name were changed, the customs would be changed likewise. Then they selected eighty senators to take counsel for the state, but the sovereignty of the entire state they granted to one hundred and eighty optimates, who had the highest power over the magistrates and the laws. They remained under this kind of government for almost thirty years. Later, when the government had been changed into an oligarchy and the nobles became quarrelsome, their command was taken away by the people. Then, having created triumvirs, whom they called *priori*, along with a gonfalonier, to whom they gave a praetorian guard to protect the state, they formed in addition four companies of urban and country men, lest they should be hard pressed by an enemy. Since the great standard-bearer was of democratic origin, he prevented the nobles from seeking honors even by lot. Afterwards very serious dissension occurred among the nobles. On that account the people were divided into various parties, and after they had for a long time been torn with civil strife, by common consent they appealed to the pope to send them a man of royal stock, whom they would willingly obey. So he sent to Florence, Charles of Valois, the king of Sicily, who at that time had gone to Rome. Charles then for some time subdued the tumult, invited the exiles and those oppressed by civil wars to return. But, recalled by his own people, he left the city not yet completely pacified. Thereupon greater tumults and slaughter than ever ensued, to such an extent that almost all the Lucchese, disturbed by the calamity of their neighbors, hurried out from the city to Florence to settle the riots. They were not stilled, however, until they were quelled by external war.

So in the year 1304 they changed the form of the state and instead of one standard-bearer, they made three, whom they called *pannonieri*, having very great power, even dictatorial. When an assembly of all the citizens had been summoned, they instituted a system of election which they have used ever since—that is, they selected certain citizens who were suited to hold offices and honors and cast their names into urns or bags, so that year by year these names were drawn by lot. This approved list was changed every tenth year, sometimes oftener. They chose by lot eight men, who headed the state for two months in association with the standard-bearer whose term was one year. For an advisory council they elected a senate of two hundred and fifty men—part of them noble, part from the people. The college of optimates was constituted of three hundred citizens. Not even with this kind of government did the Florentines remain quiet long, on account of civil discord and domestic ill feeling. So by common consent they invited Walter de Brienne, duke of Athens, the man who was afterwards killed by the English as constable at the defeat of Poitiers. To him the optimates granted yearly authority, but the plebs, with enthusiastic shouting, ordered that he be made perpetual prince. This man then attached three hundred men to himself to retain control of the government. Yet since he seemed to bear himself too haughtily, he could keep command for barely ten months; he was driven out of the city by all classes with great slaughter of his own followers.

Again, they established a standard-bearer and eight men along with tribunes of the plebs or leaders of the guilds, and they restored the nobles, whom they had kept from honors theretofore. Then a powerful faction of the nobles started to oppress the people and the plebs. The lowest class as well as more responsible people complained that although they had overthrown the tyranny of one man, several had taken control of the state; and the discords grew so that when the nobles were in great part killed, or defeated, or driven into exile they surrendered to the people and were prohibited altogether from seeking honors.

Then, with the establishment of a strictly popular government in the year 1354, when no discords against the nobles could occur, the people began to fight among themselves for power. In the same way that the Buondelmonti had quarreled with the Uberti and then the Donati with the Cerchi, all patricians, and had disturbed the state for a long time, until they were driven out by the popular party, so the Ricci and the Albizzi, men of the people, renewed the factions of the Guelphs and the Ghibellines. Then slaughter and exile followed, until the plebeian workmen, seizing the opportunity, took up arms against the people and devastated and burnt the home of every rich man. When the popular power had been altogether abased, there followed the ochlocracy of the seditious plebs, or rather anarchy. During three entire years robbery, murder, and arson were rife in the midst of the city. Ultimately the plebs, rioting furiously, fought a pitiless civil war among themselves for control. At length, somewhat weary and more broken than satiated, after they had proposed an amnesty they appointed magistrates in accordance with the old custom, and for twenty years they managed without civil war. At that time, of course, they did not strive for office, but took modestly what was offered and ruled justly. Afterwards, bored with the long-continued calm, for no reason whatsoever they condemned Cosimo de' Medici, who was called the "father of his country." [143] Yet the same man later was recalled from exile by force and civil war, and a great number of his enemies were driven forth. From this time the Medici family gained the highest power in the state without complete sovereignty, since of course he won to his side the sagacious and good men, and by their assistance the state and the sortition of magistrates was directed. But after Cosimo, who had directed the helm of state, had died, they fell back upon murder and banishment, until when every quarrelsome man had been put down, the Medici recovered their authority. This they retained for about thirty years, although the Pazzi made a conspiracy, killed Julian de' Medici before the altar, and seriously wounded his brother Lorenzo. As a result, the conspirators were punished by death and banishment. The exiles, on the other hand, invited Pope Sixtus and Alphonso to bring armies in order to conquer for a hostile power the fatherland in which the exiles themselves could not reign. Finally, when the state had been liberated, after a serious war, a senate of seventy men was established, by whose counsels public affairs were guided until Piero de' Medici, after the death of his father, Lorenzo, was not satisfied with the power he had and tried to make himself king. On this account arose greater sedition than ever, which did not cease until the more powerful citizens to a man had been driven from the city. So it happened that in the year 1494 the plebs stampeded back and forth like a flock without a shepherd, fearing the designs of men and of wild beasts. This Machiavelli reported. At length the senate, convening with reluctance, quarreled for a long time about approving a form of government, since some preferred the optimates, some the people. Then, persuaded by the rioting throngs of Savonarola and Soderini, they accepted the popular form of government, with the condition that the highest magistrate in the state, who among them was called "gonfalonier," should hold office for life and that no rogations could be made to the people (the dregs of the plebs being ignored), except about laws and magistrates and the public money. Not long after, oppressed by the power of Piero Soderini, and, later, of Francis Valori, they rebelled again and by force of arms drove the more powerful classes from control, killing Valori himself, although he was a judge and a high official, when he attempted to check an appeal to the people. Again, in the year 1512, they made the highest office of yearly tenure and gave to the senate of eighty men a six months' term. A little

[143] Machiavelli, *History of Florence*, VII. i. 349.

later Pope Leo, a prince of the house of Medici, feigning that he wished to restore the state to that form in which it had been before the year 1494, transferred the popular power to fifty men, commonly known as the *balia*, and gave them office for life after he had destroyed the liberty of the people. Nevertheless, when Pope Clement, another prince of the house of Medici, was captured, the state returned to its early form. Finally control slipped into the power of one man, for the Florentines, forced by the soldiers of Emperor Charles, received Alexander de' Medici, with a guard of soldiers, into the town. Imitating Clearchus, the tyrant of Heracleia, he then killed, proscribed, and exiled the more powerful leaders and the enemies of his name. In turn, he was assassinated by Lorenzo de' Medici, and the successor to his power was Cosimo, who with incredible cleverness escaped repeated conspiracies. The greatest flaw in that state was that popular rule was preferred to that of the optimates, then that control of the entire state was granted to a standard-bearer and eight men were chosen to serve for two months; they did not have any senate except in crises, and then it was almost powerless. This is equivalent to a body that lacks a mind. For the safety of a state rests with the senate; but there sixteen men, leaders of guilds and of working men, like tribunes of the plebs, with no mediator, opposed the greater magistrates in such a way that it was inevitable that the country should be torn by perpetual strife. At last they admitted to honors by lot both the plebs and those born in the city of foreign parents, whereby the government became more popular. But let us shift from foreign countries to our own.

FORM OF GOVERNMENT AND EVOLUTION OF THE EMPIRE OF THE FRENCH

At first our ancestors flourished for a long time under kings, as Caesar, Book VI, and Livy, Book V, bear witness. In those times they conquered almost all Europe and Asia Minor with their arms, led forth colonies, founded cities, and gave race names of the Celts and Gauls to the conquered regions, whence Celtiberia, Celtoscythia, Portogallia, Galicia, Galatia, Gallia Transalpina, Gallia Britannorum; hence the names of many regions captured by the Boii and the Helvetians, whom Tacitus calls Gauls. I omit these because they have been explained by others.

FORM OF GOVERNMENT IN MARSEILLES

However, when the kings ruled ineffectively, the optimates took over control. They seem to have done this from the example of the Massilians, who had led a colony from Phocaea to the Celtic shore. Six hundred optimates were at the head of the state of the Massilians.[144] From these every year fifteen magistrates were appointed, among whom three presiding officers had the greatest power, as Strabo wrote. Following their example the others divided the people into the three orders suited to nature—that is, in accordance with the form of reason, wrath, and lust. The druids were forever exempted from military service and freed from all tax burdens, as Caesar wrote. But they controlled the civil authority, religious affairs, and laws and constituted the final court of appeal. The knights took care of military matters, along with vassals and retainers; the plebs, the fields and handiwork. An assembly drawn from these three orders had the sovereignty of the entire state. But it is said that such was the wisdom of the druids, such the strength and majesty of their rule, that when they held the annual assembly they compelled all important leaders to obey their edicts and decisions without violence and kept each to his task, solely through fear of religion and of interdiction from sacred things, as the bitterest of all punishments.[145] From this we may understand how great was the veneration for the ancient religion, as Caesar wrote. Where fear of the divine will exists, there piety, justice, and all virtues must flourish. I say nothing of that loftiest knowledge of heavenly and natural things, which is attributed to them by the consent of all the writers. I discuss only the state.

It is inferred that their government was aristocratic from the fact that while there were two very powerful factions of the Haedui and Arverni among the Celts, the separate governments of the Belgian towns used to have a gathering of the optimates and were bound by the same rules and laws in assemblies as in the court trials of the druids, although there were many chieftains everywhere. Furthermore, almost every town had its aristocracy, as did the cities of the Germans, which are bound by the laws of the empire. If anyone attempted to establish a tyranny, it was the custom to burn him alive. To escape this penalty Orgetorix committed suicide when accused of an attempted tyranny, as Caesar himself wrote in his *Commentaries*. Of course each man was ruler of his family and had the right of life and death not only over the slaves but also over his wives and children, as Caesar himself testified. Justinian, in addition to many others, erred in alleging, in the chapter on a father's power,[146] that no people had so much power over their sons as the Romans had, for

---

[144] Strabo *Geography* IV. I.
[145] "Solely . . . punishments" is omitted from the edition of 1595.
[146] *De patria potestate* is *Institutes* I. 8.

it is evident from Aristotle and the Mosaic Law that the custom is also common to the Persians and the Hebrews. The ancients understood that such was the love of the parents toward their sons that even if they wished very much to abuse their power, they could not. Moreover, nothing was a more potent cause of virtue and reverence in children toward their parents than this patriarchal power. But that the separate towns had the aristocratic form of government may be inferred from the fact that the plebs were kept from honors and counsels and that the highest magistrates for each year were not appointed without great rivalry. When Caesar learned this from the inhabitants, he said, "It is a custom of the country to sow factions in Gaul. This is an old custom and advisedly maintained, that the plebs may be safe from the injuries of the more powerful; nowhere in the world are the plebs more despised. Indeed, this group was once regarded as in a position amounting nearly to servitude and now is excluded from all public councils." [147] He left this testimony like a secret of the ancient empire. But I am amazed that Caesar thought that those factions which brought ruin to the state had been salutary for the plebs. Of course, I confess that Aristotle's advice is prudent—in a state men having different opinions should be selected as magistrates, lest they plunder the public wealth in the same way that family servants who agree too well plunder domestic possessions. But when they regard each other with mutual hatred, they expose their own crimes, so the plebs are safer from the rapine of the magistrates when they quarrel among themselves. On the other hand, factions cannot grow among the princes without great suffering to the plebs. For whatever wrongs kings commit, as the poets say, the Achaeans pay the penalty,[148] unless there is one prince of outstanding power who can when he wishes coerce the party leaders without favoring anyone. If he wishes to defend some to the peril of others, it is to be feared that he will lose control; this happened to Henry VI, king of England, when he took up the defense of the Lancastrian party against the Yorkists; he was defeated by the latter faction and murdered in prison. Yet I do not wish to take a stand against the opinion of Caesar. I would say this only: the ruin of almost all states has had its start in the quarrels of princes. This is too obvious to everyone to need examples.

Caesar gave this evidence about our ancestors: among the Haedui the factions of the princes brought ruin to the state, when some summoned

147 Possibly based on Caesar De bello Gallico VI. 11-13.
148 Horace Epistles I. ii. 14.

troops from the Germans, others called in the Roman soldiers. In the end the country, broken by the long war with Caesar, yielded to the Romans, but under the stipulation that a great part of the cities should enjoy their own justice and liberty, as Pliny reported in Book VII. Four hundred years later, when Romans, Goths, and Hungarians were quarreling, the Franks, ancient colonists of the Gauls, gradually occupied all Gaul and established our form of royal power, so that few peoples have flourished longer in military reputation and none in civil. On the military side, indeed, it is evident that the French, under the leadership of Charles the Great, joined greater Germany, the Pannonias, Saxony, Italy, and a part of Spain to the domain of all Gaul. They governed for ninety years both Syrias and Cyprus, liberated from the most cruel servitude. They destroyed the empire of the Lombards. They gave to the Roman pontiffs a good part of Italy as a gift. They yielded to the Venetians Crete and the Peloponnesus when they invaded the empire of the Greeks, over which they reigned for fifty years. These facts, of course, are evidence of great military prowess.

But on the civil side there is no greater proof than that foreign kings and princes from the extremities of Germany, Italy, and the shores of Spain flocked in a great throng to the senate of the French, just as to the sacred asylum of justice. For example, in 1244 Emperor Frederick II took to this senate the controversies which he had with Innocent IV about the Kingdom of Naples. In 1312 the Count of Namur brought into this senate his case against Charles of Valois for the county of Namur, not questioning the influence of so great a prince, whom he defeated in the trial. In 1320, likewise, Philip, prince of Tarentum, won his case against the Duke of Burgundy in this senate, when they were arguing about the expenses incurred in recovering the empire of the Greeks. Yet in another trial the same man was fined. In 1342, with equal willingness, the Duke of Lorraine and Guy of Châtillon, his brother-in-law, received in this senate the decision regarding the division of the family estates. Moreover, in 1390 when the Dauphin and the Count of Savoy quarreled about the marquisate of Saluzzo and voluntarily betook themselves to this court, the count was defeated at the trial; he was again defeated in another trial and was condemned in 1400 to restore the entire area. Afterwards the inhabitants of Cambrai, a free people, who were called into litigation, appeared in court that they might agree to the matters decided by the senate, and they gave satisfaction in 1403. But there is no more famous example than the fact that the kings of Castile and Portugal, when compacts between them had been concluded, judged that these should have no force until they had been ratified by this body and promulgated from its open doors. It would be endless to follow all instances. Furthermore, the king, as well as private citizens, agrees to its laws and decrees.

The most ancient law of the kingdom is said to be the Salic. This may be seen in the laws of the Salians; it removes women from succession to the throne, although there is doubt as to whether it was ratified or not. However this may be, of course, Baldus and many jurisconsults acted stupidly when in interpreting the Salic Law they confused the rights of inheritance with the majesty of empire as though they were discussing booty and the possession of goods. Moreover, it is not peculiar to this kingdom, but is common to Assyrians, Persians, Hebrews, Egyptians, Greeks, Romans, Abyssinians, Carthaginians, Germans, and Scythians, who kept women far from power. Not so long ago the Aragonese accepted Petronilla, the Castilians, Isabella, the Mantuans, Matilda, the Neapolitans, both Joans, and Norway, Margaret; then Navarre and Lorraine also transferred sovereignty to women. Yet Roderick the historian definitely stated that by an ancient law of the Spanish the rule was denied to women and, moreover, that serious complaints were often heard from the people because the display and favoritism of Isabella had violated the laws. Even Guicciardini left testimony of this. Finally, the Britons, who in early days always abhorred the rule of women, recently allowed Mary and her sister to reign, whereby, of course, not only divine laws were violated, which explicitly subject women to the rule of men, but even the laws of nature itself, which gave to men the power of ruling, judging, assembling, and fighting, and kept the women away. The laws are disregarded, not only of nature, but also of all races, which never allowed women to rule. Zenobia, of course, invaded Palmyra with thirty tyrants, but in a short while she was driven from control by Aurelian. Irene herself was driven into a monastery by Nicephorus when he conquered the Greek Empire. Tomyris, Semiramis, and Thalestris ruled in the name of their sons.

The prince is restricted also by the Agrarian Law, which forbids alienation of the public domain without the consent of the Estates. Though he may want to alienate it very much, he can in no way do this, since on the death of the king the royal proctor takes perpetual possession thereof. Although princes often tried to break that law, yet they could not do it. In another clause of the Agrarian Law the prince is prohibited from claiming for himself common lands or any lands of foreigners or of condemned persons if they do not closely adjoin the royal domain, lest, enticed by an evil lure, he should be tempted by the possessions of private citizens to cruelty and rapine. But in many places in France the goods of the condemned are left to the legitimate heirs. Elsewhere the prince is required to give these things into the public treasury or to turn in the financial proceeds, as was stipulated in the law passed by Francis I of Valois. Of all the laws of the realm, however, none is more sacred than that which denies to the decrees of the princes any force unless they are in keeping with equity as well as truth. From this it comes about that many are cast out by the magistrates, and the grace granted [by the prince] is no help to the wicked. Often the voice of the magistrates is heard, "The prince can do nothing contrary to the laws." Indeed, when Henry, father of the present one, ordered that an Italian servant be put in prison without assigning a cause, the judges freed the man, yet first admonished the king for ordering him to be condemned on the pretext that he [the king] had taken the man in the basest crime, which he was unwilling to make public. Nevertheless, the judges did not wish to condemn the defendant, although the best of princes piously and solemnly swore that the man was taken in crime by him. He was angry at the judges because they did not have faith in what he said. The prisoner, however, was freed by the judges and dismissed from jail; but afterwards, by order of the king, he was plunged into the River Seine at night, lest the unusual event should trouble the people. Nevertheless, the jurisconsults think that the prince can judge according to his conscience, in the title "Concerning the office of governor," starting with "forbidden," under the paragraph "truth," [149] and Pope Paul III, influenced by this idea, punished by death a well-known man who had confessed to him, when he was still a cardinal, that he had committed homicide.[150]

But the superior courts have no regard for laws except for those which they have approved by their own proclamation, and they say that they cannot be coerced. Yet when custom grows obsolete we turn gradually away from precedent. Oh, that we might imitate the virtue of our elders! They preferred to depart from life rather than to abandon their opinions. Their children prefer the loss of both state and reputation rather than office. When Louis XI (who first is said to have liberated the kings from servitude) attempted to bring ruin on the Parlement of Paris unless it proclaimed the laws ordained by him, the fathers, realizing the import

[149] *Illicitas ¶ veritas De officio praesidis* refers to *Dig.* 1. 18. 6.
[150] "Nevertheless . . . homicide" is absent from the edition of 1566.

of the situation, approached the king arrayed in purple. Then said he, "What cause brings you hither?" Said La Vacquerie, "To seek death rather than to suffer the passage of iniquitous laws." The king, thoroughly alarmed by the speech of the president and the remarkable firmness of the magistrates, received them kindly, and the laws which he had ordered to be proclaimed he commanded should be destroyed in his presence, swearing that hereafter he would decree nothing except what was equitable. By judgment of the Parlement his father, Charles VII, was ordered to cut down a wood near the capital and to sell it at a given price, by decree of the court. He did not refuse to obey the order. By another law, also, or rather by established right, the king is prevented at his accession from revoking the office or the authority of any man, unless he shall have been convicted of crime and condemned in public trial, although in the announcement of offices by the prince that old formula is wont to be cited "as long as it please us." This law is upheld unfailingly and has become custom, although the annual vow which the judges used to take on the twelfth of November, shows sufficiently that not so long ago they held office for one year, as Budé also reported. Philip the Fair, as well as many great men of today, thought that the annual system ought to be renewed. But Louis XI promulgated a law about perpetual offices, in order that thereafter no office might be taken away from anyone except through death, or retirement, or public trial. On the other hand, when Henry II came into the Parlement once, along with the constable, to force through a law of which the court disapproved, he is reported to have said, prompted by the speech of I know not whom, the court of Paris could not legally act, unless he himself ordered it, since the jurisdiction was given from year to year to the twelfth of November.

Whether, indeed, it would be wiser to grant perpetual authority or, on the contrary, to limit the time, of course I should not dare to say, since it is of great importance; yet I believe that for the protection of popular and aristocratic rule this office ought to be granted for a short time, as seemed best to Aristotle. But I should think that in a kingdom a different opinion might prevail. What would the magistrates dare to do contrary to the power and desire of princes if they feared that their honors would be taken from them? Who will defend the weak from servitude? Who will guard the interest of the people, if the magistrate has been driven away and they must comply with the demands of the mighty? Furthermore, a magistrate's authority is of little weight when it is bestowed for only a short time, and we do not easily obey the men, nor with dignity do they command, whom we have had as companions in our daily life and who afterwards are going to be private citizens. But if the people understand that a man cannot be driven from power except for crime, that man is necessarily feared by the wicked, reverenced by the prince, and he becomes a good man either because a sense of shame forces him or because he fears punishment—lest along with his reputation he may lose life, head, and fortune. Indeed, there are censors and investigators of all his actions. Then what Alexander, otherwise a good authority, believed in the title "About Things Loaned," starting at "imperial" [151] is childish. He said that power of office given to a private citizen with this clause, "as long as it seems good to us," is valid in perpetuity. He thought this was done on the strength of the title "About Release," starting "those skilled in the law," [152] and from "About Things Loaned," starting "it is enough." [153] But this is not to our purpose. Indeed, it is of greater weight and moment to guard the secret of this kingdom—the fact that the royal power is greatly limited when perpetual honors are granted to magistrates, for nothing can be more efficacious for restraining the tyranny of a prince. On the contrary, by frequent change of officials the power of the prince more than of anyone else is considerably increased, as Aristotle wrote; and by continual increase, it becomes a tyranny. But the more you can take from the power of the prince (and on this point one cannot be wrong), the more just will be the rule and the more stable for the future, as King Theopompus is reported to have said when power was granted to the ephors. Those who by evil arts think to increase the authority of the prince err, since they are attempting the overthrow of the kingdom and of the kings. Indeed, it is more important than empire, as the Emperor Theodosius decided, that the princely power should be subordinated to the laws.

So Machiavelli is mistaken in reporting that our king is lord of our treasury. There is a precise manner of distribution defined by law; if he goes beyond this without the senate's permission, he is not obeyed, and the overseers of accounts do not place funds to the credit of the treasurers without excellent reasons. King Charles VIII, on the first of September, 1492, promulgated a law providing that the largess and gifts of the prince should not be valid unless the pension list were approved by the

---

[151] *Principalibus de rebus creditis* refers to *Dig.* 12. 1. 33.

[152] *Jurisperitos, de excusat. tut.* refers to *Dig.* 27. 1. 30. *Tut.* for *tutela* or *tutorum* does not appear in the heading in the *Digest.*

[153] *Sufficit. de rebus creditis. De rebus creditis* is *Dig.* 12. 1 or *Codex,* 4. 1, but I am unable to locate the paragraph *sufficit.*

overseers of accounts. Small donations of a hundred pounds are excepted, but even these are not valid without the assent of the paymasters. I have copied this law from the original records, which have been kept inviolable. Indeed, it is a peculiar virtue of this monarchy that the prince is arbiter of all rewards in the state, yet he cannot inflict any punishments, but relinquishes this unpleasant duty to the magistrates. Whereby it happens that he is held worthy of the love of all, the hate of none, and powerful men, condemned by the judges, have no cause to be angry at him, because he is not responsible. Everyone accepts the judicial decision, but if anyone, relying upon his own might does not recognize authority, the governors of the provinces and the leaders of marshals force him to obey by using weapons, and everyone takes up arms against one man. The opposite happens with the Germans, among whom the decrees of the imperial curia have almost no force if they are unfavorable to powerful men, because the rulers of the vassal states are unwilling to attempt by arms a policy which they fear they cannot follow out.

Nothing difficult of attainment is uselessly decreed among us. Thus the superior courts, which in great part are drawn from the third estate, coerce the might of the nobles and more powerful subjects by impartial decrees and, as it were, maintain the highest and the lowest in unbelievable harmony. Those who have been trying to overthrow the dignity of these courts seek the ruin of the state, since in these is placed the safety of civil order, of laws, of customs, and of the entire state. There are seven courts of this sort; the greatest consists of one hundred and forty judges, from whom there is no appeal. Nor may one recklessly supplicate the prince without a large fine.

Another great bond of this empire lies in the patronage of the nobles. While in all the states of Greece the weak and the plebs were oppressed by the patricians and the patricians rather often were driven out by the attacking plebs and the two classes were perpetually quarreling, it happened by a certain divine goodness that since the laws of fiefs were proclaimed the nobles have guarded the lowly from injury as their retainers. This is, perhaps, the reason why empires endure so long among peoples who use these laws. But we have this additional advantage, that the firstborn among our nobility, as well as among the Britons, take a great part of the whole inheritance, and by perpetual succession the elder sons guard the ancestral inheritance, lest if the fields were divided among many, the glory of a noble class, which maintains military discipline, might perish. This is what Lycurgus first commended so highly among the

Spartans; then Plato in the *Republic* and the *Laws*. But the latter limited the hereditary portions to 5,040, the former to nine thousand; we have no certain number. If we should maintain the custom of our elders, to which the Germans alone hold fast, that is, that women should be kept away altogether from fiefs and the next male heirs should inherit Salic land (for in an ancient testament at Bordeaux it is reported that this is the name applied to a fief, by the man who first wrote a book about the Salic Law), I should not want the laws of Lycurgus or of Plato about the succession. But when the first Capetian among us granted government of the provinces to the dukes and counts, he created an opportunity to violate the law. Afterwards parents readily obtained for women permission to take Salic land.

If among us authority is thus constituted, Jovius made a capital blunder, of course, since he preposterously attacked the French for thinking that a certain divinity of spirit inheres in kings. What if he had seen the English uncover when passing before the throne, even if it were empty? He himself was worthy of greater scorn, because all his life he did not blush to kiss more than servilely the feet of his master. Not only the kings of the Persians and of the Turks, but even the most haughty caliphs of the Arabs always abhorred that kind of worship. There is, therefore, and always has been (Oh, that it may last forever!) such sympathy and harmony between the prince and the French people that a people never surrounded a prince with greater reverence or a prince a people with greater love. Moreover, how much divinity the people think is in the prince and how much liberty they enjoy can be understood from the fact that not so long ago Louis XII permitted renewal of the custom of showing ancient comedy on the stage so that everyone's faults were commented upon facetiously. Everywhere else, especially in Venice, this was always a capital crime; but he did not wish to be spared himself, since he said that the prince could not otherwise have confidence in his policies. Oh, excellent prince and worthy to rule the world! Relying upon the integrity and innocence of his life, he did not fear the evil comments of the wicked.

Before the time of Henry, it is true, we never used the word "Majesty" in addressing the king. I mention this because many things about our customs and rule have been reported incorrectly by Italians and foreigners. It seems incredible, yet it is true, that not one king has been killed by a conspiracy of the people. One was murdered through the plot of an adulterous wife. When Charles the Simple was captured by

Herbert of Vermandois Charles, although a most bitter enemy, did not die by violence, but perished through illness and old age. Yet his son Louis executed Herbert. No greater proof of a stable state exists than was shown recently in the religious wars that flamed throughout all France. Although the leaders of the parties devastated everything with slaughter and fire, yet the splendor and prestige of the courts and of the greatest cities strangely enough was undiminished. Then many battles and great tumults were quieted in a short time by an edict of the best of kings, as swarms of bees may be checked by the throwing of a little dust. The prince forgot all injuries. Goodness of such a nature is innate in the race of the Valois. This is not a new custom, but one accepted by our elders. Charles VII was despoiled of his kingdom, and judged altogether unworthy in the court of Paris; yet when he had achieved a stronger position by the peace of Arras, he overwhelmed and defeated the English, who held control. Many thought that he would avenge his own sorrows; but he was so far from revenge that, imitating the clemency of Caesar, he kindly received the Parlement and the people of Paris into his protection.

These things produce enduring empires—when princes avenge drastically the injuries of others, but overlook their own entirely. Indeed, we find that no kingdom has flourished longer with the same form of government, except that of the Assyrians. Almost the twelve-hundredth year has now slipped away since the beginning of this kingdom, which started from the family of Waramund, then fell to the Merovingians, then to Charles the Great, and finally descended to the race of Capet; nevertheless, it could not be overthrown by civil or foreign wars. But the kings of Egypt, if we believe Josephus, hardly attained the thousandth year. I ignore the many fables about the Assyrians and the Egyptians and how easy it was in those times to establish and hold an empire, when there were no enemies to keep them from reigning. But as for those empires, limited to city walls, which are called very old, those of the Lydians, the Tyrians, the Argives, the Corinthians, the Spartans, and the Athenians, Plutarch, in his life of Theseus and Diodorus, affirmed that they were fabulous for the most part; and even if they were true, those which actually lasted for a long time did not exceed eight hundred years.

CHANGES IN THE EMPIRE OF THE CHALDEANS

It is true that the Chaldeans lived very quietly for 249 years after the flood. This period is called golden by Cato in *Origins*—if, indeed, he is the author of this book. Then Ninus invaded Asia Minor with an army;

after this man thirty-seven kings reigned 1,220 years, even to the fall of Sardanapalus. His empire surrendered to the prefects Arbaces and Beloch. After the kingdom had been divided into two parts there was a struggle between the Medes and the Assyrians for almost three hundred years, until the Persians seized control. From that time they held the helm until the reign of Alexander, who enlarged the empire of the Persians, extending it far and wide from India to the Hellespont. After Alexander died and the empire had been divided, Seleucus received Asia Major; Antipater, Asia Minor; Ptolemy, Egypt; Antipater, Macedonia; and Lysimachus, Thrace. Then, devastated by serious wars and aflame with internecine strife, after two hundred years they fell into the power of the Romans. Asia Major yielded to the Parthians 172 years after the death of Alexander. Their kingdom flourished about five hundred years from Arsaces to Artabanus and won a great reputation for military prowess. At this time Artaxerxes the Persian, having killed Artabanus, seized the throne; and the Persians held this for more than four hundred years, until Omar, the prince of the Arabians, invaded Persia and Syria.

CHANGES OF THE EMPIRE OF THE GREEKS

Let us consider the other empires in natural order of priority: that is, from Justinian, who, taking Africa from the Vandals and Italy from the Goths, broke the attacks of the Parthians and restored the dignity of the empire while he himself obtained the highest reputation for military and civil administration. Abandoning Spain to the Goths, Gaul to the French, Britain and Upper Germany to the inhabitants, he set the boundaries of the Greek Empire at the Danube, the Alps, the Euphrates, and the extended shores of Africa. In this form of government the empire flourished almost one hundred and twenty years, that is, to Constant, the grandson of Heraclius, in whose times the Arabs took from the Romans, Egypt, Syria, and Cilicia; afterwards, even Africa. They sent their army and colonies as far as Italy. On the other hand, the Slavs invaded the Pannonias and Illyricum. Earlier, the Lombards established themselves in Insubria and occupied a good part of Italy. Civil wars for the empire of the Greeks followed, when one emperor was elected by the soldiers, another by the senate. Leontius drove the younger Justinian into exile; Absimarus forced Leontius into prison, after he had slit his nose. Justinian, restored with the aid of barbarians, drove his adversaries from the empire. Philippicus followed him, but he, in turn, was most cruelly blinded by Artemius; nor was the latter's rule of long duration. A little later Tiberius, elected emperor, was killed by Leo. Still greater was the cruelty of Constantine IV, who blinded Artavasdus, along with his sons, after the conquest of Constantinople; but Constantine suffered very great defeat in his turn at the hands of the Bulgarians and died miserably. Then power was taken over by Irene, who blinded her son because she sought marriage with Charles the Great; she was put into a monastery by Nicephorus. This very man was made emperor and afterwards was killed by the Bulgarians. Two Michaels followed him, of whom the last was cruelly murdered by Basil. By that time the empire of the Greeks was much reduced in size, since they had lost Illyricum and all of Italy, and Turks and Arabs had occupied a good part of Asia. But the princes of the Greeks themselves were harassed by mutual animosities and civil wars for a long time, until the empire was occupied by the armies of the French. Yet these people were driven out after fifty-six years, and the Greeks again took command; but since the Palaeologi and the Cantacuzeni quarreled, they called in the Turks, masters of Asia, by whom a little later they were driven from the empire.

CHANGES OF THE ARABIAN EMPIRE

The empire of the Arabians also had commenced to decline when the Turks led their armies into Europe. When the Arabs broke away from the Greeks, in the year of grace 650 approximately, they seized in a short time Syria, Egypt, Persia, and Africa, even to the ocean, afterwards Spain also, Crete, Sicily, the Peloponnesus, and a part of Italy, with such a rapid succession of victories that they seemed to have conquered these many regions before they had actually traversed them. Although their history is obscure and full of fables, which our men have put into writing, yet it can be understood easily from Leo the African and William, bishop of Tyre, who inspected their antiquities and penetrated far into their country, that almost no empire of olden times except the Roman Empire ever was greater. The high priests, who were called caliphs, had so much influence through religion alone that they directed arbitrarily all laws, divine and human. To these men, as to the gods, generals and armies were subordinate. The other princes owed to them life, rank, fortunes, and finally power. But when they began to quarrel among themselves about religion, on account of the murder of Ali, the Egyptian caliphs waged very serious wars with those of Bagdad [154] and Damascus. Then, because of the strength of the French, they were forced to leave Further

---

[154] The editions of 1572 and 1583 read Babylon.

Spain and afterwards Italy, Cyprus, and Syria. At length, repulsed also by the Persians, the Tartars, and the Turks, they concentrated their strength in Egypt and Africa, about the year of grace 1100. Thus, the Tunisian kings have governed the kingdom from the first incursion of the Arabs into Africa until today, that is, for nine hundred years, as Muley Hasan boasted in the presence of Pope Paul. The sultans held Egypt 336 years, from Saladin to Touman Bey, whom Selim, prince of the Turks, executed. But the Tunisian kings developed such an intense and murderous rivalry with the Moors, while the Moors—later the sultans—quarreled among themselves, so that, broken by the strength of the Spanish and the Turks, they are now accustomed to be subordinates.

CHANGES IN THE EMPIRE OF THE TURKS

In almost the same period in which Saladin occupied Egypt, two very powerful empires were gradually developing, that is, those of the Tartars and the Turks. Hayton wrote that Genghis Khan, a prince of the Tartars, who once were called Scythians, extended his empire far and wide into Greater Asia Minor. From this same race of Turks, one legion which had come to aid the Persians accepted the religion of the Arabs and settled down in Asia Minor. Gradually, because of the discord of the Arabs and the Greeks, it grew to such power that since Selim, a private person, seized the principality of Cappadocia, in the year 1104, up to Selim, the father of the present sultan, they won not only all the empires of the Greeks and of the Arabs but also all the provinces from the Danube to the Dnieper, peopled by the most ferocious men, and both Pannonias and Illyricum, although they were involved in great wars with Persians, Christians, and Tartars. But since many men have written many things about the state of the Turks, it is enough for me to touch lightly upon them. The most important fact, however, has been overlooked by those writers. For John Huraut, councillor of the privy council, and Louis Martin, both men famous for diplomatic activities and knowledge of affairs, have told me that all lands, with the exception of only a few, belong to the soldiers, whom they themselves call "timariots," from τὸ τιμᾶσθαι as I think; the rest are taxpayers, who are wont to pay to the soldiers taxes for the fields and to rent the taxable land on a ten-year lease.[155] When a timariot dies, the military office is arbitrarily awarded by grace of the prince, as once fiefs and benefices used to be given. If war is declared, the soldiers are available without stipend. Yet about seven praetorian

[155] "ab decimo quoque anno censualia praedia reconducere."

legions do receive their pay out of the public treasury, collected from the head tax. This system makes the state invincible. Charles V used the same law for the Indians, collecting only the capitation tax, whence an infinite store of gold (the taxes gathered from the customs are light) was taken to the treasury.

CHANGES IN THE EMPIRE OF THE POLES

Meanwhile the Poles, separated from the Germans politically, successfully administered the kingdom founded by their leader Pyastus in the year of grace 800. Before this time no definite narrative can be gathered from the historians. The deeds of the Poles are well known, however, from the fact that for a long time they waged very serious wars with the Turks, the Germans, and the Russians. They have, nevertheless, maintained until the present the prestige of their empire, have taken Prussia from the Germans, and are defending themselves bravely even today against the resources of the Turks. Moreover, their kingdom increased considerably in size when the race of Pyastus became extinct in the male line. At that time Jagellon, king of Lithuania, who had accepted the Christian religion, married Hedwiga, queen of Poland, in the year 1386. By this alliance the family of the Jagellons received the throne by legitimate right. Their last representative is the man now ruling, Sigismund. The Marquis of Brandenburg and the Voivode of Transylvania, on the other hand, trace their origin from the women of the Jagellons.

CHANGES OF THE EMPIRE OF DENMARK AND SWEDEN

In that same age in which Pyastus established himself in Poland, Charles the Great took control in France and Nicephorus, in Greece; Godefricus set up the kingdom of Denmark. It was based on force, as well as law, and from him to Nuba the monarchy lasted for 140 years. Then Henry the Fowler, emperor of the Germans, reduced that kingdom to the form of a province. When the Danes later seceded from the empire, they were again conquered by Otto; but once more they rebelled, under Sweyn their king, who was driven away by his brother Waldemar. From him the kingdom was carried by succession 211 years later to Margaret, who ruled over the empires of Denmark, Sweden, and Norway and adopted the duke of Pomerania. Thirty-five years later Engelbert, revolting from the Danes, invaded the kingdom of Sweden, which he afterwards abandoned, due to civil strife. Once more this triune dominion obeyed the rule of one man, a Bavarian. After him Christian was elected, and others descended from this ancestor have ruled down to the present time. Yet not so long ago Gustavus took the kingdom of Sweden by force from Christian II, whence great wars arose between the Danes and the Swedes, not yet quieted, even though Henry [Eric], king of Sweden, was captured by his own men and deprived of power by a conspiracy of his younger brother with the citizens of Stockholm. This happened on that very day (the thing is worthy of note) on which King Charles IX was almost defeated by the arms of his own people on the field of Meaux, that is, in the year 1567, on the 28th day of September. Moreover, what I learned from Holster, a Swede, is worthy of notice, that the princes have the right to select whom they wish from several children. This custom is reported common to the Poles, the Lithuanians, the Hungarians, and the Abyssinians. In truth, the governments of the Danes and the Poles may be called aristocracies, since among them the nobility have the right to make laws and peace, to carry arms, and they have power over life and death. Their elected prince can fulfill none of these functions without the approval of the nobles. On the contrary, a nobleman cannot even be judged by the prince or by a magistrate other than the optimates, where it is a question of his rank, his life, or his reputation.

CHANGES IN THE EMPIRE OF THE BRITONS

Next come the Britons, who, like almost all peoples, had a monarchy at first. Polydore Vergil, using ancient authors, either authentic or legendary, wrote that sixty-eight kings had commanded the Britons for about a thousand years before Caesar; but they obeyed the Romans for about five hundred years after they had been conquered by Caesar, that is, until the reign of the younger Theodosius. In these times, since they were hard pressed by the Scots and the Picts and had commenced to despair of Roman aid, they summoned from Germany the help of the Angles and the Saxons. These people, having defeated the Britons, easily got possession of the kingdom, but in such a way that seven kings ruled the divided empire and were engaged in perpetual civil wars. About three hundred years after the English had driven the Britons into France, however, that is, in the year of grace 800, Egbert ruled practically alone. Afterwards the Danes and the Scots, sometimes defeated and sometimes conquerors, harassed the island in the manner of pirates for almost one hundred and fifty years to Edward the Elder, who took command after the Danes had been driven out. A hundred years later, vexed by civil strife, they summoned William the Norman. This man, having killed Harold and founded a state, handed down the power in succession to his sons, who ruled effectively almost 110 years [*sic*]. Stephen, count of Blois, of the French race, followed, who guided the kingdom humanely by laws and civil training in the year of grace 1136. Afterwards Henry II, also of the French race, and, as many say, the son of Stephen, by paternal right the count of Anjou, Maine, and Touraine, obtaining England and Normandy through adoption by Stephen and maternal inheritance, and acquiring Aquitania and Poitou in the dowry of his wife, ruled a very great empire for a long time; then his posterity for four hundred years so governed this flourishing kingdom, abounding in military glory, that they occupied almost all France, a part through legitimate right, a part through force, a part through trickery, when the French were hard pressed by civil war. At long last the French conspired together and won a rapid series of victories, driving the English from the whole territory of France. But when the foreign war was over, these people waged civil wars with such great cruelty that the things which are reported about the tragic ferocity of the Thebans seem child's play beside those which are narrated by Polydore. Although he is said to have written many things in favor of this race, yet it ought not to seem remarkable that Philip de Comines has written that in the thirty years during which the civil wars were waged, more than eighty men of the royal family were killed in his own time. I omit twelve kings, who were killed or driven from power in a popular uprising or conspiracy of princes.

CHANGES OF THE SPANISH KINGDOM

We must now consider briefly the Spanish also. We see among them no empire more ancient than the Carthaginian, unless perchance the Celts and the Gauls had subdued a great part of Spain before the time of the Carthaginians, and we should assume that the Gauls named the region, as the Spanish confess. But since these things are not recognized in authentic history, we must start with the Carthaginians, who under their leader Mazeus occupied a great part of Spain, as can be understood from Justin and Orosius. They held the rule until they were driven out entirely by the Romans. Yet Spain was not completely conquered in the age of Scipio, for the farther region had its own leaders even in the time of Caesar. From Scipio Africanus to King Gonderic (who was the first of the race of the Vandals to invade Spain) 660 years elapsed. Afterwards, when the Vandals had crossed into Africa, Alaric the Pannonian, from the family of the Balthi, succeeded to power. He was then leader of the Goths. The Goths ruled in Spain for three hundred years after him, that is, to Roderick, in whose times the Arabs and the Moors subdued all Spain to their rule, except the Cantabrians and the Asturians. This happened in the year of grace 717, in the seventh year of the rule of Roderick, as Tarafa wrote. The prince of the Celtiberians created the occasion for this change, since he called the Africans into Spain to avenge the insult done to his wife by Roderick. Afterwards the French, first under Charles the Great, then under Louis, his son, reclaimed a great part of Spain from Arabian servitude and governed through legates until Louis the Pious gave complete authority to Jamfred, his deputy. Later the Spanish, having recovered their strength under the leadership of Alfonso V, drove the Arabs from almost all Spain. But when the legitimate line of the Goths became extinct in Bermudo, the son of Alfonso, Ferdinand, the first king of Aragon, took control. Afterwards the empire of Spain was cut—first into four parts and soon into five parts; then a very cruel slaughter followed, not only among the princes themselves but also among brothers, parents, and children. Alfonso III, prince of the Asturias and Galicia, blinded all his brothers and even killed one, when he seized part of the kingdom. Likewise, Alfonso IV was blinded by his brother Ramiro. Peter, too, the legitimate son of Alfonso XI, was driven forth and killed by Henry, his bastard brother; Garcia, also, by his brother Sancho; the latter by Bellido. A little while thereafter Alfonso VIII, French by race, son of Raymond of Toulouse, united the three empires into one and the same. Again the Moors attacked Spain with a great fleet, and they held a good part until the time of Ferdinand, the maternal ancestor of Philip. Thus, at length, the empire, greatly increased partly by force of arms, partly by legitimate succession also, now flourishes in the highest glory of civil and military pursuits. It has been a kingdom for 852 years, from the time of Pelagius. It is even more glorious that they have carried into Africa and as far as America their arms and their laws, not without a thriving and profitable commerce and zeal to inculcate the religion of Christ. They will spread farther, since from all those empires ruled by the authority of one man there is none so extensive in which less is allowed to the prince. That is the best proof of a well constituted empire.

The other empires—of the Tartars, the Russians, the Indians, and the Ethiopians—which history has not clearly revealed, I pass over. Yet from those which we have investigated it is plain that no empire has been more lasting than that of the Gauls or less given to civil wars. It is true that many things in customs, laws, institutions, and trials need correction, but the form of government of a state approved by such long continued existence cannot be changed without the most serious danger. The finest warning of Aristotle cautions us against changing anything in a state which has flourished for a long time in the same form. But since many men of this age, serious and learned men, prefer the rule of optimates, and some even a democracy, we must speak briefly about the best type of government, after we have repudiated their opinion. We have already refuted the opinion of Polybius and those who came from his school, with arguments, as we think, demanding assent.

THE BEST TYPE OF STATE

Altogether there are three kinds of government—that is, the rule of one, of several, and of all—and so we must consider not only how to avoid the degraded forms, but also how to select the best among the worthy. The tyranny of one man is pernicious; even worse is the tyranny of more than one, which is called oligarchy; worst, finally, is that dominion of the mob, released from all law, which the Greeks called ochlocracy and Cicero even called tyranny. It is next to anarchy, in which no one obeys and no one commands; there are no rewards for good deeds, no punishments for crimes. Then, if we reject these forms we must choose a popular form, an aristocratic form, or a kingdom. About the popular form I should think nothing ought to be written if it were not supported by the opinions of many people. N. Machiavelli, for example, is convinced by arguments and reasoning that it is the most excellent. But on this question I think he is less creditable, especially since he overthrows the premises of his discussion. In the *Institution of the Prince,* at the very beginning, he assumed only two forms of rule, monarchy and republic. The same author, in his book on Livy, affirmed that the Venetian state is the best of all, yet he thought it was popular, for in the third book he wrote that popular forms of government always have been more praiseworthy, in opposition to the approved opinion of the philosophers, historians, and of all great men. To omit the others, Xenophon, that good general and philosopher, testified that popular power is altogether inimical to virtues; it cannot be established or retained except by driving out all the good men. This Seneca put with brevity, "For who, if he admires virtue," said he, "can please the people?" Aristotle also supported the same position, especially in that passage where he asserted with effective arguments that some were born to rule, others to obey. But the error originated with Plato, who, after he had established a popular state, introduced dangerous equalization. Then the Academicians who came from his school amplified his reasons, assuming that society is maintained by harmony, harmony by equality of justice, and equality by a popular state. Then all the citizens are made one and the same in the most perfect equality and likeness, and this should be the aim of human society. Aristotle did not confute the hypothesis of Plato, but he thought that Plato had erred especially in trying to make the citizenship one and the same; in that way the state is destroyed and becomes a family. This reasoning seems to me to be ineffective; but I judge the hypothesis not only absurd, as Aristotle would have it, but also clearly false. For if we refer all things to nature, which is chief of all things, it becomes plain that this world, which is superior to anything ever joined together by immortal God, consists of unequal parts and mutually discordant elements and contrary motions of the spheres, so that if the harmony through dissimilarity is taken away, the whole will be ruined. In the same way the best republic, if it imitates nature, which it must do, is held together stable and unshaken by those commanding and obeying, servants and lords, powerful and needy, good and wicked, strong and weak, as if by the mixed association of unlike minds. As on the lyre and in song itself the skilled ears cannot endure that sameness of harmony which is called unison; on the contrary, a pleasing harmony is produced by dissimilar notes, deep and high, combined in accordance with certain rules, so also no normal person could endure equality, or rather that democratic uniformity in the state. On the other hand, a state graduated from the highest to the lowest, with the middle orders scattered between in moderate proportion, fits together in a marvelous way through complementary action. It is true this gives rise to that blight of all public affairs, the fact that people who are alike from a certain aspect think that they are altogether unlike; but, those who are in a certain degree unlike, think that they are altogether alike. If, therefore, such is the disparity of men among themselves, such the disparity of natural talent, who would divide authority, resources, honors, and offices on the basis of equality? It is as if the same food and clothing were given to boys, grown men, old men, the sick, and the strong and by this reasoning they think to preserve equality. Since Plato, in the

Republic, forbade equality of possessions (for he enrolled four classes of citizens with different ratings), and those who followed after, the Academicians, who supported popular states, always forbade equal distribution of goods, lest they overthrow the foundations of states set up chiefly to protect their own possessions—why did they not also eliminate equality of power?

The popular form of government is no other than this sharing of sovereignty. It was not so absurd to equate all the resources of everyone as to equate their share of power, because every man can enjoy wealth, but wisdom for ruling is the natural capacity of very few. What stupider than the plebs? What more immoderate? When they have been stirred up against good people, what more hysterical? Rightly Livy said, "The nature of the multitude is such that it either serves meekly or rules insolently." There is no need of examples. Oh, that so many did not exist! Those who praise the popular rule of the Romans seem not to have read their histories. What more tragic than the frequent secessions of the plebs from the patricians? What more shameful than that citizen with citizen so many times fought with stones, scythes, and swords, in the midst of the town, in the market place, in the camp, in the assemblies, in the senate, in the temple of Jupiter Capitolinus? Said Cicero, "In the Forum we have often seen stonings; not often, but yet too often, swords." Appian wrote that Apuleius Saturninus, tribune of the plebs, made laws backed by workmen and armed bands and killed the lawfully elected consul [156] after citizens were driven from the scene by other citizens in a disgraceful stoning. Indeed it used to happen with good reason that candidates came to the meetings with weapons beneath their togas, in the company of a veritable army. I omit the assemblies broken up by trickery, the largess, the murders, and the frequent summonings of the people from the fields and important pursuits into the town; I omit the countless introductions of law, repeals, modifications, additions, and invalidations, the many plebiscites and *senatus consulta* mutually contradictory, which in a brief time could be changed according to the whim of the plebs. These things occurred not only at Rome, but also at Athens; among the Athenians access to the councils of state, which ought to be sacred, was coveted by the plebs; that is, wisdom by the unbalanced and furious. As Anacharsis said pithily, at Athens wise men express opinions in the assembly, but the stupid judge. So when Philip invaded Attica, the people, who had heard the news, gathered to-

[156] Appian *Roman History* "The Civil Wars" I. 28.

gether in the theater at dawn, as we may read in Demosthenes. They had not been summoned by any magistrate, and such great terror was felt that no one dared to address the crowd. The same Demosthenes, in his speech about the state, reported that the orators were the leaders of the government; to these the generals were subordinate, and the laws and decisions were made by the votes of about three hundred people; the rest of the citizens were at their mercy. Among the Florentines, likewise, a share in the counsels was desired by the plebs, although often they were besieged by the enemy. So the fact that both states lasted for a long time (although in a wretched condition) must be attributed to Aristides, Pericles, Conon, and Cosimo and Lorenzo de' Medici, who, however, were exiled by their people or heavily fined. I know not why Machiavelli, a Florentine, praised popular rule so highly, since from his history it is plain that of all states none more unhappy than Florence existed as long as it was democratic.

ROYAL POWER BETTER THAN THAT OF THE OPTIMATES

Since the popular state has been repudiated by the consent of great men, we must consider whether the power of the optimates is any more desirable than royal power. There are those who think that Plato gave control to the optimates; but they are really mistaken. The functions which, we have shown, are of the highest importance in the government Plato himself gave to the people, that is, to the multitude of all the citizens: the power of passing laws, I say, creating magistrates, and selecting the senators also—finally, the power over life and death. Moreover, he gave all public trials to the people, because the offense was against the people as a whole. By this reasoning it would have been necessary for the man who had been injured to have been judge in his own case. Plato wished that all citizens should be made participants in the private trials also, then added the reason—lest if they should be excluded from the trials, they would not think themselves citizens. The commentators on Plato thought that this was a moderate form of the popular state, but this idea has been refuted by us earlier. Yet those who have come from his school approve more highly the rule of the optimates, which lies halfway between a democracy and a monarchy. They err, however, in this respect, that they seem to place virtue in the average thing or number, not in the mean proportional. Indeed, if this is true no prince will ever be good, nor will any oligarchy be quarrelsome, because between one and many they place the mean of a few, like the mean of virtue. Yet if there is any excellence in numbers, I suppose that unity is most to be praised of all, as Plato himself most divinely wrote, in the book about entity and unity.

But how much better is Aristotle, who opposed three lawful types of state to three depraved; kings to tyrants; optimates to quarrelsome oligarchies; the people to the turbulent plebs. In the end he affirmed that royal power is more excellent than the others, yet he did not refute this dictum of Plato, accepted by many and discussed by Contarini: that is, it would be very difficult ever to find any one man of integrity and the highest virtue. Certainly this objection is not worthy of refutation, for it is self-refuting, because it would be more difficult to find many good men than one. Since in a multitude of optimates only a few are good, the few are swamped by the votes of the many; for in a democratic or aristocratic state the votes are counted, not weighed. But if a tyrant should be feared, how much more ought a multitude of tyrants to be feared? Omitting these truisms, however, why in establishing a state, as in all things, do we not imitate nature?

ROYAL POWER IN ACCORD WITH UNIVERSAL EMPIRE

If we should inspect nature more closely, we should gaze upon monarchy everywhere. To make a beginning from small things, we see the king among the bees, the leader in the herd, the buck among the flocks or the bellwether (as among the cranes themselves the many follow one), and in the separate natures of things some one object excels: thus, adamant among the gems, gold among the metals, the sun among the stars, and finally God alone, the prince and author of the world. Moreover, they say that among the evil spirits one alone is supreme. But, not to continue indefinitely, what is a family other than the true image of a state? Yet this is directed by the rule of one, who presents, not a fictitious image, like the doge of Venice, but the true picture of a king. If, then, Plato were to change the nature of things and set up several lords in the same family, several heads for the same body, several pilots on a ship, and finally several leaders among bees, flocks, herds (if only the farmers will permit); if at length he would join several gods into an association for ruling, then I would agree with him that the rule of the optimates is better than a kingdom. But if the entire nature of things protests, reason dissents, lasting experience objects, I do not see why we ought to follow Plato or anyone else and violate nature. What Homer has said, "No good thing is a number of masters; let one man be master, one man be king," [157] Euripides has repeated, "Power belongs to one man in the homes and in the cities." [158] For this reason Sibylla is said to have prophesied in her poems that the safety of the Roman Republic is founded upon a kingdom, that is, the citizens cannot be protected unless they have a king. In the year 1552 Soliman made this plain by a memorable example. When Mustapha, his eldest son, had exhausted the resistance of the Persians and had returned without an escort to his father, trusting to a safe-conduct, he was received with such a clamor by the army, with such favor, as no mortal ever had before. His father could not endure his son's popularity, but ordered him to be strangled in an inner bedroom and then thrown to the army. Thereupon he commanded the herald to proclaim in a loud voice: "There is one God in the heavens; on the earth one man, Soliman alone, ought to be emperor." The whole army was silent, struck by terror. Two days later a younger son was carried off by poison because he grieved for his brother's death. The third, for fear of his father, fled to the king of the Persians. Immediately he was brought back by envoys and beheaded. There remained only the present Selim, whom his father would have threatened if he had not been the surviving son. This was customary among the race of Ottomans, because the hope of empire will come to all, but attainment to one alone. It is not only most salutary, as Tacitus wrote, but also necessary in the administration of great affairs that power should rest entirely with one man. Three tribunes with consular power, indeed, were a warning, as Livy reported, of the ineffectiveness of the rule of several men in time of war. L. Paulus and Terentius Varro had a similar experience against Hannibal; the Christian princes, against the king of the Turks; the leaders of the Greeks, against Philip; not so long ago, the princes of the Germans opposed to Charles V learned at great cost that nothing can be properly directed by many people. So the Greeks and the Romans, when a serious war or civil rebellion disturbed the state, had recourse to the rule of a dictator or an archon or a harmost as to a sacred refuge, just as Florentines, Genoese, and Venetians in crises of the state often granted to one general the highest power over war and peace. Indeed, why discuss it, when in countless centuries it has been found that democratic and aristocratic states are dangerous for human kind? Great are the empires of the Turks, the Persians, the Indians, and the Tartars; greater even, those of the Abyssinians and the Spanish, who have subordinated

[157] Homer *Iliad* II. 204.   [158] Euripides *Andromache* l. 484.

a new world to their laws. Of wide extent are the kingdoms of the Moors also, of the French, the Muscovites, the Poles, the Goths, and the Britons, who do not know the rule of optimates and dislike democratic rule. Moreover, from earliest memory the people of America always have retained the royal power. They do not do this because they have been taught, but from custom. They were not trained by Aristotle, but shaped by their leader, nature. Furthermore, when they hear that the rule of optimates exists in some corners of Italy or Germany, they marvel that this can be. Many of our men wonder that the state of the Venetians has endured so long, that is, for eight hundred years, since this is constructed contrary to nature. Yet Donato Giannotti, who of all has written most accurately about the Venetian state, reported that the highest power was lodged with the doges; and the Venetians had an entirely monarchical government up to the period of Doge Sebastian Ciani, that is, up to the year 1175, at which time the great council was established in the state, as he himself wrote. Therefore it happens that it has flourished in this form for only about three hundred and sixty years. But the Indians are not surprised that the kingdom of the French, unlimited by narrow swamps and extending far and wide, has flourished through incredibly glorious deeds for twelve hundred years, since nothing in line with nature ought to seem wonderful. Unless I am mistaken, Contarini, Manutius, Machiavelli, and many others say that the Venetian state is the most excellent of all, for reasons that I am about to explain. When Michael Suriano, the Venetian, a man of the highest erudition and virtue, acted as ambassador at Paris, through his good will to me he often questioned me learnedly about our state, and I probed him about his. He preferred to discuss all things dispassionately, with a view to acquiring the actual facts, rather than to judge; and I do not assume to judge about so difficult a matter, but since we have chosen the rule of one man, we should seem to deny ourselves, if we were to approve the government of the optimates. Then the fame of the Venetians must be due to military prowess, or the equity of the laws, or the size of the empire and its resources, or the variety of the arts. In martial renown they are inferior to almost all peoples; in size the empire is superior to only a few; in the art of governing and profitable trade they yield to the Spanish and in variety of arts to the Germans. How each cultivates his religion in private, they do not particularly care, and they refused to allow the popes to investigate heresy. There remains the excellence of the laws, which may be understood from the customs of the citizens. Plato called the Spartans brave and moderate, yet unjust; the Romans are regarded as brave and just; the Hebrews, religious; the people of Marseilles, just and moderate; the Athenians were celebrated for the arts, other peoples for other virtues. If the Venetians excel in any virtue, I suppose they excel in counsels and sagacity. I should not wish to deprive them of the reputation for other virtues or to concede more to them than to others. But those who extol the resources of the Venetians are very much in the wrong, for the public treasury is in need of funds. The system of pawnshops is an evidence thereof; it exhausts the public revenues with interest at five percent, as Donato Giannotti confessed.

Of course the Venetians maintain zealously the ancient laws of their city; in this is their greatest merit. Such is the prestige of tradition and its majesty that Aristotle justly doubted whether a new and better law ought to be placed ahead of an ancient law, and he did not think that the question should be settled by him. It is indeed worthy of great praise that they grant their allies and resident aliens the highest equity of the law; foreigners also they treat with much kindness; and if there are any who have large resources, they seek an alliance with them so that no dowry seems more important than noble birth. In taking counsel about the state, in undertaking wars, in concluding alliances, and in maintaining peace they use great sagacity. Although these things are very significant, yet more vital for the defense of the government is the fact that because of inaccessibility of location they can very easily defeat all attacks. The Genoese once tried to conquer them and not so long ago Louis XII, king of the French, would have taken control away from the Venetians if he could have besieged the city. So they have nothing to fear from an enemy. Moreover, today people who lack experience with arms and in military discipline cannot engage in civil wars or successfully attempt to revolt. The Romans, on the contrary, were involved in civil wars as soon as they had withdrawn from foreign wars. Although a city well constituted in military and civil discipline ought to be supported not by laws alone but also by arms, they guard the one with highest praise, it is true, yet they abandon the other altogether, as Contarini himself confessed. Therefore, when the enemy attacks, they are forced to use not only foreign soldiers but even foreign generals— how wisely, I do not know. Yet for a long time all military leaders have unanimously disapproved of this; certainly they do not recall any more frequent cause of the destruction of cities than this. Wherefore Bartolomeo Colleoni, to whom the Venetians erected a golden statue for good service to the state as general, is said to have rebuked them, because they unwisely entrusted themselves and the state to an alien. Corinth fell into the hands of a tyrant for no other reason than that it had called in Timophanes, a foreign general. The Britons, likewise, were driven from control by the Angles, the Spanish by the Moors, the Greeks by the Turks, whom they had called in for protection. Contarini wrote that for the sake of domestic order and the maintenance of peace military discipline is neglected, yet it is to be feared that if they neglect the one they will lose both.

It contributes not a little to the stability of the government, also, that the optimates are united among themselves and with the state, so that they may not be easily overwhelmed by the multitude of aliens as if they were disunited. For the concordant power of a few rulers is not easily shaken, said Aristotle. That harmony may be more stable, they feast rather often in public and solemn banquets, in accordance with an old custom of the Cretans and the Spartans. The doge is forced to prepare these banquets and with gifts to unite his citizens to each other and to the state. It is a further advantage, as Aristotle reported, that large cities are less suited to sedition, because they have a great throng of the middle class, who join the highest to the lowest in the same society. But there is no more effective safeguard for protecting an aristocratic state than the fact that authority is not perpetual, and it is invariably shared; offices are limited to a two-month, or a three-month, or a six-month period, or at the most a year. However, no authority is given to those offices which are perpetual and chiefly honorary; for example, that of doge, procurator of St. Mark, or chancellor. But if anyone exceeds the others in the highest virtues, or resources, or popularity, he is admitted with reluctance to the greatest honors, lest by the splendor of his gifts he might blind the eyes of his fellow citizens. And that secret of empire which the Athenians and the Ephesians rashly disclosed by ostracism, too openly declaring war on virtue, was understood in the death of that Loredan who so terrified the citizens by his mere nod when they were rioting and making murderous attacks on each other that they fled, casting aside their arms, even though no power of the magistrates could have coerced them. They could not, however, endure the superiority of a private citizen who had freed the state from a serious defeat, but poisoned him, as many Italians report; I do not wish to affirm this, and I cannot persuade myself of it. They were, however, accustomed to choose as doge a man whom they kept at home unarmed and bound with golden chains—not too energetic or desirous of glory, but a good and simple man. They feared lest the same thing should happen to them as happened to the frogs in the marshes, seeking a king from Jupiter. When he gave them a log, as Aesop writes, they were angry; then Jupiter sent a frog-eating crane. Finally, the fact is that the Venetians enjoy authority in turn and the greatest liberty, for the protection of which the citizens and foreigners willingly keep the peace.

This is the principal reason why men praise the state of the Venetians so much—one lives there in the greatest freedom. However, states are not established for the sake of liberty, but for the sake of living well. Of course there is hardly ever any place for virtue in a city where each man indulges his own habits and desires so eagerly. If we measure the happiness of man by his resources, honors, dominion, pleasure, and unrestrained freedom, happy is the country which abounds in all these; but if we consider virtue preferable, I do not see why Venice is the most outstanding of all states. No evidence of a badly constituted state seemed to Plato greater than a multitude of magistrates and physicians—and there never were more than among the Athenians long ago and today among the Venetians. So it ought not to seem strange that they usually spend the greater part of the year in choosing magistrates. Moreover, this excessive number of magistrates is due either to an insatiable desire for honors and command, or to an endeavor to restrain frauds and crimes, or to both. But the state of Lycurgus, which is praised in the words of everyone, had no magistrates at first except the senate of thirty men who held office for life. The great *paedonomus*, master of the youths, lacked power. They are really mistaken who think that a multitude of officials inspires a love of virtue in the citizens, since nothing increases more the desire to rule and to seek riches. Indeed, those who have once enjoyed the sweetness of command not only have forgotten how to obey but also cling to power beyond their term and lay it down reluctantly.

Wherefore among us recently, with the approval of all orders, a law has prudently been passed that the great number of magistrates, which under King Henry was endlessly increased by the evil arts of certain men, should be reduced to the former number; for what does this accumulation of magistrates result in if not thefts, avarice, corruption, extravagance, a lust for domination, and multiplying of lawsuits? Certainly there was never greater impunity for crimes and excesses. Therefore a few magistrates are sufficient, provided that they are sought for excellence alone. By this system all citizens are necessarily inspired to virtue and well-doing, so that they may attain honors as a reward. The hope for these will come to everyone; the attainment, to a few.

Then authority, magistrates, and honors do not make happy citizens, much less too great liberty, which brings ruin even to a well-constituted state. Servitude is base; yet sinful license is even more base. Still, if it is servile to bear the authority of a king, it ought also to seem servile to obey one's parents. Often it has seemed remarkable to me that the Venetians, who so wisely arrange all [other] things, do not allow censors to be chosen, as once the Romans did and today the men of Lucca and the Genoese also. This could be done very conveniently by the procurators of St. Mark who have reached their present office by rising through the ranks. The popes whose function this properly is and who used to guide temporal rulers along the path of duty by appealing to their piety, now themselves need the most severe censors. The office of censoring is so solemn and so necessary in the state that it appears to have contributed more definitely to the success of the Roman government than any other single factor. This was understood after the censorship had been removed, for then the splendor and majesty of the state along with the virtue of the early Romans disappeared. The Venetian state suffers also from the danger that when they admit a countless multitude of foreigners and resident aliens, they risk being driven from control by these newcomers. An actual example of such an occurrence is not lacking. For on this account the Achaeans drove out the men of Troezen; the Samians, the Messinians; and the Chalcidensians, the Amphipolitans, by whom they had been admitted into the city without honors, as Pausanias and Aristotle reported. Such an event is the more to be feared if the optimates differ among themselves. In the case of the Cnidians, the nobles first enjoyed the honors alone; but after they commenced to quarrel, they were cast out by the aliens and the plebs. This happened also among the Mitylenians, the Ostians, and the Phoceans, and not so long ago among the Sienese, the Genoese, and the Genevese, who were driven from power by the plebs when the optimates quarreled among themselves for position. The men of Corcyra acted more cruelly, since they had the quarrelsome nobles all thrown into prison, where they suffered together the most horrible death, as Thucydides wrote. The sojourners of Cologne, with equal fury, killed a great part of the patricians because they alone had obtained honors and had imposed too heavy tribute. The resident aliens of Lindau, having killed the optimates, created tribunes of plebs.

This danger, therefore, is to be feared in the case of Venice. For when a census of the whole city was taken in the year 1555, there were counted 159,459 resident aliens in addition to the patricians. Women and boys over six years were included in this number. About 1,500 patricians controlled these people, for the juniors under 25 years are not admitted to the assembly and to a share in power, except a few occasionally. The Venetians do not seem to have acted wisely in counting the people; first, since by divine law it is forbidden; then, when strangers and poor people understand their numbers ana strength, of course there is danger lest they form some plot against the optimates. When the senate of the Romans once decreed that the slaves should be distinguished from the freeborn citizens by ornaments and clothing, Seneca said it would become dangerous if the slaves started to count their number. Moreover, the Cretan wars showed how much love the allies and sojourners had for the Venetians. So did the surrender of Padua, Verona, and other towns to the French. At that juncture the optimates exempted the allied towns from tribute and taxes, as Bembo tells us, from whom, especially in that crisis, they ought to have received aid. This is sufficient proof that they were feared more than they were loved.

But we pour out all our fortunes and our blood for the safety of king and country, especially after we have been defeated. Not to be too diffuse, there is no better proof of a good and effective state than to drive off foes valiantly, and to maintain the citizens in a state of contentment. Usually the Venetians are easily conquered by the enemy; and they could not restrain the citizens from punishing eighteen doges by death or exile. Sabellicus reported this number, from the time when they set up a government of the optimates. But even the heirs of the Doge Loredan were forced to pay fifteen hundred golden crowns into the treasury, according to legal decision, because Loredan had not been sufficiently generous to the citizens, as Donato Giannotti wrote. I omit the civil wars, which were waged too often in the midst of the city when the Venetians still upheld military training. I omit the conspiracies of the Bocconi, the Falieri, the Tiepolo, and the Bajamonte,[159] which devastated the state woefully after the senators had been surrounded and a most sanguinary struggle had taken place between the citizens. I

[159] Either Bodin means Querini, or Bajamonte should precede Tiepolo as a personal name.

omit the very serious and incessant rioting of the Giustiniani, of Scaevola's men, of the Selii, the followers of Bassus, the exiles and the murders—for no other cause than that they had no trust in those sharing
the government. Too often the same thing happened that happens in a
ship without a pilot. Polybius used this example; when one man tries
to turn the helm, another makes sail, and another tries to reverse, the
passengers with so many pilots are in danger. At length they display
to the spectators in the port their calamitous shipwreck.

Moreover, who has not seen Germany terribly devastated by the
armies of the Turks and the Swiss, the Spanish and the French, then of
the Italians, and finally of their own citizens, although when it was governed by royal power it easily overcame all peoples by the strength of
its arms. From this we understand that a kingdom is far better than the
rule of optimates. We ought to refute the opinion of Josephus and of
those who think that in the Sacred Scriptures God execrated a kingdom
and set up the rule of optimates among the Hebrews. Josephus made
such a statement, Book VI, chapter 6, *Of Antiquities*,[160] although Philo
the Jew, in the book about the creation of a prince, taught that the rule
of one prince had been established by the command of God.

But let us refute the opinion of Josephus. As far as concerns the words
of Samuel,[161] then, he did not describe a kingdom, but a tyranny, contrary to what Melanchthon thought. For who even slightly learned in
the Hebrew tongue does not know that מלך means "king" as well as
"tyrant"? Thus, Abraham is said to have been turned away from the
slaughter of kings. But the word משפט signifies in this place, not the
rights of a king, but the custom and usage, as all the best interpreters
say. Unless a tyrant is described, why did Moses, in Deuteronomy 17,[162]
order the king to learn the separate precepts of the law and to rule the
people by divine law? According to this chapter, not only are popular
and aristocratic power rejected, but royal power is even approved. Then,
too, this: thou shalt not speak ill of the prince of the people; it assumes
the rule of one man. And in the book "Sanhedrin," chapter 2,[163] the
royal majesty which existed among the Hebrews is described very fully.

FORM AND CHANGES OF THE EMPIRE OF THE HEBREWS

It is inferred, of course, that Moses had royal power from the fact
that regardless of the will of the people and the optimates he ordered

[160] Josephus *Jewish Antiquities*, paragraphs 36–37.
[161] I Samuel 10: 18. [162] Deuteronomy 27. [163] From the Talmud.

laws, chose the senate, selected magistrates, created the priests, condemned to death at one time more than forty thousand seditious citizens without trial, and at last of his own accord announced that Joshua was to be prince, for nothing greater than this could be done. When Joshua was dead the senators chose Othoniel as leader, then Ehud. So Peter Martyr wrote correctly that aristocracy started when Othoniel was appointed leader by the senators, although the interpreters are pleased to say that the leaders were chosen, not by human counsels, but by divine order. In this way Gideon was elected leader. "I will not rule over you," quoth he, "nor my son, but God will rule over you." [164] Finally when the sons of Eli and Samuel behaved badly and the power of the optimates degenerated into factions, the plebs in their vexation sought a king. Then, indeed, the riots died down. For this reason Maimonides [165] wrote that it was forbidden by divine law to build the temple until the Jews had a king who might check the tumults by his power to command. These things are written in the third book of the *Guide of the Perplexed*, chapter 47. From these instances it is evident that the royal power was pleasing to God, and tyranny displeasing. When the king had been chosen, the senators were first admitted, not to sovereignty, but to the council, as Moses had arranged. As for the fact that Romulus wished the less important cases to be judged by the senate, the more important by himself, as we read in the pages of Dionysius, Moses also decreed the same thing in creating the senate, as is written in Numbers, chapter 11.[166] Hence, when the Chaldean interpreter on Jeremiah wrote that a senate of seventy-one men (whom the Hebrews call שפטים but he himself called Sanhedrin, a corrupt Greek word) had the highest power of ratifying the law and of judging even under the kings themselves, he referred to the promulgation of law and trials; among us the superior courts proclaim the law, which the inexperienced think is ratification, but that belongs to the prince alone. The same Chaldean interpreter added that trials about the tribe, about the high priest, about majesty, and about false prophecy cannot be settled except by the senate. But Moses Maimonides, in the *Guide of the Perplexed*, the last chapter of Book III, wrote, "The senate had the power of the sword." From that same senate there were twenty-three chief men who were set

---

[164] Judges 8: 23.

[165] Maimonides (Moses the Egyptian), 1135–1204, an Aristotelian, was author of *Guide of the Perplexed*, and works on astrology, astronomy, the Talmud, law, and philosophy.

[166] Numbers 11: 16, 17.

up in the separate towns as judges of souls, and seven men, judges of money and goods. Of these, three arranged the trials, five took cases of first appeal, seven decided about the second appeal. Furthermore, ten judges of commercial matters, like aediles, were created including one priest. For these things three arbiters were added of whom each litigant chose one. The two selected chose a third. All these things are explained fully in the *Pandects* of the Hebrews under the title "Sanhedrin," chapters 1–3. Finally, it is evident that the senators were usually selected by that very senate whose power was perpetual; yet all these things were ratified by command of the kings, so that beyond decrees the senate had no power. This is to be seen in the judgment of Herod, who, when he demanded the slaughter of the children, stated his case before the senate of the Hebrews. Yet he did so at the command of Hyrcanus, king and high priest, by whom Herod was absolved, not by the senate, as Josephus wrote, Book xiv, chapter 16. Long before that, after the death of Solomon, when his son established a tyranny, the people were divided, and two kingdoms, or rather two tyrannies were set up—one from the tribe of Judah and Benjamin, the other tyranny from the remaining tribes, so that the senate had as much authority as was permitted by the kings or the tyrants. In the same way, each Roman emperor according to his will weakened the senate. As the Roman senate declared certain emperors to be enemies or condemned them to death, such as Nero and Maximinus, so also the senate of the Hebrews judged in the case of Herod when he was still a young man, and it would have condemned him for nefarious murder if it had not been checked by King Hyrcanus. When Herod became older and gained complete control, he killed King Hyrcanus and all the senators except Shemaiah, who really was the greatest enemy of all, yet Herod spared the glory of the name, as we find in the pages of Josephus, Book xiv. With this form of government, then it is evident that the state of the Hebrews from its origin flourished one hundred and sixty years under a king. Afterwards it was ruled by optimates for two hundred and forty-four years. Then the Hebrews had a monarchy, which was soon divided into a twofold tyranny for four hundred and ninety-six years, and in the end it was overthrown by the Assyrians. First the kings of Samaria and the ten tribes were taken into Chaldea; then the kings of Jerusalem with the rest of the people. After they had suffered for seventy years in exile, they came back again into the fatherland and flourished under kings and priests until, weakened by civil strife and neighboring wars, they fell first under the power of the Egyptians, then under that of the Greeks, and later under that of the Idumeans. In the end Judea was reduced to the level of a province by Augustus and accepted the rule of the Romans, from whom it broke away one hundred years later. In those times Jerusalem was taken and razed to its foundations. Since all the neighbors conspired for the destruction of this one people, such a great slaughter ensued in both Asia and Africa, that the Hebrew race was believed to have perished altogether. The number of killed given by Josephus certainly exceeds three hundred thousand. The rest were led away into degrading slavery, and since then they have been dispersed over the face of the earth.

ROYAL POWER THE MOST EXCELLENT

Now, since the royal power is natural, that is, instituted by God, the father of nature, chosen in a remarkable decision by the Magi, praised by Homer, Xenophon, Aristotle, Plutarch, Dio, Apollonius, Jerome, and Cyprian, later established by Augustus after serious discussions with Maecenas and Agrippa, and, lastly, approved by the unanimous agreement of all peoples, or of those best known to fame, and by a lasting experience—what more must be said about the best form of state?

IN A MONARCHY ELECTION SHOULD BE AVOIDED

We must now advance suitable arguments to refute the theory of elective monarchy. Aristotle thought it dangerous and clearly uncivilized that kings should be dynastic. Others have made no distinction between elective and dynastic kings. In Book III,[167] at the end, he believed that the Spartans were inferior to the Carthaginians because the latter elected kings; the kings of the former were descended from Hercules. Then the Egyptians also must have been uncivilized—Assyrians, Macedonians, Phoenicians, Ethiopians, Abyssinians, Turks, Indians, Tartars, Russians, Poles, Danes, Swedes, Britons, Italians, French, Spanish, and Americans—finally, all the peoples of the earth except Germans, Swiss with their allies, Venetians, Ragusans, Lucchese, and Genoese, who are ruled by the power of optimates or have popular governments. But if so many people are uncivilized because they have hereditary kings, oh, where will be the abode of culture? The fact that Aristotle thought it disastrous, however, seems to me much more absurd. For in the first place an interregnum is clearly dangerous, since the state, like a ship without a

[167] Aristotle *Politics* II. 8. 1269a 15.

pilot, is tossed about by the waves of sedition and often sinks. This happened after the death of Emperor Frederick II. The country, in a state of anarchy, was without an emperor for eighteen years on account of the civil war among the princes. Moreover, what could be more wretched than the unchecked plundering of the plebs by the mamelukes in an interregnum between the sultans of Egypt. What more wicked than that in the interregnum between the popes of Rome all things were given over with impunity to slaughter and violation.

Furthermore, the system of electing a prince is plainly impracticable. It cannot be done well by the whole people, as Aristotle would like it, since logical ability and wisdom are lacking. Therefore it must be done by the few and the best. But the people will resent this, and the army will refuse. Hence came those serious and lasting discords between the Roman senate and the praetorians. Each man who pleased the senate displeased the legions. Often the legions in various places and contemporaneously created several emperors, so that at one moment there were thirty. Hence civil wars arose, murder, proscriptions of goods, and a most unhappy chaos in the whole empire. It is even more disastrous that every very wicked man gains power, while the good repudiate such a burden voluntarily. If by chance a prince were so sage that he wished to proclaim a good man as his successor to power, as Nerva, Trajan, Hadrian, and Antoninus Pius wisely did, electors of kings would think it uncivilized. But since the hope of power comes to all, though attainment to only one, after the pilot has been killed the approach to power must lie open to robbers and poisoners. Because there is no more stable foundation for a state than the respect of the subjects for their prince, how can it happen that the people do not scorn the rule of a man who is thought to have been born in an obscure station or was once an equal, or has sought control through crime or riches? Nothing was more commonplace than the slaughter of Roman emperors like cattle by their own men. No less than thirty can be counted. The state never was more quiet than when the son had inherited the power of his father, which Aristotle thought was dangerous. Among the German princes wars for control did not cease until the father designated his son as Caesar. For example, Henry III had his son elected when he was only a boy. He, in turn, adopted his grandson. Charles IV arranged that his son should be his successor; the latter, his brother Sigismund, who adopted his son-in-law. Frederick selected Maximilian; the latter, his grandson. The rest for the most part died, through conspiracies or poison—Rudolph, Albert, Henry VII, Frederick III, Louis the Bavarian, Charles, grandson of Henry, and Gunther.

But those assemblies of the kings of Poland and Hungary, which they themselves called *cari*, are held in arms; because of which too often civil wars arise. If the family of the Jagellons had not won the suffrage by right of blood, that empire would have perished long ago. There were not more than fifteen elected sultans of Egypt. Seven were killed by the mamelukes, by whom they had been elected, namely, Tughi, Malik Shah, Kotuz, Bunduqdar, Mohammed, Chirkouh, and Janbalat. But Saphadin, the brother of Saladin, having been elected by his people, cruelly killed the ten sons of his brother so that he might reign safely. The Turks, who determined the succession by the vote of the Janizaries, do not actually attain power by any means other than mutual slaughter. Finally, it is reported that the Roman popes are poisoned, although chosen when aged lest they may reign too long. Sometimes those who rule prefectures or provinces are unwilling to accept dismissal from power—for instance, dukes and counts among the Germans. Likewise, with us dukes and counts seized the provinces of the kingdom on this account, as soon as they had chosen a king by their own right, as it were —so Julius Pflug and Aemilius confessed. In order to become king, Hugh Capet agreed that each count should have his province by right of dominion. So, little by little fiefs, empires, and jurisdictions came to be hereditary possessions. There exists in the library of Beauvais the ancient form of consecrating a king and of election by the people, by which Henry I is said to have been elected here. But I do not see that any one of the older or following kings was created by election; certainly the kingdom would not have stood so long if we had descended to voting.

So it happened to the Germans also. The province of Saxony was given to Henry I in this way in the year 913. Another lord obtained another province and little by little the princes freed the towns from taxes that they might more easily obtain the empire, as in the case of Nimwegen. To certain towns, when a definite price had been paid, autonomy was completely restored as Rudolph restored it to all the towns of Etruria, in the year 1230.[168] The Lucchese redeemed their liberty with twelve thousand golden crowns; the Florentines, with six. Afterwards Rupert granted three imperial towns to his son. Charles IV

[168] Misprint for 1273?

sold Milan to his governor; Otto, Isnia; [169] Louis, Eger; Frederick, Nuremberg. Ulm won its own liberty, as did many others. The same thing happened to the Roman popes, so that their officers set up a tyranny over the provinces, as we have shown before. But when there was certain hope of power and legitimate succession, the provinces could not be torn away.

How much more happy, then, were the Assyrians, the Persians, the Egyptians, the Macedonians, and the French, who have flourished for so many ages and so many centuries in tranquillity for no other reason than that the kings were selected from a royal house? I suppose, though we seek everywhere, we shall find no better evidence of a well-constituted state than its long continuance. The Abyssinians, who for eight hundred years have held the greatest empire of all Africa, have always sought their kings from one and the same family. In order that the family might not at some time fail and that several claimants might not divide the people into various parties because of eagerness for dominion, as often happened among the Turks and the Persians, or dishonor themselves by parricide, like Deiotarus, who killed all but one of his numerous progeny so that this one might reign more safely—the relatives of the king (whom they call the "sons of the Israelites") are brought up together in a very strong fortress—the lofty mountain Anga, as Alvarez reported, which one cannot reach except through steep and narrow places. They fortify these areas with a very strong guard. When the king dies, they do not usually proclaim the nearest male relative, but the one who seems to the optimates and the guardians the most suitable. This custom also is implanted among Danes, Swedes, and Hungarians, so that from many children they choose arbitrarily the one they wish. Then the Abyssinians, taking this man from the fortress like some God fallen from the sky, attend him with the greatest honors and loyalty. Although fifty provinces are governed by this one man, yet there are no towns surrounded with walls and no citadels, lest the prince should seem to trust in any other defense than in the benevolence of the people or to offer to the seditious any occasion for rebelling. Moreover, what brought the empires of the Parthians and the Turks such glory? Was it not that both appealed to the admiration and loyalty of their peoples, the Turks relying upon the race and the faith of the Ottomans, while the Parthians trusted the sons of Arsaces. Machiavelli was mis-

[169] Isnia may be a misprint for Ivrea.

taken when he thought that the empire would collapse if the prince of the Turks were killed, along with his children, because then there would be no leaders to whom the empire could rightfully go. There remain four families which for splendor and antiquity of race have for a long time equaled the Ottomani: the Michalogli, the Ebrenes, the Turacanii, and the Malaconii, who are descended from the same stock as the Ottomani. These men are, however, wisely removed from the environs of the prince and the government, lest they might be tempted to stir up rebellion. Yet Carthaginians, Persians, French, Britons, and Spanish can maintain their empire in no more convenient way than by an act of succession. Even the Florentines, after they had won their liberty and had disgraced the city and themselves for a long time in a civil war, seeing no end to it, unanimously begged the pope, through their ambassadors, to send them a man of royal family, to whom they would tender the right of dominion. He therefore sent Charles of Valois, by whose presence the seditions suddenly were brought to an end, so potent is the reverence for blood and race, to bind men together by mutual deference and good will. This alliance, of course, is the objective of all states, and dominion should be given by law not only to the nearest agnates but also to the first born. Otherwise murder and civil wars will often occur among the descendants. Indeed, wars between subjects of the same state are much more dreadful than those between strangers, since dissensions among brothers are much more serious. We have as evidence those horrible parricides of the Turks, which at length will bring ruin to that state. Since Selim, the predecessor of the reigning sultan, had such a foreboding, he cast away all desire of begetting children after he had acknowledged his son Solyman. The latter, imitating Deiotarus, did not rest before he saw all his sons slain except one. If the first born alone should have the hope of empire, the rest would be loyal to him, as may be seen among us, where they do not record that any parricide of brothers has taken place.

In this way, then, is royal power constituted, the most excellent of all, as indeed it seems to me, especially helpful for the citizen body and, like harmony, tempered by sweet concord. As for the fact that Plato wished his state to be governed according to geometric ratio, Aristotle decided subtly and cleverly that this concerned rewards only. Arithmetic ratio he related to honoring pledges and to penalties. How rightly, I will not discuss; but about the harmonic ratio neither said anything. Yet I think this ratio, as the most beautiful of all, pertains to the form of the best empire. First because it is developed from arithmetic and geometric ratios alone, yet is unlike each. The harmonic ratio cannot pertain to penalties or rewards, or to pledges, since in pledges an arithmetic equality inheres, in penalties and rewards an equable geometrical similarity. In the harmonic alone inheres the relationship of the superior and the inferior. As the first interval, that is, the octave, with its one to two ratio, embraces all the intervals, so in one and the same prince is the sovereignty, and from him it flows to all the magistrates. The second and third intervals are obtained by adding to the original string half itself, or one third, respectively. The former, with the ratio $1 : 1\frac{1}{2}$, produces a "fifth"; the other, with the ratio $1 : 1\frac{1}{3}$, produces a "fourth." Together they constitute the first interval. The fourth interval is not consonant.[170] The following intervals make violent discords, and the second then is distributed into innumerable parts. When the multitude of numbers is increased more and more, then the strength of the interval is correspondingly decreased until one reaches nothing. Therefore if we should follow our investigation through a perpetual series it becomes plain that the division of authority among several is as abhorrent to nature as is harmony among many numbers. Moreover, that characteristic peculiar to a musical proportion—that is, that the interval is more important than the separate notes and if the ratio were reversed the notes would harmonize well among themselves—is fitted to a monarchy alone, in which authority is carried down gradually to the magistrates. As they govern the lower classes, so in turn they obey their superiors, until unity is achieved in the prince, from whom, like a fountain perennial, flows the majesty of the entire kingdom. Furthermore, the number one is separated from other numbers and stands in a special category. But whether the harmonic ratios are suited to powers and empires, I prefer to let others judge in a matter so obscure than to be the first to affirm it.

Yet these three types of proportion—arithmetic [A.3.4.5.6] [171] geometric [G. 1.2.4.8], and harmonic [H. 2.3.4.6]—seem to me to signify

---

[170] An obscure passage. The Latin reads as follows: "Quemadmodum primum intervallum scilicet ab uno ad binarium in dupla ratione concentus omnes amplectitur: sic in uno et eodem principe summum est imperium, et ab eo fluit ad omnes magistratus. Alterum intervallum duorum aut trium, ratione sesquialtera diapente, tertium diatessarωn complectitur, et utrumque primo intervallo comprehensum est, quartum nullum efficit concentum." See F. M. Cornford, *Plato's Cosmology*, pp. 66–71, and Macrobius *In somnium Scipionis* II. 1. I am indebted to Dr. F. W. Sternfeld, of Wesleyan University, for assistance with this passage.

[171] These mathematical expressions were given in the margin by Bodin.

the three daughters of Themis, as the poets imagine, Eunomia, Dike, and Dikaiosyne; [172] the middle one unites the others in her embrace. They are interpreted as order, justice, and peace. For peace, fitting the harmonic ratio in the most remarkable way, is the most excellent and best objective of empires and states. Nor do I think that those ancient lawgivers had any other goal when they united their citizens by means of public banquets. Hence Minos ordered the gatherings of the Cretans to be celebrated with festive dinners, which they themselves called *andreia*, Lycurgus the *pheidika* or *philika*, Plato *symposia*, Moses *skenopegia* and great *pasach*, which the Greeks corruptly called *pascha*; following him, the early Christians instituted love feasts, as may be seen in the pages of Clement, fourth letter, to the church of Jerusalem. In this list, also, belong the public dinners of the Athenians in the Prytaneum and the banquets during the *panathenaea* and the *thesmorphoria*. Hence the *caristia* of the Romans among near relatives and feasts in the Capitol and at the public sacrifices. To this end the *epulones* were created, by whose example the Venetians instituted four public festivals. Moreover, the legislators of the Swiss wished to have mutual drinking bouts in the *schaffae*, which are now prohibited by edict on account of drunkenness, so that the citizens who were wild and crude might be recalled not only to culture and dignity but also away from hatred, vindictiveness, and quarrels, to peace, love, and benevolence. All these things relate to the rule which has come down to us from heaven and is used so frequently by Christ in the holy supper—that is, that we should love one another.

The other things which can be said about excellent legislation in states are for another place and discussion. We are not talking now about the best state, but about the best type of rule. However, all laws concerning the best state are directed toward the best education of the prince. For nothing more divine ever was said by a prophet than what was said by Plato, "As are the princes in a state, so will be the citizens." By lasting experience we have found this abundantly true. For examples it is unnecessary to seek farther than Francis I, king of the French. As soon as he began to love literature, from which his ancestors had always turned away, immediately the nobility followed suit. Then the remaining orders studied the good arts with such zeal that never was there a greater number of learned people. But since it is difficult to mold in the

---

[172] Hesiod *Theogony*, l. 920. The edition of 1583 of the *Methodus* gives δύναμις, "force," instead of εὐνόμια, "order."

virtues the few optimates who some day will be leaders of the state, even more difficult to mold the many, and most difficult, all the citizens, it follows that the best teachers and guides to learning should be won over by great rewards to the education of the prince, not to imbue the flexible mind of the young prince with a foreign language—which we noticed had once been done, stupidly and unprofitably—but with true religion. Of all topics of discussion about the laws and the government, none is greater or more worthy of zeal and study than that the prince should understand that he has come into this world for the true worship of God. In this alone consists the supreme safety of the state and of all the laws. For the prince so informed by training that he realizes that God is the judge and spectator of all his actions will do nothing impious or wicked, will not even think anything base. This one man his subjects will love and fear. They will shape their lives and customs by his example, as is said of King Louis IX and King Edward I, who on account of the unqualified integrity of their lives were ranked among the saints. The empires of the French and of the English have lasted for a long time because of their laws and their excellent ways of life. Often the kings of the English have been driven from the throne when they spurned the people who were asking for the laws of Edward the Confessor. This, then, is the foundation of the kingdom, without which laws are offered to the prince in vain, because the wicked are not deterred from a life of injury and crime by religious scruples, but by fear of the magistrates.

Yet what magistrate, what laws, what authority will coerce the prince if he is not restrained by fear of God? Such is the strength and the majesty of religion that by itself it not only expels vices and bestows all virtues, on which the highest final good of man depends, but also it is essential to the prince himself, so that power is more effectively supported by this than by anything else. Even Aristotle, at first, then Polybius and Epicurus confessed this, although they despised the divine power. On this account Trebatius [173] the Epicurean found it proper to write books about religion. But since princes have so many desires which are not easily restrained, the second important matter in the education of a prince will be that he shall be nurtured upon solid and true merit. In this atmosphere he should gradually develop. Thus St. Thomas, following the opinion of Aristotle, thinks that a prince ought to be trained, since if he is not content with glory, he will become a tyrant. He will

[173] Trebatius was a contemporary of Cicero. He had a great knowledge of civil law.

seek wealth and pleasure; hence he turns to theft and excesses. This happened to Dionysius the Younger, whom his father reared in ease and delight so that he was not brought into the public eye from the training field, was not hardened by any discipline at all, and had no appreciation of true merit. So he indulged his many desires in company with the most dangerous flatterers, until he was driven from that tyranny as from a citadel. Yet he who is eager for glory not only flees from infamy and baseness of life but also understands that true worth consists of the acts of virtue alone, by which, indeed, he may control the wicked, guard the good, and honor the deeds of the brave and the wise with praises and rewards to the everlasting shame of the wicked.

CHAPTER VII

REFUTATION OF THOSE WHO POSTULATE
FOUR MONARCHIES AND THE
GOLDEN AGE

A LONG-ESTABLISHED, but mistaken, idea about four empires, made famous by the prestige of great men, has sent its roots down so far that it seems difficult to eradicate. It has won over countless interpreters of the Bible; it includes among modern writers Martin Luther, Melanchthon, Sleidan, Lucidus, Funck, and Panvinio—men well read in ancient history and things divine. Sometimes, shaken by their authority, I used to think that it ought not to be doubted. I was stirred also by the prophecy of Daniel, whose reliability it is a crime to disparage, whose authority it is wicked to question. Yet afterwards I understood that the obscure and ambiguous words of Daniel could be twisted into various meanings; and in interpreting the prophecies I preferred to take that formula of the courts, "it doth not appear," [1] than recklessly to agree with anyone because of the opinion of others which I did not understand. I thoroughly approve the reply of Calvin, not less polished than sagacious, when he was asked his opinion about the book of the Apocalypse. He candidly answered that he was totally at a loss regarding the meaning of this obscure writer, whose identity was not yet agreed upon among the erudite. Similarly, I do not see how we are to relate the wild beasts and the image discussed by Daniel to those empires which flourish everywhere now-a-days and have flourished for so many centuries.

At the beginning of the argument we must assume that a monarchy has certain limits of dominion and area or is famous for the origin of its prince or people, so that we may understand what is this thing which they call monarchy. Although it is the main issue of this discussion, the interpreters of the prophecies have not defined it at all clearly. They suppose from this vision of four beasts and an image that an equal number of empires was signified: that is, of Assyrians, Persians, Greeks, and Romans. They augured that there will be no more. Eventually the Germans were to control the Roman Empire. Since it was explained in this way by Germans, I judged it was written for the glory of their name

---

[1] *Non liquet.*

and empire, for it is altogether strange to the interpretation of Daniel. I desire, therefore, to refute them with their own arguments.

In the first place, Philip Melanchthon says that a monarchy seems to him that sovereign power of a state which can subjugate the riches and resources of others. In that case we should use the word "empire," since "monarchy" cannot be applied to the popular form of government of the Romans. Yet if we should weigh the matter without considering the technicalities of terms, surely the Germans do not relevantly claim the monarchy of the Romans, since they hold beneath their sway hardly the hundredth part of the world, and the king of Spain has an empire greater than that of the Germans, in both number of people and extent of domain—omitting the American regions (over which in great part he rules), three times greater than Europe. But the Germans are not even equal to the king of Portugal, if we define empire by the magnitude of the area. He seized almost the entire shore of Africa by force, and by means of the strongest defense works frequently he has driven off the attacks of barbarians. At this point someone will say, we must take into consideration, not the number of men or the extent of territory, but power and endurance, and of course I agree with them in this. Yet I do not see in what way Germany could have resisted the legions of Spain and Italy under the leadership of Charles V, who, if he had not been restrained by the valor of the French, would have reduced that empire to the form of a province, as the Germans in famous and still extant documents have testified. They render equal thanks to us.

Turning to foreign nations, what has Germany to oppose to the sultan of the Turks? Or which state can more aptly be called a monarchy? This fact is obvious to everyone—if there is anywhere in the world any majesty of empire and of true monarchy, it must radiate from the sultan. He owns the richest parts of Asia, Africa, and Europe, and he rules far and wide over the entire Mediterranean and all but a few of its islands. Moreover, in armed forces and strength he is such that he alone is the equal of almost all the princes, since he drove the armies of the Persians and the Muscovites far beyond the boundaries of the empire. But he seized provinces of the Christians and the empire of the Greeks by force of arms, and even devastated the lands of the Germans. I shall not discuss the prince of Ethiopia, called by his people Jochan Bellul, that is, precious gem, whose empire is little less than all Europe. What of the emperor of the Tartars, who rules tribes barbarous in their savagery, countless in number, unconquered in strength? If you compare Germany with these, you compare a fly to an elephant.

The way in which the Germans define a monarchy is absurd, that is, according to the interpretation of Philip Melanchthon, as the most powerful of all states. It is even more absurd that they think they hold the empire of the Romans, which of course would seem laughable to all who have well in mind the map of the world. The empire of the Romans was most flourishing under Trajan. Never before had it been so great, and afterwards it constantly diminished, as may be seen in the pages of Appian and Sextus Rufus, who wrote in the time of Trajan. It was, in truth, bounded by the Danube and the Orkneys on the north, Cadiz on the west, the Euphrates on the east, and Oenopolis on the south, when Trajan, by throwing a stone bridge over the Danube, added Dacia to the empire and triumphed over King Decebalus. Then, having defeated the legions of the Parthians, he crossed the Euphrates and annexed Mesopotamia and a great part of Arabia Felix to the empire of his ancestors. Pompey had been reluctant to attempt this in earlier days, even though he told the king of the Parthians that the dominion of the Romans was limited not by rivers, but by justice, when that king asked that the Euphrates should be the frontier between the Roman and the Parthian empires.

The Germans, however, hold no part of the Roman Empire except Noricum and Vindelicia. Germany is bounded by the Rhine, the Danube, the Vistula, the Carpathian Mountains, and the ocean, but all authority ends at the foothills of the Alps in the south; by the Rhine and a few cities this side of the Rhine in the west; by Silesia, in turn, on the east; by the Baltic regions on the north. How much truer it is of the king of the Turks, who took Byzantium, the capital of the empire, from the Christians, the region of Babylon, which is discussed in the book of Daniel, from the Persians, and joined a great part of his dominion beyond the Danube, up to the mouths of the Dnieper, to the old Roman provinces? Now, if we identify monarchy with force of arms, or with great wealth, or with fertility of areas, or with the number of victories, or with size of population, or with etymology of the name, or with the fatherland of Daniel, or with the seat of the Babylonian empire, or with the amplitude of sway, it will be more appropriate, certainly, to interpret the prophecy of Daniel as applied to the sultan of the Turks.

Even in that case there are, and have been until now, not only four, but almost an infinitude of empires greater than the Babylonian. They disregard the empire of the Chaldeans, who first built the foundations of Babylon. They ignore the empire of the Medes, who drove out the Assyrians, and certainly Nebuchadnezzar was a Mede by race, not an Assyrian. They forget also the empire of the Parthians, who drove out the Greeks, frequently broke the power of the Romans, often led the emperors captive or more often invaded their provinces. They overlook the Arabs, who seized the Babylonian Empire and conquered by force a great part of Asia, Africa, and Europe. But if they include Chaldeans, Medes, Assyrians, and Parthians under this same name of "empire," why not add the Persians also, their neighbors—especially since the Medes were by far the more remote? The Parthians, indeed, were very far from Babylon, which nevertheless they seized. If a change from a Median prince to a Persian, that is, if the conquest by one man, Cyrus, produced a change of dominion, although by race and customs he was closely united to the Medes, why is not the same thing true about Chaldeans, Parthians, Medes, and Arabs? On the same basis, then, that Cyrus, a Persian, established a new monarchy, they also will create monarchies: Trajan, a Spaniard, created a Spanish monarchy; Caracalla, Carus, Carinus, and Antoninus, French by birth, a Gallic monarchy. We shall make the same decision about Alexander and Heliogabalus, who were Syrians; about Philip the Arab; and about Totila, Witigis, Theodatus, and Alaric, Goths, who invaded not only the provinces but even the capital of the Roman empire itself, oppressed Italy, and finally put the city to fire and sword. In the end they held Italy by force of arms for seventy years, although Alexander the Great, who broke the power of the Persians, governed barely twelve years, but, like a flash of lightning, shone here and there and then vanished. So his empire was given over to four princes, and it disappeared soon after.

Indeed, it seems more stupid that Charles the Great (who first seized what they call the monarchy), by race French, born in France, and educated in the language, customs, and institutions of the French, as well as his ancestors, is called German by some, or Alemannic by others. Although many may think that he derived his origin from the Frankish colonists of the ancient Gauls, yet they do not deny that he used French arms and legions to unite Germany, Italy, and a great part of Spain with the empire of the French, and to his first born gave France as the seat of empire, to others other regions, torn from this empire, until Henry the Fowler, by birth a German, proclaiming himself king, seized

Germany, part of this empire. More truly, then, and more equitably, the term ought to be applied to the French monarchy, which was achieved by the valor of the French before the Germans had heard the word "monarchy." Moreover, who can deny that the Britons also established their monarchy under Constantine the Great much more truly than the Germans? He was by race British (although born illegitimately of a Roman father); contrary to the will of the senate and the Roman people he came into Italy from the farthest shores, defeated the Roman emperors in war, abolished the religions and institutions of his elders, introduced the name of Christ to be worshiped, transferred the seat of empire to Byzantium, deprived the Romans of all importance, and at length called the capital itself by his own name. But if the descent of Cyrus, although he was by blood and fatherland a neighbor to the Assyrians, determines the monarchy of the Persians, why will not this equally new and unorthodox dominion of Constantine make a monarchy, since it brings about so conspicuous a change in race, area, laws, and religion?

It is, indeed, remarkable that defendants of this theory omit the monarchy of the Arabs, who forced almost the whole of Africa and a great part of Asia to use not only Arabian arms and laws, but also their religion and language. The Mohammedans defeated the armies of the Persians and reduced them to such servitude that they were forbidden to use their own literature and customs in any way. It ought also to seem strange that such theorists forget entirely the empire of the Tartars, when it can be ranked with all the rest. Or was this because it is far from Babylon? But the Germans are farther away, and they have no part of the Babylonian empire. The Tartars, on the other hand, devastated Bactria and Sogdiana, seized broad provinces of that empire, and under the leadership of Hulagu, overthrew Babylon itself from the foundation, as Marco Polo wrote. When I ponder at length over what the prophet wanted to say, nothing more fitting occurs to me than to apply it to Babylon, which came into the power of Medes, Persians, Greeks, and Parthians, a city which has been devastated rather often and at one time completely destroyed. What is commonly called Baldach is not the same as ancient Babylon, but rather ancient Susa, as Marco Polo explained. But if this is true, the prophecy about the government of Babylon, the changes and the destruction, was not vain, especially when the words of Daniel and all the Prophets were intended for Christ and his times as a goal. As evidence, there is that stone (by which Paul eloquently affirms that Christ was symbolized—in these words, "the Rock, moreover, was Christ") [2] cut from the top of the mount, which destroyed the image.[3] Although Daniel himself, in interpreting, explained the many beasts of his oracle, as well as the many horns of the beasts, what prevents their referring to the successors of Alexander the Great and to those empires which flourished on the site of his? However, I should dare affirm nothing in matters so hidden and obscure. Only this much: the words of Daniel can in no way suit the desired interpretation.

Josephus the Jew, the best interpreter of Daniel, wrote that Medes, Persians, and Greeks were summoned by Daniel to rule over Babylon. About the Romans, from whom he himself acquired the name of the Flavian family, the citizenship, and a statue,[4] he noted no reference by Daniel. But in that way spread the mistaken custom that each man should interpret the prophecies of Daniel according to his own judgment, not according to accurate history. Hence they think that there ought to be only five kings of the Persians, because Daniel said that there would be only five kings to come. But the unanimous verdict of all writers places the minimum at eight; some even at ten, on account of seditions and civil wars. By a similar error, from the oft-mentioned image of Daniel (whose head of gold, chest of silver, legs of bronze, shins of iron, and feet of clay, they say, were put together badly with iron) historians established four or even more ages.

Once there was a golden age, afterwards a silver, then a bronze, and then an iron. At length clay followed. But this opinion must be adjusted, for if anyone examines the meaning of historians, not of poets, certainly he will decide that there is a change in human affairs similar to that in the nature of all things; nor is there anything new under the sun, as that sage master of wisdom says.[5] The age which they call "golden," if it be compared with ours, would seem but iron. Who doubts that the flood came about through divine will on account of the sins of men, which were so many and so great that God himself was grieved that man had been created? Let us then consider the ages which followed the flood and are called "golden," not only by the poets, but also by Cato himself in his book *Of Origins*. He reported that Cameses and Saturn flourished at that time. But no one doubts that Cameses was called the son of Noah by the Hebrews; Saturn, Nimrod by the consent

[2] I Corinthians 10: 14.
[3] Daniel 2: 34.
[4] See note 16 in Chapter II.
[5] Ecclesiastes 1: 9.

of all; it was his son Jupiter Belus who made an end to the golden age. From this it is plain that the golden age seemed a brief moment if an epoch of six thousand years is taken into account. Cato, following the fables of the poets, limited it to two hundred and fifty years. But how innocent was Cameses, who violated the honor of the best of parents by some new and disgraceful indignity! On this account he earned the curse of his father. It was even so in the case of Nimrod, grandson of Cameses, whom they call the founder of the golden age. What his character was is understood sufficiently from his very name, which in Hebrew means "rebel." He was termed by Moses a "mighty hunter," but he used this word everywhere to indicate robbers and wicked men, as even Aristotle placed piracy among the kinds of hunting. The next was Jupiter Belus, who with greater audacity, or shall I say impiety, hurled his aged father from power as if from a bridge. I observe there have been other Jupiters (for antiquity worshiped three hundred), but whichever is the one who drove his father from the throne, according to the poets, he is well known not only for parricide but also for all kinds of debauchery and incest with his sister. In that same era someone tried to snatch the tyranny from Jupiter. On this occasion the brothers [6] plotted to rend the skies, and when they had built towers and ramparts, they brought an accursed war against immortal God. They tried to cast him headlong from the sky [and would have succeeded], if they had not been prevented by a thunderbolt or by the confusion of tongues which made it impossible for the rebels to coöperate. On this account the name of Babylon was given to the tower which we call also Babel.

Of course Moses to a certain extent agreed with the poets (who confused the truth of the matter with fables). Yet what significance is there in the statement that the giants bring war against the gods—other than the struggle against nature, as Cicero says?

This, then, is that golden age which produced such monsters for us. I make the same judgment about Hercules who, Manetho reported, was the greatest of the pirates. He allied Theseus and Pirithous with him in criminal association, and when they had carried off Helen and

---

[6] The Latin reads: coniurati coelum rescindere fratres, qui turribus et aggeribus extructis, immortali Deo nefarium bellum intulerunt eumque de coelo praecipitem deturbare sunt conati, nisi tum fulmine prohiberentur vel ipsa linguarum confusione, unde turri nomen Babylon ab inscitia loquendi, quam nos quoque babil appellamus. In this sentence Bodin is combining two legends dealing with revolt against the Deity: the first is the revolt of the Titans, and the second, of the descendants of Noah who put up the tower of Babel in defiance of God.

had tried to take the daughter of King Molossus from her father, he threw them into prison. The one was torn by the Cerberean hounds; the other would have been torn in a short time, if he had not been called back from the infernal regions by the prayers of Hercules, or rather if he had not been saved for crueler punishments. Furthermore, who was stronger in all kinds of lust than Hercules, or shall I say more abominable? But lest these things should seem like fables, let us rather agree with Thucydides, the most truthful father of history. He left witness that a little before his time such was the barbarity and ferocity of men in Greece itself that by land and sea piracy was openly practiced. Without any shame travelers usually asked whether those they encountered were robbers or pirates or not. Yet since fortifications did not exist at that time and there were no defenses, justice resided in force, and the old colonists were continually driven from possession by new ones. This custom in Greece little by little became permanent. Moreover, the nations farthest removed from culture lived in this savagery for a long time, as Caesar wrote about the Germans. Piracy committed beyond the frontiers of each state is considered no disgrace among the Germans, and they recommend that this practice be used to train youth and to diminish laziness. From that custom, it happened, I suppose, that robbers, who are commonly called "brigands," take their name from the Brigantini, who hold Lake Podamicus or Brigantinus,[7] as the assassins do from that tribe of Persians which for a long time has labored under the bad reputation of being robbers and murderers. The Spartans, too, thought that there was no crime in the theft of edibles, but only in being caught stealing. Of course both opinions are more criminal than stealing, in so far as it is more wretched and base to permit freely by law anything which is wrong by nature.

These were the golden and the silver ages, in which men were scattered like beasts in the fields and the woods and had as much as they could keep by means of force and crime, until gradually they were reclaimed from that ferocity and barbarity to the refinement of customs and the law-abiding society which we see about us. Thievery, which once incurred only a civil judgment, not only according to the laws of the Hebrews but also to those of the Greeks and the Latins, now everywhere in the world is repaid by capital punishment. On the contrary, if human affairs were becoming worse, long ago we should have reached

[7] Lake Constance.

the extreme limit of vices and improbity, whither indeed I think in times gone by they had arrived.

Since wicked men cannot progress any farther or stand any longer in the same place, it becomes necessary for them to retrace their steps gradually, forced either by shame, which inheres in men naturally, or by necessity, because society can in no way be developed by such crimes, or else they are forced by the goodness of God, which is the truer solution. This, indeed, becomes plain from books of annals and records of our elders, in which so many and such dreadful enormities are reported (and yet not all) that we cannot very easily say which was the worst. The witnesses are Suetonius, Tacitus, Lampridius, and Athenaeus. What more criminal could be conceived than that the most horrible vices should be regarded as virtues? This is to be seen not only in depraved states but also in that republic which flourished under the institutions of Lycurgus and was thought most laudable by the consent of all writers. To omit the abandoned lusts of these people (Oh, that they were buried in eternal oblivion!), what is so impious as that men should be sacrificed most cruelly both at funerals and in religious rites? But this used to be done among almost all peoples. What more cruel than that the most innocent, under pretext of slavery, should be torn to bits in public spectacles, or should wound and kill each other for the delight of the people? Yet nothing was more commonplace among the Romans, who enjoyed the highest reputation for justice. By some divine retribution, in a spectacle of gladiators at Fidenae fifty thousand persons were overwhelmed in the collapse of one amphitheater. Certainly our men, much more wisely than the Romans (may it be said with due apologies to them), eliminated from the Christian state mortal contests among human beings, as well as the bloodthirsty spectacles of wild beasts, and set up instead a fruitful and useful kind of disputation on all subjects. How much better it is, then, to be formed for the good arts and true ornament than to be trained for the gymnasium? Yet we have not omitted suitable exercises for the body or neglected military training. Our records have also their Catos, Fabricii, Camilli, Alexanders, to say nothing of the others, and Titan did not fashion their hearts of a finer clay than our own.[8]

Was military glory greater in Alexander than in Charlemagne? The former, indeed, was great, but only against the soft Asiatics, as

[8] Juvenal *Satire* XIV. 34.

Caesar was wont to say about Pompey after he himself had experienced the strength of our men; the latter, our leader, conquered the most ferocious nations of Europe. Did an equal piety exist in Antoninus and in Louis the Pious? Moreover, what prince of all antiquity can be compared to St. Louis the king? Omitting the laws promulgated by him upon which this kingdom rests, certainly no such devotion of any prince toward God, responsibility to his country, love toward his subjects, and justice to all have ever been recorded. Not only the virtues of our men are equal to those of the ancients but also the disciplines. Literature suffers changes of fortune. First the arts arise in some places through the practice and the labor of talented men, then they develop, later they flourish for a while at a fixed level, then languish in their old age, and finally begin to die and are buried in a lasting oblivion by the eternal calamity of wars, or because too great abundance (an evil much to be feared in these times, of course) brings satiety to the frivolous, or because God inflicts just punishments upon those who direct useful knowledge to the ruin of men. Although disciplines had gradually developed among the Greeks, so that they believed these arts had reached their peak, such a change came about afterward that Greece herself, to judge from her present predicament, seems never to have existed.

What of the Latins? Among them talented men were so abundant that almost simultaneously they excelled all peoples in warlike glory and in superiority of culture. Yet by a similar fall they also started to lapse into their early barbarity when the forces of the Scythians, pouring into Italy, burned the well-stocked libraries almost everywhere and all the monuments of antiquity. This horrible deed destroyed all disciplines, so that for about a thousand years they lay prostrate without any prestige and indeed seemed to be dying, until Mansur, prince of Africa and Spain, stirred up the talents of the Arabs with offers of great rewards for the revival of letters. I omit how Egypt, India, and Ethiopia teemed with many philosophers, geometrists, and astrologers; how many well-known mathematicians were in Chaldea before Greece had any literature. I come back to our times in which, after a long eclipse of letters throughout almost the entire world, suddenly such a wealth of knowledge shone forth, such fertility of talents existed, as no age ever excelled.

Not even the Goths themselves have lacked the finest talents in modern times. Olaus Magnus is an evidence of this, as well as Holster and many others, as if nature had decreed that the wounds of knowledge should now be healed by those very people who once inflicted them. Although until recently they retained the custom of their ancestors and the voice of a herald ordered men of letters to depart from the senate (for we have evidence of this in their history), now everywhere they are wont to cultivate letters. This is so definite a change in all respects that no one ought to doubt that the same process occurs in human talent as in the fields, which are wont to repay with greater abundance the privilege of lying fallow. Some one will say, however, that the ancients were inventors of the arts and to them the glory ought to go. They certainly did discover many things—especially the power of the celestial bodies, the calculated courses of many stars—but yet not all—the wonderful trajections of fixed stars and of those called "planets." Then they noted carefully the obscurities of nature and explained many things accurately, and yet they left incomplete many of these things which have been completed and handed down to posterity by men of our time. No one, looking closely into this matter, can doubt that the discoveries of our men ought to be compared with the discoveries of our elders; many ought to be placed first. Although nothing is more remarkable in the whole nature of things than the magnet, yet the ancients were not aware of its use, clearly divine, and whereas they lived entirely within the Mediterranean basin, our men, on the other hand, traverse the whole earth every year in frequent voyages and lead colonies into another world, as I might say, in order to open up the farthest recesses of India. Not only has this discovery developed an abundant and profitable commerce (which formerly was insignificant or not well known) but also all men surprisingly work together in a world state, as if in one and the same city-state. Indeed, in geography, one of the most excellent arts, one may understand how much advance has been made from the fact that information about India which used to seem fabulous to many (for Lactantius and Augustine said that men who believed in the antipodes were crazy) have been verified by us, as well as the motion of the fixed stars and the trepidation of the great sphere. Moreover, what is more remarkable than that abstraction and separation of forms from matter (if I may speak thus)? From this the hidden secrets of nature are revealed; hence healthful medicines are daily brought forward. I pass over the method of investigating celestial longitude from equal hours,[9] which could not be calculated by the ancients from the normal to the

---

[9] Hour in this sense was an angular measure of right ascension or longitude, the 24th part of a great circle of the sphere, or 15 degrees.

ecliptic without great error. I will not dwell upon the catapults of our ancestors and the ancient engines of war, which, of course, seem like some boyish toy if compared with our [instruments]. I omit finally countless arts, both handicraft and weaving, with which the life of man has been aided in a remarkable way. Printing alone can easily vie with all the discoveries of all the ancients.

So they who say that all things were understood by the ancients err not less than do those who deny them the early conquest of many arts. Nature has countless treasures of knowledge which cannot be exhausted in any age. Since these things are so and since by some eternal law of nature the path of change seems to go in a circle, so that vices press upon virtues, ignorance upon knowledge, base upon honorable, and darkness upon light, they are mistaken who think that the race of men always deteriorates. When old men err in this respect, it is understandable that this should happen to them—that they sigh for the loss of the flower of youth, which of itself breathes joy and cheerfulness. When they see themselves deprived of every kind of delight and instead of pleasure they feel sharp pains, instead of having unimpaired senses, they suffer weakness in all their members, it happens that they fall to these sad meditations and, deceived by the false picture of things, think that loyalty and friendship of man for man has died. As though returning from a distant journey, they narrate the golden century—the golden age —to the young men. But then their experience is the same as that of men carried out of port into the open sea—they think the houses and the towns are departing from them; thus they think that delight, gentle conduct, and justice have flown to the heavens and deserted the earth.

CHAPTER VIII

A SYSTEM OF UNIVERSAL TIME

THOSE WHO think they can understand histories without chronology are as much in error as those who wish to escape the windings of a labyrinth without a guide. The latter wander hither and thither and cannot find any end to the maze, while the former are carried among the many intricacies of the narrative with equal uncertainty and do not understand where to commence or where to turn back. But the principle of time, the guide for all histories, like another Ariadne tracing the hidden steps with a thread, not only prevents us from wandering, but also often makes it possible for us to lead back erring historians to the right path. So we see all very good writers have so much regard for time as to include not only the years, but even the separate parts of the year. Others do not omit even the very months and days, or the moments of the day, in which a thing has happened, because they understand that without a system of time hardly any advantage is culled from history.

Then, since the most important part of the subject depends upon the chronological principle, we have thought that a system of universal time is needed for this method of which we treat. Both on account of its great usefulness and also on account of the discrepancy which appears among historians concerning the antiquity and the succession of events, I should like to shed some light on this topic also.

First, then, let us establish the beginning of time, without which this discussion would be empty, settling this not so much by authority, which has no value among those who wish to be led by reason, as by necessary arguments. It is true that if the sacred founts of the Hebrews and the revelations of divine law bear witness that the world had a precise beginning of creation, to seek further would seem a crime—to doubt, seems wicked. Such is the authority with me of Moses alone that I place him far ahead of all the writings and the opinions of all philosophers. He subjected to capital punishment those who violated the Sabbath, chiefly for this reason, that by violation of the Sabbath they seemed to call into doubt the creation of the world, as Rabbi Moses the Egyptian wrote. But since the wicked do not suffer themselves to be awed by his authority and recklessly scorn his attendant warnings, it is necessary to refute and to weaken their arguments with corresponding arguments. If by the authority of philosophers and the force of reasoning it should be clearly understood that the world was not everlasting, but founded by immortal God at a precise moment of time, we shall put greater trust in sacred history. In that case the creation of the world, depending upon a belief in so splendid a first cause, will increase in us a special awe and love of God. That teaching is not only Hebraic but characteristic also of Chaldeans, Pythagoreans, Stoics, Academicians, and Arabs, and, finally, it is approved and confirmed by the weightiest teachings of many men. Epicurus himself was of this same opinion, as we find in the pages of Plutarch. Among the Latins, indeed, although only a few treated philosophy in earnest, M. Varro, who is called by Tully the most learned of the Latins and the Greeks, reached this same conclusion in the book which he is reported to have written about the end of the world. The authority of all these men, assenting to this same principle, ought to be of no small weight and importance even among philosophers.

But since Aristotle first of all, dissenting from his predecessors and from his master Plato, dared to assume that the world is eternal,[1] all this discussion is undertaken in opposition to him. Galen, indeed, refuted his reasons in one word—he wrote that they seem probable, yet are not necessary. In the book *About the Heavens* Aristotle said that since the opportunity for demonstration was denied to all, the statements of others, compared with his own, made the conclusion more certain. These are not the words of physicists or of geometrists, but of logicians doubtful of the subject under discussion, as Rabbi Moses the Egyptian, who is called interpreter of doubtful things, observed with acumen. Demonstrations suffer no one to doubt, but by their own light are manifest, so that like applied torture they wring assent from the unwilling. Therefore, if Epicurus and Galen, men not at all religious, denied that Aristotle's arguments had any force and if Origen, Avicenna, and finally the schools of all theologians and philosophers refute these things by adverse arguments, it may be sufficiently understood that they are only probable and uncertain, not inevitable.

But I come to Plato, who imagined that God, after the production of such a great work, addressed His speech to the created things.[2] He affirmed that they are mortal because they had a beginning, yet by His divine will are to be immortal. With regard to this Aristotle, taking up the words of Plato, said that if the world is not perishable, then it does

---

[1] Aristotle *De caelo* I. 10. 283b 26.   [2] Plato *Timaeus* 41 A, B.

not have a beginning, because things that have a beginning sometime must decay, and things which die must necessarily have been generated. These things he learned from Plato in *Phaedrus* and *Timaeus,*
where the latter said that for this reason souls do not have a beginning [3]
(as Augustine also wrote in *De civitate Dei,* Book x),[4] lest sometime
they might perish, and that the form of the world would always be the
same under divine command. Which, then, errs more seriously in a philosophical sense, the one who leaves to all-powerful God the free faculty
of deciding about His own affairs, or the other who confesses that He is
the governor of the world and indeed the efficient cause, yet takes from
Him all power of changing His work, so that if He wishes to destroy the
world He cannot? By this argument Aristotle, in making a decision
about the eternity of the world, recklessly, I would say rather, impiously,
tried to enervate and weaken not only the decrees of natural philosophy
but also the strength of divine majesty. Yet in every discussion undertaken, especially about matters so difficult and so far removed from our
perceptions, we must be careful that nothing whatsoever shall be said
scornfully against the majesty of God; this Aristotle ignored. When he
was hard pressed everywhere by the force of reasoning and had to confess that the world had an initial stage if he granted to God free will—
he affirmed that the world is ruled by necessity, not by volition. All the
discussions revolve around this point. Yet the same man, disputing
against the Stoics, who assumed a fatal compulsion in all things, showed
by many arguments that certain things were done by necessity, others by
will, many by spontaneity, and most by chance.[5] He even divided fortune and chance into three parts and placed divine actions and nature
among the inevitable things. From this it may be understood that the
matters which he discussed in the book *About the Heavens,* because they
indicated an inescapable urge, he so altered in the book *About Interpretation* that to man, indeed, he gives a will released from all restriction;
but God and nature he binds by necessity. Yet what more impious, more
arrogant, finally, more mad than to give free will to himself, but wish
to take it from God? The consequence is that God cannot stay the course
of the sun, or check the power of the celestial stars, or change anything
in universal nature; not even the impulses and the volitions of man can
He impel whither He wishes. Since these things seem absurd and full
of impiety, it follows that we should remove this compulsion from the

[3] Plato *Phaedrus* 245 D. [4] Augustine *De civitate Dei* X. 4.
[5] Aristotle *Physics* II. 6. 198a.

world. When it has been removed, the result is that God is bound by no force, but governs all things by pure choice. Since Aristotle felt ashamed of himself—that is, for granting freedom to man, but taking it away from God—he granted free will in words, yet in truth a will forced by necessity (Moses the Egyptian noticed this). He permitted volition, but of such a kind that it could not be changed, as Jupiter in the fables is held by the laws of Nemesis, although in his book "About Customs" [6] he taught that the force and the nature of this volition is such that unless it can be changed it loses the name "will." So when he saw that many things in nature occur in different ways—now in this manner, now in that—he fell into this error of preferring to establish fortune and chance according to the opinion of the mob rather than to ascribe to God liberty to do different things differently. Moreover, what is more unworthy of a philosopher than to think a thing can happen without a cause, that is, to leave anything to fortune and to chance? These problems belong to that group which the Peripatetics could in no way solve, so they are refuted by Plutarch in the book "About Fortune" and also by Lactantius [7] with most effective arguments.

Let us consider of what kind are the remaining matters, or at any rate the most important. It would be interminable to follow all things. Some philosophers postulated as the basis of the entire discussion that nothing is born of nothing, which gave rise to all the errors. But they are in difficulty with the conclusions, since this very thing remains to be proved. Then they are annoyed because they think it is wrong that their premises should be denied. But what are those premises, ultimately, which seem more obscure than the conclusions? No one ever denied the postulates of geometry, because they are clear by their own light. But if these things seemed clear, why do so many schools of philosophy so constantly deny them? Why does Philoponus [8] clearly demonstrate the premises are false? Moreover, what more stupid than to postulate a condition which if it were actually denied would block their further advance?

However, let us refute that famous principle, if agreeable. I wonder why our men have not done this, since they have exercised themselves so much in this dispute. Philip Melanchthon and the theologians have

---

[6] "De moribus," Aristotle *Nicomachean Ethics* III. 3. 1113a 10.

[7] Lactantius, c.260–c.340, wrote *Seven Books of Divine Institutions* and *Concerning the Death of the Persecutors.*

[8] Philoponus was an Alexandrian of the fifth to sixth centuries. He wrote a commentary on the Mosaic cosmogony and *Adversus Procli de aeternitate mundi argumenta.*

made a distinction and say that in ordered nature this principle is true; but this argument takes us back to the start, as the logicians say. For how can we imagine nature disordered? Either it is complete and joined in all its parts, that is, in matter and form, or it is nonexistent. Let us, then, use more precise arguments. This subject we shall understand easily from the excellence of forms. Form is noble and, as Aristotle wrote, an essence having something divine, the chief part of nature itself, because all things exist by its benefit. Moreover, it is not drawn from matter, as I shall make plain, or from itself only, since forms separated from matter totally perish and cannot exist alone, as Aristotle reported in *Metaphysics*. It may not be a small fragment of God, since from pure and eternal mind body does not arise. A certain wise Moor taught this when he said God established the celestial orbs from the light of his vestment. It follows that the form is produced in matter out of nothing. So Aristotle, Book II of the *Physics*, wrote that natural form is the purpose of nature itself, the efficient and formal cause.[9] Yet he separated God from the beginnings of nature and placed mere privation, which is not essence or true accident, among the principles.[10] But since the individual forms rise and fall in some perpetual flux, as he confessed in Book I, chapter 9, of the *Physics*, he produced grave doubts in the later Peripatetics as to whence these forms come. In the end the Peripatetics believed that the forms developed from the depths and power of matter, an idea which never came into the mind of Aristotle. From this it followed that primeval matter possesses forms not potentially, but actually united with itself, and it is inaccurate to call it amorphous, or form, immaterial; or to say that what is shapeless shapes itself, or that forms develop through the tempering of matter, finally, that they increase in extension and intensity. Aristotle taught that these theories are false in Book VIII of the *Metaphysics*, and also in *The Soul*, Book I, chapter 3. Then they say form is not a principle, but has its origin in matter itself; they say it is not a simple principle, but mixed and composite. Finally, they say matter gives to things themselves their existence, that is, their being. If these things are not easily credible from the teaching of Aristotle himself, not even the former doctrines, whence the latter are derived, can be proved: that is, that forms are drawn from the interior of matter. Therefore we must assume that they are added from the outside.

[9] Aristotle *Physics* II. 8. 199a. 30. "Since the term nature is applied both to material and to form, and since it is the latter that constitutes the goal, and all else is for the sake of that goal, it follows that the form is the final cause."   [10] *Ibid*. I. 7. 191a.

Aristotle denied this in Book II, chapter 3, *About the Generation of Animals*, except in the case of the form of man, which he himself confessed did enter from without. We shall wrest this concession from him, then, that the form of man is generated from nothing in matter, and the same judgment will apply to all forms, for in truth matter has no fashioning force. Certainly it is as stupid to think that forms are drawn from the bosom of matter as that the figure of Mercury was drawn from a log, since it comes from the mind, work, and concept of the artificer.

Then what they postulated is false—that from nothing nothing is derived. The basis of the discussion having been overthrown, the rest is threatened with ruin. Philoponus argued against Aristotle in this way: if it does not seem absurd that forms flow from pure privation, why does it seem absurd that from privation primordial matter also flows? When Theophrastus himself saw that plants were created without seed not only in soil but even in stones, he could find no other cause than the power and peculiar nature of the heavens: *About the Causes of Plants*, Book I, chapter v.

Let us look to the rest. Similar is the saying that nothing in the heavens is contrary to itself and that therefore nothing must be feared from the end or hoped from the beginning. Whence come then the contrary powers of mutually discordant elements? They admit that these things are stirred up by the force and agitation of superior things and that from these causes come contrary dispositions. But since one effect is derived from one simple cause, a contrasting effect from a contrasting cause, it must be confessed that warring causes exist in the heavens, not so much in their effect, as is erroneously thought, but in the very character of nature, as they say, formally. That they infer the everlasting motion of the sphere from the fact that time cannot endure without motion is equally deceptive and sophistic, as if anyone should say that hours did not exist before clocks or that if the clock were taken away there would be no [hours]. So Plotinus, Book VIII, and Pico della Mirandola *About the Vanity of Pagan Teachings*,[11] Book VI, long since laughed at the problem of Aristotle, Book IV of the *Physics*, that is, whether if the soul which does the counting were taken away, time would cease to be. Indeed, to escape this empty chattering, Basil, Ambrose, Augustine, and Moses the Egyptian separated time altogether from eternity.

Yet one argument was brought forward by the interpreters of Aris-

---

[11] *Investigation of the Vanity of Pagan Teaching*, by the nephew of the more famous Giovanni Pico della Mirandola.

totle which really disturbed Moses: they said that the existence of the world was necessary, or possible, or impossible. If impossible, the world would never have existed; if necessary, it has always existed; if possible before it existed, the power of existing, or to use their words, that potentiality, was in some entity. Therefore there was something which evolved from power into actuality. But I concede all this, and that possibility which they seek I will place in a being, that is, in the everlasting effective cause; nor do I see what can be said in opposition.

But if they think that power ought to be in underlying matter also, the proof will be more sophistical than necessary, somewhat like this: if the first Creator came from pure privation to actuality, there was something which enticed and incited Him to action. I say He was incited by Himself, just as the architect who has no matter or space for building, yet by himself is stirred to the thought of building. It is much more repugnant to reason and to truth to think that the world exists necessarily —that whether the Creator wishes it or not, He is bound by the necessity of fate. These are the chief arguments of the Peripatetics and Averroës. Proclus [12] has three arguments. Differing from his master Plato, he thought that the world is eternal and wrote that Plato meant to say this. Simplicius,[13] Plotinus,[14] Marinus, Syrianus, Apuleius, and Iamblichus [15] also thought so, and among modern men Cardinal Bessarion and Fox-Morcillo.[16] The latter, in order to reconcile Aristotle with Plato, all assumed a beginning of the world in [the sense of a beginning of that] defense of its safety which has always been God's concern. Others think that Plato spoke hypothetically; but Plutarch and Philo refute them.

Philoponus refuted Proclus in eighteen books, but all the discussion is, I think, covered in these three arguments: God, said Proclus, could make the world everlasting. Therefore he wished to. If He wished it, the thing was done. It becomes plain that He wished to do so from the fact that only an ill-willed person hesitates to do good when he can, or a

[12] Proclus, A.D. 410–485, was a celebrated Neoplatonist of Athens, who wrote *In Platonis theologiam.*

[13] Simplicius lived in the sixth century A.D. He was one of the last members of the Neoplatonic School to which Syrianus, Proclus, and Marinus also belonged. It was the center of efforts to maintain Greek mythology against Christianity. Simplicius was the author of commentaries on Aristotle's *Physics, Metaphysics,* and *De anima.*

[14] Originator of the Neoplatonic system in the third century A.D.

[15] Iamblichus lived in the fourth century A.D. He was a Neoplatonist who differed somewhat from the views of his master Porphyry, and studied the philosophy of Pythagoras.

[16] Sebastian Fox-Morcillo, c. 1528–1560, a Spanish philosopher, the tutor of Don Carlos, son of Philip II. He wrote *De historia institutione dialogus.*

man who envies the advantages and rejoices in the misfortunes of another; this could not be true of God. Therefore that opinion would not hold. Yet to be carried from quiet to activity, from what you do not want to actually willing, indicates change and variety very foreign to the divine nature, which is simple and always constant. This argument, however, will follow if we grant that for countless centuries God remained inactive and that He thought only recently about the founding of the world. Finally, if the world does not feel an approaching decline, it is evident that it did not have a beginning. Since the hypothesis is true, the conclusion follows. Every collapse, said Proclus, is due to external or internal force. In this case no internal strength can be brought to bear; outside, nothing is to be feared. Therefore the world will never perish in any lapse of time.

The remaining arguments of Proclus are easily refuted by themselves. This first is false, that whatsoever good things God can create, those very things He wishes to create. For He can so direct all men to the pursuit of virtue that even if they wished they could not fall into error. Of course, to Proclus nothing seemed greater than this good or more to be desired. Moreover, He could have put this world together in such a way that in no minds, in no matter or form, could any blemish or any seed of evil exist. Yet He did not want to do this. Therefore, if Proclus did not accuse immortal God of any crime because He did not prohibit those evils which He could have prohibited, much less can he do so if He did not create the world from eternity when He could have done so. The second argument is more forceful—that to be carried from rest to action involves a change, that is, as the writer himself said, alteration, which is very far from that everlasting mind. But it is false that God was borne from rest to action, from quiet to work, when He started to found the world. Indeed, Proclus erred in the very principles of nature when he attributed to God quiescence, which is nothing but absence of motion. If God cannot be moved, neither can He be at rest. For He is by the demonstration of Aristotle (*Physics*, Book VI), not only immobile in the movements of the spheres, but also unchangeable in guarding the safety of the world; therefore he has not altered since the Creation.

Aristotle regarded it as settled that God is lord and director of all things, not only the effective cause, but also the preserver of this world; not only immobile, but also devoid of all struggle and effort, rejoicing in His power and excellence. The same author also wrote that the wise man does not change when he is thinking or the architect when he is building. How much less will a change take place in God when He is engaged in the care of the world? And so no less stupidly than impiously certain petty theologians think that God can be implicated in any humdrum occupation, which, of course, offered an opportunity to Epicurus to say that he preferred to be a porter rather than God. Since Christ accepted without question the evident benevolence of his Heavenly Father toward Him, so He said He might have, if He wished, twelve legions of angels for a guard. From this He wished to imply that this world is full of immortal souls whose service God uses like that of servants.

These arguments of Proclus resemble those evil sayings of the Epicureans: If the world had a beginning or is doomed to die, what action did God take in the past and what is He going to do ultimately? To these sinful men who demand from God a reckoning of past time, I repeat only what Spiridion, at the Council of Nicaea, answered to a question of this kind: He founded places of eternal punishment for men so inquisitive, in order to be occupied. This reason seems to me not only witty but also sound.

Yet, if the steadfast opinion of all philosophers is that the highest happiness of man abides in contemplation and if the wise man is called by Plato a very god, by Aristotle self-sufficient, because, although set in desert solitudes, he is, nevertheless, happy because of that blessed state of mind whereby he despises human affairs here below and gazes upon the Divine, how much the more content is God in Himself and happy in the contemplation of Himself alone? Yet He can contemplate nothing greater or better than Himself. Therefore Aristotle (Book xiv of the *Metaphysics*) called God absolutely self-sufficient in the same way in which the Hebrews call him שדי, that is, as Moses the Egyptian interpreted, He who is content in Himself. Indeed, if Origen had considered this more attentively, he would not have thought that God founded countless worlds in succession, as he wrote in the book *On First Principles*, fearing, I think, either that God might languish from inertia or, what Plato feared, that if the race of men should be entirely destroyed, He would be without sacrifices and praises. Yet it is easier to hold this opinion than to think that the world has existed always along with God. Many Hebrews, indeed, believed this, as Moses wrote, and in our age Leo the Hebrew.[17] But both groups are involved in the greatest error, the one, that they measured the Divine felicity by the existence of the

---

[17] Leo the Hebrew (Judah Abravanel) died at Venice 1535. His most important work was *Dialoghi di amore*, written in Platonic vein. An astronomical treatise composed at the request of Pico della Mirandola is unpublished.

world; the other, that they measured His glory by the sacrifices of men and mortal things. Yet none errs more perniciously than those who think that God is contaminated by any concern for the world or can become wearied of maintaining its safety.

Since we have repudiated the opinions of Proclus and the Peripatetics, we must conclude that the world had a beginning and that therefore it will have an end, if we assent to the doctrines of Aristotle. There are, however, three opinions in the discussion held about the world: one, of those who think it had no beginning and will have no end; the second makes both affirmative; a third group, by striking a mean, say it had a beginning, but will never have an end. Supporters of this third opinion were Panaetius,[18] Posidonius, Boethius, and Seneca among the Stoics; Thomas Aquinas among the theologians; Philo among the Hebrews; then also the leader of the Academy, Plato, the actual author of this theory. Philo defended his position by the opinions of Moses and Solomon, but Isaiah, Esdras, and Peter openly rebelled against them, so that from their words no one can have any doubt about the end of the world. We read in Plutarch that Epicurus was of this opinion, and his disciple Lucretius also, from these lines:

"One day will consign [this threefold nature] to destruction, and the mass and fabric of the world sustained for many years will fall into dissolution."[19]

But since the theologians twist the passages of the Sacred Scripture into various meanings, and Moses the Egyptian and Thomas Aquinas gave an interpretation contrary to that of Philo, it is well to advance arguments [dealing with the nature of the universe]. Of these none seems to me more definite than the one which can be inferred from the dicta of Avicenna and Alexander of Aphrodisias. The latter affirmed that the world is everlasting because it is moved by God. An infinite action belongs to an infinite and everlasting mind. On the other hand Avicenna denied that the first sphere was moved by God. If this, indeed, is true, as it is, the end of the world necessarily will follow, since the action of a finite mind must be finite. If the action of the Prime Mover is finite, this entails the end of the world, whose safety depends upon motion, according to the opinion of Aristotle. From this motion is derived the

---

[18] Panaetius died in Athens before 111 B.C. He was a Stoic philosopher, who passed for a Platonist among the Neoplatonists.

[19] Lucretius *De rerum natura* v. 96.

origin of all things. The fact that the first sphere is not moved by God becomes plain because it would be absurd to join an infinite mover to a finite body, like the world, since finites have no ratio nor connection nor relationship to the infinite.

What is more absurd than that which Aristotle and Averroës did, i.e., joined the same God whom they called infinite in action to the world, that is, a finite body, in such a way that it cannot be separated from Him? Moreover, what is less worthy of a philosopher than thus to unite the efficient cause, which is infinite, with a finite effect, so that if one exists, the other must exist? Aristotle philosophized about the world and God in the same way as about fire and heat or about the sun and light; the one is the sufficient cause of the other, but yet clings so closely to that other that they cannot be torn apart even in thought. However, according to this reasoning it was necessary that the world should be mind, or that God should have corporeal nature, if the cause were to be such that it could not be torn from the effect. From this it would follow that the God of Aristotle, whom he attached to the world like a sponge to a rock and wearied by perpetual motion, not only is not infinite but also plainly is fused with the world and finite, as the light to the sun. But he himself confessed in the books of *Metaphysics* that all minds are free and released from uncontaminated corporeal substance. God is, then, not a cause of a kind that cannot stand apart from its effect, and since He is infinite in action He cannot be compared with a finite and limited body by any relationship, of origin, of condition, or of motion. Even if a small seed has a definite relation to the entire world, as Archimedes explained, when he taught how to define sand by number, because each body is determined in place and size, yet no ratio of the world to what is infinite can be conceived.

This reasoning means that God cannot make God, since the infinite cannot flow from the infinite. So that world which He girded with the rather narrow circumference of the sphere, He could no more equip with eternal motion than with infinite size. On this account Averroës could not refute the argument of Philoponus—if the world is finite, it has finite power. Then, as Proclus argued against Anaxagoras and Metrodorus, who postulated regions of infinite size and countless worlds, infinity excludes God. Thus, from the same sources we shall draw this argument: if infinity of spaces or bodies excludes God, then in assuming everlasting motion or infinite time, which depends upon motion, we must of necessity exclude God, since eternal motion includes an infinity of centuries, from which if six hundred thousand years had passed, it would not be even a moment in relation to the infinite.

In this matter Scaliger was mistaken when he rebuked Philoponus and said that time did not actually exist as infinity, but only in sequence like individual forms. He did not see that to the infinite mind and ever-lasting God nothing was earlier or later, but that this whole time which he assumed everlasting and actually infinite was possessed by Him as though it were the present and the moment by which time is limited. Other-wise the mind would not be actually infinite. Rightly then, Augustine wrote, nothing in events, or in places, or in times, or in motion is infinite except God.

If we imagine that God is the moving principle of the first sphere, it will be no less preposterous to reduce Him to the rank of those so-called lesser intelligences and to involve the divine will of that most splendid mind in the same actions in which the lower minds of the spheres [are involved]. This cannot be conceived without sin. Since, then, the majesty of God is far distant from the class of souls, it follows that He is not the mover of the first sphere. In like manner, if a lower mind is the mover, it must be finite as to function, power, and action. Furthermore, the order, sequence, and dignity of things demand that certain orders be moved only, such as forms mixed with impure matter. Certain others may be moved and move, such as the celestial spheres, which are moved by intelligences and in turn move these lower things. Still others may move only and may not be moved, such as the minds which propel the heavens and the stars, for they themselves are immobile, as Aristotle demonstrated in Book vi of the *Physics*. The last gradation is something which does not move and is not moved; this, then, is God.

From this analysis we may understand that the first sphere is moved by a mind other than that of God, from whom just as from a fountain perennial spring the lower minds; from which in turn, since they are finite, the spheres start and cease to be moved. Ficino held a contrary opinion, for he wrote that the mind of man was infinite. But by that reasoning, since a second mind proceeds from God, infinite would flow from infinite, which is entirely repugnant to the principles of nature. What, then, is more absurd than to unite those things endowed with perception and corporeal to intelligences—good with evil, infinite with finite, incorruptible with transitory—and finally by the entire chain of reasoning to unite by the same bond of everlasting nature things discordant with each other and obvious contrasts? In order that there may be the same bond between infinite good and evil, between God and the evil demon?

Scaliger also advanced the argument, not without weight, that all motion tends to rest, as may be seen in the individual natures of things. Therefore the celestial spheres also incline to rest; it is evident that this could not happen without the end of the world. By this argument he inferred that the world will perish.

But this is to be understood in the sense of ordinary death, since rest is merely absence of motion in a thing which can be moved again. Leo the Hebrew also had this interpretation, and Lactantius and the men of old, who thought all things were mingled in unwrought matter before the order, condition, and shape of this world. To this idea belongs the argument which disturbed Theophrastus, as may be seen in the pages of Philo in the book he entitled *The Eternity of the World*. It is as follows: there ought to be the same rule for the parts and for the whole. Then if parts of the world are falling into ruin and degenerating, sometime it must happen that the whole thing will come to an end, at least by ordinary death. Since living things, plants, and bushes are devoured by fire and take on the paltry nature of ashes after they have lost the nobler form, we must reach the same decision about the heavens also. Proclus, when he could not escape falling into the same difficulties, said that these elements and the bodies composed from them are not part of the world, but only a product of stars, and as it were an appendix, as we find in the pages of Philoponus. This utterly absurd opinion, however, does not need refutation. Yet Theophrastus seemed to solve it in such a way as to concede that the destruction of the world would come to pass if the whole went to ruin at the same time as the separate portions in their turn. When a finger is cut off, nothing prevents a man from living, said Philo. However, we do not ask whether a man lives when he has been deprived of certain members, but whether any part of the body can lose life. For from this fact is judged the transitory nature of the whole body, as the savor of the spring from a drop of water. Theophrastus did not distinguish in that conclusion homogeneous parts from heterogeneous. Otherwise it will be confessed that one part, and that indeed corporeal, of the same animal (this world is animal by the consent of all the Academicians and of Theophrastus himself) is so composed that part of it dies and part is not liable to death.

To me this seems as ridiculous an argument as that which Aristotle advanced, relying upon the record of his ancestors: he said that no one remembers the destruction of the heavens.[20] But by this method he might affirm gold, adamant, asbestos, which is more durable than adamant, or even that iron which is said in Darie not to melt in fire, to be everlasting, since no one remembers that these things have passed away because of internal weakness. Yet from the arguments of all, none seems greater than the argument of Philo, which flows from the secret and sacred sources of the Hebrews. He said, God is not the author of disorder and of confusion, but of order. If, therefore, he takes care of the world, he will not suffer it to pass away and come to an end. The same reason induced Moses the Egyptian to say that God cared for no individual forms except for immortal man. This fits the doctrines of Aristotle and of Alexander, who did not think anything would perish for which immortal God cared. From this it follows that God protects the universal forms indeed, but neglects the individual forms, which are changing and transitory.

The same argument impelled the Manicheans to establish two principles of equal power—one the author of all good and order, the other the author of evil, death, and confusion. To avoid this, Moses the Egyptian and Augustine explained death, evils, and confusion, not by nature, but by the mere absence of good.[21] If, however, following the teaching of Aristotle, we assume a nature for evil things, as many theologians do, I do not see what absurdity follows, since God is not on this account in Himself the cause of evil and death, but by accident only, so that when He fails to guard a wicked man or even a good man, as is said in the case of Job, He thereby abandons him to the prince of darkness, who arranges a miserable death for a wicked and sinful man. This is the opinion of Moses the Egyptian. It seems that we must make the same decision about the destruction of the world and of all things. As soon as He abandons the care of these, they will collapse. Lest anyone should doubt this, He Himself is said to have created for Himself Pharaoh, whom the Hebrews interpreted as the prince of darkness, so that He might reveal His own glory in him by restoring Himself whatever things he would overthrow and destroy.

But I am glad to refute Philo the Jew and Plato with a most effective argument of Leo the Hebrew. They said that the sky and the stars and

---

[20] Aristotle *De caelo* I. 3. 270b 14.

[21] Augustine *De civitate Dei* X. 9, "for evil has no nature, but the loss of good, that is evil."

whatever had been created would perish because they had a definite moment of origin. Then God contradicted Himself if He made anything corruptible which He did not really want to be corrupted. But if it is true that the heavens are built up from fire and water, as Philoponus explains from the teaching of the Academicians, and as the wisest Hebrew interpreters of nature affirm—for they comprehend the idea of fire and water in the very word שמים, that is, אשמים, or as others, שסמים — who doubts that the heavens also will perish? Lest Aristotle be forced to confess this, he assigned a fifth nature to the heavens; but what it was, he never explained. Then he should not have affirmed that the heaven was everlasting if its nature was unknown. Let this be the final consideration, lest we discuss endlessly. I do not see by what argument this difficulty can be solved. If the world is a natural body, it consists of matter and form, as all the physicists report. In like manner, it is mixed; moreover, nothing mixed and made up of parts can be produced by itself, according to the teaching of Aristotle himself. Therefore, the world has an efficient cause of its being. This also Aristotle confessed. Cardan did not sufficiently understand him and denied that God is the effective cause of the world, which was not fitting for a philosopher or for a Christian. But from this admission of Aristotle it follows that the cause of the world precedes the effect not only in its very nature but also in time. Otherwise the natural body can be created without time and in an instant, and indeed out of heterogeneous parts dissimilar to itself. This is repugnant to the principles of nature and the doctrines of Aristotle.

Therefore it is fitting that God is not only prior to the world in nature but also prior in time. Then, too, the world from its very nature as a material body is perishable. But it is helpful to hear the response given when we ask where states and empires for so many thousands of years lay hidden, where the memory of deeds done so many centuries ago. In return we are told that by fires and floods oft recurring on the earth men die, and in turn from the earth, pregnant through new warmth and seed, they are reborn. Solon disseminated in Greece this opinion, which he had received from the Egyptians; then Anaxagoras confirmed it; then Plato, in *Menexenus* and *Timaeus*; afterwards Aristotle, in *Problems*; then Avicenna, in the book *About the Floods*. At last Aristotle, in Book I of the *Metaphysics*, seems to have abandoned this opinion, and Averroës also in Book III of his treaties *On the Soul*, where they denied that there ever were such floods as to inundate the whole earth. I think they were influenced by the fact that in this period no giants were born, not even little myrmidons, as once upon a time came forth from the earth; perhaps because the soil was not sufficiently rich. Aristides would deny it, for in the *Panathenaeia* he thought that the Athenians alone might rightfully boast of nobility of race, because they alone were indigenous of mother earth, that is, autochthonous; although no soil seems more sterile than the Attic. But in Egypt, where there are rich inundations of water, and the earth, as the poet says, "fruitful without a cloud," [22] it is reported that no men were generated from the soil. Was this because the sun is very old, or the earth effete? How many times do they think that this world, like an animal, is taken with dropsy or acute fever, when it totters through fires and floods? Certainly they confess that matter dies from age and that the world will die from debility. This universal nature clearly shows.

Pliny, Book VII, reported that all writers complained that the race of men cannot be compared with the ancients in number, size, or strength. Wherefore it happens that it seems fabulous to our generals when they hear of the countless armies of Xerxes or that Alexander or Caesar defeated sometimes three hundred or even four hundred thousand men in one battle; yet this is in keeping with the Holy Scriptures. Crete, indeed, which was called by Homer "hundred-citied"—"a hundred great cities they dwell in," [23] quoth he—in this age can hardly boast of three. Moreover, Diodorus wrote in Egypt eighteen thousand famous cities were once mentioned in their sacred books. Later, at the time of Ptolemy Lagi, three thousand existed. Indeed, in this age in Egypt and Asia together hardly that number are said to be standing. Of course, the remarkable size of the bones, preserved entire even until these times, presents the most certain proof of the unusual size of the men. But of all things nothing is more wonderful than that, for the recollection of posterity forever, Copernicus in the books *About the Motion of the Heavenly Bodies*, then Reinhold, and afterwards Stadius, well-known mathematicians, showed with clear demonstrations that the apsis of the sun was nearer to the earth than it was in the age of Ptolemy (for he lived when Hadrian was emperor) by twelve degrees, that is, thirty-one semidiameters of the earth, or as the Germans measure, 26,660 miles German, which is said to be twice as much in French miles. When Philip Melanchthon verified their theory by frequent experiments and tried demonstration, he thought it ought to be attributed to the wasting nature

---

[22] Claudius *Carmina minora* xxviii. 5.   [23] Homer *Iliad* II. 649.

of celestial and terrestrial bodies, so that these elements may be warmed more comfortably by the heat of the sun. When Scaliger heard this, he thought people who wrote such things were worthy of the lash. He himself was not worthy of the lash, because from ignorance of these matters he erred often and indeed childishly.

Since, then, the celestial matter is flowing and transitory, we infer that it had a beginning and will sometime end. This being the case, it is evident that time has a beginning and an end. But this is what we were seeking.

SEQUENCE OF TIMES

Now our system of chronology from the Creation must be taken out of historical documents; this cannot be obtained from the arid sources of the Greeks. They had nothing older than the Trojan history, which Thucydides said was fabulous for the most part, and since Homer himself, the most ancient writer after Orpheus and Linus, flourished two hundred years after the Trojan War, it is natural that they reported common errors and fables instead of true history. However that may be, Plutarch, beginning the lives of the princes with Theseus, affirmed that the earlier events were mixed with fables. Theseus is said to have flourished about five hundred years before Romulus, in the time when Abimelech was the leader of the Hebrews. The year is 2740 from the Creation. For that reason let us inquire about the antiquity of time from [sources] other than the Greeks. From all writers of other races I see no one older than Moses. Herodotus, the oldest, Ctesias, Hellanicus, and Xenophon, contemporaries, are younger than Moses by 1,800 years. Thucydides follows immediately after Herodotus. Then Berosus, the Chaldean, is younger than Herodotus by two hundred years. Manetho the Egyptian followed Berosus; then Megasthenes the Persian, in the time of Alexander the Great. Of these, however, only a few fragments remain, if indeed they were written by these men. About Megasthenes and Ctesias there is less doubt, except that the latter is adversely criticized by Diodorus, Book III [11] in *The Kings of the Assyrians*. He is praised by the same author in the *History of the Persians*. In contrast is Eusebius, who compiled correctly the affairs of the Assyrians and carelessly those of the Persians. So we must come to Josephus, the Hebrew, the son of Mathatias, not of Gorion (whom Munster thinks to be the same, although he is clearly refuted by the *Jewish War*). In a treatise in two sections, *Against Apion*, he compared the most ancient historians who were then available with Moses and appraised them carefully. From these passages it is first understood that what Apion took from the *Timaeus* of Plato is false—that is, that the Egyptians had the history of eight thousand years hidden in records.[24] Even more absurd is the tale Herodotus heard—that there had been a kingdom among the Egyptians for 13,000 years.[25] Most absurd, what Cicero wrote in the book *About Divination:* that the Chaldeans boasted they had for 470,000 years tested the talents of men. Diodorus adds 404 in Book III, but he affirmed that this was fable. Josephus, however, by gathering a most definite system of chronology from the history of the Phoenicians and of Manetho, who made known the secrets of the Egyptians given in their sacred literature, openly refuted the inane stories of the Egyptians and the Greeks by adding the ages of the kings of the Egyptians and of the Phoenicians. Although Diodorus went to Egypt before the time of Josephus to make a thorough investigation of the antiquities of that people, he discovered that all the history of the Egyptians which could be obtained was included within 3700 years. He gave evidence of this in Book II, where he refuted the lies of the Egyptians, who in order to seem to excel others in antiquity of race, boasted that they had an antiquity of 33,000 years. I have compared the chronology of Diodorus, extracted very faithfully from the secrets of the Egyptians, with the history of Philo, which all very learned men follow. From this I understood that there was a discrepancy of about two hundred years, after subtracting the interval which came between Philo and Diodorus, that is, a little less than a hundred years. From the Creation to Philo (who was sent as an ambassador to Caligula by the Jews) there are counted four thousand years. I have drawn an even weightier argument from Simplicius. For although he proved a most bitter enemy of the Hebrews and the Christians, especially when he defended Proclus against the Christians, nevertheless in the commentaries on the first book of *On the Heavens,* he left witness that Aristotle had written a letter to Calisthenes, asking him to collect the antiquities and records of the Chaldeans while the others, intent on booty, plundered Babylon. Then Calisthenes wrote back that he had diligently collected the Chaldean records and had found there the history of 1,903 years. This number exactly fits the sacred history of Moses and Philo, if we count back from Alexander the Great to that time in which first he reported that the sons of Noah were dispersed over the earth and that the race of Shem sought an abode in

---

[24] Plato *Timaeus* 23 E.   [25] Herodotus *History* II. 142.

the land of Sinar, to the east of Armenia, in which the ark came to rest. Now Chaldea is east of Armenia, a little to the south. It is, then, especially worthy of notice, no less than of wonder, that Calisthenes and Moses, who drew the truth from the purest sources, agreed so far as concerns a universal system of time. This also fits in very well with Diodorus, if we count time from the Creation even to his age. Not less corroborative to Moses are the work of Xenophon *About Ambiguous Times* and that of Archilochus *About Times* (if, indeed, they wrote these fragments). Both wrote that Ninus ruled 250 years after the flood. One actually acquired this information from the epitaph of Ninus which Semiramis inscribed on a column to him. This time agrees nicely with the systems of Philo and the Hebrews. With reference to these things Megasthenes the Persian, when he was seeking a chronology from the earliest memory of kings, differed only slightly from the Hebrews, on the testimony of Berosus the Chaldean himself, of the work, I say, which was then complete and uncorrupted. It is worth noting what Josephus in *Apion* showed—that the floods were mentioned in the writings of Berosus and that the ship which preserved the seedbed of animal life and of the human race came to rest on the mountain of the Cordyaeans, so that even at the time of Alexander fragments remained, whence people were wont to collect bitumen to use as talismans.[26] These things he confirmed by the authority of Jerome the Egyptian and of Mnaseas the Damascene.[27] Jean Bourrel from Dauphiné makes plain by a geometrical demonstration that the size of this ship was large enough for the food and the health of all the living beings.

I omit the fact that the ancient poets transformed into stupid fables the truth of a matter received from their elders. Janus is given that name by them because he is said to have discovered the vine called *iain* by the Hebrews; thus they transfer to Jove what the Holy Scriptures say about Cham, who revealed his father's nakedness. Others apply it to Saturn, because he also exposed the genitals of his father. But many interpreters of the Hebrews transmitted this very fact about Cham, as Rabbi Levi wrote in his commentary on Genesis, chapter 9. Similar is the history of the Giants [28] and of Androgynus, which all the interpreters of the Hebrews say is very true. Plato turned it into fables. Moreover, for the purpose of confirming the sacred history of the ages

[26] Josephus *Jewish Antiquities* I. 93.

[27] Mnaseas came from Patara in Lycia. He was an antiquary and a disciple of Eratosthenes.

[28] Pliny *Natural History* II. cvi. 238.

no more certain proof can be opposed to the wicked (for the good do not need such arguments) than that Berosus the Chaldean is in agreement from Noah himself up to Sardanapalus; from this point Megasthenes, from the history of Susa to Alexander; then Ctesias, the most ancient after Herodotus, who brought annals into Greece from the very court of the Persians, on the witness of Diodorus; finally the chronology of Manetho [29] the Egyptian himself—all agree with Holy Scriptures and with Calisthenes's history well enough so that the Chaldeans and the Hebrews differ from the Egyptians by not more than three hundred years. This fact ought to seem astonishing in such a number of writers and variety of periods. Josephus made plain from the most ancient history of the Phoenicians (from whom the Greeks learned to write and to talk, as they themselves confess) that the temple was built by Solomon 140 years before the founding of Carthage. This was done by compiling the ages of the separate kings. Then Danaus, the brother of Rameses the Egyptian, the most ancient prince of the Greeks, fled from Egypt into Greece, in the 393d year after Palestine had been occupied by the Jews and three hundred years before the destruction of Troy. The same man also showed that Cadmus, the founder of Thebes, brought the alphabet into Greece in the same period in which Pharaoh Menophis flourished among the Egyptians and among the Jews Othoniel, the third leader from Moses, had control. Indeed he gave to Apion, his adversary, the proof that he had obtained the epochs of the kings from Manetho the Egyptian and the history of the Phoenicians. So great a man did not wish to lie about a history known even to Apion.

Herodotus, who is older than Manetho by almost 500 years, and Diodorus, the junior of Herodotus by 800 years, covered almost the same princes of Egypt as did Jeremiah, whose history Herodotus seems to follow to the letter after the period of Apries, whom Jeremiah, his contemporary, called Hophra. Afterwards Herodotus followed through the epochs of the successive kings even to Psammetichus,[30] who was captured by Cambyses, king of the Persians, and despoiled of his kingdom. Then the Persians held Egypt. Herodotus, however, ceased at the flight of Xerxes, which happened in the year of the world 3486. He started with Gyges, prince of the Lydians, who ruled in the time of Manasseh. But since the period of Egyptian history seemed to him

[29] Manetho lived in Ptolemaic Egypt. He wrote in Greek a history of his country, basing his information on sacred books, and starting with Menes.

[30] Psammetichus III.

short, in comparison with one reported to be of eight thousand years, he wrote this: the Egyptians boasted that before Menes, whom he called the first king of Egypt, they had the histories of thirty kings written down in sacred books, yet they did not remember the name of any of these, or the deeds. But by many arguments fables of this sort can be refuted, and in truth no fable is greater than that Claudius Ptolemy, an Egyptian, sought out the starting and stopping points of the fixed stars from the time of Nabonassar, as though the Chaldeans had taken their first observations from that period. Nabonassar, who was called Shalmaneser [31] in the Book of Kings, was famous in the year 3000 after the Creation, 980 years before Ptolemy, as he himself wrote in the *Almagest*. The other matters which he learned from Hipparchus, Meton, Eudoxus, and the Egyptians are included in these cycles of time. But if the Egyptians and the Chaldeans had noted on tablets the celestial motions of 470,000 years, why did Ptolemy the Egyptian, a neighbor to the Chaldeans, collect the motion for only 800 years? This larger body of information would have been essential for demonstrations which he had undertaken. But he did not explain the motion of the fixed stars or of the trepidation, as the Arabs first, then Regiomontanus and Copernicus, plainly demonstrated. He could not even grasp all the motions of the sun, since he said that the apsis of the sun does not move. Yet after the age of Ptolemy, that is, in 1,360 years, it was discovered to have moved through an entire sign.

There are not lacking those who calumniate the things said to have been written by Moses about the ages of men, although Moses will readily withstand their scorn. Nevertheless, Josephus in *Jewish Antiquities*, Book 1, chapter 3, praised ten historians who reported that the life of man sometimes exceeded six hundred years, sometimes nine hundred. To wit, Manetho, Berosus, Mochus,[32] Hestiaeus, and Jerome, who collected the ancient history of the Phoenicians, Hesiod, Hellanicus,[33] Acusilaus,[34] and Ephorus. To these, also, we shall add Xenophon, whose authority Pliny and Valerius used. He covered some eras of the maritime kings and said that one of them actually had lived six hundred years, another eight hundred. Who then will deny confidence to so many writers?

[31] Nabonassar ruled in Babylonia contemporaneously with Shalmaneser (Salmanassar) in Assyria.

[32] Mochus was the author of a non-extant work on Phoenician history.

[33] The work of Hellanicus of Lesbos is extant in fragments only.

[34] Acusilaus came from Argos. His works are only fragmentary.

But if anyone thinks that the years were months, as many childishly do think, why ought it to seem marvelous to Xenophon that a maritime king lived for 600 monthly years, which makes fifty solar years? Xenophon himself lived to be more than ninety. Moreover, in this old age of the world it is agreed by the consent of many writers that John, who was called timeless (? de temporibus), lived to be three hundred years old. Pliny, indeed, from the most reliable tables of the censors, reported that some people lived 150 years. But if they were monthly years, it would be necessary for men in the pages of Moses, who produced children in their thirtieth year, to have begot at two and three years. Moses freed us from this error, since in chapter VII of the Book of Genesis he included 365 days in the annual revolution. So Plutarch laughed at those who thought the Romans before Numa Pompilius completed a year in ten months, because all peoples always limited the year to twelve months, although intercalary days make the system of counting uncertain.

Now that we have determined the origin of the world and the limits of time which, by agreement of Egyptians, Chaldeans, Phoenicians, and Jews are placed at 5,700 years at the most, we must account, as well as possible, for that discrepancy of about two hundred or three hundred years which separates Megasthenes from the Jews, then the Jews among themselves, later Eusebius also from the others. Although Lucidus, Funck, and Panvinio made many diligent observations on this subject, yet up to this time there are still many things which require explanation. The origins of the error are manifold; and when these things have been noted, the mistake is the more easily corrected. In the first place, the Persians called the leaders of the Persians and the Assyrians by names different from those the Greeks used, and the Hebrews used still others. From these the Egyptians also differed, for each wished to retain the force and purity of his own idiom. Sometimes the names were even obliterated. In this way were created problems about the kings of Assyrians, Persians, and Egyptians, from whom the system of chronology was derived. Another error also developed from the fact that the Greeks and the Latins did not know the ancient history and language of the Hebrews and the Egyptians. Eusebius, following the interpreters of the Greek Bible, included 1,200 more years than the Jews from the creation to Christ; although Moses reckoned 1,656 years from the founding of the world to the flood, Eusebius counted 2,241, because the seventy interpreters, or rather copyists, in the fifth chapter of Genesis made the life span of men two hundred and sometimes three hundred years longer than the scriptures of the Jews permitted. Not the least cause of error seems to be the fact that the Greeks commenced the years from the summer solstice; the Latins from the winter; the others, who live to the westward, start from the springtime; the Arabs, from the entrance of the sun into Leo, as Solinus [35] and Firmicus [36] (in Book III) reported. The orientals, on the contrary, that is, Chaldeans, Persians, Indians, Egyptians, and Jews, from the autumn; in that time the world was created by God, as Josephus wrote in *Antiquities,* Book I, chapter 3. Rabbi Eleazar, on Genesis, [said]: בראשה, that is, at the beginning, בהשוי, that is, in the month of September; he thought that the secret of the month is explained by this same change of letters. Rabbi Abraham also concurred, writing on chapter 8 of Daniel, although Moses placed first in order Nissan, which is called Xanthicus by the Macedonians, but April by the Latins, because God in this month liberated the people; yet Moses made no change in other customs, as Josephus bore witness. This can be understood from the orders of Moses, Exodus, chapter 23: "Thou shalt celebrate the day as a feastday," said he, "at the end of the year, when thou hast gathered in thy fruits into the storehouse." For this reason Garcaeus was mistaken when he reported that the Jews commenced the year with the vernal equinox because they thought that the world was created at that time. Rabbi Josue held this view, but Rabbi Eleazer refuted him. Plutarch discussed that question in the *Symposiaca,*[37] but let us omit the discussion. If at the beginning of spring the unformed fruits were not ripe, God would likewise have made living things imperfect or suckling, and would have provided nurses. Not less did Mercator err, since he thought that when the world was born the sun was in Leo. On the basis of this incorrect premise, other things about the motion of the stars which he reported on the authority of history are doubtful. I omit the frivolous conjecture concerning an olive branch after the floods and the other things of this kind which are too trifling to merit refutation.

Let us then accept the system of Moses, and of the Jews, who in private and public business began from the month of September, as did the Greeks also. This is plain from the clock of Mitylene. It is evident that another cause of error was the fact that Egyptians, Persians, and

[35] Solinus was a polyhistorian of the third or fourth century A.D. His work is based on Pliny.

[36] Firmicus Maternus wrote a formal introduction to judicial astrology in the fourth century A.D.   [37] Plutarch *Morals* II. 213 and III. 244.

Hebrews had no certain epoch or initial point of time, but defined time by the ages of kings. Greeks and Latins did better; the former computed their time by the Olympiads, the others from the founding of the city. The Christians also, although somewhat late, that is, in the six hundredth year of Christ, commenced to date the system of time from the delivery of the Virgin. The Arabs start from the Hegira, that is, from the flight of Mohammed, which occurred in the year of Christ 592 [*sic*], and this year, 1565,[38] they call the year 988 [*sic*]. They do not use any other initial point, as may be observed from the history of Leo the African, who in only one passage of the third book dated the Hegira according to the Christian era, as well as from Moslem edicts, which we have seen promulgated. From this it is understood that people who begin the Hegira from the year of Christ 491 are blundering, as well as Genebrard, who begins with the year 621.[39] The Spanish recently, that is, before Ferdinand, called the Catholic, in 1490, took the beginning of an era and, as it were, the initial point which they themselves call the epoch, from the sixteenth year of the rule of Augustus, when he issued the edict from Tarragona to define the limits of the world. But a census was made in the year 42 of the empire, from which the starting point is understood to have been 26 years before the nativity, as Antonio of Gerona wrote. On the other hand, Roderick of Toledo,[40] in his last chapter, made twenty-eight years of difference. However, the councils which were held in Spain under the rule of the Goths started their reckoning of time from the year in which the edict of Tarragona was promulgated; after the time of Ferdinand they followed the Christian era. Later the Jews, in public and private acts, commenced to date their era from the creation. It is five thousand, three hundred, and twenty-five, in the year of our Lord 1565. Those who follow Philo add 202 years, so that this year from the Creation is 5325 [*sic*].[41] But it is the fourth year of the 259th Olympiad; of the flood, 3872; of the Hegira, 1014; the tenth year of the 84th indiction.[42] We must use these numbers in the history of the world, so that the date may be in all cases

---

[38] The edition of 1595 gives the year 1570, but makes no other correction. The edition of 1583 gives 1565. The edition of 1566 gives 551 in place of 592 and omits the end of the sentence. After "Christian era" there is an omission of several lines to "Later the Jews . . ."

[39] But see p. 150, above.

[40] Rodrigo, 1170–1247, archbishop of Toledo, author *De rebus Hispaniae*.

[41] The edition of 1566 reads 5327. That of 1572 reads correctly 5527.

[42] This last method of dating gives 1583, which would be satisfactory for the edition of that year, even though the author failed to correct the earlier blunders. Unfortunately

more definite. The indiction is a kind of tribute in Asconius and Pliny the Younger, and it does not commence to signify the course of time before Constantine the Great. Then it began in the year of our Lord 313, the 8th day before the calends of October, Constantine and Licinius being Augusti, and consuls for the second time. This was written in the *fasti* of the Greeks in these words: the beginning of the indictions of Constantine is here. On this day Maxentius Augustus was killed by Constantine the Great and the peace of the Christian Church restored. So it was decreed in the Council of Nicæa that in documents the indictions should be reckoned, as Bede wrote, because they did not yet use the year of our Lord, but the years of the emperors; the fact that they were changed repeatedly rendered the reckoning of time obviously uncertain. It was decreed that the cycle of the indictions should take 15 years, since one Olympiad consisted of four.

But no cause of error was greater than that due to the unknown courses of the sun and the moon. Although all antiquity engaged itself in this problem, it could not really be solved so that we might have a definite system of years and months. The cycles of eight years of Leostratus were found to be faulty and were not at all useful; the golden rule of nineteen years which is said to be Meton's is imperfect; so that after the three hundredth year the course of the sun had gained on the moon by one day and almost eighteen hours. Faulty, also, was the year of Calippus. Erroneous rules of Hipparchus showed an error of one hour in the 304th year thereafter, nor were the intercalations of Philolaus and Democritus much more certain. Finally, the year of Caesar has this inconvenience, that it eliminated lunar months and is now full of error. For little by little the summer holidays are going back to the winter months.

Although the Greeks knew the solar year, despite such great errors about stellar motion, still they used the lunar years of 304 days, which, however, they intercalated in every other year, or every third year, since one day was left over. In addition they added the intercalary month, which they placed either in every third year or every fourth year. They could not recognize equinoctials, or solstices, since the months for all the year fluctuated through a period of thirty-three years. But the Romans erred much more seriously in this respect, for they established at first a year of 304 days, as certain men think (yet Plutarch for one de-

---

for this theory, the edition of 1566 also reads "the tenth year of the 84th indiction," as well as the edition of 1572.

nied this); then, when Numa added two months, the years were made lunar. But such was the variety and confusion of the intercalaries that the system of *fasti* was changed sometimes for the winter months, sometimes even for the summer months, on the authority of Suetonius. The Jews, of course, used lunar months, but every third year they inserted an intercalary month, which was called by them Vaadar, that is, Adar doubled. For this reason Garcaeus was in error when he wrote that the Jews as well as the Egyptians used solar years. The Egyptians had a regular year of 365 days, but the extra quarter brought it about that in 1,460 years the revolution of the entire year had returned to its starting point, and a whole Sothic year was intercalated. Although great errors followed because they took a whole quarter of a day, yet it was less than a whole quarter, as the event afterwards showed.

Since these things are so, it is not remarkable that with such discrepancies of the years a definite system of time could not be developed. Theodorus Gaza was seriously wrong in his little book about the Attic months, as well as interpreters of the Greeks and the Latins. These antiquarians think their months are analogous to the months of the ancients, which were so indefinite that they always fluctuated uncertainly. In proof of this we have the fact that the year defined by the Julian law, which is regarded as the most definite of all, turns back the proper place of the solstices and equinoctials by about fourteen days from the time of Caesar and struggles in vain to make the motion even. In my judgment celestial motions are ineffable and inexpressible, or as the mathematicians say, deaf,[43] since they can be comprehended by no numbers and there is always something left to be counted; this may be seen in the separate revolutions of the planets. Then what certitude could exist before the Julian law when days and months had been intercalated with such irregularity? It is, however, worthy of attention that from the creation the Hebrews and the Chaldeans made the very same reckoning of the year which the Arabs now use: that is, 354 days, collecting the intercalary days in every third year. This is plainly evident from the Holy Scriptures. In similar fashion the Egyptians always inserted additional days in the Sothic year. Whence it happens that in round numbers dealing with periods and years which have passed since the creation almost no mistake can be made by them, although with respect to the separate actions of princes, victories, or the beginning or end of each empire they differ from the Greeks, and both differ from the

[43] Surds.

Latins. The long-continued and endless discussions of writers about the death of Christ are due to this variation. One man says it took place on the sixth day before the calends of April; another, such as Panvinio, on the seventh. The majority say on the fourth day, like Lucidus, who started the controversy about this matter. They quarrel considerably among themselves not only about the day but also about the year. Bede, Chrysostom, Nicetas, Gaurico, Albertus Magnus, Bernard of Modena, and Panvinio declared that he suffered in the year 34. Apollinaris, Lucidus, Nicolas of Lyra, Marianus Scotus, and Paul of Burgos, in 33; Tertullian and Irenaeus, in 31. Not less disputed is the question among the Greeks and the Latins, and even among the Latins themselves, about the year of the founding of the city. Since this plainly cannot be settled, Panvinio, in the *fasti*, collected from all the opinions the two most probable and included both in the *fasti*, so that each man may follow that which he pleases, with a difference of one year.

For various deeds of princes and memorable matters, it is unwise to note the date carelessly, but when there is an error in [the date] for the beginning of empires, or in the era or origin of epochs, endless mistakes result. Yet everyone, as well as may be, ought to be corrected according to the system of the Jews and the Chaldeans, which differ not at all, or certainly very little, from Philo. The Talmudists, too much tied to their own way, took two hundred years from the age of the world in order to interpret the divine lots and prophecies in the light of their own judgment and not to agree with the Christians. For example, Rabbi Nasso, as often as he mentioned Christ, with great scorn called him התלוי and the Christians נלוו ערים [?]. However, this variation does not exist among them before the year of the world 2239. This is the year of the journey of Jacob into Egypt. It was 430 years from this date to the departure. This is reported very fully in Exodus 12, Galatians 3. About this passage Josephus, in Book 11, chapter 6,[44] and also Philo and Rabbi Levi, Gerson's son, said that the period of 430 years commenced with the advance of Abraham himself into Egypt when he was 76 years old. From the time when Jacob went into Egypt along with his family to the exodus they count 210 years. In this respect almost all the Jews agree. Philip Melanchthon and every learned man followed them, except Genebrard, a man of erudition and outstanding piety. He held fast to the words of the Scriptures. Funck thought that the mistake originated in the word *triakosious* [300] instead of *tetra-*

[44] Of *Antiquities*.

kosious [400], and Theodore Beza suported this. The error may, indeed, have occurred in the Epistle to the Galatians and the Acts, which are written in Greek, but the passage of Exodus, being written in Hebrew, does not admit of this. In this discussion, then, it is safer to support the interpretations of the Jews, especially when they almost all agree with Megasthenes. I think there should be a similar procedure for the rest. Philo seems to have followed this method very nearly, and therefore I agree with him more readily when he counts 920 years from the departure of the Jews to the founding of the temple. Josephus on the other hand estimated 1062 (Book x, chapter 12). The former reckoned 440 years from the founding of the temple to its fall; the latter, 470. The younger Jews thought it should be 419. Philo struck a mean. He also counted 3,373 years from the creation to the destruction of the temple, Josephus 3,513. The former reckoned 1,717 from the flood to the overthrow of the temple; but the latter, 1,913. The Jewish interpreters give considerably less for both, but Philo adopted a compromise. Then to reconcile these various authorities among themselves, let us in the first place reject Alphonso's period of 8,549 years of the world to today, that is, A.D. 1565, since he offers no support for his opinion. Neither does Eusebius, by whose testimony 6,760 years have passed from the creation. According to Augustine there have been 6,916; according to Bede, 6,893; according to Jerome, 6,605; Theophilus of Antioch, 6,831; Isidore, 8,171. Let us accept the Jews, the Chaldeans, and the Persians, whose history says that not more than 5,730 years have passed since the creation. Let us combine Megasthenes, or Ctesias, or Herodotus, or Berosus with the Jews. Among the Jews, Baal Seder reckoned 5,133 years from the creation up to now; Rabbi Nasso, 5,172; Rabbi Gerson and Kimhi, 5,301; the younger Jews, 5,349; Philo, 5,628, Josephus, 5,720. Then the difference between Josephus and Philo, most accurate writers, is about two hundred years, and this was caused by that passage which I have mentioned in Exodus, chapter 12, which Josephus examined very closely. But since the rest of the interpreters of the Bible count a lapse of 430 years from the advance of Abraham into Egypt even to the time of Moses, and since the system of Ctesias agrees pretty nearly with Philo, who struck a mean between Josephus and the Talmudic writers (for he exceeded these by 200 years and was exceeded by Josephus to an equal amount), it follows that Philo is more reliable than all the rest. The younger Jews too stubbornly distorted the times of Daniel, so that against the authority of all writers, they counted only five emperors of the Persians, whereas Megasthenes, Ctesias, and finally the Greeks reported that there were ten, giving the age of each prince. They did this, however, so that they might not seem to differ from the oracles of the Prophet which they had misunderstood.

It is necessary to refute them, on the authority both of Josephus and of Philo, then also by the motion of the celestial spheres, whose precise beginning from the reign of Nabonnassar is given by Ptolemy in the *Almagest*. Astrologers, since they have nothing in their reckonings any older, are accustomed to begin with this. Then it is worthy of notice that, from that initial point of motion, the order and system of universal time most precisely agrees with Jews, Chaldeans, Greeks, and Latins, from the 3,218th year of the creation, in which Nabonassar took over the rule. This is inferred in the following way.

All historians allege that Alexander the Great died in the first year of the 114th Olympiad; but Ptolemy counted 424 years from Nabonassar to the death of Alexander, that is, 106 Olympiads. This would imply that Nabonassar began to reign in the first year of the eighth Olympiad. That year was the twelfth of the reign of Ahas, the king of the Jews, as is written in Book IV of Kings, but the sixth after Rome was founded. Now according to Varro and Dionysius the foundations of the city were laid in the fourth year of the sixth Olympiad. This reckoning of universal time, then, can mislead no one, although in separate events some authorities will often differ from others.

From the tables of Ptolemy precise dates are obtained from Nabonassar to Hadrian (under whom Ptolemy flourished). In Book IV, chapter 2, he covered 853 years, from the second year of Mardocempedus (whom Jeremiah called Merodach) to the 19th year of Hadrian. The fact that Nabonassar is the same who is called Shalmaneser in the Holy Scriptures is clear from the fact that from the fall of Samaria to the destruction of the temple the years are 133 according to the Holy Scriptures. From this we gather that Hezekiah ruled for twenty-three years, Manasseh fifty-five, Amon two, Josiah thirty-three, Jehoiakim eleven, Zedekiah eleven. He was captured at the occupation of Jerusalem. But Ptolemy reckoned 140 years from the first year of Nabonassar, who took Samaria, to the ruin of the temple. For he said in Book V, chapter 14, that the fifth year of Nabopolassar (who is called Nebuchadnezzar in the Scriptures) was the 127th of Nabonassar. If you add thirteen years of his rule, up to the capture of the city (it was taken in the eighteenth year of Nebuchadnezzar), the years are one hundred and forty. This number is less [more?] by seven years than the one which the Holy Scriptures use, but the years of Nabonassar's era must be extended to the captivity. If we examine the history of the world in accordance with this rule of celestial revolutions, it will be made plain that Megasthenes reckoned a shorter period. This happened on account of interregna, when the princes of the Assyrians and the Chaldeans waged internecine wars among themselves with great cruelty, and in time one drove out the other. Meanwhile there was no regard for chronology or for the lapse of time. It serves as proof that neither Berosus nor Megasthenes included an interregnum or the months of any reign, but only the years of each rule, and without any definite point of departure. Ctesias, a diligent writer, did not omit the months and interregna, but we have nothing beyond scant fragments. However, Diodorus and the rest followed this writer. Moreover, Plutarch (who in his life of Artaxerxes calls Ctesias most untruthful) thought he ought to be believed in so far as pertains to chronology, especially when he rebuked Herodotus for lying; and he was praised by Xenophon himself (in whose times Ctesias flourished), by Strabo, Athenaeus, and Diodorus. In the history of the Phoenicians Manetho and Dius [45] collected the months and interregna, as may be seen in the pages of Josephus, but the history of this people has altogether vanished. Manetho ceased in the fifth Olympiad, five years before the founding of the city, twelve before Shalmaneser, three hundred and twenty-five after the destruction of Troy, with which the Roman tables of Sempronius agree. This variation does not exist among the Greeks and the Latins in the system of time which began from the [first] Olympiad, since the founding of the city followed in the sixth Olympiad. Hence it is easy to compare the *fasti* of the Romans with the Olympiads up to the invasion of the Goths, which happened under Odoacer in the year of Christ 351. Then from the era of Christ the most precise dates are computed to the present. We must deduce from the universal system of chronology the ages of the kings and the reigns, making a choice of each best writer. We must also be warned in reading history that it is necessary to observe the system of the bissextile year, if ever it occurs, so that we may read the preceding or following years more certainly and easily. For example, Marcellinus wrote in Book XXVI, that on the occasion when Jovinian died near Ancyra, Valentinian was created emperor on the seventh day before the calends of

---

[45] Dius was the author of a history of the Phoenicians, of which a fragment is preserved by Josephus.

March, and did not want to take up the insignia of empire on the mor-
row, because by chance the bissextile day occurred then, and he feared
the time was unpropitious. From this passage of Marcellinus, the *fasti*
of the Romans, made inaccurate by civil wars and interregna, were corrected and restored, since with each fourth year the bissextile recurs.
Hence, when we count the years from Caesar to Valentinian, there are
408 from the fourth consulship of Caesar the Dictator, who established
the bissextile year. From the founding of the city, however, there are
1,116 years.

Now this Marcellinus whom I have mentioned was called Ammianus
and lived in the age of Julian the Emperor. The other Marcellinus, a
count, and of honorable rank when Justinian reigned, started a chronicle 1,130 years from the founding of the city. He distinguished carefully by indiction and consulate, although the consuls in that time had
ceased to exist, but the title remained in the emperors. Last of all was
Flavius Basilius, Junior, of honorable rank, consul of the East, in the
year of our Lord 541, whom Procopius often mentions in the book
About the War of the Goths.

We have discussed these things about the system of universal time
and the origin of the world. When its fall will take place, not even the
angels know—certainly no one of the mortals, unless perchance we may
agree to the conjectures of Rabbis Elia and Catina. In the books of the
Talmud, under the title "Sanhedrin," chapter "a share," [46] then also
under the title "Idolatry," chapter "before," these rabbis limited the
age of the world to six thousand years because of the fact that the world
was made in six days. This conjecture many accept like an oracle, since
they think that Elia was a prophet. Rabbi Isaac writing on chapter 1
of Genesis, along with Augustine, Book 11 of the *City of God,* embraced
that prophecy as fallen from the sky. Leo the Hebrew thought, in addition, that in the perpetual agitation of six thousand years there will
come a change of the elemental world and that in the seventh millennium there will be quiet, until, when 49,000 years have elapsed, a fiftieth
millennium will bring the fall of the celestial spheres and the quiet of
the Great Jubilee. But to investigate more subtly these matters, which
cannot be grasped by human wit, or inferred from reason, or approved
by the divine prophecy, seems not less stupid than impious.

[46] Bodin has transliterated from the Hebrew. These references are to the tract Sanhedrin
xi. 302, and to the tract Idolatry i. 16.

CHAPTER IX

CRITERIA BY WHICH TO TEST THE ORIGINS OF PEOPLES

No question has exercised the writers of histories more than the origin of peoples; they record the decline of states or the course of civil wars for no reason more frequently than to attest the fame and splendor of their race. Some people, having achieved noble rank through riches, or crime, or the valor of their ancestors, prefer to separate themselves from the others and repudiate their affinity with them. The extreme type of arrogance is seen in those who, forgetful of their human nature, boast that they are descended from gods. This happened not only in the case of foolish and stupid men but also of men who achieved the highest reputation for wisdom and virtue. Caius Caesar was not ashamed to boast in the assembly of the Roman people that in the maternal line he was descended from kings, but in the paternal from the gods. Aristotle also traced his family back to Aesculapius and Apollo. From this idea grew pretensions to divinity on the part of some men who thought they would be gods when they had ceased to be human. The haughty pride of powerful men is reflected even in the humblest, who, because they did not know their own racial origin, or because they concealed it on account of dislike for foreigners, called themselves sprung from the parent land, that is, autochthonous and earth-born. Aristides, in the Panathenaea, claimed for the Athenians the boon of highest nobility, because they traced their descent from no other source than from this very earth, mother of the gods.

This error is common not only to the older writers but to the younger ones also, since Polydore Virgil, otherwise a reliable author, affirmed that the Britons lived in the interior, were indigenous there, and had not come from any other place—following Caesar, I suppose. Althamer, imitating Tacitus, also wrote that the Germans were born in Germany itself and were not descended from any other race; he did not hesitate to credit this story relying on the authority of Tacitus, Sabellicus, and Sipontinus.[1] What more stupid, shall I say, or more impious can be

---

[1] Sipontinus is a name applied to Nicolas Perotti, 1430–1480, archbishop of Siponto and author of *Cornucopiae* and of a translation of the *Histories* of Polybius. Possibly some other Sipontinus wrote a history of Germany, or may we guess from Bodin's own bibliography that he meant Aventinus?

imagined than this? The ancients, of course, in a certain sense deserve indulgence; but modern people are guilty either of great error or of sin, both because they openly contradict the statements made by Moses about primitive times in the Holy Scriptures (although no reason is submitted) and because they separate these races altogether from association and friendship with others by assuming for them no source other than the ancestral soil. By divine will many things led Moses to write about origins, and I think especially this reason, that all men whom his story might reach should understand clearly that they are of the same blood and allied by the same bond of race. I know of no conviction more powerful than that of consanguinity for developing and maintaining the good will and friendship of mankind. Not only Diomedes and Glaucus but also countless hosts armed for mutual destruction, by the mere semblance of racial affinity often abandoned their enmities. On the other hand, do not men who boast that they are indigenous and born of the earth violate the very bond of human society? Hence come those implacable and threatening words of the Egyptians against the Jews, of the Greeks against the Latins, when one called the other barbarian with scornful disrespect. For the same reason foreigners once were called "enemies" by the Romans; and now-a-days "Welsh" by the Germans, with even greater scorn. This word is not in keeping with the hospitality of their ancestors, which has won so much fame for them. Finally, to the same cause are due the famous books against foreigners by those who more truly ought to be called, not priests of the muses or of Minerva, but priests of Mars, who swing burning torches between the lines of battle and inflame to hate with taunting affronts men whom they ought to conciliate by mutual love. It is not necessary that I should name anyone or that I should commemorate things written against us by those who have brought greater infamy to themselves than to us. But how many times more righteous it was to associate with foreigners in the same bond of blood and propinquity than to depart haughtily from that common kinship with scornful words? For that reason I cannot approve the laws of Lycurgus [2] or of Plato, which emphatically forbade citizens of Sparta or of Athens to trade with strangers. Then, too, they prohibited the export of domestic products and the import of foreign goods to their own people. What is this but the removal of human association from human concerns? If the natives are better, they ought to train strangers through their own virtues and make them happy, not

[2] Plutarch *Lycurgus* 15.

keep them away. Of course, Moses thought that the foreigner ought to be treated with no less benevolence than the citizen; and he commanded the injuries of the foreigners to be avenged more severely than those of the citizens. Now-a-days, by the highest wisdom of immortal God, we have seen it come about that no region is so fecund that it does not urgently need the resources of others. India, says the poet, sends ivory; the soft Sabaeans, their incense; and the naked Chalybes, iron.[3] Then a little later, nature constantly imposed these [economic] laws and lasting alliances on certain regions. For what purpose, finally, if not that the peoples should unite their possessions and ideas in mutual commerce and thus strengthen peace and friendship?

Thus, I think it happened by divine vengeance that the Greeks were subject for a period to the Latins (whom they used to call barbarians) and in turn the Latins for some time were subject to the Goths and the Scythians (from whom once they had invariably turned away as from wild animals). Then, too, because of the many colonies all peoples were fused together and recognized that they were related.

There are three proofs in the light of which origins can be known and evaluated when reported by historians: first, in the proved reliability of the writer; second, in traces of language; third, in the situation and character of the region. We have spoken earlier about the choice of historians and how much credit can be given to a writer who deals with his own fellow citizens or with an enemy. Conrad Peutinger,[4] Irenicus, Hermann Neuenar,[5] Lupold of Bamberg,[6] Jacob Wimpheling,[7] Andreas Althamer, Wolfgang Lazius, Paul Jovius, Antonius Sabellicus, and among us Robert Ceneau [8] wrote so vaingloriously about their own fellow countrymen, that they made no concessions to others and thought that the gods themselves were not their equals. More truthful were Beatus Rhenanus and Abbot Trithemius.[9] Others in praise of

[3] Virgil *Georgics* I. 57, 60–61.

[4] Conrad Peutinger, 1465–1547, a German humanist, author of *De mirandis Germaniae antiquitatibus* and owner of a famous map.

[5] Hermann von Neuenar, 1492–1530, author of works on the history of France and of Belgium, such as *Brevis narratio de origine et sedibus priscorum Francorum*.

[6] Lupold, bishop of Bamberg, died in 1362. He wrote *De juribus regni et imperii romani tractatus*.

[7] Jacob Wimpheling, 1450–1528, author of *Epitome rerum Germanicarum usque ad nostra tempora*.

[8] Robert Ceneau, 1483–1560, prelate, historian, and controversial writer. He dedicated his *Historia Gallica* to Henry II.

[9] Johannes Trithemius (von Heindenberg) was born in Trittenheim in 1462 and died

their own names wrote many things which, though they may be true, still could be written in more moderate vein without scorn for others. Let us grant that the Franks originated among the Germans. What can be more excellent for the fame of our name, or better for forming alliances and friendships, or more useful for the vigor of both states than to trace the origin of the Franks to the valiant and noble race of the Germans? However, for questions of this sort let us use the tests which I have mentioned to obtain definite and well-authenticated origins of all peoples.

It is evident, then, that the Chaldeans were the most ancient of all peoples, by the weighty testimony not only of Moses but also of Megasthenes, Herodotus, Ctesias, and Xenophon. More recent writers agreed with this, Diogenes Laertius and Philo, as well as Porphyry [10] in a certain letter to Boethus, Clement of Alexandria [11] in his *Miscellanies*, Eusebius in *Evangelical Demonstration*, Theodoret in Book I, *About the Cure of the Troubles of the Greeks*, Rabbi Moses Maimonides, *Guide of the Perplexed*, Book III, chapter 30, and other interpreters of the Jews also. These all credit learning, literature, the arts, and praise of all the great disciplines to the Chaldeans. Hence, they imagined that the Chaldean Prometheus, because he had forced men from wild and uncivilized life to one more humane, had recorded the calculated courses of the constellations, the trajections of the planets, and the whole mystery of nature to the race of men, drew down the sacred fires from the sky with the fennel giant of Pallas, and breathed a celestial soul into man, who had been molded out of clay.

Then the word "indigenous" must be abandoned, and the origin of all peoples must be sought in the Chaldeans; since in their country, or certainly near it, came to rest that ship which served as nursery of the human race. From there men scattered hither and thither and propagated their kind in the way in which Moses and the teachers of the Jews have most truthfully and fully described. But I omit what each reader may obviously find in the same books.

I will explain only this one thing which our writers about origins have not made sufficiently plain, that is, the linguistic traces, in which

in 1516. He was a Benedictine, who wrote *De luminibus sive de viris illustribus Germaniae* and *Introductio in Claudii Ptolemaei opus de effectibus astrorum.*

[10] Porphyry, 233–c.304, was a disciple of Plotinus. He wrote *De vita Plotini, De vita Pythagorae,* and *Sententiae ad intelligibilia ducentes.*

[11] Clement of Alexandria, c.150–c.216, a native of Athens and a convert to Christianity. He influenced Christian thought through his disciple Origen.

the proof of origins chiefly lies, as well as in the character of the lands occupied. If the region nearby was fertile and uninhabited, it was, of course, seized by some neighbors. After population began to be abundant, colonies were led forth into the farthest solitudes and most sterile areas. Who, abandoning Asia or Italy, would lead colonies into the country of the Goths, unless driven by the most pressing need? For this reason we need no longer wonder whether the Egyptians are older than the Scythians, or the Greeks older than the Latins. This question was anxiously debated by the ancients, as we may see in the pages of Diodorus, Justin, Cato, and Dionysius of Halicarnassus. Those who occupied the deserts of Arabia and of Lybia or Ethiopia, although they were older than the Greeks and the Latins, nevertheless were content with these areas, since they closed the approaches to Asia and Europe. As evidence of this we have the fact that the Arabs and the Carthaginians, as soon as they began to trust to arms, sent colonies and armies into Asia and Europe. Leo the African wrote that the caliph of Babylon kept the Arabs within their territories by means of religious awe until, in approximately the two-hundredth year after the Hegira, he wished to open the approaches of the Nile to countless legions, so that he might take revenge on the rebelling princes of Africa. But the most striking fact, by which the Epicureans can easily be refuted as well as others who maintain that men are autochthonous, is that the nations named by Moses retain traces of the Chaldean and the Hebrew languages—differing in dialect alone—which never have decayed even in so many diverse tongues. It is that first idiom which was given to his race by Abraham the Chaldean.

Before any semblance of the Greek and the Latin languages existed, peoples and regions used the Jewish names. It is Japhet, the son of Noah, from whom the Europeans are said to have sprung, and this not only the Jews confess but the Greeks and the Latins also. Bold, they say, is the race of Japhet. This is taken from Homer and Aeschylus. It is remarkable how the Greeks search about in vain to find the etymology of Japhet. Some wished it to be taken from τὸ ἰάπτειν, that is, "damage"; some, from τὸ ἰᾶσθαι, that is, "to heal"; some, from τὸ ἴεσθαι καὶ πέτεσθαι (hasten and fly), although it signifies in Hebrew, "swelling." In the same way Tacitus made the Jews (Judaeos) as *Idei* take their rise from Mount Ida in Crete, hence he led them into Mauritania, finally into Palestine, although by this word the Hebrews signify worshipers. By a similar error Strabo and Livy thought that the Germans were given that name as brothers of the Gauls, even when this word, like "Alemanus," also signifies a whole man or a strenuous man in the mother tongue, as Althamer showed. By the same error Ion, or as Homer has it Iaon, the Greeks derived from "flower." In Hebrew it signifies defrauder. From him the Ionians in Asia and in Greece were descended. Hence Daniel foretold that Alexander the Great, that is, Iaon or Ion or Javan, would rule in Assyria. The Greeks, indeed, have tried to distort these names as their own, but they could by no means appropriate those which signify nothing at all to the Greeks or the Latins and are the oldest of all, from which peoples acquired names understood by the Jews alone—for instance, Danaus, which in Chaldean means "judge." From this comes Danai, and Dardania, the home of judges. *Dar* is to dwell. Hence they are said to be Dardani. Another example is Janus, that is, "full of wine," whom Dionysius of Halicarnassus called Oenotrius with the same significance. He first led colonies into Italy. *Iain* is "wine" to the Jews, "grief" to the Achaeans, "narrows" to the Egyptians. Nimrod means "insurgent." Philip Melanchthon interpreted it incorrectly as "cruel ruler," for *marad* is "he rebelled." Ninus is "son"; Nineveh, the home of Ninus. Solon, "peaceful," instead of Solom, since the Greeks did not allow the letter "m" as a final letter. Furthermore, the word means nothing to the Greeks. Likewise Cadmus, the founder of Thebes and of the alphabet which the Greeks use, is called the father, but [the word Cadmus] means "eastern" and "ancient"; Medes, "measured out"; Armenians, "uplifted"; Canaanites, "traders"; Hebrews, "crossing over"; Dodoneans, "rulers"; Chusitae, "negroes," whom the Greeks called Ethiopians in the same sense; Muscovites, "spread out"; Riphaei, "giants"; Persians, "divided"; Assyrians, "blessed"; Libyans, "fiery." The Greeks said that Africa meant "without intense cold"; Emathii means "truthful," for it cannot come from ἄιμα, since the practice of the Greek language would not permit it. Misrim [means] "narrow" (Philip Melanchthon erred in interpreting it as "insurgent"); the Egyptians were said to be narrow and in these days also they retain the ancient appellation. The Scythians, "shooters," is from Cethim, "son of Japhet"; this is a truer etymology than that which is alleged by Melanchthon from the Macedonians, whom he called Macethim. But this "m" is a particle of a different origin. Vagabonds are called "heneti" by the Jews, "nomads" by the Greeks. Homer calls them ἐνετοί and places them in Paphlagonia. These men really seized lower Germany, later the Wendish Gulf, then they settled in

Italy and in Gaul also. The very name itself shows that the Cimbri are descended from the Cimbri of the Chersonese, and the Danes from the Danaians. Elam is "adolescent," the name which the Jews give to the Persians; hence the race of Elymais in the pages of Xenophon, where he means the Persians. Lydians [means] "born"; Sarmatians, "leaders of another"; the Secani, "inhabitants"—thus the first settlers of Sicily were called, and those who seized the region of Burgundy. The Thracians, "destroyers," are from Tiras, the son of Japhet. Hence the name of the river in Thrace. Phut, the son of Camesis, means "a pivot." The Moors were called this by Ptolemy, as well as the river by the same name, even the city of Phut in Mauritania, because it is in the pivot [12] of Africa.

I pass over matters explained by Philip Melanchthon; among these, however, I cannot approve his opinion that Aescanazim (the name by which the Jews call the Germans) is derived from אש and [בתו]סהו, as it were, "priests of fire." For the Jewish tongue does not allow that the root ו be elided, and ה is silent in Cohen. It is more probable that it means "scattered inhabitants," from *sacan* and *naza;* hence, also, the Ascanian region of Asia Minor and Sicania.

These appellations are Chaldean and Hebraic; they mean nothing in Greek or Latin and show that the primary origin of all races ought to be attributed to the people from whom the idioms flow. They indicate that of all races the most ancient are the Chaldean, Armenian, Egyptian, Jewish, Arab (whose tongue differs very little from Hebrew), the Phoenician, Ionian, Asiatic, Persian, Indian, Medes, Ethiopian, and Sabaean. Not inconsistently did the Egyptian priest taunt Solon with the fact that the Greeks seemed to him mere children, because they had nothing old. More appropriate, even, the taunt of the Christian who told the Greeks that Moses the lawgiver was older than the gods of the Greeks, for Greece has almost nothing older than Danaus and Cadmus. Of these the one was founder of the race, the other brought letters to the Greeks. But in those same times the Jews flourished, having the highest reputation for valorous deeds. The empires of the Chaldeans and of the Egyptians seem to have grown old.

Chaldeans, Egyptians, and Jews are as much older than the Greeks as these are older than other races, and this becomes plain because of the three criteria of the system used—as I said, the tested reliability of writers, the old roots in language, and the situation of the area. Pausa-

---

[12] *Cardo* is "pivot" or "hinge"; possibly "watershed."

nias and Strabo said that all the Greeks were either Ionians or Aeolians or Dorians. The Ionians, of course, came from Asia into Greece, as we stated above, supported by the authority of great writers. What Hecataeus testified in the pages of Strabo also fits in with their evidence— that the first inhabitants of Greece came from barbaric regions. In similar fashion Pliny wrote that the Meander River, which watered a good part of Asia Minor, bathed Ionia. In addition, the Athenians, the most ancient of the Greeks, for they alone are said to be autochthonous, are called Ionians by all writers. But Pausanias and Strabo were mistaken in calling Attica the old Ionia, since Asia had been cultivated by these people earlier, whence came that name. Although the twelve colonies of Athenians were led into Asia, as Strabo and Pausanias reported—a number which, Pliny recounted later, grew even to eighty—yet it does not follow on that account that the Athenians were older than the Asiatics. By this system the Gauls would be more ancient than the Greeks and the Asiatics, and the Greeks than the Chaldeans, since the Greeks often sent forth colonies into Chaldea, the Gauls into Asia and Greece.

In contrast are the Aeolians, that is, diverse and mingled, because their stock came, I think, from the Ionians, the Egyptians, and the Phoenicians. All peoples beyond the Isthmus of Corinth, except the Athenians and the Megarians, were called Aeolians, as Strabo wrote. The fleet of Danaus came to the shore of Achaea, and this very man won control of the Argives, who were famous among the Aeolians. He afterwards sent colonies into the Peloponnesus. Cadmus the Phoenician led a colony of Thebans into Boeotia. That the Dorians, however, were no other than Aeolians at first becomes plain from Pindar himself, who calls his poem written in Doris "an Aeolic song." To coin a new designation from that of Prince Dorus could indeed change their name, but not their origin. However, if anyone wishes to know what is the origin of each people in Greece, Pausanias and Strabo explained this very fully. To follow through the details of this is not the task of one who writes a *Method*.

This only—that the Greeks originated in Asia, Egypt, and Phoenicia and united first in Europe. Then colonies were led by them into Italy. Authors such as Fabius, Cato, Piso, Gellius, Sempronius, Varro, and Dionysius of Halicarnassus himself, who often quoted the authority of these other men, gave evidence of this fact. From this we can refute the error of the people who think that Cato was the writer of the fragments which we have. Dionysius reported that Cato's opinions about the

Greeks indicated that the Italians must have descended from them. But in the fragments mentioned the Greeks are blamed for effrontery, because they affirm their forefathers were the ancestors of the Italians. A greater proof of this origin, however, is that Italy is outstanding for fertility and moderation of climate, that it is a neighbor to Greece, and that the journey to it is very short. Last is the fact that traces of the Greek language have not disappeared.

Caesar proved that the maritime Britons originated from the Belgic Gauls by the following arguments: first, that the island is a neighbor to the Belgians; then, that the British towns have the same place names as the Belgian towns; last, he learned these facts from the inhabitants of both regions. Tacitus, also, to show that the Gothini, from whom the Goths are thought to have come, are descended from the Gauls, said, "The Gallic tongue proves that the Gothini are not Germans." Likewise, the Greek tongue proves that the Italians are derived from the Greeks. For Italy was called Oenotria by the ancient Greeks, from Oenotrius the Arcadian; others think it was [from?] Janus, because to the Hebrews that means the same thing as Oenotrius to the Greeks, "vinitor" to the Latins. But to the younger Greeks it was Hesperia, a Greek word, because it was situated to the west of Greece. Dionysius thought that formerly it was called Ausonia. This also is Greek, τὸ αὖσαι, τὸ καῦσαι or τὸ θεγεῖν [to kindle, to burn, or to provoke]. Finally it was called Italy on account of the size of its cattle, as Hellanicus recounted. For Italus means to the Greeks "calf" (*vitulus*) or ox, as Herodotus and Timaeus have written. Varro also followed this etymology. Moreover, Cicero said, "In the reign of my ancestor, that is, Servius Tullius, Pythagoras came into Italy, which then was called Greater Greece." Furthermore, the Doric language was common to almost all Italians, as their writings bear witness. Then, too, the Italian regions for the most part keep the Greek name: of this sort are Lucania, Umbria, Cumae, Phlegraean Field, Elaea, Pandosia, Pandataria, Neapolis, and Peuceria.

Changes of language are wont to be made chiefly for three reasons (I omit the one alleged by Moses, which occurred at one instant, not gradually). One is the passage of time, by which not only the tongues but also all things are changed, and the entire nature of things grows old. So Polybius wrote that in less than fifty years from the time when the alliance was made between the Carthaginians and the Romans the words of the alliance, which he himself called ancient, could with difficulty be understood. Indeed, the songs which were sung in the rites according to the ancient formula were understood by very few. Thus we see all the languages of all peoples gradually changed in one way or in another.

Another cause is the fusion of colonies and of peoples. For proof, we have Italy and Greece, which for so many centuries kept the purity of the Greek and the Latin speech and spread those languages throughout the whole world. After Scythians and Goths invaded each country such a change came about that Latium and Attica seem never to have existed on their present sites. So the colonies of Tusci, who were driven by the Gauls from Italy, and of the Gauls, who once wandered in deserted Germany, developed a third kind of speech different from both. Colonies of the Angles sent into Britain and of the Saxons sent into Belgium by Charles the Great, and also of Gauls into Saxony, produced a variety of dialects. Likewise, Parthians corrupted the Persian language; the Arabs, the Punic; the Turks, the Tartar; the Slavs, the Greek; and the Latins, the Gallic and Spanish speech.

Finally, the cause of the change of language depends on the very nature of the area. For it is characteristic of all peoples who live in a northerly region to make words with consonants striking sharply without vowels from the inner chest, and with frequent aspirations. This happens on account of the great strength of their breath and the inner heat rushing out. The Saxons and those living near the Baltic Sea almost universally pronounce the media for the tenuis, and aspirates for the media.[13] The following is an example: Per theum ferum pibimus ponum finum. But the southerners, in whom the heat is tempered and the breath is weak, pronounce gently. More softly, even, the women, because they have a weaker breath than a man and less heat. This is easily understood in the colony of the Saxons, whom Charles the Great led among the Belgians. When the Saxons call a horse *pfert*, the Flemings, brought up under a kinder sky, pronounce it *pert*. I omit discussion of the nature of each place appropriate to and inherent in it on account of the waters, which change voices and languages; for instance, in the Labdanian field of Gallia Narbonensis all stammer in using "l"; and in the Vaux [14] region of the Turini. The ancient Sabines also used to say *foedus* instead of *hoedus*, *fircus* instead of *hircus*, as Varro wrote. Among us the Gascons use *hocus* instead of *focus*; *hilius* instead of *filius*.

---

[13] An aspirate is a consonantal sound followed by the sound of *h*. A media is a voiced or soft mute. A tenuis is an unvoiced, or voiceless, or breath stop.

[14] Vaux? The text reads *in Valedoca*. See above, p. 142.

Then, too, the Parisians and Orleanists, in accordance with the custom of the ancient Etruscans, use *Valesius* and *Fusius* instead of *Valerius* and *Furius*.

From these three causes chiefly, the many dissimilitudes of language arise, and yet the early speech cannot be so totally lost but that manifest traces of the old will still endure. For example, the ancient Celtic tongue was for the most part Greek, because our ancestors are derived from that people. Bouillus, Picardus, and Perionius formed countless words, yet not all—not painfully or inappropriately as Lazius did in his own tongue, but very easily, sometimes even with no change from the Greek sources. In this, however, there seems to me not so much of weight and importance, as in those expressions which are common to us and to the Greeks; then, also, in the elegant use of participles, infinitives, and articles which sufficiently proves that the origin of the Gauls must be Trojan or Greek, or both, since they both used the Ionian tongue. Ammianus Marcellinus, Book xv, wrote that he had read in the records of the Gauls and had learned from the inhabitants that the origin of the Gauls went back to the Trojans, although the story was that the Gauls had come from the Dorians. Josephus traces the race from Gomer, the first born of Japhet the elder. But I think this reference is to the descendants of Gomer. Lucan writes that the Arverni say that they are brothers of the Romans and calls them people of the blood of Ilium. Certainly we have two cities of Paris and one of Troy, for thus the inhabitants call that city which is named Tricassium or Trecensis.[15] Furthermore, it is clear that the Venetians, a people of the Celts, are descended from the Venetians of Paphlagonia. Indeed, in Book iii Strabo derived the people who control the Adriatic Gulf from the Venetians of the Celts,[16] although Livy thought otherwise. Finally, the name Celts, which interpreters of our antiquity have omitted, is always used for "knights" by Homer, Pindar, and other early writers. Appian traced it from Celtus, son of Polyphemus, as absurdly as our men [traced] the Franks from Francio, the son of Hector, who never existed. Even more preposterous is Lazius, who affirmed it is derived from Galatians, for the name Galatians is of course not used by the ancients. Κέλης, moreover, is a riding horse, unharnessed, which the Latins call *sellarius,* but κελετίζειν and κελετᾶν in Homer and Pindar are nothing but "to ride upon unsaddled horses," as Eustathius wrote. Thence κελεταί and κελταί by contraction. The reason the Gauls were first called Celts, however, is that of all peoples they especially were able

---

[15] Troyes.   [16] Strabo IV. 4.

horsemen. This is true, although the Moors were praised by the ancients because they excelled in horsemanship and won famous victories for Hannibal over the Romans (whose chief strength lay, as Caesar wrote, in the infantry). Even more outstanding was the cavalry of the Gauls, which Caesar always used in the civil wars. Thus, Hirtius said, "An incredible thing happened in the African war. Less than thirty Gallic knights put to flight two thousand of the Moorish knights." The same man said, in *The Spanish War:* "With a great force Afranius attacked a few Caesarian troops. Swiftly the Gallic horsemen got into motion, and when the battle was joined, a very few withstood a great number of the enemy." Moreover, in the life of Antony, Plutarch wrote that when the armies of Antony were hard pressed everywhere, the Parthians could not be coerced or broken by any force except the Gallic cavalry. This passage was pointed out to me by Christopher Auger, my colleague, a specialist in history and law. Pliny's statement is equally fitting—that Hipporedia, a city of Gallia Togata, was so called from the best horse tamers. Caesar, when he divided the people of Gaul into three classes—druids, knights, and farmers—allotted military disciplines to the knights. Since many seemed to share the name Celts, Caesar at the beginning of the first book reported that those who dwell between the Seine and the Garonne rivers were truly and properly called Celts. Although they were called Gauls by the Latins, yet in their own tongue they were Celts. Plutarch, lest there should be confusion, called them κελτόριοι in the life of Camillus.[17] Moreover, it happens that almost all peoples are by foreigners given names different from their own. The Italians were called by the Greeks, Hesperians; Hellenes, by the Latins, Greeks; Libyans, by the Greeks, Africans. Yet the Italians did not use the name Hesperians, or the Hellenes, Greeks, or the Libyans, Africans. Likewise the Scots called the Angles, Saxons; so, also, those whom we call Turks dislike that name intensely and the name Saracen is not heard in Asia and Africa. Yet on account of affinity of language, or origin, or of both, or of frequent emigration of colonies, the Greeks called our ancestors Celts, in their own and the same Celtic tongue. Where the name Gaul came from or what it signifies, in truth, no one has explained so far as I know. It is odd to interpret it "snatched from the waves," as Rabbi Samuel did. It is more accurate to derive the word from "coming" and "wandering." We are called Wallons by the Belgians, because it happened that the ancient Gauls, when they were wandering about the world, inquired of

[17] Plutarch *Themistocles* 15.

each other, "Où allons nous?" that is, "Whither now do we go?" From this it is credible that they were called Ouallones. The Latins never took this letter "W" into their language, but used the letter "G." Moreover, Gaul is properly "most fertile field," and in the territories of the Parisians is thus called Oualesia. Unless we may trace the word from *wal*, which in the Celtic language meant "wood," a word which the Germans use, so the *wali* may be the same as "druids."

As in those days the Celts lived between the Seine and the Garonne, so the Gauls lived beyond the Seine. But Strabo bounded the Celts by the Pyrenees, the Alps, the Rhine, and both seas. Lazius, Peutinger, Althamer, and Xylander [18] were not sufficiently accurate in wishing to use Celtic for all the peoples of Germany and Gaul; they were influenced by the authority of Herodotus, by whom they themselves are easily refuted. He placed the Celts near the sources of the Ister (which he himself traced from the Pyrenees). What greater conflict exists with geographical knowledge than this? But if the name Celts is applied properly to the Germans, why did Strabo, according to the opinion of the ancients, allocate to the four quarters of the world, the Indians in the east, the Celts in the west, the Ethiopians in the south, the Scythians in the north? Gaul is situated in the farthest western region; but Germany is east of Gaul. In another passage Strabo placed Celts and Iberians in the west, Nomads and Scythians in the north.

After the Gauls had filled Germany, Italy, Spain, Britain, Greece, Asia Minor, and even farthest Scythia with colonies, founded cities, cultivated the areas, established laws, they stirred up such a reputation among all peoples that all races of Europe boasted that the fame and the splendor of their stock descended from the Celts, as though they were Trojans. Thus Plutarch in the life of Marius called all the lands of Europe sloping to the north and west Celtic. The Greeks themselves, of course, flourishing in the renown of learning and heroic deeds, were wont to seek examples of bravery from the Celts. This may be seen in the pages of Aristotle, in the books *Ethics* and *Politics;* then, also, in the pages of Aelian, in the book of *Diverse Histories.*

What of the German writers? Of course Peutinger and Neuenar (I omit the others) while they claimed a Celtic name for themselves and took it away from our ancestors, at the same time vilified Gaul with words of scorn and despoiled her of all triumphs as far as they could.

[18] Xylander was the Hellenized version of Holtzmann of Augsburg, who lived from 1532 to 1576, and annotated translations of various classical works.

Since men trained in a more polished discipline and specialists in all antiquity openly exclaimed against this, Lazius tried another method, and having repudiated their opinions, he covered the Gauls with praise while he affirmed that the Germans first were called Tuiscones and Teutons, then Galatians, afterwards Germans or Alemanni, then Celts and Gauls. Thus he wrote in the preamble. Well, Lazius! By doing this you will vindicate from reproaches the Gallic name, recklessly and unwisely desecrated by your compatriots, and I have a great hope that it will come about that when the Germans and the Gauls regard themselves as blood brothers (as Strabo wrote more truthfully and appropriately for his purpose) they may unite themselves in a perpetual alliance and friendship.

It only remains for us to discuss whether our ancestors were originally descended from the Germans. Lazius affirmed it, but the following took a negative stand: Polybius, Caesar, Livy, Pliny, Strabo, Plutarch, Athenaeus, Josephus, Tacitus, Justin, Berosus, Pausanias, and Diodorus. However it may be, so greatly are both races praised, according to the words and books of so many men, that neither the Germans nor the Gauls ought to envy the origin of the other. The fact that Herodotus and then Diodorus extended the Celtic limits into Scythia from the west, while Plutarch took them even as far as Pontus, makes it sufficiently clear that the Celts, wherever they may have had their origin, have filled all Europe with a multitude of colonies. The chief indication of their origin is that they extended the frontiers of their empire and gave racial names to the subject peoples, like clearly marked footprints for the everlasting record of posterity, as almost all peoples have done. Then, from the Celts come the Celto-Scythians. The Celtiberians, whom Livy called the strength of Spain, are also from the ancient race of Gauls, by combining the name Celt with the Spanish. What Caesar wrote about the Gauls in Book VI, Valerius in Book II reasserted about the Celtiberians. It was always sinful for them to survive in a battle when the man had fallen to whose safety they had pledged their lives. From these same Celts, who afterward were called Gauls by the Latins and Galatians by the Greeks, Gallicia and Portugal of Spain had their names as well as North Wales, South Wales, and Cornwall of Britain, Galloway of Scotland, Westphalia of Germany, Gallia of Italy, and Galatia of Asia Minor; even the Ruteni, a people of Germany, from the Ruthenian Gauls; likewise the Carnians of Germany, from the Carnians and the Carnutians, and Lombardy from the Langones, whom Livy called a people of Gaul, and from bards, poets. This is too plain to require proof. In Thrace, in which the Gauls ruled for a long time, as Polybius reported, likewise in Byzantium and Syria, whose dominion they held not so long ago, no traces remain, and they did not deny the original name to the conquered regions. Bohemia, indeed, has retained up to now the name of a particular clan of Gaul from the Boii, a people of Gaul, said Tacitus. But the regions of the Scordisci, the Tanisci, and the Helvetii, whom Pliny, Caesar, and Tacitus called Gauls, have no trace of the ancient name. The early Gauls invaded Gallia Togata from the Ufente River to the Alps and the Adige after they had driven back the Tuscan people, as we may read in the pages of Livy, Book XLVIII. This area finally lost the name of the clan, although Milan (there still exist with us two towns of this name), Como, Vicenza, Verona, Brescia, and many towns of Lombardy, Liguria, and the Etruscans, which Du Bellay mentioned, are said to have been founded by our ancestors. But from Olbia, a town of the Tectosages, five most famous cities are derived, as may be seen in the pages of Pliny and Strabo, one even of Bithynia, another of Pamphylia, a third of Cilicia, a fourth of Celtoscythia near the mouths of the Dnieper, a fifth this side the Rhine, which is called Tolbiac, for τὸ ὀλβιακόν. There is no greater proof that the four in Asia were founded by Olbiacs of the Tectosages than the fact that the Tectosages seized the whole region of Asia, the most fertile of all, as Trogus Pompey and Livy witnessed. It is credible that the Isle of Albion, which later was called Britain, has its name from this. But these things, Lazius will say, were done by the Gauls or the Celts (for those whom Polybius called Celts, Livy everywhere called Gauls), peoples of Germany. What said Caesar? He was not a Gaul or a German, although a most bitter enemy of the Gauls. Said he, "There was formerly a time when the Gauls excelled the Germans in valor and voluntarily started wars. On account of the pressure of population and the lack of land they sent colonies across the Rhine, hence the Volcae Tectosages seized those sections of Germany which are most fertile, around the Hercynian Wood, and settled there." [19] Caesar reported these things, and Tacitus confirmed them. Livy also wrote [20] in agreement, that is, that Ambigatus, king of the Celts, sent Bellovesus and Segovesus, the sons of his sister, to what abodes the gods might assign, because in his reign Gaul was so populous that this abounding multitude seemed difficult to direct. To Segovesus was given the Hercynian highlands. Bellovesus received Italy. Pausanias

[19] Caesar *Gallic Wars* VI. 24.   [20] Livy V. xxxiv.

also wrote that the Celts advanced into Pannonia and Greece, and from them the Alps were called Celtic. Athenaeus likewise reported in Book v that the Celts who had crossed over into Greece moved their abodes into Pannonia. Strabo plainly confirmed this in Book v, Pliny in Book IV, and lastly Polybius in Book II repeated that Boii, Eganes, Senones, and Ananes had migrated from Gaul into Germany and, in Book III, that the Celts, under their leader Brennus had penetrated into Thrace and held this kingdom even to the time of Clyarus.[21] So Beatus Rhenanus properly smiled at certain German writers who thought that Brennus and the Senones came from the Germans. But Polydore Virgil affirmed that Brennus was a Briton, which no one ever dared to write before. Lazius merits the same reproach, since he reported that the Cimbri advanced along with Brennus into Italy and Greece. The same author is the only one who brings the Boiarii, who it is well known were by origin Gauls, from Armenia [Arvernia?] into Germany.

But it is worthy of note that everywhere the Latins use the word Gauls, whereas the Greeks use κελτοί in the same narrative of events. Livy in Book XLVIII, admitted that the Gauls (he does not call them Cimbri, or Germans, or Tuiscones, whom he always distinguished from the Gauls) peopled Italy, Illyricum, Pannonia, Greece, Macedonia, Thrace, and Asia with their colonies, as well as all the region on this side the Taurus mountains and the Halys river, and made the kings of Syria themselves pay tribute. But when he wrote about the Germans, he called them by a racial name, as Josephus in the speech of Agrippa to the Jews and Posidonius in the work of Athenaeus distinguished fittingly and appropriately between the names German and Celt in the case of the banquet of the Celts and also in the banquet of the Germans. Now Justin, indeed, made plain from Trogus Pompey that that memorable migration of the Gauls happened in the time of Tarquinius Priscus, when, after they had driven forth the Etruscans, they seized the greater and better part of Italy; but the Tuscans went into Rhetia and Vindelicia of Upper Germany. At the same time, from another direction, Bellovesus occupied the most fertile parts of Lower Germany (on the authority of Livy). We understand from this that Germany in that time had no inhabitants. It is not believable that the inhabitants of the north, who in strength and greatness of courage exceed the southerners, would have admitted the Italians and the Gauls, whom they could have barred from the approach to Italy by the broad ditch of the Rhine or

---

[21] Polybius mentions a Cavarus, *The Histories* IV. 52.

the peaks of the Alps with no great difficulty. Because of these considerations, then, I decide that the Tusci, a people of Italy (which Wolf
and Funck admitted), and the Gauls were the sources of the western
Germans. It is ridiculous to assert that they were descended from Hercules or from Tuisco, the son of Hercules.

The farthest shore of Scythia was occupied by the Heneti and the
Cimbri, who descended from the Venetians of Paphlagonia and the
Cimmerians, peoples of the Tauric Chersonese recorded by Homer.
Hence the Baltic Sea is called Venedicum.[22] Pliny wrote that the inhabi-
tants of Germany are made up of "Ingevones" (Peucer explained this
as a variation of "indigenous," although they really are the ancient
Heneti and Cimbri) or, near the Rhine, Istaevones, offspring of the
Gauls; or around the Danube, Hermiones, who also take their origin
from the Gauls, as we have shown formerly, or Vandals, that is,
"strangers" in the German tongue, who landed from Scandia on the Baltic shores, now Vindelici; finally, Bastarnae and Peucini in the vicinity of
Dacia, who travelled from Scythia into Germany. Although we do not
have classical authority for this, nevertheless, the very topography of
the country leads us to this decision. Tacitus, to show that the Germans
were born in Germany (a thing which is evidently absurd and impious),
gathered his evidence from the very description of Germany.

Those who wanted to change their habitation [said he], used to set sail in a
fleet and the great ocean is visited by few ships from our side. But who, apart
from the perils of an awesome and unknown sea, would have left Asia or Africa
or Italy to go to Germany, with its wildernesses, severe climate, barbaric culture
and appearance, unless, indeed, it were his fatherland?

A little later:

It is well known that the Germans have no inhabited cities. They do not even
permit the houses to be joined together. They dwell in separate habitations,
where a grove, a spring, a field pleases them. Each man has a cleared piece of
ground around his house, either against accidents of fire or from lack of skill in
building. Indeed, the use of cement or of tiles is not known among them. They
use rude material for all purposes, and without consideration of appearance or
attraction.

So Tacitus wrote in his own era, that is, in A.D. 120. If Germany seemed
to him then to be rather the home of wild beasts than the residence of
men, without cities, without towns, without camps, without connected

[22] The Frisches Haff.

buildings, what should we think it was when Tarquinius Priscus was reigning, that is, about eight hundred years before Tacitus?

But in those days Livy wrote that Gaul was prolific of men, so that it sent forth colonies into Germany and all Europe. Then, neither the Gauls nor the Celts came from the Germans, who did not exist at that time, but the Germans are descended from the Gauls, the Tusci, the Scythians, and the Heneti. For this reason, when inquiry is made about the origin of the Franks, who were the last to invade the kingdom of Gaul, I do not trace them from the Trojans, as do Gregory of Tours and the Abbot of Ursperg, or from the Phrygians, as our Du Bellay, or from the Cimbri or Phrysii, as Lazius did. I trace them from the inhabitants of eastern Franconia beyond the Rhine, near the Gauls, where, as Caesar said, lie the most fertile regions of Germany, occupied by Gallic colonies around the Hercynian Wood. It is now called by the inhabitants the *Schwartzwald*, that is, "black wood," around the sources of the Danube, the Neckar, and the Main. Beatus Rhenanus, following Tacitus, wrote that there were two valleys, Bellovacens, from Beauvais, and one which is called Andegaust, from the Angevins, my people. Then the river Maine itself, which waters Anjou, is the same as the Maine of the Hercynian Wood. They pronounce it Mein, taking away the "e." Furthermore, there are also two cities not far from Basel, beyond the Rhine, called by the Gallic names Angers and Breisach [Brissac]; then, too, the grove of Senon from the Gallic Senones, who, as Polybius recounted in Book III also led colonies into Germany. Indeed, what is called Westphalia of Germany, that is, western Gallia, which lies between the Weser and the Rhine and borders the regions of Franconia and the Sicambrians to the east, shows well enough that it originated by analogy with Eastphalia, that is, eastern Gallia, beyond the Weser, subjugated by the Gauls. I do not see how Lazius could satisfy these arguments.

Such were the origins of the Franks; such the beginnings. The name itself is plainly Celtic, not used by the Germans, as I have learned from them. Moreover, Frank is, in the Gallic tongue (not Latin or Greek, much less Hebrew) no other than "free" and "exempted." From this it becomes not only probable but even manifest that the peoples of Gaul, impatient of servitude to the Romans, migrated across the Rhine to the old colonies of the Gauls, and then went back again to their fatherland as soon as they could, when they had shaken off the Roman yoke. Meanwhile, they had received the name Franks, that is, "freemen." We have as evidence the fact that Tacitus, who counts innumerable peoples of Germany, does not mention the Franks. I omit the ridiculous guess [that they are] the βρέγκων of Pannonia, which some allege on the authority of Ptolemy, although it is plain enough from the above that more properly the Pannonians are of Gallic origin. Therefore the Franks overflowed into Gaul from those regions beyond the Rhine in the neighborhood of Gaul, that is, from Franconia (as Ammianus, Agathias, Vopiscus, and Procopius reported), in the days when Aurelian was prince, and they accomplished so much by strength of arms that they often conquered the Romans, drove the Huns off with Roman aid, then put to flight the Goths, and finally drove the Romans themselves from the possession of Gaul. When the former rulers had been driven out, the Franks first forced the Burgundians to serve them, then the Alemanni, after the defeat of Tolbiac, and crossing the Rhine, they brought under their rule and laws Rhetia and Vindelicia and later Swabia, Carnia, Pannonia, and Saxony.

The final proof of this matter is in linguistic traces, so that it is plain that the Germans originate from the Gauls, not the Gauls from the Germans. This is clear from the actual writings of the Germans and of the ancient Latins, so we arrive at survivals of words as the most important proof of origin. Since the Latins come from the Greeks and the Latin tongue is composed of Greek words and yet is not the same, so also the origin of the French tongue was Greek, contrary to what our men have written. Greek is the intellectual discipline of the French. Although we have many traces of the Greek, almost a countless number, yet the Celtic language was not the same as the Greek, as Lazius affirmed from what Caesar wrote: "The Gauls in public and private acts used the letters of the Greeks, and the number of Helvetians who had gone away from home was counted in Greek letters." This is analogous to thinking that the Germans have the Latin language for their common speech because they use Latin letters in public and private accounts. Caesar wrote letters to Quintus Cicero, his lieutenant, in the Greek language lest they should be intercepted by the enemy and understood. Furthermore, he could not understand Divitiacus the Aeduan except through an interpreter. This is sufficient proof that Divitiacus was ignorant of the Greek language (in which Caesar was skilled). Massilians, of course, spoke Greek, as we find in the pages of Strabo, when Marseilles was still of the original stock and the colony of the Phocaeans had not mingled with the Gauls. It is credible that the druids also were instructed in the Greek

language, since Caesar wrote that they were well versed in the same
religions and disciplines as the Greeks. Lucian wrote that he had heard
a Gaul really skilled in Greek learning discussing that famous statue of
the Celtic Hercules. The language of the Germans also differed very
much from the Celtic, although Lazius by the same error wrote that
Celtic and German were one. Why, then, did Tacitus say that the
Gothini are by origin Gauls, not Germans, because they used the Gallic
tongue? Why did St. Jerome write that the Galatians of Asia Minor
spoke the same language as the Treveri (whom Tacitus calls Gauls), but
not German? Such a great man, who had traveled throughout the world,
was not ignorant of this distinction. Why, finally, would Ariovistus, a
German, by continuous practice for fourteen years, during which he had
lived in Gaul, have learned to speak Gallic? Yet Celtic fitted no less
easily into the German tongue than into the Gallic. Omitting that large
number of Greek words which, I have said, has been collected by others
and overlooking phrases omitted by those who have written about this
matter, as well as names ending in "on" according to the Greek custom,
such as Platon, Caton, Hoqueton, that is, ὀχίτων, in which we see the
image of the Greek tongue clearly reflected (for the Latins are wont to
say Plato, Cato, Dio, Melanchtho), we shall find no greater proof than
in our own old place names, which our authors have neglected altogether.

I will therefore introduce a few from many. Rhodonii Mountains,
from "roses"; Pyrenees, from "flames," as the well-known fragments
of Berosus show, are called *shenni*,[23] "extinct," as it were. The inhabitants use this name for that mountain called Cemenus [24] by Strabo;
thence Mount Pelion. Tholosa means "muddy," as is the nature of the
plain, or "covered." Olbia, which in the Doric manner we call Albia,
means "happy," of which town and etymology I have been advised by
Jerome Chandieu, secretary to the king, famed no less for his erudition
than for the splendor of his race. Limoges, the "land of hunger"; or in
feminine fashion, Limosaea. The Dorians use *gaian* and *aian* by elision.
It is a region exceedingly sterile and plainly unfruitful. Do not assume
"pestiferous" from confusing the words λοιμοῦ and λιμοῦ. Moreover, the
old form of "town" is *lan* (for thus our men take over the Doric *lan*),
yet the inhabitants pronounce it *laon*, in the Aeolic fashion. It has acquired its name from the rocks or peoples. Antibes,[25] which is situated

---

[23] From σβέννυμι which in the passive means to be extinct.
[24] Cevennes or Cebenna.   [25] Antipolis.

opposite Nice, was named by the Greeks, as well as the Stoechades Islands, from their arrangement; Alexia of the Mandubians from "safety"; Cape Aphrodisium, from Venus; likewise the Tectosages, from "makers of arms," and the Rhone, from τὸ ῥοδανίζειν, on account of the cataracts. Macon, moreover, is a town in the territory of the Burgundians, so called because it is extensive. Philibert Bariot, a judge of Macon and a man of the highest integrity, famed for his erudition, reminded us of this town and its etymology. The unskilled, however, call it Matiscon. In the territories of the Carnutes there are also two neighboring walled cities; they call the one οὔχ, the other ἔχομεν. There is the town called by the Greek name Euros, as well as our Boeotia. I omit the name "druid," plainly Greek, and that of the wise Semnothei of Gaul, although others think they are called Schamotae, as if "celestial" in Hebrew. But in this field each man can investigate many things in accordance with his own ability. From these characteristic place names a truer and wiser decision can be made about origins. Moreover, the Celtic tongue has been almost abandoned on account of the customary speech of the Romans and their numerous colonies, especially in Gallia Narbonensis and Aquitania, where the vulgar tongue is not very far away from the Latin speech. There have been more colonies led into Gaul than those counted by historians. This is evidence—that Lectoria, a town of Aquitania, from the name, as well as from the ancient inscriptions of the town, has been judged a colony of the Romans. No writer, so far as I know, has included this among the colonies. Narbonne is known to be a very ancient colony; Lyons is a colony; as well as Cologne, Valence, Nîmes, Grenoble, Arles, and the one retaining the name Coloniac, in the territory of the Sequani. Moreover, since the legions of the Romans were habitually stationed in Gaul, we naturally forgot altogether the language of the fatherland and accepted Latin. But into Germany the Romans led almost no colonies except to Augsburg and Constance. From this circumstance it happened that the Germans seem to have retained more traces than we of the Celtic tongue, acquired from us, on account of the sending of colonies and of commercial contacts.

To select a few from many, it is evident from Caesar himself that *Vergobret* is a Celtic word. Glareanus [26] interpreted it as "the highest

---

[26] Heinrich Loriti, called Glareanus, 1488–1563, was a Swiss. He was a pupil of Cochleus, a professor of music, and poet laureate of the empire. His most famous work is *Dodecachordon*. He also edited Boethius and wrote *Compendiaria Asiae, Africae, Europaeque descriptio.*

executive," and the Germans and Helvetians use it. *Rheda,* a word for chariot which Caesar attributed to the Gauls, is used by the Germans with the same significance. Moreover, this goes back to the Greeks, who called a chariot ῥέδιον as we find in Hesychius. To the present we retain *alauda.* Pausanias wrote that a horse is called *marc* by the Celts, whence marquis and Marcoman, that is, "horseman." *Marca* means "limit," *marché,* a "market," to the Germans as well as to ourselves. But a marquis has greater dignity than a knight. Po comes from *pades,* a Gallic word, meaning "pitch pine," because there is a great deal around the source of the Po, as Metrodorus has written, but it is more probable that in Gallic it means "deep," said Pliny, for the Ligurians use *bodingum* for "deep." He asserted that the ancient city Bodincomagum,[27] where the river flows deeper, is a proof. Similarly, Lake Constance is called Boden by the inhabitants. The great gulf in the interior of Gothia is called Boding with the same significance, and the people who dwell in the large city of Pannonia are Bodini. Indeed, we take personal and family names from this appellation (there are almost countless examples of this name in Gaul). We do not keep its meaning, but use a Latin word; yet from this we can guess that these names have traveled from the ancient Celts to the Germans with the migrations of peoples.

Many have asked, and Athenaeus explained, the meaning of the word *dunus.* He wrote that the masters were called *douni* by the Celts. This word the Spanish, for the most part descended from the Gauls, and the Sicilians retain in the same sense; but our men abandon it to the monks. Yet thence come the old names Lyons, Verdun, Issoudun, Nevers,[28] unless we are to say that *dune* means a loftier place or a hill. Our men call *dunes* "levées." But what *magum* is, neither the Germans nor our men have revealed. We were shown this by Pliny, however, when he interpreted *Bodincomagum* the "deep town." I omit the stupid interpretations of *magum.* Hence come Nimwegen, Rouen, and Nyon.[29] The Germans do not have this word *magum,* since once they had no towns. They themselves received from us *burg,* which plainly is Greek. We learned *villa* and *castrum* from the Latins. *Berg* is an old Celtic word meaning mountain. The Germans use this even now; we, the Latin word. Thence comes "berger," that is, in the old tongue, "mountaineer," by which name we call the shepherds. Countrymen learned the Latin words with more difficulty. From *berg* the Germans make the composite names of

---

[27] Turin.   [28] Lugdunum, Virodunum, Isodunum, Noviodunum.

[29] Noviomagum, Rhotomagum, Neomagum.

towns and fortresses situated in the mountains: Bamberg, Hildeberga, Clarberg—we say Clermont. Likewise the name bard, which to the Germans today means "priest," was learned from our ancestors, for Caesar wrote that the Germans had no education, no sacrifices, and no religions. Sulpitius showed in his commentary on Lucan and Ammianus, and Diodorus also indicated, that the poets of Gaul were once called "bards" by the Gauls, and in the Celtic tongue *bard* means "singer." Since poets of this sort seemed stupid and barbarous to the Latins, they called unlearned and stupid people "bards." Hence Dagobard, the heroic singer or poet; Sigebard, the conquering poet; Albard, active poet; Robard, ruddy poet. Hence Lambardi and Langobardi are interpreted by the Germans "heroic priest" and "ruddy priest." For the Langones and Bardi are neighboring peoples.

Hard is also Celtic, meaning "robust" to Germans, and to us *"bold."* We add a vowel at the end which the Germans for reasons of diction oftener remove. As they call a cohort a *band*, we *bande*, so they call an uncultivated region *land*, we *lande;* so also they use *hardimant*, we *hardiment*. Hence, also, we use the word "hard" for a twisted branch, for nothing is stronger, and we call a certain punishment "hard," that is, strangulation, which the ancients used instead of ropes. Moreover, there is this composite word *Bernard* from the German *Bern* and the Celtic *hard*, that is, master of a bear, and also *Leonard*, that is, the strength of the people, made up from Greek and Celtic words. The Greeks would say Leosthenes and Demosthenes. Likewise they have that family name Caenomani, which is from the Celtic *man*, very frequently used by Germans, Scythians, Turks, and Tartars (we, however, use the Latin word, calling it *homo*), and it is fused with the Greek. From this it seems likely that the Caenomani, that is, "new men," came into Gaul from elsewhere before the times of Tarquin, since afterwards colonies of Caenomani were sent by the ancient Celts into Insubria. They are called the Caenomani of Italy.

Reix is also old Celtic, that is, *rex*. The Germans make it *reich*. Caesar, in the custom of the ancient Gauls, wrote it *rix*. From this are derived the names Dumnorix, "king of rulers," Ombiorix, "king of hosts," Orgetorix, Graeco-Celtic, that is, "king of the mad," for *orgé* is "madness" and *orgelos* in Gallic *orgueilleux*—that is, a vice common to the insane. Friederich is the same as "king of peace." In the pages of Livy, Lonnorius and Lutarius are Celtic; Caesar properly should have written Lonnorix. The Germans translate it *rich*, not accurately enough in my judgment: so they obtain "rich in madness," "rich in hospitality." Although both Germans and Gauls translate *rich* "rich," the Gauls have added the feminine "e," which the Germans take away. Yet there is a certain elegance of figure in it, because riches are suitable for kings. For illustration, the Germans call the kingdom of France *Frankreich.* Then *Ostreich* and *Westreich* (which we correctly call Austria and Neustria) are applied to the eastern kingdom and the western kingdom by the Germans. The *könig,* which means "king" among the Germans, originated among the Goths and the Slavs.

Mar also is old Celtic, common to the Germans as well as to us. They pronounce it "mair," we "maire," for the highest official of the city. Hence those ancient names Viridomar, Suemer, Condomar, that is, master of Condomus, and so forth, as the Latins said "dictator" for master of the people. Furthermore, the last king of Sweden and Denmark of the old stock, the father of Margaret, was called Waldemar. There are countless old Celtic forms which the Germans even now use, such as *platz, robes, sot, froit, feu, foyer, mantel.* Yet many seem twisted unnecessarily by them, as when Lazius sought the Franks from Phrygia: first Phrygians, then Frisians, afterwards Franci, then Bregkones, and Frianci, at length he reported that they were called Francs. The Cimbri were first Gomeri, then Gimri, then Cimri, afterwards Cimbri, at last Sicambri. The same author reported that the word *beccus,* used by Herodotus, meant "bread" in the Phrygian tongue, although a goat's bleat was produced by the child, who had never heard anything else.[30] We can believe more easily what is written in the *Franciade,* by Pierre Ronsard, my fellow citizen (the town of Vendôme is situated in the region of Anjou)—that Astyanax was called Frank by the ancients, as if φερεέγχον.

But the words which are German and sprung from German soil not only have a different meaning, but even a different pronunciation from the Gallic. For instance *bald* to the Germans means "light" and "quick," but we use the Celtic word *leger,* a name which once was given to a great river of Gaul, on Caesar's testimony. We never enunciate the particle *bald,* except with the diphthong *au.* Thus, what they call Gerbald, Thedobald, and Widbald, we on the other hand call Gerbaud, Thibaud, Widebaud. *Land* is old Celtic, which the Germans use for "region." For us *lande* means "uncultivated area," such as all Germany once was. Among them the names of regions are therefore Friesland, Grotland,

---

[30] See Herodotus *The History* II. 2. for the story of the infant brought up in isolation.

and so forth. Those words which among the Germans end in "ther," of course, are Celtic, such as Deither, Luther, Deiotarus, Lutharius, who, it is evident from the history of the Latins, were kings of the Galatii. In the same way, the regions and names of the winds which were given by the sailors, that is, east, west, north, south. From these the others [like north-west] are composed. That they are Celtic is apparent from the fact that wherever the Gauls have fixed their abode the regions are found to be distinguished by these words: for instance, North Wales and South Wales, of Britain, Westphalia, of Germany. West Germany is not found, or West Britain. Furthermore, we use Latin place names, that is, of the orient, occident, meridian, septentrional, so that it appears plain that the former are old.

Countless are the examples of this sort which each man can seek out according to his judgment and talent. Yet from these examples of words which we have produced from Athenaeus, Pausanias, Caesar, Pliny, and Diodorus, I think it is plain that the German language in great part is derived from the purest Celtic sources. But if this is so, it also follows that they owe their origin, arms, laws, and finally their culture to the Gauls. Lazius was gravely mistaken when he affirmed that our ancestors came from the Germans.

This evidence from linguistic remains indicates well enough that the Armorican Bretons are descendants of the Britons, because only those Britons who dwell in the narrow region of Wales understand the speech of the Bretons, as I have learned from the English. The combined authority of all historians also supports this view. But whence came these Welsh, if not from the Gauls? On this account many think that their language is the tongue of the ancient Celts. I do not dare to affirm this, since, of course, to me that language is unknown. Since in the time of Caesar the story was spread abroad by our ancestors that the inhabitants who hold the inmost recesses of Britain did not originate in Gaul, but were born in that island and are therefore indigenous, I have doubted whether this can be substantiated from the linguistic evidence. If we grant that it was first called Albion by the Albion Gauls, it follows that Britain (for thus Aristotle called it) was named by some other newcomers who had expelled the first settlers. Then, too, among the Cantabrians there is a word *breta* which means "earth." Hence Alphonso VII is called Abreta, because he always slept on the ground and came in contact with earth, as Tarafa the Spaniard wrote. For this reason it seems probable to me that the Britons had their origin from the Cantabrians, who, when first they saw the Island (as sailors are wont when land is seen) called it Britain. The Spanish, however, do not know that word. After the Saxons had expelled the Britons, they changed the language. They call the land by the same name by which the Germans, Goths, and northern peoples do, that is, by the Hebrew word *ertz*, although *barath* also means "field" to the Jews. I am convinced that they were sprung from the Cantabrians by the linguistic evidence, also by the very short stretch of sea, finally by the traditional belief of the inhabitants of the neighboring Hibernia, who say that they had the Hiberians (that is, the Spanish) as ancestors. But Hiberia seems to have been cultivated first by Africans, living near Spain, or certainly by Hiberians of Asia, whose ancient language differed only a little from the Hebrew, as men learned in that language have written. In the first place, the word Hiberi itself means nothing to the Greeks or the Latins. So the Greeks called them by the Jewish word Heberi, the Latins by the Greek word Hispani, that is, "few," because once they were handicapped by lack of men, even if Cicero called Spain crowded in his times.

Furthermore, the [name of the] largest river of Spain, which the inhabitants call Ebro, the Latins, Hiberus, and [the name of] the Bethis [31] seem to me to be derived from Palestine itself. Finally all writers of history report that the Secanians (who are called Sicani by the Greeks and Latins) came from Spain into Sicily and have given it their own name. But *secani* means nothing in the Greek or Latin tongue, while in Hebrew it means "inhabitants." I think the people of the Sequani, who dwelt in Burgundy and Sucana [32] (for thus Caesar called them, taught by the inhabitants) have their name from the same Sucanians. The idea of Josephus that the Spanish are descended from Jubal the son of Lamech, of course, is remote from probable conjecture, unless the reference is to his ultimate posterity, from Heber, the grandson of Shem, who was forefather of the forefather of Jacob, the parent of the Hebrews, and from his stock it is plain that countless other branches could arise.

Only the origins of that people whom alone God chose are explained in the Scriptures, not of the others. These origins can be understood from the stock of Israel himself, from whom the twelve tribes are derived by the Jewish interpreters. Thence have come the Arabs, who like the Jews have kept the ancient history of their race intact and have tribes defined by precise origins and names, as may be seen in the pages

---

[31] Guadalquivir.   [32] Soissons.

of Leo the African. Although I think it is sufficiently evident that all peoples have for a long time been so intermingled in the numerous colonies, wars, captivities, and wanderings that none except the Jews could isolate themselves from the intermixture of other peoples. This is easy to understand, if anyone remembers that the Vandals and the Goths led colonies from the farthest shore of the north into Africa; the Arabs, into Persia, Syria, Africa, Italy, and Spain; the Spanish, into America and India; French and Italians, into Asia and even Scythia.

There are four reasons for sending out colonies: either the inhabitants have been driven out by the strength of the enemy and have sought other homes, as the Trojans, after the overthrow of their city, went into Latium, or as the Etruscans, who are also called Tusci, driven from Italy by the Gauls, led colonies into Rhetia, whence the first name for the Germans was Tusci. So, also, a colony of Egyptians under their leader Danaus went into Greece; the Normans, into France; the Britons, driven by the Angles, to the Celtic shore; men of Phocaea, disturbed by the tyranny of the prefect of the Persian king, moved their abode into Celtica, as Justin wrote, and set up the most flourishing state of all which have ever existed, on the affirmation of Tully. Canaanites, driven by the Jews from the plain of Palestine, sailed into Illyricum and Pannonia, as Rabbi David Kimhi averred at the end of his commentary on Obadja. The Vandals, driven by the arms of the Franks, fled into Spain; driven thence by the Goths, they crossed into Africa. Not so long ago the Rhodians, defeated by the Turks, migrated into Crete. Of this migration there is an infinite number of illustrations in the pages of Pausanias and Strabo.

Another kind of colony is due to surplus population, lack of arable land, or intemperate climate. In 570 Miletus sent people in different directions, as Seneca wrote in the book "To Helvia on Consolation." The same man says "An Athenian throng is in Asia." That whole shore of Italy which is watered by the lower sea was Greater Greece. Asia claimed the Tusci for itself. The Tyrians inhabited Africa; in Spain were the Carthaginians; the Greeks were settled in Gaul; the Gauls, in Greece. The Pyrenees did not prevent the crossing of the Germans. Some, exhausted by long wandering, did not select a site wisely, said he, but from very weariness seized upon the nearest. Some by force of arms won for themselves possessions in a strange land; the ruin of their own cities sent out others to spend their excess strength; domestic strife, still others; the press of a superabundant population, or pestilence, or frequent earthquakes, or unendurable poverty of the soil drove forth many. Some other cause drove others from their homes. Certain people settled where lack of supplies had left them. The sea engulfed certain other peoples when they sought the unknown. A little later [Seneca said] what need to mention Antenor, the founder of Padua, and Evander, who founded a kingdom on the banks of the Tiber? How many colonies did the Roman people send into all provinces? The Roman was dwelling everywhere. The wandering colonists freely gave names to places. You will find hardly any land which indigenous peoples now cultivate. At last Seneca concluded in this fashion: it is manifest that no one remained in the same place where he was born.[33]

This migration of the human race is constant; daily they lay foundations of new cities, new names of races arise from earlier ones, extinct or altered. Yet I see the Scythians almost always betook themselves with countless legions from the north into the middle regions. Cimbri and scattered bands of their descendants, Advatici, Nemetes, Ubii, Tungii, Vangiones, Sicambrians, Saxons, Goths, Lombards, Gepidae, Vandals, Pictones, and Normans, Olaus even adds Getae, Alani, Heruli, Huns, Turcilingui, Winuli, Rugii, and Sueci (who now are called Swiss) invaded Europe from Scandinavia. Moreover, Procopius and Albert Krantz report that the Slavs from the same Scandinavia burst into Pannonia in the time of Justinian. Afterwards that race filled all Europe with the fame of its name and tongue. I hear that Poles, Bohemians, Russians, Lithuanians, Muscovites, Bosnians, Bulgarians, Serbians, Croatians, Dalmatians, and Vandals use the same language the Slavs used in Scandinavia and differ only in dialect. Likewise, the Parthians, the Turks, and the Tartars take their origin from the Asiatic peoples of Scythia.

The third kind of colony is undertaken for the sake of extending and protecting the dominion. The Romans used this most effectively, both that they might free the state from domestic sedition and also that they might retain the loyalty and obedience of the conquered peoples. This is one reason why they extended their empire so far and wide. In the same way the Genoese led into the Crimea the colony of Theodosia, which is called Capha. The Venetians led forth colonies into the islands; the Spanish, into America and the Indies.

The last kind of colony is penal, for instance, the transporting of ten tribes of Jews into Chaldea, to be followed eighty years afterwards by

[33] Seneca "To Helvia on Consolation" vii *passim.*

the remainder. The ten tribes are reported to have been scattered hither and thither in Asia. The tribes Judah and Benjamin obtained permission to return into the fatherland. Six hundred years thereafter they were again reduced to servitude by the Romans and spread over the whole world from the farthest shores of Europe and Scythia into Africa and all Asia. They serve as an example that all peoples are intermingled in innumerable colonies, because this one race today also seems to have scattered into Chaldea, Parthia, India, Gaul, Greece, Italy, Spain, Germany, and Africa. What of the Romans? They propagated their colonies, arms, and legions from Oenopolis even to the Danube, from Britain even into Persia. Then the peoples of Italy are mixed and blended from Arcadians, Trojans, Sicanians, Gauls, Greeks, Goths, Huns, Vandals, Heruli, Lombards, Carthaginians, and Normans. Thus we see that it was not without admirable foresight that the Jewish people, who suffered the violence and tyranny of the cruelest of all princes, alone retained the antiquity of their race.

But the powerful king of Ethiopia derives from that same people the splendor of his race and calls himself and his relatives Israelites. It may seem even more remarkable that from these people flow as from a fountain the religions which are accepted by the whole world.

Since we see this people scattered over all the earth, what must be thought of the other races? The fecundity of nature is such that in a short time we observe countless numbers are procreated from the stock of one man. Justin left a quotation from Trogus Pompey that Herotinus, the king of the Parthians, begot six hundred sons. The progeny of Jacob alone grew into countless legions within two hundred years. One legion of Turks, which the Persians summoned against the Arabs, increased rapidly into such a multitude of men that the Arabs, trying in vain to drive them out, yielded to them their own scepter and power. Likewise, the migration of the Tartars into Asia Minor under the leadership of Tamerlane mixed the tribes of Asiatics and Turks. Why do I commemorate what will seem incredible to posterity, the fusion of Circassians with Egyptians, of Spanish with Americans, of Portuguese with Indians, or the relationship of Goths and Vandals with Spanish and Africans? From these illustrations, then, it is understood that all men for a long time have been so fused in migrations and also in the teeming colonial populations, as well as in wars and captivity, that none can boast about the antiquity of their origin and the great age of their race except the Jews.

Those princes seem to me to be gravely mistaken who trace the dignity of their noble rank from earliest times or hope that it will be everlasting. The stock of Aeacus and Heracles, which was most famous among the Greeks, or the Julian among the Latins, did not last longer than twelve hundred years. The other patrician families—Potitii, Pinarii, Geganii, Sergii, Cornelii, Fabii, Manilii, Aemilii, Curiatii, and Claudii —hardly attained eight hundred. So it was necessary for Caesar to enroll among the patricians both new men and those from official families. The Darii flourished for two hundred years; the Arsacidae, about six hundred; the Ottomans, for three hundred. The Spanish princes claim the highest degree of nobility from the Goths, who in the opinion of everyone are reckoned barbarians. The house of Austria has control of Italians, Spanish, and Germans, deriving from the counts of Hapsburg the splendor of their race. They are entirely ignorant concerning the condition of their family before Rudolph, the father of Albert—that is, three hundred years ago. The very ancient Saxon house cannot discover an ancestor earlier than six hundred years ago—that is, before Otto, the father of Henry the Fowler. Then the race of Merovingians, who laid the foundations of this empire, ceased after the four-hundredth year. The race of Charles the Great became extinct in Charles, duke of Lorraine, after two hundred years. Now the Capets rule, risen from Widukind the Saxon. He was brought into Gaul and trained in the Christian religion by Charles the Great, and created count of Anjou; or, as others think, left descendants of his race, from Otto his brother—a race most famous in glorious deeds and the most ancient of all now in Europe. From Widukind a little less than eight hundred years are counted. The princes of the Normans and the Angles ceased in Henry I; of Anjou, in Richard III. The line of Henry VII, in Edward VI. Of Lancaster and York no males remain. The first kings of Scotland end in Alexander III; the Bruce, in David II; the Stuarts, in James V; the Castilians, in Henry III; the Aragonese, in Ferdinand V; the Swedes, Danes, and Norwegians, in Margaret, the daughter of Waldemar; the kingdoms of Pomeranus and of Bavarus seem to have become extinct before they were created. The Aldeburgers followed, who now hold control of Denmark. The father of Gustavus, starting as a private citizen, not so long ago got control of Sweden, and not much more lasting in the rule over Pannonia was the race of Stephan, to whom Charles of Anjou, king of Naples, succeeded. Then came Otto of Bavaria; then Sigismund of Luxembourg, whose house Mathias Corvinus succeeded, the first and the last of his race called king. But the kings of Poland seek their antiquity no farther back than Pyast, a peasant, whose posterity, however, ruled for barely six hundred years. The Jagellons, from the dukes of Lithuania, succeeded them, yet they could not compare with the Pyasts in antiquity or in glorious deeds. The Venetians, in truth, are wont to claim for themselves the nobility of Italy. Yet the most eminent of them, tracing his origin from the earliest times, cannot recall his ancestor earlier than seven hundred years ago. The next after them are the Colonna, the Orsini, the Savelli, and the Petilii, the remains of Roman nobility, to which neither the Estes nor the Gonzagas can be compared. The Medici glory, not in the antiquity of race, but in valor. It is sufficiently evident that the patricians in all the towns of Italy which flourished under a popular government have either been most cruelly slaughtered or driven away, abandoning their property.

In Gaul and Spain, in truth, the most ancient race of all is believed to be the Leva, on the authority of the famous Francis Vallesio, who is said to have investigated the origins of patricians. Yet the Leva trace their stock to the Levites, as the kings of the Abyssinians to the Israelites, for thus they call the nobles. Yet they do not precisely define the source of their own people, nor does Alvarez contribute anything. Therefore, only the Jews excel all peoples in the certainty of their antiquity, yet not one can now trace his tribe. All, blended together, acknowledge the stock, but are ignorant of the branchings. It is true that a race of priests which claimed the loftiest glory of nobility from Aaron and flourished for two thousand, three hundred years is believed to have died in the disasters of the Goths and the Vandals, not without marked evidence of divine vengeance.

CHAPTER X

THE ORDER AND COLLECTION OF HISTORIANS

ONE MUST START from the shortest chronicles, for example, of Bullinger, Luther, and the like; then to chronologies, that is, of Funck, Phrygio, and Eusebius; hence we come to histories somewhat more diffuse, such as those of Carion, Melanchthon, and Peucer; at last to the finished history of each period, embracing all subjects, or all the most illustrious.

Writers of Universal History

Moses, the book of origins embraces the history of the world for two thousand four hundred and fifty years, from the Creation to the migration of the Jews out of Egypt into Palestine.
Fl. 1519 B.C.

Berosus the Chaldean, Fragments of universal history, as they are called, from the Creation to the year of this world 3130. He ceased with Sardanapalus, as Megasthenes writes.
Fl. 330 B.C.

Herodotus of Halicarnassus, nine books concerning the deeds of the Greeks, Egyptians, Medes, Persians, and Lydians, from the year of the Creation 3210 up to 3500.
Fl. 425 B.C.

Polybius the Megalopolitan, concerning the affairs of the Greeks, Romans, Carthaginians, and Celts, from the exile of Cleomenes and Pyrrhus, king of the Epirotes, to the war of the Romans with the Achaeans and Philip, king of the Macedonians: that is, from the year 3630 of the Creation to the 3766th. From forty books the first five are extant, and an epitome of the following up to the fifteenth.
Fl. 200 B.C.

Trogus Pompey, epitome by Justin, included in forty-four books covering briefly the deeds of almost all peoples from Ninus to Caesar Augustus.
Fl. A.D. 150

Diodorus of Sicily, The Library of universal history, chiefly of famous peoples, from the earliest memories of the Egyptians to Caesar. Of forty books, fifteen are extant.
Fl. A.D. 40

Philo the Jew, two books concerning events from the Creation to Tiberius. Fl. A.D. 38

Eusebius, chronicle from the Creation to the year of Christ 300. Fl. 312

    Jerome added fifty years, Fl. 340
    Prosper of Aquitaine sixty,
    Palmieri of Florence 1040,
    Palmieri of Pisa, thirty.

Julius Africanus, concerning events from the Creation up to the year of Christ 320. [As re-arranged by Eusebius?] [Fl. 221]

Freculph, epitome of histories from the Creation to the year of Christ 550. Fl. 560 [830]

Bede the Englishman, chronicle from the Creation to the year of Christ 700. Fl. 730

Ado of Vienne, concerning the six ages of the world to the year of Christ 900. Fl. 980

Helmand [Helinand?], chronicle from the Creation to his own times. Fl. 1066

Hermann Contract, the Swiss, about the six ages to his own time. Fl. 1067

Marianus of Fulda, a Scot, chronicle from the Creation to his own time. Fl. 1088

Zonaras, a combined history from the Creation up to the year of Christ 117, divided into three parts; the first part is of the Jews, the second of the Greeks, the third of the Latins. Fl. 1120

Honorius of Autun, chronicle from the Creation to his own times. Fl. 1120

Sigebert the Gaul, chronicle from the year of Christ 381, that is, from the end of the tripartite history, to the year 1113, with appendix of uncertain authorship to the year 1216. Fl. 1130

The Abbot of Ursperg, chronicle from the Creation to Emperor Frederick II. Fl. 1219

Vincent of Beauvais, history from the Creation to the year of Christ 1250. Fl. 1260

Antonine, Archbishop of Florence, combined history from the Creation to the year of Christ 1470. Fl. 1480

Fascicule of the times from the Creation to the year 1484 of uncertain authorship.

Antonius Coccius Sabellicus, eleven Enneades of history Fl. 1490 from the Creation, and corresponding to these the synopsis of Caspar Heid.

Donato Bosso of Milan, history from the Creation to the year 1489. — Fl. 1496

John Nauclerus of Tübingen, chronicle from the Creation to the year of Christ 1500. — Fl. 1510

Philip of Bergamo, history from the Creation to the year of Christ 1503. — Fl. 1515

Martin Luther, the Saxon, sequence of years of the world up to his own age. — Fl. 1519

Achilles Gasser, epitome of chronicles of the world, from the Creation to the year of Christ 1530. — Fl. 1530

Paul Constantine Phrygio, chronicle from the Creation to the year 1523. — Fl. 1540

John Carion of Lübeck, three books of chronicles from the Creation to the year of Christ 1530 to which is added an appendix to the year 1555. — Fl. 1550

Philip Melanchthon, chronicle included in three books taken in great part from Carion himself, to Charles the Great. — Fl. 1540

Gaspar Peucer, chronicle from Charles the Great, where Melanchthon left off, to his own age. — Fl. 1550

Paul Jovius, the history of almost all peoples of his time from the year of Christ 1494 to the year 1540. — Fl. 1540

Henry Bullinger, chronicle from the Creation to his own age. — Fl. 1545

John Funck, the Prussian, chronology from the Creation to the year of Christ 1553. — Fl. 1550

Mercator, chronology. — Fl. 1570

Universal "Geographistorians"

Strabo of Cappadocia, sixteen books, in which he unites the brief history of all peoples with geography. — Fl. 20 B.C.

Pomponius Mela, the Spaniard, about the position of the world along with the history of the peoples. — Fl. in the time of Christ.

Pausanias of Caesarea, the Grammarian, affairs of Athens, Corinth, Laconia, Messenia, Elis, Achaia, Arcadia, Boeotia, and Phocis. — Fl. A.D. 140

Raphael Volaterranus, thirty-eight books in which he included universal history with geography. — Fl. A.D. 1500

Munster, cosmography, embracing histories and origins,   Fl. A.D. 1540
along with the description of the regions.

To this can be joined historians of various matters, such
as Athenaeus, Aelian, Tzetzes, Leonicus, Solinus, Valerius Maximus, Pliny, Suidas.

*After the History of the Universe the Ecclesiastical Writers May Appropri-
ately Be Added, and the History of Those Sects Which Established and
Retained Power, and Especially about the Religion, Antiquities, and Deeds
of the Jews*

The Holy Bible.

Philo the Jew, who can be called a "philosophistorian,"   Fl. A.D. 38
all the writings.

Flavius Josephus the Jew, twenty books of Jewish An-   Fl. A.D. 99
tiquities and seven books about the Jewish War.

Josephus, the son of Gorion, History of the Jewish War,   Fl. A.D. 99
written in Hebrew.

Hegesippus, the history of the Jews from the Maccabees   Fl. A.D. 130
to the year of Christ 72.

Historians of Pagan Superstition

Irenaeus, the bishop of Lyons, one book against the pagans.   Fl. A.D. 75
         [175]

Clement, bishop of Alexandria, eight books of miscellane-   Fl. A.D. 200
ous writings.

Arnobius, seven books against the pagans.   Fl. 300

Lactantius Firmianus, about false religion, and his com-   Fl. 320
plete works.

Paul Orosius, seven books against the pagans.   Fl. 1515
         [415]

Lilio Giraldi, about the gods of all peoples.   Fl. 1550

John Caules, a book in French [or] Italian, about the   [1150 in
religion of the ancients.   ed. 1595]

Historians of the Christian Religion

The New Testament

Justin Martyr, Apology   Fl. A.D. 120

Q. Septimius Tertullian of Carthage, apology for the faith.   Fl. 150

Irenaeus, bishop of Lyons, five books against heretics.   Fl. 175

Origen, the book about martyrs.   Fl. 260

Eusebius, ten books of ecclesiastical history.   Fl. 312

Socrates, Sozomenus, Theodoret, and Cassiodorus, ecclesi-   Fl. 400

astical history from the birth of Christ to the year 454.

Gennadius, the presbyter of Marseilles, the book about famous ecclesiastics.   Fl. 496

Evagrius, the Scholastic, six books about the Roman Church and Empire, from the year of Christ 435 to the year 595. He starts where the tripartite history ends.   Fl. 610

Nicephorus Callistus, eighteen books of ecclesiastical history from Christ to Heraclius.   Fl. 1100

Marcellinus, Count, a history from the times of Eusebius to the year of Christ 500.   Fl. 700

John William, archbishop of Tyre, twenty-three books about the Crusades.   Fl. 1150

John Foxe, the Englishman, ecclesiastical history from Wycliffe to the year of Christ 1552.   Fl. 1555

State of the Church of uncertain authorship from the birth of Christ to the year of Christ 1560.

John Sleidan, ecclesiastical history, from the year of Christ 1517 to the year 1555.   Fl. 1548

The Magdeburg history, twelve centuries, from the birth of Christ to the year 1200, in which are fully explained the writings on ecclesiastical history of all the ancients.

About the state of religion and of the Church under the Kings Henry II, Francis II, and Charles IX, of uncertain authorship. French.

Historians of the Arab Sect

Coran or Furcan, collected from all the Korans which were collected in the name of Mohammed in the 110th year after Mohammed.   Fl. 600

Historians of the Chaldeans, Assyrians, Medes, Egyptians, Persians, Phoenicians, Jews, Parthians, Whose Deeds Are Covered by Almost the Same Writers

The Books of Kings, the Books of Chronicles, and of Esdras.

Herodotus of Halicarnassus, nine books of histories.   Fl. 445

Ctesias of Cnidos, Agatharchides, and Mennon, fragments about the kings of the Persians and of the Assyrians.   Fl. 375 A.D. [B.C.]

Xenophon, the Athenian, about the expedition of Cyrus (whose lieutenant he was) into Persia.   Fl. 370 B.C.

Berosus, the Chaldean priest, the so-called Fragments, included in five books.   Fl. 340 B.C. [280]

Megasthenes, the Persian, a book about judging times and the annals of the Persians.	Fl. 330 B.C.
Manetho, the Egyptian priest, the so-called Fragments, about the kings of almost all peoples.	Fl. 330 B.C. [250]
Josephus, two books against Apion the Grammarian, and twenty of Jewish Antiquities.	Fl. A.D. 99
Hegesippus, one book about the Parthian War.	Fl. 130
Appian, Parthicus.	Fl. 140
Procopius, two books about the Persian War.	Fl. 540

Historians of the Greeks, under Which Names Come the Ionians, Aeolians, Dorians, Who Settled Asia Minor and Europe from the Danube, the Acrocераunians, and Mt. Haemus, to the Ionic Sea, on the Islands and on the Continent

Dictys of Crete, six books about the Trojan War, converted into Latin from the Carthaginian tongue by Q. Septimius.	Fl. 1129 B.C.
Dares of Phrygia, six books about the Trojan War, translated from Greek into Latin song by Cornelius Nepos.	Fl. 1129 B.C.
Herodotus of Halicarnassus, nine books, where he deals here and there with the Greeks, up to the flight of Xerxes, embracing the history of 211 years.	Fl. 425 B.C.
Thucydides, the Athenian, eight books, in which he has written the history of 90 years, from the flight of Xerxes, to the twenty-second year of the Peloponnesian War.	Fl. 340 B.C. [400]
Xenophon, the Athenian, seven books in which he follows the narrative of Thucydides about the things that happened in Greece in 43 years, to the battle of the Spartans and the Thebans at Mantinea.	Fl. 310 B.C. [360]
Megasthenes, Theopompus, Philostratus, Hellanicus, Timaeus, Acusilaus, Ephorus, Mochus, Estiaeus, Jerome, Isidore, and Nicolaus of Damascus, have written consecutive histories, as may be observed in the pages of Plutarch, but their writings have completely vanished.	
George Gemistus, two books, in which the history of Xenophon is prolonged in a continued series from Plutarch and Diodorus, from the battle of Mantinea to the defeat at Chaeronea.	Fl. 1520
Diodorus of Sicily, the sixteenth book follows the continued narrative of Gemistus about the deeds of Philip and Alexander the Great.	Fl. 40 B.C.

Polybius, the second, fourth, and fifth books, with epitome of the following, and the fourth decade of Livy, with fragments of the fifth decade covering the affairs of the Greeks, which occurred under the successors of Alexander.	Fl. 200 B.C. [150]
Plutarch's lives of Aratus, Philopoemen, and Demetrius contribute a great deal to the understanding of later histories of the Greeks.	Fl. A.D. 120
Procopius, seven books of deeds under Justinian.	Fl. 540
John Zonaras, the third volume, from Constantine the Great to the death of Alexius Comnenus, that is, from the year of Christ 300 to 1113.	Fl. 1120
Anna, the daughter of Alexius, twenty books of the deeds of her father Alexius the Emperor, in which she continues the narrative of Zonaras.	Fl. 1130
Nicephorus Gregoras, the history of a hundred and forty-five years from Theodore Lascaris to Andronicus Palaeologue the Younger.	Fl. 1280
Nicetas Acominatus of Chone, the history of eighty-six years from the year in which Zonaras ceased to the death of Murzufulus the Emperor, that is, to the year 1203, in nineteen books.	Fl. 1460

Historians of the Romans and Carthaginians, and of Italian Affairs Generally

Fasti Consulares restored by Charles Sigonius and Panvinio.	Fl. 1560
Sextus Rufus, of consular rank, epitome about the deeds of the Romans from the founding of the City to the Emperor Valentinian.	Fl. 450
Florus, epitome of Livy.	Fl. 200
Velleius Paterculus, the proconsul, two books on the general history of the Roman people.	Fl. 210 [30]
Eutropius the Presbyter, ten books about the deeds of the Romans.	Fl. 370
Q. Fabius Pictor, two books about the origin of the city of Rome.	Fl. 280 B.C.
M. Cato, the so-called fragments from his Origins.	Fl. 260 B.C. [184]
Polybius, the sixth book about the military and civil system of the Romans.	Fl. 280 B.C. [150]
Dionysius of Halicarnassus, eleven books.	Fl. 280 B.C. [35 in ed. 1572]

C. Sallust, two books about the Jugurthine and Catalinian wars.	Fl. 35 B.C. [45 in ed. 1572]
Polybius, the first and third books, with epitome of the following.	
Xiphilinus the Patriarch, epitome of Dio.	Fl. 54 B.C. [A.D. 1070 in ed. 1572]
Dio Cassius, twenty-three books which have been preserved from eighty about the deeds of the Romans.	Fl. 1070 [215 B.C. in ed. 1572]
C. Caesar, three books about the Civil Wars.	Fl. 34 B.C. [43 in ed. 1572 and 1595]
Appian, five books of the Civil Wars.	Fl. 215 [145]
T. Livy of Padua, forty-five books, which remain from one hundred and forty-four, from the founding of the City to Augustus.	Fl. 120 B.C. [35 in ed. 1572]
Cornelius Tacitus, annals from Augustus, where Livy ceases, to Nerva, twenty-six which remain from twenty-one (sic).	Fl. 120 B.C. [A.D.]
Ammianus Marcellinus, knight, of Constantinople, eighteen books which have survived from thirty-one. He started from Nerva, where Tacitus left off. He ceased with Valens. The rest Eutropius can supply. Then also the separate histories of the princes, of Suetonius, Cassius, Spartianus, Capitolinus, Vopiscus, Herodian, Lampridius, and Egnatius.	Fl. A.D. 360
Prosper of Aquitaine, a continuation of Roman history, from the year 382 to 447, when the City was taken by King Genseric.	Fl. 480
Procopius, twelve books of affairs under Justinian, which ought to be used with the above.	Fl. 1130 [530]
Aeneas Sylvius, twelve books of affairs in Italy in his times.	Fl. 1420
Flavius Blondus of Forli, secretary of Pope Eugene, thirty books from the decline of the empire to his own times, and ten books about Rome triumphant and Italy illustrated.	Fl. 1440
Niccolò Machiavelli, history of the Florentines, from the year of Christ 1215 to 1494.	Fl. 1500
F. Guicciardini, the history of Italy, from the year 1494 to the year 1536.	Fl. 1520

Joannes Pontanus, about the Neapolitan war.	Fl. 1490
Pandulph Collenuccio, about the kingdom of Naples, from Augustus to Charles V, emperor.	Fl. 1540
Michael Coccinius of Tübingen, about the Italian Wars.	Fl. 1540
Galleazzo Capella, about the Italian Wars under Charles V.	Fl. 1540
M. Antonius Coccius Sabellicus, thirty-three books of the history of Venice.	Fl. 1490
P. Bembo, twelve books of the history of Venice.	Fl. 1540

Historians of the Celts or Gauls, and of the Franks; under This Name Come All Peoples Who Are Surrounded by the Rhine, the Pyrenees, the Alps, and Both Seas

Julius Caesar, seven books about the Gallic War, and the continuation by Hirtius.	Fl. 43 B.C.
Hunibald, eighteen books about the Franks whom he traces from the Trojan War to the death of Antenor in the six earlier books; in the following six to Waramund; then he ends in the times of Clovis.	Fl. 500 B.C. [A.D.]
Appian, Celticus; or, about the Gallic War.	Fl. 1550 [155]
Jean du Tillet, Parisian, epitome of histories, from Waramund to Henry II.	Fl. 1550
Hubert Leonard, one book about the origin of the Franks.	Fl. 1490
Paul Aemilius of Verona, a history of the Franks from Waramund to Charles VIII.	Fl. 1530
Jean Le Feron, Frenchman, histories of the successive kings to Francis.	[Fl. 1540; see *infra*, p. 379]
Johann Trithenius, German, about the deeds of the Franks, from the year 433 B.C. to the year 1500 A.D.	[Fl. 1500; in ed. 1572]
Gaguin, history to Charles VIII.	[Fl. 1497]
Nicholas Gilles, the annals of the Franks.	Fl. 1500
Bochet, the annals of Aquitaine.	[?]
Count Herman, about the affairs of the Franks to the year 1525.	Fl. 1530
Aemund, concerning the dukes of Burgundy, Flanders, Brabant, and Holland, from the Trojan War to Emperor Charles V.	Fl. 1520
Beyssel, concerning the deeds of the Flemings.	[?]
Jean Lemaire, history of the Belgians.	Fl. 1480
Annals of Burgundy of an unknown author.	

William Paradinus, one book concerning the ancient state   Fl. 1555
of Burgundy.

Gregory, bishop of Tours, ten books of the history of the   Fl. 630
Franks from their origin to the year of Christ 600.

Antony the Monk, five books about the kings of the Franks,   Fl. 830
from the year of Christ 420 to the year 826.

Rupert, ten books concerning the deeds of the Gauls   Fl. 1120
against the Saracens.

Froissart, history of the wars of the French and the Eng-   Fl. 1420
lish from the year of Christ 1335 to the year 1499.

Enguerrand de Monstrelet, history of the subsequent years,   Fl. 1500
to Louis XII.   [1450]

Philippe de Comines, history from the year of Christ 1462   Fl. 1488
to the coronation of Louis XII, continuing Monstrelet.

Galleazzo Capella, concerning wars waged in Italy be-   Fl. 1530
tween Charles V and Francis, king of the French.

William Paradinus, history of the following years to the   Fl. 1555
year of Christ 1555.

Rabutinus, concerning the expedition of Henry against   [Fl. 1556, in
Charles V in the year of Christ 1552, undertaken in   ed. 1572 and
behalf of the liberty of the princes of the Germans.   1595]

*Historians of the Germans and of All Peoples Who Dwell from the Alps to
the Baltic Sea, and from the Rhine to the Vistula; to Which is Added the
History of the Goths, Vandals, Huns, Heruli, Helvetians, Lombards,
Poles, Muscovites, Danes, and Swedes*

AT THE BEGINNING ARE MENTIONED THOSE WHO HAVE WRITTEN ABOUT
ALL THE GERMANS GENERALLY; THEN ABOUT THE SEPARATE PEOPLES.

Cornelius Tacitus, the little book concerning the customs   Fl. A.D. 120
of the Germans, explained by the commentaries of Alt-
hamer.

Beatus Rhenanus of Schlettstadt, three books of German   Fl. 1500
affairs.

Jacob Wimpheling, the epitome of German affairs.   Fl. 1549

Francis Irenicus Helingiacensis, twelve books of German   Fl. 1519
exegesis.

Huldreich Mutius Hugwaldus, thirty-one books about the   Fl. 1551
first origin of the Germans, customs, institutions, laws,
and memorable deeds in war and peace.

Johannes Aventinus, explanation of German affairs, in-   Fl. 1510
cluded in ten books.

Munster, Cosmographia, or rather Germanographia. Fl. 1550

The Abbot of Ursperg, whose name is unknown, chronicle from the Creation to Frederick II. He wrote very fully on German affairs, on the rest very briefly.

Lupold, the bishop of Bamberg, about the zeal of the early leaders of the Romans for religion. Fl. 1340

AUSTRIA

Chronicle of the dukes of Bavaria and Suabia of uncertain authorship.

Wolfgang Lazius of Vienna, history of Austria, included in four books. [Fl. 1550]

Ricciardo Bartolini of Perugia, twelve books of Austrian affairs. Fl. 1500

HUNGARY

John of Thurocz, Hungarian, chronicle of Hungary in three books. [Fl. 1500]

Melchior Soiterus, about the Pannonian war. Fl. 1530

Antonio Bonfini of Ascoli, thirty books of Hungarian affairs up to Matthias Corvinus. Fl. 1440

POLAND

Chronicle of the Poles

Martin Cromer, thirty books about the affairs of the Poles. Fl. 1552

Philip Callimachus, Polish history against the Turks (*sic*) [Fl. 1475]

SLAVONIA

Helmold, presbyter, history of the Slavs from Charles the Great to Frederick Barbarossa. [Fl. 1177]

DENMARK AND SWEDEN, OR GOTHIA

Chronicle of uncertain authorship about the origin of the Franks, Vandals, Goths, and Burgundians.

Albert Krantz, the history of Denmark, Norway, Sweden, which is called Gothia and Scandia, from their origins to the year 1504. Fl. 1520

Olaus Magnus, Goth, prince and Christian priest, twenty-two books concerning the affairs of the Goths. Fl. 1530

Saxo Grammaticus, sixteen books about the history of the Danes. [Fl. 1203]

Procopius, three books about the wars of the Goths. Fl. 530

Agathias of Smyrna, five books about the wars of the Goths.	Fl. 550
Idacius, chronicle from Theodosius the Great to the year of Christ 400.	Fl. 410
Sidonius Apollinaris, a Gaul, who was famous among the men of Toulouse at the court of the Goths under king Alaric, various narratives of deeds by the Goths.	Fl. 470
Jordanes, the bishop of the Goths, two books about the wars of the Goths and the Romans.	Fl. 540
Aurelius Cassiodorus, passages about the deeds of the Goths and the Romans.	Fl. 575
Leonardo of Aretino about the war of the Goths.	Fl. 1420

LOMBARDY

Paul the Deacon, the chancellor of King Desiderius, six books about the affairs of the Lombards.	Fl. 780

SAXONY

Albert Krantz, the history of the Saxons.	Fl. 1520
Widukind, the Saxon, three books about the affairs of the Saxons.	Fl. 950
Three books about the Saxon War, of uncertain authorship.	
Sebastian Boisseliner, about the siege of Magdeburg.	Fl. 1560

LÜBECK

Five books of chronicles of Lübeck.

PRUSSIA

Erasmus Stella, the antiquities of Prussia.	[Fl. 1500]

NETHERLANDS

Gerard of Nimwegen, history of Batavia.	Fl. 1530

BOHEMIA

Aeneas Silvius, Bohemian history.	Fl. 1416
John Dubravius, Bohemian history.	[Fl. 1550]

SWITZERLAND, OR HELVETIA

John Stumpf of Zurich, history of the Helvetians included in three tomes. In German.

Idem; the epitome of the whole history of Joseph Simler.

ORDER AND COLLECTION OF HISTORIANS

Historians of the Britons, Who Afterwards Were Called
Anglo-Saxons and Scots

Gildas, a Briton, historian of the Angles.	[Fl. 550]
George Lily, Englishman, chronicle from Hengist, that is, from the year of Christ 600 to the year 1560.	Fl. 1560
Ponticus Vitruvius Tarvisinus, six books of British history.	Fl. 1520
Polydore Vergil of Urbino, twenty-six books of English history.	[Fl. 1530, in ed. 1572]
Bede, an Englishman, five books of the histories of the Anglo-Saxons, to his own age.	Fl. 732
Geoffrey Arthur, an Englishman, eight books about British affairs.	[? 1150]
Hector Boetius, history of the Scots.	Fl. 689 [1550?]
Nicholas Trivet, Englishman, English annals from the counts of Anjou, that is, from the year of Christ 1135 to 1307.	Fl. 1420 [d. 1328]

Historians of the Spanish

Francis Tarafa, a Spaniard, a brief epitome of all the histories and kings of Spain from the Creation to Emperor Charles V.	Fl. 1530
Chronicles of Spain of Peter Antonio, in Spanish and Italian.	
Appian, Hiberica.	[Fl. 140]
Roderick Valentinus, about the affairs of Spain, in Spanish.	Fl. 200
Peter of Medina, about the affairs of Spain, in Spanish.	[d. 1567]
Maria, a Sicilian, Aragonese history.	
Antony of Lebrija, about the deeds of Ferdinand.	Fl. 1494
Jacob Bracellus, five books about the Spanish War.	Fl. 1496
Charles Verardus, about the siege of the kingdom of Granada, and the Betic history of the same man.	Fl. 1468
Damian Goes, about the deeds of the Lusitanians in India.	Fl. 1510

Historians of the Arabs, Who Once Held Control of Africa, Syria, Persia,
and Spain, Commonly Known as Saracens

Leo the African, the "Geographistorian," accurate description of all the regions and peoples of Africa.	Fl. 1510
Herman Dalmata, chronicle of the Saracens.	
Rupert the Monk, eight books about the war against the Saracens.	Fl. 1187

William, archbishop of Tyre, twenty-three books about the Crusades.   Fl. 1150

Historians of the Turks

Andrea Cambini, about the origin of the Turks, in Italian.

William Postel Barentonius, three books about the customs, religion, and state of the Turks, in French.   Fl. 1150 [1550 in ed. 1572]

An arrangement of the administration of the Turks by an unknown author.

Leonicus Calcondila, history of Turkish affairs.   Fl. 1490

Christopher Richer Torignaeus, five books of the affairs of the Turks.   Fl. 1530

Martin Barlet, about the resistance to the Turks and the life of Scanderbeg, the king of the Epirotes, included in thirteen books.   Fl. 1488

Paul Jovius, Books 12, 13, 14, 15, 16, 17, 32, 33, 34, 35, 36, 37.   Fl. 1540

Henry of Penia, about wars waged between Ishmael and Selim.

Historians of the Tartars and the Muscovites

Hayton of Armenia, one book of history of the Tartars.   Fl. 1290

Marco Polo, three books about oriental regions and the empire of the Tartars.   Fl. 1280

Matthias of Miechow, two books about Sarmatia, Asiatic and European, in which the history of the Tartars and Muscovites is briefly contained.

Paul Jovius, of Como, Book I about the embassy of the Muscovites.   Fl. 1540

Historians of the Ethiopians, Indians, Americans, and Almost All the Peoples of Africa

Leo the African, nine books of description of Africa, in Italian and in French.   Fl. 1500

Francis Alvarez, description of Ethiopia, in Spanish, Italian, and in French.   Fl. 1496

Aloysius Cadamustus, journey to the new lands.   Fl. 1504

Christopher Columbus of Genoa, journey to islands hitherto unknown.   Fl. 1512

Peter Aloysius, the journey.

Albert Vespucci, epitome of journeys.   Fl. 1510

Amerigo Vespucci, four journeys.   Fl. 1497

Joseph, the Indian, journeys.   Fl. 1500

Louis, a Roman patrician, seven books of journeys to Ethi-   Fl. 1515
opia, Egypt, and both Arabias, on the hither and further
sides of the Ganges.

Paul Jovius, Book XVIII.   Fl. 1540

*After the Histories Common to All Peoples and Those Which Are Peculiar to
Each State Follows the Separate History of Illustrious Men*

FIRST ABOUT ILLUSTRIOUS MEN OF ALL PEOPLES; AFTERWARDS ABOUT SEPA-
RATE INDIVIDUALS

Raphael Volaterranus, about famous men of all races.   Fl. 1500

Pliny the Younger, or as some think, Cornelius Nepos,   [Fl. 60 B.C.]
about seventy-seven illustrious men.

Paul Jovius, about illustrious men.   Fl. 1540

Francis Petrarch, about illustrious men.   Fl. 1374

Polydore, about the origin of famous kings.   Fl. 1530

Giovanni Boccaccio, about the fortunes of famous men.   Fl. 1370

Gaspar Ursinus, about the lives of kings, emperors, and   Fl. 1540
Roman pontiffs to Charles V.

Jean Le Feron, pedigrees, with deeds of famous families,   Fl. 1540
partly published, partly still to be published, in French.

Plutarch and Philip of Bergamo, about famous women.   Fl. 120

Diogenes Laertius, ten books about the lives of philosophers.   Fl. 200

Baptista Egnatius, about Roman emperors, from Caesar to   Fl. 1530
Charles V, emperor.

Joannes Cuspinian, about the Caesars to Charles V.   Fl. 1540

Plutarch, fifty lives of the leaders of the Greeks and Ro-   Fl. 120
mans.

C. Suetonius Tranquillus, twelve lives of the Caesars from   Fl. 120
Caesar to Nerva.

Dio of Nicaea, lives of the emperors, from Nerva to M.   Fl. 140
Aurelius.

Aelius Spartianus, about the lives of Hadrian, Antoninus   Fl. 240
Pius, and M. Aurelius.

M. Aurelius, the life, written by himself in twelve books.   Fl. 170

Julius Capitolinus, three books about the lives of both An-   Fl. 307
tonines, Verus, and Pertinax.

Dio Cassius, history of the princes of the Romans, from   Fl. 240
Augustus even to Alexander Severus, whose epitome
Xiphilinus made.

Aelius Lampridius, about the lives of Didius Julianus, Heliogabalus, and Severus.   Fl. 300

Herodian, eight books, from the death of M. Aurelius to the younger Gordian.   Fl. 200

Sextus Aurelius Victor, about the lives of the emperors from Augustus to Theodosius the Great.   Fl. 420

Pomponius Laetus, about the lives of the successive emperors, from Gordian to Heraclius.   Fl. 490 [1490 in ed. 1572]

Trebellius Pollio, about the reigns of Valerian, Galienus, Claudius, and the Thirty Tyrants.   Fl. 310

Flavius Vopiscus, about the lives of Aurelian, Tacitus, Florian, Probus, Firmus, Saturninus, Proculus, Carus, Carinus, Numerianus.   Fl. 320

Eusebius, about the deeds of Diocletian, Maxentius, Constantine.   Fl. 312

Eutropius, epitome of the Roman princes to Jovian.   Fl. 340

Ammianus Marcellinus, about the deeds of Constantius, Julian, Jovian, Valentinian, and Valens.   Fl. 360

Michael Ritius, about the kings of the Franks, Spanish, Naples, Sicily, Hungary, Jerusalem.   Fl. 1505

Q. Curtius, eight books, left from ten, about the deeds of Alexander the Great.   Fl. 1482

Turpin, Eginhard, and Acciajuoli, about the life of Charles the Great, the two former of the period of Charles the Great, the third 1490.

Platina, about the lives of the bishops of Rome from Peter to Sixtus, in the year of Christ 1472.   Fl. 1480

Paul Vergerio, about the deeds of the princes of Mantua.   Fl. 1540

The succession of the princes of Montferrat, by an unknown author.   Fl. 1550

Charles Stephan, epitome of the dukes of Milan.

Jacob Bracellus, about famous Genoese.

Xenophon, about the deeds and sayings of Socrates.

Philo, about the life of Moses.

Otto of Freising, about the deeds of Frederick Barbarossa.

Philostratus, eight books about the life of Apollonius Thyanaeus.

Laurentius Valla, about the deeds of Ferdinand, the king of Aragon.

Staphylus, about the deeds of Charles V.

FINIS

BIBLIOGRAPHY

Aemilius, Paulus. De rebus gestis Francorum libri x. Basel, 1601.

Aeschines. The Speeches of Aeschines; with an English translation by Charles Darwin Adams. London and New York, 1919. The Loeb Classical Library.

Agricola, Georg (Georg Bauer). De veteribus & novis metallis lib. ii. Basel, 1546.

Allen, Don Cameron. The Star-Crossed Renaissance; the quarrel about astrology and its influence in England. Durham, 1941.

Allen, John William. "Jean Bodin," in F. J. C. Hearnshaw, ed., The Social & Political Ideas of Some Great Thinkers of the Sixteenth and Seventeenth Centuries. London [1926].

Althusius, Johannes. Politica methodice digesta; with an introduction by Carl Joachim Friedrich. Cambridge [Mass.], 1932.

Alvarez, Francisco. Narrative of the Portuguese Embassy to Abyssinia during the Years 1520–1527; tr. from the Portuguese, and ed., with notes and an introduction, by Lord Stanley of Alderley. London, 1881. Works issued by the Hakluyt Society, No. LXVI.

Ammianus Marcellinus. The Roman History of Ammianus Marcellinus; tr. by C. D. Yonge. London and New York, 1902. Bohn's Classical Library.

Apocrypha and Pseudepigrapha of the Old Testament, The; ed. in conjunction with many scholars, by R. H. Charles. Oxford, 1913.

Appianus of Alexandria. Appian's Roman History; with an English translation by Horace White. 4 vols. London and New York, 1912–1913. The Loeb Classical Library.

Apuleius Madaurensis. Opera omnia; ed. by G. F. Hildebrand. Leipzig, 1843.

Aristotle. The Basic Works; ed. by Richard McKeon. New York [1941].

—— Meteorologicorum libri iv; ed. by Julius Ludovicus Ideler. 2 vols. Leipzig, 1834–1836.

—— The Nicomachean Ethics; with an English translation by H. Rackham. New and revised edition. New York and London, 1934. The Loeb Classical Library.

—— The Works of Aristotle; tr. into English under the editorship of Sir William David Ross. 11 vols. Oxford, 1908–1931.

Arrianus, Flavius. Anabasis of Alexander and Indica; tr. with a copious commentary, by Edward James Chinnock. London and New York, 1893. Bohn's Classical Library.

Athenaeus. The Deipnosophists; with an English translation by Charles Burton Gulick. 7 vols. London and New York (Vols. VI and VII, Cambridge, Mass.), 1927–1941. The Loeb Classical Library.

Augustine, Saint. The City of God; tr. by John Healey in 1610. 3 vols. London, 1903. The Temple Classics.

Battaglia, Felice. Lineamenti di storia delle doctrine politiche. Rome, 1936.

Baudouin, François. De institutione historiae et coniunctione eius cum jurisprudentia. Paris, 1726.

Benoist, Charles, and others, "IVᵉ Centénaire Jean Bodin," *La Province d'Anjou, Novembre-Décembre,* 1929.

Berriat-Saint-Prix (called Jacques Saint-Prix Berriat). Histoire du droit romain suivie de l'Histoire de Cujas. Paris, 1821.

Bible, The. King James Version.

Bodin, Jean. Le Theatre de la nature universelle; tr. by François de Fougerolles. Lyons, 1597.

Born, Lester Kruger. "The Perfect Prince; a study in thirteenth and fourteenth century ideals," *Speculum* III (1928), 470–504.

British Museum. Department of Printed Books. General Catalogue. London, 1931–

Brock, Arthur John, ed. and tr. Greek Medicine. London and Toronto; New York [1929]. The Library of Greek Thought.

Brown, John Lackey. The Methodus ad facilem historiarum cognitionem of Jean Bodin. Washington, D.C., 1939.

Brunet, Jacques Charles. Dictionnaire de géographie. Paris, 1928.

—— Manuel du libraire. Paris, 1928.

Burtt, Edwin Arthur. The Metaphysical Foundations of Modern Physical Science. Rev. ed. New York, 1932. International Library of Psychology, Philosophy and Scientific Method.

Bury, John Bagnell. The Idea of Progress. London, 1920.

Busson, Henri. Les Sources et le développement du rationalisme dans la littérature française de la Renaissance. Paris, 1922.

Cabos, Alban. Guy du Faur de Pibrac. Paris, 1922.

Caesar, C. Julius. The Civil Wars; with an English translation by A. G. Peskett. London and New York, 1914.

—— Commentarii rerum in Gallia gestarum VII, A. Hirti Commentarius VIII; ed. by T. Rice Holmes. Oxford, 1914.

Carlyle, Sir Robert Warrand and Alexander James. A History of Mediaeval Political Theory in the West. 6 vols. Edinburgh and London, 1922–1930.

Cassius, Dio Cocceianus. Dio's Roman History; with an English translation by Earnest Cary. 9 vols. London and New York, 1914–1927. The Loeb Classical Library.

Charbonnel, Roger. La Pensée italienne au XVIᵉ siècle et le courant libertin. Paris, 1919.

Chauviré, Roger. Jean Bodin. La Flèche, 1914.

Chevalier, Cyr Ulysse Joseph. Répertoire des sources historiques du moyen âge. Paris, 1903–1907.

Cicero, Marcus Tullius. De natura deorum; Academica; with an English translation by H. Rackham. London and New York, 1933. The Loeb Classical Library.

—— De republica, De legibus; with an English translation by Clinton Walker Keyes. London and New York, 1928. The Loeb Classical Library.

—— De senectute, De amicitia, De divinatione; with an English translation by William Armistead Falconer. London and New York, 1923. The Loeb Classical Library.

—— M. Tullii Ciceronis opera quae supersunt omnia; ed. by J. G. Baiter and C. L. Keyser. Ed. stereotypa. 11 vols. in 6. Leipzig, 1860–1869.

—— Rhetorica; ed. by Augustus S. Wilkins. 2 vols. Oxford, 1902–1935.

—— The Treatises of M. T. Cicero; tr. by C. D. Yonge. London, 1853. Bohn's Classical Library.

—— Tusculan Disputations; with an English translation by J. E. King; London and New York, 1927. The Loeb Classical Library.

Claudius Claudianus. "Carmina Minora," in his [Works] with an English translation by Maurice Platnauer. 2 vols. London and New York, 1922. The Loeb Classical Library.

Columella, Lucius Junius Moderatus. On Agriculture; with an English translation by Harrison Boyd Ash. Cambridge, Mass. and London, 1941. The Loeb Classical Library.

Cornford, Francis Macdonald. Plato's Cosmology. London, 1937.

Corpus juris canonici; ed. by C. H. Freisleben. Basel, 1735.

Corpus juris civilis Romani; ed. by Theodor Mommsen and Paul Krueger. 3 vols. Berlin, 1928–1929.

Dean, Leonard F. "Bodin's *Methodus* in England before 1625," *Studies in Philology*, XXXIX (April, 1942), 160–166.

Demosthenes. Olynthiacs; Philippics; Minor Public Speeches; Speech against Leptines; with an English translation by J. H. Vince. London and New York, 1930. The Loeb Classical Library.

Dick, Hugh G. "Thomas Blundeville's True Order and Method of Wryting and Reading Hystories (1574)," in the *Huntingdon Library Quarterly*, III (1940), 149–171.

Du Cange, Charles du Fresne. Glossarium mediae et infimae latinitatis; new ed. by Léopold Favre. 10 vols. in 11. Paris, 1937–1938.

Duhem, Pierre. Le Système du monde. 5 vols. Paris, 1913–1917.

Erasmus, Desiderius. The Education of a Christian Prince; with an introduction by Lester K. Born. New York, 1936. Records of Civilization, Sources and Studies. No. XXVII.

Febvre, Lucien. A Geographical Introduction to History. A translation of La Terre et l'évolution humaine, by E. G. Mountford and J. H. Paxton. New York, 1925. The History of Civilization.

Feist, Elizabeth. Königsmacht and Ständefreiheit. Dresden, n.d. Reprint from the *Historische Vierteljahrschrift.*

—— Weltbild und Staatsidee bei Jean Bodin. Halle, 1930.

Flach, Jacques. "Cujas, les glossateurs et les Bartolistes," in *Nouvelle Revue historique de droit français et étranger,* VII (1883), 205–232.

Garosci, Aldo. Jean Bodin, politica e diritto nel rinascimento francese. Milan [1934].

Gellius, Aulus. Noctium Atticarum libri xx; ed. by Martin Hertz. Leipzig, 1877.

Gilbert, Felix. "The Humanist Concept of the Prince and *The Prince* of Machiavelli," *Journal of Modern History,* XI (1939), 449–483.

Gilmore, Myron Piper. Argument from Roman Law in Political Thought, 1200–1600. Cambridge [Mass.], 1941.

Goes, Damiao de. Fides, religio moresque Aethiopum . . . Paris, 1541.

Hauser, Henri. La Modernité au xvie siècle. Paris, 1930. Bibliothèque de la Revue historique.

—— La Prépondérance espagnole (1559–1660). Paris, 1933. Peuples et civilisations.

Heath, Sir Thomas Little. A History of Greek Mathematics. 2 vols. Oxford, 1921.

Herodotus. The History of Herodotus; tr. by G. C. Macaulay. 2 vols. London and New York, 1890.

Hesiod. The Homeric Hymns, and Homerica; with an English translation by Hugh G. Evelyn-White. London and New York, 1914. The Loeb Classical Library.

Hippocrates. Hippocrates, with an English translation by W. H. S. Jones. 2 vols. London and New York, 1923. The Loeb Classical Library.

Hitti, Philip Khûri. History of the Arabs. London, 1937.

Homer. The Iliad; rendered in English hexameters by Alexander Falconer Murison. London, New York [etc.], 1933–

—— The Odyssey; tr. by Sir William Marris. London, New York [etc.], 1925.

Horace. Satires, Epistles and Ars poetica; with an English translation by H. Rushton Fairclough. London and New York, 1932. The Loeb Classical Library.

Jervis, Walter Willson. The World in Maps. New York, 1937.

Johnson, Francis Rarick. Astronomical Thought in Renaissance England. Baltimore, 1937. Huntingdon Library Publications.

Johnson, Francis Rarick, and Sanford V. Larkey. "Thomas Digges, The Copernican System, and the Idea of the Universe in 1576," in *The Huntington Library Bulletin,* No. 5 (April, 1934), 69–117.

Josephus. Josephus; with an English translation by H. St. John Thackeray. 9 vols. London and New York, 1926–1937. The Loeb Classical Library.

Julianus Apostata. The Works of the Emperor Julian; with an English translation by Wilmer Cave Wright. 3 vols. London and New York, 1913–1923. The Loeb Classical Library.

Juvenalis, Decimus Junius. Satirarum libri quinque; ed. by C. F. Hermann. Leipzig, 1904. Bibliotheca scriptorum Graecorum et Romanorum Teubneriana.

Kimble, George Herbert. Geography in the Middle Ages. London [1938].

Klibansky, Raymond. The Continuity of the Platonic Tradition during the Middle Ages. London, 1939.

Kristeller, Paul Oskar. "Augustine and the Renaissance." Reprint from *International Science*, I (1941), 7–14.

Kristeller, Paul Oskar, and John Hermann Randall, Jr. "The Study of the Philosophies of the Renaissance," *Journal of the History of Ideas*, II (1941), 449–496.

Lavisse, Ernest, ed. Histoire de France, illustrée, depuis les origines jusqu'à la Révolution. 9 vols. in 17. Paris, 1911–1926.

Leo the African. The History and Description of Africa; done into English by John Pory in the year 1600; ed. by Robt. Brown. 3 vols. London, 1896. Works issued by the Hakluyt Society, Nos. XCIV–XCVI.

Livius, Titus. Livy; with an English translation by B. O. Foster. New York, 1919–1938. 13 vols. The Loeb Classical Library.

Lovejoy, Arthur Oncken. The Great Chain of Being. Cambridge [Mass.], 1936.

Lucanus, Marcus Annaeus. Pharsalia; ed. by Carl Friederich Weber. 3 vols. Leipzig, 1821.

—— The Pharsalia of Lucan; literally tr. into English prose . . . by Henry T. Riley. London, 1903.

Lucretius, Carus Titus. On the Nature of Things; tr. by John Selby Watson. London, 1882. Bohn's Classical Library.

Machiavelli, Niccolò. History of Florence from the Earliest Times to the Death of Lorenzo the Magnificent. New York, 1901. The World's Great Classics.

Macrobius, Aurelius Theodosius. In somnium Scipionis; ed. by Franz Eysenhardt. Leipzig, 1868.

Meuten, Anton. Bodin's Theorie von der Beeinflussung des politischen Lebens der Staaten durch ihre geographische Lage. Bonn, 1904.

Minar, Edwin L. Early Pythagorean Politics in Practice and Theory. Baltimore, 1942. Connecticut College Monograph, No. 2.

Moreau-Reibel, Jean. Jean Bodin et le Droit public comparé. Paris, 1933.

Paris. Bibliothèque nationale, Département des imprimés. Catalogue général. Paris, 1907–

Pausanias. Pausanias' Description of Greece; with an English translation by W. H. S. Jones. 5 vols. London and New York, 1918–1935. The Loeb Classical Library.

Philo Judaeus. Philo; with an English translation by F. H. Colson and G. H. Whitaker. 10 vols. London and New York, 1929– The Loeb Classical Library.

Pidal, Ramon M. Primera cronica general. Madrid, 1906.

Plato. The Dialogues of Plato; translated by Benjamin Jowett. 5 vols. London and New York, 1892.

—— Laws; with an English translation by Richard G. Bury. 2 vols. London and New York, 1926. The Loeb Classical Library.

—— Phaedrus; with an English translation by H. N. Fowler. London and New York, 1914. The Loeb Classical Library.

—— Phaedrus, Ion, Gorgias, and Symposium; with passages from the Republic and Laws; translated into English . . . by Lane Cooper. London, New York, Toronto, 1938.

—— The Republic; with an English translation by Paul Shorey. 2 vols. London and New York, 1930. The Loeb Classical Library.

—— Timaeus; with an English translation by H. N. Fowler. London and New York, 1929. The Loeb Classical Library.

Plautus, Titus Maccius. Ausgewählte Komödien; ed. by A. O. F. Lorenz. 4 vols. Berlin, 1866–1876.

Plinius Secundus, C. Letters; with an English translation by William Melmoth. 2 vols. London and New York, 1915. The Loeb Classical Library.

—— The Natural History of Pliny; tr. by John Bostock and Henry T. Riley. 6 vols. London, 1890–1900. Bohn's Classical Library.

Plutarch. Plutarch's Lives of the noble Grecians and Romans; Englished by Sir Thomas North anno 1579. 6 vols. London, 1895–1896.

—— Plutarch's Morals; ed. by Wm. W. Goodwin. 5 vols. Boston, 1879.

—— The Roman Questions of Plutarch; tr. by H. J. Rose. Oxford, 1924.

Polybius. The Histories; with an English translation by W. R. Paton. 6 vols. London and New York, 1922–1927. The Loeb Classical Library.

Pomponazzi, Pietro. Les Causes des merveilles de la nature; ou, les Enchantments; tr. by Henri Busson. Paris, 1930. Les Textes du christianisme.

Ponthieux, A. "Quelques documents inédits sur Jean Bodin," *La Revue du xvi*^e *siècle*, XV (1928), 56–99.

Procopius. History of the Wars; with an English translation by H. B. Dewing. 7 vols. London and New York, 1914–1940. The Loeb Classical Library.

Propertius, Sextus Aurelius. Propertius; with an English translation by H. E. Butler. London and New York, 1912. The Loeb Classical Library.

Ptolemaeus, Claudius. Composition mathématique; traduite pour la première fois du grec en français par M. [N.B.] Halma (avec le texte grec). Réimpression facsimilé. Paris, 1927. Half-title: Almageste.

Randall, John Hermann, Jr. "Development of Scientific Method in the School of Padua," *Journal of the History of Ideas*, I (1940), 177–206.

Renouard, Philippe. Imprimeurs parisiens, libraires, fondeurs de caractères et correcteurs d'imprimerie, depuis l'introduction de l'imprimerie à Paris (1470) jusqu'à la fin du xvi⁰ siècle. Paris, 1898.

Renz, Fritz. Jean Bodin; ein Beitrag zur Geschichte der historischen Methode in xviten Jahrhundert. Gotha, 1905.

Sandys, John Edwin. History of Classical Scholarship. 3 vols. Cambridge, 1908–1921.

Savigny, Friederich Karl von. Histoire du droit romain au moyen âge; traduite de l'allemand . . . par M. Charles Guenoux. 4 part. en 3 vols. Paris, 1830.

See, Henri. "La Philosophie d'histoire de Jean Bodin," *La Revue historique,* CLXXV (1935), 497–505.

Seneca. Moral Essays; with an English translation by John P. Basore. 3 vols. London and New York, 1928–1935. The Loeb Classical Library.

Shepard, Max Adams. "Sovereignty at the Cross Roads; a study of Bodin," *Political Science Quarterly,* XLV (1930), 580–603.

Shotwell, James Thomson. The History of History, Vol. I. Revised edition of An Introduction to the History of History. New York, 1939.

Singer, Charles Joseph. From Magic to Science. New York, 1928.

Sohm, Rudolph. The Institutes; a text book of the history and system of Roman private law; tr. by James C. Ledlie. Oxford, London, and New York, 1901.

Strabo. The Geography of Strabo; with an English translation by H. C. Hamilton and W. Falconer. 3 vols. London, 1889–1893. Bohn's Classical Library.

Strong, Edward William. Procedures and Metaphysics; a study in the philosophy of mathematical-physical science in the sixteenth and seventeenth centuries. Berkeley, 1936.

Suetonius Tranquillus, C. Lives of the Caesars; with an English translation by J. C. Wolfe. 2 vols. London and New York, 1914. The Loeb Classical Library.

Tacitus. Dialogus, Agricola, Germania; with an English translation by William Peterson and Maurice Hutton. London and New York, 1914. The Loeb Classical Library.

—— The Histories; with an English translation by Clifford H. Moore . . . The Annals; with an English translation by John Jackson. 4 vols. London and New York, 1925–1937. The Loeb Classical Library.

Talmud, The Babylonian; ed. by Michael L. Rodkinson. Boston, 1918.

Taylor, Eva Germaine R. Tudor Geography. London, 1930.

Taylor, Henry Osborn. Greek Biology and Medicine. Boston, 1922.

Theophrastus. Enquiry into Plants; with an English translation by Sir Arthur Hort. 2 vols. London and New York, 1916. The Loeb Classical Library.

Thompson, James Westfall. History of Historical Writing. New York, 1942.

—— Medieval Library. Chicago, 1939.

Thorndike, Lynn. A History of Magic and Experimental Science. 6 vols. New York, 1923–1941.

—— Science and Thought in the Fifteenth Century. New York, 1929.

Thucydides. History of the Peloponnesian Wars; with an English translation by C. Forster Smith. 4 vols. London and New York, 1923–1931. The Loeb Classical Library.

Tilley, Arthur. "Humanism under Francis I," English Historical Review, XV (1900), 456–478.

Valerius Maximus. Valerii Maximi factorum et dictorum memorabilium libri novem; ed. by Carolus Kempf. Leipzig, 1888. Bibliotheca scriptorum Graecorum et Romanorum Teubneriana.

Varro, Marcus Terentius. On the Latin Language; with an English translation by Roland G. Kent. London and Cambridge, Mass., 1938. The Loeb Classical Library.

Vergilius Maro, Publius. Georgics and Eclogues; with an English translation by H. Rushton Fairclough. London and New York, 1930. The Loeb Classical Library.

Viard, Paul-Emile. André Alciat. Paris, 1926.

Vitruvius, Pollio. Ten Books on Architecture; tr. by Morris H. Morgan. Cambridge, 1926.

Warmington, Eric Herbert, ed. and tr. Greek Geography. London, 1934. The Library of Greek Thought.

White, Lynn. "Christian Myth and Christian History," Journal of the History of Ideas, III (1942), 145–158.

Wright, John K. "Notes on the Knowledge of Latitudes and Longitudes in the Middle Ages," Isis, V(1923), 75–98.

Yung Chi Hoe. The Origin of Parliamentary Sovereignty or Mixed Monarchy. Shanghai, 1935.

Zulueta, Francis de. "The Science of Law," in The Legacy of Rome; ed. by Cyril Bailey. Oxford, 1923.

INDEX

Abraham, Rabbi, 325
Absimarus, *see* Tiberius Apsimarus
Acciajuoli, Donato, 45, 380
Accursius, jurist, 173
Acilian law, 181
Acusilaus, 323, 370
Ado, bishop of Vienne, 77, 366
Aebutian Rogation, 2
Aelian, Claudius, 106, 141, 368
Aemilius, Paul, of Verona, 27, 45 f., 57, 83, 284, 373
Aemund, 373
Aeschines, 169
Aeschylus, 48, 110, 141, 338
Agathias, 53, 97, 352, 376
Agesilaus, Spartan king, 64
Agis, Spartan king, 187
Agrarian law, French, 253
Agrarian laws, Roman, 185, 203
Agricola, George (George Bauer), 112, 133
Agrippa, Marcus Vipsanius, 132, 282
Ahas (Ahaz), King, of Judah, 331
Alaric I, King of Visigoths, 294
Alaric the Pannonian, 266
Albert I, Emperor, 168, 284, 363
Albertus Magnus, 329
Alciati, Andreas, ix, 61, 70, 100, 141, 173, 176
Alcibiades, 238
Alexander (Aristotle?), 97
Aleander, Jerome, the Elder, 226
Alexander III, King of Scotland, 363
Alexander III, Pope, 221
Alexander VI, Pope, 226
Alexander of Aphrodisias, 96, 312, 316
Alexander of Phera, 216
Alexander Severus, Emperor, 170, 203, 216, 294
Alexander the Great, xxi, 13, 41 f., 47, 61, 227, 229 ff., 260, 294, 296, 299, 318, 320, 321, 331, 339
Alexius I, Comnenus, Emperor, 54
Alfonso I, King of Asturias, 222
Alfonso III, King of Asturias, 266
Alfonso IV, King of Asturias, 266
Alfonso V, King of Leon, 266

Alphonso VII (the Emperor), of Leon and Castile, 358
Alfonso VIII, King of Castile, 266
Alfonso X, King of Castile, 168
Alfonso XI, King of Castile, 266
Aloysius, Peter, 378
Aloysius, tyrant of Piacenza, 216
Alphonso V of Aragon, I of Naples and Sicily, 12
Alphonso, duke of Calabria, 248
Althamer, Andreas, 105, 334, 336, 339, 346
Alvarez, Francisco, 47, 54, 57, 79, 87, 107, 114, 128, 137, 285, 364, 378
Alviano, Bartolomeo d', 76
Ambrose, bishop of Milan, 81, 236, 308
Ammianus (Ammianus Marcellinus), 46 f., 51, 54, 71, 82 f., 121, 130, 215, 332 f., 344, 352, 369, 372, 380
Amon, King of Judah, 331
Amyot, Jacques, 90
Anacharsis, 86, 113, 269
Anafesto, Paoluccio, doge of Venice, 188
Anaxagoras, 116, 313, 317
Ancients, achievements of, compared with modern men, xxi f., 299 ff.
Andrea, John (Giovanni d'Andrea), 119
Androtion, 194
Anna, daughter of Emperor Alexius, 371
Antigonus, Greek historian, 21
Antigonus, King of Macedon, 166, 209
Antiochus I, 37, 151
Antiochus the Great, 181, 218
Antipater, 238, 260
Antonine of Florence, 77 f., 366
Antoninus Caracalla, *see* Caracalla
Antoninus Pius, Emperor, xv, 155, 283, 294, 300; law of, concerning status of individuals, 162
Antonio of Gerona, 326
Antonio, Peter, 377
Antony, Mark, 36, 64 ff., 99, 129, 149, 161, 199, 211, 228, 345
Antony the Monk, 374
Apicius (Apicius Caelius), 31
Apion, 320, 322
Apocalypse, 291 ff.